NOSOTROS

 LATINOS IN THE UNITED STATES SERIES

NOSOTROS

A STUDY OF EVERYDAY
MEANINGS IN HISPANO
NEW MEXICO

ALVIN O. KORTE

Michigan State University Press • East Lansing

⊖ The paper used in this publication meets the minimum requirements
of ANSI/NISO Z39.48-1992 (R 1997) (Permanence of Paper).

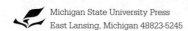 Michigan State University Press
East Lansing, Michigan 48823-5245

Printed and bound in the United States of America.

18 17 16 15 14 13 12   1 2 3 4 5 6 7 8 9 10

LIBRARY OF CONGRESS CATALOGING-IN-PUBLICATION DATA
Korte, Alvin O.
Nosotros : a study of everyday meanings in Hispano New Mexico /
Alvin O. Korte.
p. cm.
Includes bibliographical references and index.
ISBN 978-1-61186-029-0 (pbk. : alk. paper) 1. Hispanic Americans—New
Mexico—Social life and customs. I. Title.
F805.S75K675 2012
305.8680789—dc23
2011029499

Cover and book design by Charlie Sharp, Sharp Des!gns

g green press Michigan State University Press is a member of the Green
INITIATIVE Press Initiative and is committed to developing and
encouraging ecologically responsible publishing practices. For more
information about the Green Press Initiative and the use of recycled
paper in book publishing, please visit *www.greenpressinitiative.org*.

Visit Michigan State University Press at *www.msupress.org*

Contents

RUBÉN O. MARTINEZ

Foreword

HISPANOS ARE THE DESCENDANTS OF THE SPANISH/MEXICAN FAMILIES THAT settled the northernmost province of New Spain and are today indigenous to New Mexico and parts of Colorado and Arizona. La Provincia de Nuevo Mexico became part of Mexico in 1821, when the latter gained its independence from Spain, then became part of the United States in 1848, when the northern half of Mexico was taken over at the conclusion of the American-Mexican War. The earliest Spanish settlement in the region, Ciudad de Nuestro Padre San Francisco, was established by Juan de Oñate y Salazar in 1598, near the confluence of the Rio Grande and the Rio Chama near Caypa, which came to be known as San Juan Pueblo (San Juan de los Caballeros), and which lies just north of present-day Española, New Mexico. This settlement served as the "capital" of the province until 1609, when Oñate's successor, Pedro de Peralta, established the settlement La Villa Real de Santa Fé de San Francisco (present-day Santa Fe), which became and continued as the capital city of New Spain's northernmost province. The province included the geographical areas of New Mexico and Arizona and portions of present-day Colorado and Utah. The cradle of the culture that evolved in the region was centered in the area that came to be known as Rio Arriba, or today's Upper Rio Grande, in contrast to the

Rio Abajo, or the Lower Rio Grande (southern New Mexico, today known as the Middle Rio Grande).

Military installations and settlements in the region remained relatively stable, though not without problems or threats, until the Pueblo Indian Revolt of 1680, when the Pueblos killed hundreds and drove out the Spanish settlers, many of whom fled beyond while others only as far as El Paso del Norte, which became New Spain's northernmost settlement for just over a decade. In 1692, the reconquest by Diego de Vargas brought the region back under Spanish control. Although another revolt was attempted by the Pueblos in 1696, it was unsuccessful. From then on the culture of Hispanos evolved in relative stability, but not without constant threat and conflict, blending somewhat with indigenous cultures, and in relative isolation from the mother culture given the distance to and the difficulty of traveling to the Spanish provinces to the south. For example, the Camino Real de Tierra Adentro extended 1,600 miles between Mexico City and Santa Fe. As a result of this relative isolation, the Hispano culture took on, among others, three particular characteristics: (1) although increasingly clipped as an oral form, the Spanish language remained relatively unchanged until the last century, when the influence of English became more and more pronounced; (2) local adaptation features such as the emergence of *penitentes* and their political importance once the region became part of the United States; and (3) the institutionalization of communal *acequia* (irrigation ditch) governance structures.

One of the interesting cultural aspects resulting from the relational dynamics of these features is the self referential term "manitos," which emerged from the penitente brotherhoods, the members of which addressed each other as "hermano," with the term ultimately being clipped to "mano." For example, when addressing each other, elder Hispanos in the 1950s would use "mano" as a title preceding a person's first name (for example, Mano Juan, or Brother John). The brotherhoods emerged in the second half of the eighteenth century to "commemorate the Passion and Death of Christ during the Lenten season and especially during Holy Week" (Espinosa 1993, 455). Engaging in self-flagellation as a form of penance, a practice that swept devout Catholics in Europe in the first half of the second millennium, American outsiders viewed the *hermandades* (brotherhoods) as fanatical and outdated (although the practice is still found among some devout Catholics across the globe today). Over time, their compatriots in Texas and California, the Tejanos and Californios, referred to them as "manitos" (the diminutive form giving the term several additional meanings). Indeed, when the United States took over Mexico's northern region in the middle of the nineteenth century, it incorporated three regional "Mexican" groups: Tejanos, Manitos, and Californios. The longest established settlements were those of the manitos.

This volume is a study of the everyday meanings of "manitos," particularly those living in the north central region of New Mexico, including the eastern foothills of the Sangre de Cristo Mountains. This is the land of Pueblo Indians, Spanish settlers, nomadic tribes and, later, American outlaws; conflict and cooperation over time among the groups gave rise to various cultural forms due to cultural mixing. French, German, and British immigrants, for example, became Hispanos over the generations. This is also the land of revolts and rebellions. In 1837, Hispanos and Pueblos revolted against Mexico and held their ground for a year before they were defeated. Ten years later, in Taos, they revolted against the Americans, killing the first American governor, among others. This, too, was a short-lived revolt, with battles taking place just north of Santa Fe and in the Mora Valley, on the front range of the mountains near Las Vegas.

While the early settlements along the Rio Grande were established in the first part of the seventeenth century, those on the eastern foothills were established at the start of the nineteenth century. The remains of Cicuyé (later named Pecos), the pueblo visited by Francisco Vásquez de Coronado in 1540, are geographically located between these two types of communities, with Santa Fe representing one type and Las Vegas the other. During its day, Cicuyé was the gateway to the plains to the east and the Pueblos to the west. It is in this geographical and cultural area that Alvin Korte's work is situated, where the beautiful Sangre de Cristo Mountains meet the llano, which extends to the east into the Llano Estacado, one the largest mesas or tablelands region on the continent. Korte's work is also situated from the vantage point of an insider, or an Hispano.

This volume breaks new ground in bringing social phenomenological and ethnomethodological approaches to the study of Latinos, in this case Hispanos. Few works have utilized social phenomenology and ethnomethodology to study Latinos, and none are available that focus on Hispanos in a systematic fashion. Indeed, the study of Hispanos is quite limited, although slowly a body of knowledge is emerging. Perhaps the first major work by an American on the peoples of New Mexico was by Hubert Howe Bancroft (1889), for whom it was part of a broader historical work on Mexico. Bancroft held that the early Spanish settlers of Mexico were from Castile, Andalusia, and Estremadura, and later colonists were from Catalonia and Galicia in Spain. All of these dialects were present in New Mexico, although by the eighteenth century most new colonists were born in New Spain and likely were *mestizo* (mixed Spanish and indigenous person).

Bancroft's work, which seems inevitably judgmental, was followed by that of Charles Fletcher Lummis (1893), whose traveler journalist chronicles covering the 1846–1848 period presented the Hispano orientation as a "mañana" orientation, and held that this was the land of unhurried life, the "land of poco tiempo." Lummis presented Hispanos as despots and religious fanatics (Gutierrez 2002). Lummis's work was followed by the 1926 publication of the diary of Susan Shelby Magoffin, an early white female traveler on the Santa Fe Trail. Magoffin and her trader husband arrived in Santa Fe in 1846, following Kearny's Army of the West, en route to Mexico. Her perceptions, too, are judgmental and ethnocentric, constantly making comparisons in terms of civility and casting locals as heathens, although she was at times reflexive relative to her own cultural background. She was, however, relatively open to other cultures and learned to speak some Spanish and to make tortillas during that trip into "New Spain."

Aurelio Espinosa's dissertation in 1909 began the systematic study of Hispanos by Hispanos. Espinosa, a manito from southern Colorado, conducted a study of New Mexican Spanish for his doctorate at the University of Chicago. The body of scholarship that began to emerge went beyond language to include folklorist accounts of music, dramas, stories, and dichos, mostly through the works of Arturo Campa, Juan B. Rael, Aurora Lucero-White Lea, and Rubén Cobos. Written from a more sociological perspective, *The Forgotten Americans*, by George I. Sanchez, was published in 1940. Sanchez held that the U.S. government had failed to integrate and support the people of northern New Mexico, leaving them to fend for themselves as the agro-pastoral economy of the region was transformed into capitalism.

Meanwhile other American scholars were conducting research on "manitos." These included Charles Loomis (1958), who conducted a series of community studies in El Cerrito (near Las Vegas) beginning around the start of the 1940s. He was followed by Munro Edmonson (1957), a multilingual anthropologist of Russian ancestry who grew up in Nogales, Arizona. Following service in WWII, Edmonson spent a year in New Mexico under the tutelage of Clyde Kluckhohn and his Comparative Study of Values in Five Cultures. His study of three "Spanish American" or Hispano villages became the basis for his doctoral dissertation at Harvard. Like other Americans before him, Edmonson was overly impressed by American individualism (as innovative, progressive, and egalitarian) and cast Hispanos at the middle of the twentieth century as fatalistic, especially in religion, death, and politics. Interestingly, he traced fatalism among Hispanos to maternal discipline and an overbearing paternal authority within the culture. These and other studies set the stage for the critiques of social science stereotypes by the emerging Chicano intelligentsia in the 1960s (Roman-V 1969; Vaca 1970a, 1970b).

During the first part of the last century literary writers also took an interest in Hispanos, beginning with Willa Cather's *Death Comes for the Archbishop*, published in 1927, and Frank Waters's *People of the Valley*, published in 1941. The former, set in the period following the conclusion of the American-Mexican War, is a portrayal of the struggle for control by the U.S. Catholic Church and local Hispano priests, namely

Father Antonio José Martinez, a religious and political leader in Taos who opposed the occupation of the territory by Americans. Cather portrays the local priests as avaricious and gluttonous. On the other hand, Waters's portrayal of a family in the Mora Valley is much more emic-like, and more effectively captures the sensibility, changing lifestyles, and traditional culture of manitos. In 1953, Joseph Krumgold produced a docudrama titled *And Now Miguel* as part of a project on Latino rural workers for the Department of State. For a brief period in the 1880s, in response to American military supply needs, northern New Mexico became the sheep capital of the nation. Krumgold caught the final phase of that industry near the middle of the twentieth century through his focus on a sheep-raising family near Taos. That same year he also published a children's novel by the same title. The novel , set in the Taos Valley, captured aspects of the sheep-raising culture of Hispanos through the coming-of-age of a young boy. The book won the Newberry Medal in 1954 and led to the production of a movie by the same title in 1966.

With the renewal of the land grant struggles and the emergence of the Chicano Movement in the 1960s came a new generation of Hispano scholars who took an interest in studying manitos. This new pulse is best exemplified by Corky Gonzales's *Yo Soy Joaquin* (1972) and Ricardo Sanchez's *Canto y Grito mi Liberacion* (1971), a collection of poems and essays by an ex-pinto (con) which call for liberation from racial oppression and the humanistic redemption of humanity (also see Delgado 2011). Sanchez thanks Tómas Atencio, a manito, for helping him deal with an overzealous parole officer in El Paso as he struggled to establish Míctla* publications. Atencio was one of the leading founders of La Academia de la Nueva Raza in Embudo, New Mexico, which focused on gathering knowledge from elders, treating it as nuggets of gold produced by the disappearing traditional pueblitos. Atencio collaborated with several others on and provided the introduction to *Entre Verde y Seco,* a compilation of pieces by different authors highlighting the cultural gold of Hispano communities (Arellano 1972).

About this time Rudolfo Anaya's *Bless Me, Ultima* was published. This work also probed the cultural changes taking place in rural New Mexico through the coming of age of a young boy, and through the novel Anaya seeks to tap the collective memory of Hispanos, that reservoir of ancestral knowledge handed down across the generations. Though regarded as one of the best Chicano novels, *Bless Me, Ultima* has only recently been produced as a movie. In 1974, two years after *Bless Me, Ultima* was published, the first volume of John Nichols's well-known trilogy was published. The *Milagro Beanfield War* was adapted into a movie by the same title in 1988. The

---

*Míctla is a reference to the lowest layer of the Aztec underground—where the souls of the dead find eternal rest.

novel and movie take a light comedic approach to the water struggles experienced by *acequia* communities in northern New Mexico.

Since the 1970s numerous other literary and scholarly works focusing on Hispanos have appeared—too many to review here. Studies of communities, land grant struggles, environmental justice, acequias, and other aspects of Hispano life have been conducted and published. Important in this period is the work of Olibama López Tushar (1975), who provides a useful historical account of the early Hispano settlements (1850s) in the San Luis Valley in Southern Colorado, along with detailed descriptions of cultural features. Another useful study is that by Paul Kutsche and John Van Ness (1981), who provide an anthropological study of Cañones, a small rural community in northern New Mexico. As in the work of other scholars, the contradictions and difficulties of cultural change are highlighted. My "The Rediscovery of the 'Forgotten People'" (1988) continues the emphasis on the changes taking place in northern New Mexico due to the intensification of capitalism and the continued in-migration of Americans.

Finally, another important contribution worth mentioning is that by Tómas Atencio (Montiel, Atencio, and Mares 2009), who for years has promoted the metaphor of *resolana* (the sunny side or south face of buildings where manitos and others gather to talk about local news and events, especially during the winter months). Atencio uses the concept of resolana as a tool to investigate and recover the subjugated knowledge (*el oro del barrio*) of Hispanos for the promotion of wholesome, healthy and happy lives—a perspective, he contends, that is difficult for Americans, with their notions of incessant progress and achievement, to understand. Alvin Korte's work in this volume makes significant contributions to the stock of "el oro del barrio" and the recovery of Hispano culture. That is, it provides a profound examination of the ways by which Hispanos make sense of their experiences and construct meaning in their everyday lives. In doing so, Korte sheds new light on their cosmological views of the world, including the meanings of life and death. While a study of this sort should have been conducted in the 1940s and 1950s, when the manito culture was more intact and less influenced by Americans and the technology of recent decades, it would have been impossible because the perspective and the Chicano intelligentsia were not yet robust enough to conduct it. In hindsight, the forgotten existence lamented by George I. Sanchez in 1940 may have perpetuated the Hispano culture longer than it would have otherwise persisted, allowing Korte to capture and interpret elements of how manitos have constructed meaning in the structures of everyday life. Importantly, Korte's work provides an archimedean point against which changes in the manito culture can be assessed in the future. The rapid pace of acculturation already is dizzying.

REFERENCES

Anaya, R. 1972. *Bless Me, Ultima.* Berkeley: Quinto Sol.

Arellano, E. 1972. *Entre Verde y Seco.* Dixon, NM: Academia de la Nueva Raza.

Bancroft, H. H. 1889. *History of Arizona and New Mexico, 1530–1888,* vol. 17. San Francisco: The History Company Publishers.

Delgado, Abelardo L. 2011. *Here lies Lalo: The Collected Poems of Lalo Delgado.* Houston: Arte Publico Press.

Edmonson, M. S. 1957. *Los Manitos: A Study of Institutional Values.* New Orleans: Middle American Research Institute, Tulane University.

Espinosa, M. J. 1993. "The Origin of the Penitentes of New Mexico: Separating Fact from Fiction." *The Catholic Historical Review* 79, no. 3: 454–77.

Gonzales, Rodolfo. 1972. *Yo Soy Joaquin.* New York: Bantam Books.

Gutierrez, R. 2002. "Charles Fletcher Lummis and the Orientalization of New Mexico." In *Nuevo-mexicano Cultural Legacy,* ed. F. A. Lomeli, V. A. Sorell, and G. M. Padilla, 11–27. Albuquerque: University of New Mexico.

Krumgold, J. 1953. *And Now Miguel.* New York: Crowell.

Kutsche, P., and J. R. Van Ness. 1981. *Cañones: Values, Crisis, and Survival in a Northern New Mexico Village.* Albuquerque: University of New Mexico Press.

Loomis, C. P. 1958. "El Cerrito, New Mexico: A Changing Village." New Mexico Historical Review 33: 53–75.

López Tushar, Olibama. 1975. *The People of El Valle: A History of the Colonials in the San Luis Valley.* Denver: Hirsch Graphics Enterprise.

Lummis, C. F. 1893. *The Land of Poco Tiempo.* New York: Charles Scribner's Sons.

Martinez, R. 1988. "The Rediscovery of the 'Forgotten People.'" In *In Times of Challenge: Chicanos and Chicanas in American Society,* ed. the NACS Editorial Committee, 115–145. Mexican American Studies Monograph Series No. 6. Houston: Mexican American Studies Program, University of Houston.

Montiel, M., T. Atencio, and E. A. "Toney" Mares. 2009. *Resolana: Emerging Chicano Dialogues on Community and Globalization.* Tucson: University of Arizona Press.

Nichols, John. 1974. *The Milagro Beanfield War.* New York: Holt.

Romano-V, O. I. 1968. "The Anthropology and Sociology of the Mexican-Americans: The Distortion of Mexican-American History." In *Ghettos and Barrios,* ed. R. McGabe and S. Anthony, 89–118. New York: MSS Educational Publishing.

Sanchez, R. 1971. *Canto y Grito mi Liberacion.* El Paso: Míctla Publications.

Vaca, N. C. 1970a. "The Mexican-American in the Social Sciences: 1912–1970. Part I: 1912–1935." *El Grito:A Journal of Contemporary Mexican American Thought* 3: 3–24.

———. 1970b. "The Mexican-American in the Social Sciences: 1912–1970. Part II: 1936–1970." *El Grito: A Journal of Contemporary Mexican American Thought* 4: 17–51.

Waters, F. 1941. *People of the Valley.* New York: Farrar and Rinehart.

Preface

IN THIS BOOK, I USE PHENOMENOLOGY AND ETHNOMETHODOLOGY TO TAKE a closer look at elements of Hispano(a) life in northern New Mexico—everyday things that most people do not pay attention to as they go about their lives. In this exploration, I use ideas from a variety of sources, including newspaper obituaries, real events, the roles people play, their attitudes, belief systems, *dichos* (folk sayings), folklore, popular songs, poetry, film, opera, religious rituals, tombstones, prayer, psychotherapy, and scholarly work. The book is about northern New Mexicans, specifically Hispanos, among whom I have lived my whole life. It is an attempt to analyze the mundane things that have interested me over a thirty-year period. It does not cover everything about Hispanos. Such a task is far too big. In recent years there has been talk of a *Nuevomejicano* experience in New Mexico. I do not believe that a pure *Nuevomejicano* culture exists per se, but that Hispanos are influenced by the broader U.S. society and, to a lesser extent, by Mexican culture. Despite these influences the definitive aspects of an Hispano(a) culture can be observed in people's daily lives. It is sometimes seen and reflected in our folkways (Montaño 2001), music (Sagel 1990b), use of the Spanish language (Cobos 2003), or oral culture (Espinosa 1913, 1914, 1926; Rael 1977). Some of these forms are still extant, to a greater or lesser extent. A exciting literature is developing, for example, the work of Montaño (2001), Gonzales (2007), and other writers, artists, and poets.

The book is not intended to be a study of terms and practices that may not be in vogue anymore. However, I have found it useful to use older terms and to expand an inquiry about these terms in order to examine Hispano(a) life. Such terms may refer to phenomena that affect all levels of society and can be found in other cultures and places. For example, few Hispanos(as) know the meaning of the term *mancornadora*, which is used in many Mexican songs, yet are familiar with such old songs as "Rosita Alvirez," "El 24 de junio," or "La güera Chavela" in which a social context is provided for the term. These songs refer to a dance where a woman dances with a stranger; the old boyfriend walks in, and a killing ensues. As a person who has worked in the field of mental health and domestic violence, this kind of thing has interested me for many years. I name the event and then attempt a close examination of the topic. I make use of whatever is at my disposal for the analysis. As an example, a killing ensued in a northern New Mexico community when a jilted boyfriend waited until the former girlfriend left the Saturday night dance before committing murder ("Affidavits Filed" 2005, 4). Is this the Rosita Alvirez myth being played out?

My purpose is to inquire about events, situations, attitudes, and values; to wonder about them; and to suspend our understanding, at least until one can reconsider what we know about these daily events, and then come to a new understanding of ourselves. The phenomenological method asks us to suspend what we think we know about a social event and then to inquire about it. In addition, is it important to consider the cultural historical roots and its significance, and to place the behavior in a structure of universalized meaning.

The Culture of Words

Language is touted as the memory of a culture. Luis Rosales of the Royal Academy of Spain says in part: "Las palabras nos unen más que lo que pensamos. Son la memoria que se ha ido entretejiendo año tras año entre los vivos y los muertos. La lengua es la memoria total de sus habitantes" (Words unite us more than we think. Language is thus a memory that intertwines year after year both the living and dead. Language is the total memory of its inhabitants) (quoted in Mondragón and Roybal 1994, 7; my translation).

If a memory can be resurrected, as Antonio Medina (1983) of Mora, New Mexico, said, then "Our culture is not lost if we still have words for it. We can use words to resurrect the culture." It is indeed a living memory. Some of us do not "hunger for memory" if we still have our words to depict experience. It is a living thing within us—it revitalizes us to rediscover culture via the living word. Adherents of the "culture is dead" orientation have died to the word. *Pobresitos difuntos ya no son paisanos* (Poor dead souls; they are no longer *paisanos*). The New Mexico educator, poet, and writer Sabine Ulibarrí also depicted language as the living word, using a biblical metaphor to convey his meaning:

> In the beginning was the word and the word was made flesh. It was so in the beginning and it is so today. The language, the word, carries with it the history, the culture, the traditions, the very life of a people, the flesh. Language is people. We cannot even conceive of a people without a language, or a language without a people. The two are one and the same. To know one is to know the other. (Quoted in Abeyta 1995, 39)

Finally, that eminent student of Hispano culture Aurelio Espinosa wrote these words in 1911:

> The Spanish language as spoken by nearly a quarter of a million people in New Mexico and Colorado, is not a vulgar dialect, as many misinformed persons believe, but a rich archaic Spanish dialect largely Castilian in source.
>
> The influence of the English language on the Spanish of the entire Southwest is one of the greatest importance, and of the most intense interest to the philologist and ethnologist. The Spanish language in New Mexico and in the entire Southwest has had a great influence on the English vernacular of these regions, and its study is the greatest influence. (Quoted in Córdova 1970, 105)

Ernest Becker proposed that we are basically verbal edifices—we are word structures. For Becker, the power of the word was that it had to be delivered just so, because it impelled the other to answer. Words frame the structure of our interaction with others. "Words are the only tools we have for confident manipulation of the interpersonal situation. By verbally setting the tone for action by the proper ceremonial formula, we permit complementary action by our interlocutor" (Becker 1971a, 95). The culture of everyday life provides the meaning structures (i.e., the right words) for our action. Moreover, flawless performance means that we create ourselves in the performance. "As the individual exercises his creative powers in the social encounter, and basks in the radiation of fabricated meanings, his identity is revealed to himself. He forms himself into a meaningful ideational whole, receiving affirmations, banishing contradictions" (Becker 1971a, 99). Becker, of course, means all human beings of both genders.

Words give us meaning. On learning about the term *mancornadora* and its theme, one person I knew finally had a word for what had happened to her. She could now name the "other" woman as the *mancornadora* who took her man and disrupted her marriage. In writing chapter 5, I was preoccupied with some of the subtle messages in popular music. It still piques my interest when I hear the words of the "El asesino" and "El 24 de junio" and their underlying *mancornadora* themes: both songs have great rhythms for dancing, but underneath is the message of cuckoldry, stalking, and death. I often wonder whether the lyrics have an impact on someone at a bar drinking a beer and musing on a failed relationship. Perhaps the word may trigger an evil impulse to stalk and kill his love rival. I did not write chapter 5 to glorify violence, as one "educated" person accused me of doing. I was following a typification—an abstraction that arises in the daily lives of humans—to its logical conclusion (Schulz 1971). What is more astonishing to me is to hear music with these themes of violence played on the local radio stations or at Fourth of July parades! Rosita Alvirez is still around, if only in a song commemorating her death. These are some of the things I focus on in this book: words, culture, daily actions, everyday meanings, and how people make sense of them in their daily lives.

This book is not intended to be a social problems book or a prescriptive "what do you do about it" book. Some chapters do offer support for people who find themselves in dire situations. My primary purpose is to explore typifications and, in the process, to have a dialogue with myself and with any readers so inclined. If they find some of the ideas captivating, I will be pleased. I investigate "everyday meanings" as we find them in northern New Mexico. "Meaning" is an elusive term, but the context in which it is used in this book follows Ernest Becker's basic premise that people create meaning just by taking an action. It is when we reflect on these acts that we imbue them with meaning. We provide words for our actions. Thus, this book is an interpretation of the interpretations made by people in everyday life.

The Structure of the Chapters

Chapter 1 presents the theory of typifications as found in the work of Alfred Schutz, and provides the foundation of the remaining chapters. It provides the reader with an understanding of how existential phenomenology and ethnomethodology can assist in the study of everyday life.

Chapter 2 presents a view of the oral tradition of Hispanos. Some of these traditions such as using *dichos* are well known. There is considerable poetry to be found in *recuerdos*, remembrances for the dead. In this chapter some poetry is presented that depicts major events such as working *en la borrega* (sheepherding) or having been called to duty in World War II. Much of this poetry is influenced by the structure of the *corrido* and its predecessor from Spain called the *romance*.

Besides poetry one also needs to consider other aspects of the oral tradition known as *trovos* defined as the philosophical discourse between two opponents. Extending meaning to also include the use of everyday things is also covered in this chapter. Needless to say an incredible amount of oral material has been collected in the past and this chapter is only a small survey of all that exists

Chapter 3 is based on Erving Goffman's work. It is a study of the meaning of the term *mortificación* and its derivation from the monk Jonas Sufurino's *mortificar el cuerpo* (self-flagellation) as it was practiced around 1000 C.E. It can also refer to trouble we fret over, such as parents' loss of control over a child's behavior. The parents' inability to deal with such concerns is often experienced as their *mortificación*—a death of the self. One *viejito* (elderly man) said, "La mortificación puede tambien causar la muerte" (Mortification can also cause death).

Chapter 4 is about *la carría* (sometimes called *carrilla* or *cabula*) and dates to my doctoral studies many years ago. It shows that *carría* is antithetical to such cardinal values as *respeto* and *vergüenza*, and it examines how these values guided behavior in another time. Yet a recent discussion with a school principal suggested that the meanings of *la carría* remain alive, and so I also briefly discuss the social role of the *picaro*. This chapter owes much to the work of Erving Goffman and Mexican philosopher Jorge Portilla's *Fenomenología del relajo* (1966).

Chapter 5, my exploration of the *mancornadora* theme in Mexican music, has received considerable development. It is a study of songs that carry the core concept of "one woman, two men," and features such songs as "Rosita Alvirez," "La güera Chavela," "Lagunas de pesar," and "La mancornadora." The analysis proceeds from the idea that *mano y cuerno* (hand and horn) are the metaphors for this genre of songs, which are basically about being cuckolded. It is a study of the violence perpetrated in such situations.

Chapters 6 and 7 deal with interviews conducted with convicts in the maximum-security part of a Southwest prison. Chapter 6, on the *veterano pinto*, considers the role of the older, more experienced convict who has been in several prisons and has made crime a career. The *pintos'* core values, called the "convict code," play into the enactment of the role insofar as contact between friends is possible in a maximum-security prison. Roles are part of everyday life. In prison the convict code can help to explain many behaviors in relation to group cohesion and values. Some of these values parallel family values, for example, sharing of food.

Chapter 7 concerns a confrontation between two groups of convicts over a petition. This "naturally occurring trouble," as Reyes Ramos would describe it (1982, 120), happened because one group signed a petition and the other did not. The assumption that a *pinto* would "naturally" sign a petition being circulated against a guard led to two sets of expected behavior and conflict. In the chapter the group explored contrasting definitions of a situation that created consternation and divided loyalties among a group of convicts. This chapter illustrates how people deal with trouble and helps to uncover the reality of everyday life, even in a penitentiary.

In chapter 8, I focus on the term *desmadre*, which is used to describe situations that are out of control. If often indicates personal chaos—as in the statement *Estoy desmadrado* (I'm in a bad way). Poet Ricardo Sánchez writes about life in prison as his personal "desmadrazgos." The chapter deals with the scheming that goes on in organizations in which *lambes* "rat" on each other and lie to gain privilege. The chapter takes an existential phenomenological approach to analyze the origins of the term.

The ubiquitous crosses along New Mexico's highways led me to a consideration of *despedidas* in chapter 9. This technically refers to the formal leave-taking in a social encounter, but it means much more: the unique form of poetry of the basic corrido is used to create a remembrance for the dead, most often published in newspaper obituaries. These recuerdos (remembrances) are meant to console the living. The *Taos News* used to publish these recuerdos. Much depended on the writer's skill in presenting the death of a community individual. I have collected a number of them from the *Taos News* and elsewhere and have taken numerous pictures of roadside crosses (*descansos*) from all over New Mexico.

The last three chapters collectively focus on *el ciclo de vida y muerte* (the cycle of life and death). I amplify the basic idea by considering the metaphors that exist in life that support the notion of this *ciclo*. Antonio Medina, from Encinal in Mora County, first proposed the idea of a *ciclo de vida y muerte* to me, which seemed natural to him because he is a rancher and farmer. The idea for chapter 10 comes from the agrarian experience of Hispanos in northern New Mexico. The harvest plants die in winter but are reborn in the spring. In considering this cycle, I came to look at other possible *ciclos*, natural events that can also be metaphors for life and death. It ends with a personal odyssey in which I explore my own ending in time and my own meanings. In chapter 11, I reflect on the meaning of light and darkness. What happens when darkness prevails? The Tinieblas ceremony on Good Friday, as presented by the *La Cofradía de Nuestro Padre Jesús Nazareno*, presents a powerful contrast between death in darkness and light as resurrection. The term *tinieblas* also means being in the dark because one has not been educated about something one needed to know. The final *ciclo*, discussed in chapter 12, concerns despair and transcendence as another metaphor for death and resurrection. If psychotherapy is successful, one may think of oneself as finding a new self and a new life. *Dando gracias* is the giving of thanks for life itself. This last chapter also looks at the question of how apocalyptic thinking was part of the Hispano(a) experience of another generation. These three *ciclo* chapters cap my exploration of everyday meanings by examining the cosmic questions we all have about life and death.

A conclusions chapter attempts to round out the discussion by pointing to areas of possible research, the shortcomings of the method, and a call for more research based on phenomenological precepts.

Acknowledgments

How does one thank all the teachers and friends one has had over a lifetime? This task would involve thanking not just those in the university setting, but also lay teachers—the ones who were interviewed in one way or another for this book. Some of these folks worked as janitors, some were in prison, others were ranchers, neighbors, students, and colleagues. One colleague that deserves mention is Gabino Rendón from the Department of Behavioral Science, New Mexico Highlands University. It is important to recognize that he was instrumental in the development of the School of Social Work at New Mexico Highlands University. He was always committed to principles. Good listeners and excellent colleagues were David Engstrom and Katie McDonough. Robert C. Warren helped by opening possibilities for research. Others contributed to this book by being co-interviewers. I thank especially Hilbert Navarro for that. Former students took an interest in the project. Jake Lucero asked me many times, "¿Cuando vas acabar ese libro?" (When are you going to finish the book?) My reply was, "Ya mero, ya mero" (I'm almost done). That question, too, was an inspiration to continue. Some read the chapters and made comments. I thank my wife, Marie, who accompanied me and saw me through various graduate schools over the years. Thanks should be extended to former students Connie Buck, Sandra Yudilevich, Brian Kimber, Father José R. Vigil, Cecile J. Zeigler, Judge Matthew J. Sandoval, Patsy Andrada, and the social gerontologists who made life in the university bearable. At the University of Denver David Franks in the Department of Sociology opened the doors to phenomenology, symbolic interaction, ethnomethodology, and the works of Ernest Becker, R. D. Laing, and Peter Marris. Others like Annie Barva and David Estrin helped in immeasurable ways to get the text into shape. Anselmo Arellano, Julian J. Vigil, and Tomás Atencio were pioneers in the study of everyday life and an inspiration. Linda Gegick, administrator at the City Museum in Las Vegas, deserves special recognition for helping with the organization and presentation of the drawings and some translations by Sara Harris and Jorge Thomas. I also should thank the reviewers selected by Michigan State University Press, who provided valued comments. Special thanks should go to Rubén Martinez from the Julian Samora Research Center, Michigan State University, who provided valued guidance.

Clark Knowlton was a professor at New Mexico Highlands University teaching sociology in my undergraduate days. In those years this enlightened man was teaching us about "our people," which was indeed rare anywhere in the University in the mid-1960s. He had a passion for Hispano people and the land grant issue! Over the years, I learned to appreciate his vast store of knowledge. His letters always explored new ideas and offered support and assistance. We once had a conversation at the Western Social Science Conference in which I asked him if what I was writing at the time might be developed into a full-fledged book. He was more than encouraging, but it was only after retirement that a project of this sort was possible. It is to his memory and friendship that I dedicate this book.

•   •   •

An earlier version of chapter 3 was previously published in *Our Kingdom Stands on Brittle Glass*, edited by Guadalupe Gibson (National Association of Social Workers, 1983). Chapter 8 was previously published in *Expressing New Mexico: Nuevomexicano Creativity, Ritual, and Memory*, edited by Phillip B. Gonzales (University of Arizona Press, 2007) © 2007 The Arizona Board of Regents. Reprinted by Permission of the University of Arizona Press. Portions of chapter 9 appear in "Despedidas as Reflections of Death in Hispanic New Mexico," in *La Familia: Traditions and Realities*, edited by Marta Sotomayor and Alejandro García (National Hispanic Council on Aging, 1999). This chapter was also previously published in *Omega: Journal of Death and Dying* 32 (1996): 245–68.

Phenomenology of Everyday Life: *Fenomenología Cotidiana y los Hispanos*

> It is impossible to derive the basic logic of a science of persons from the logic of non-personal sciences. No branch of natural science requires us to make the particular type of inferences that are required in a science of persons.
>
> R. D. Laing, *Self and Others*

THIS BOOK IS A STUDY OF EPISTEMOLOGY, WHICH I DEFINE AS WHAT PEOPLE know in their daily lives. Becker and Laing are used as starting points for a general depiction of Hispano thought, which includes the study of how language develops an understanding of the world of everyday life. Language usage is the vehicle for understanding how people name events, interactions, attitudes, and values. Understanding how words are used to construct the edifice of everyday life is best accomplished by using concepts from phenomenology.

Phenomenology allows one to study the elements of everyday life as phenomena. In order for us to make a reasoned inquiry about something (e.g., *mortificación*) as a lingual event, we must be willing to suspend whatever beliefs and preconceptions we have about this term in order to develop an understanding of it and what it signifies. We need to learn how this word is understood and used by people in everyday life. In this approach, I treat everyday life—that is, "lived experience"—as phenomena and not as part of that which is taken for granted. I need to become a stranger to this reality—and sometimes to my own reality—in order to reexperience it and be able to say something about its nature. The world of everyday life is structured in terms of words. Hispanos, like other people, have a vast array of words and concepts that they use in dealing with daily life.

In 1964, Ernest Becker called for a "quiet revolution" in psychiatry, in which an invasion of psychiatry by philosophy and the social sciences would change the reductionist medical view of human problems. Becker's work in part sets out to redefine and reexamine psychiatric symptoms and, in his words, "to merge [psychiatry] into a broad, human science so that the study of man in society, to which an enlightened social psychiatry will be a contributing discipline" (Becker 1964, 2). Philosophy, sociology, anthropology, and the other perspectives (e.g., existentialist thought) would enlarge the psychiatric view of man. This proposed revolution in psychiatry was prompted by two converging sources of dissatisfaction: the medical model as a perspective for the amelioration of human ills, and the physical science model for research on human problems. Part of the dissatisfaction with these concepts, argues R. D. Laing, is that the technical vocabulary used to describe psychiatric patients splits human beings into such dichotomies as *inner* and *outer* reality, *mind* and *body*, *psych* and *soma*, and *physical* and *psychic* reality. These terms serve to isolate humans from each other and from the world (Laing 1976, 24–26).

When parts of this chapter were written many years ago, my intent was to break loose from reductionist views of Hispanos as portrayed in the social sciences, and also from a "science" perspective that defines concepts in terms of how they are to be "operationalized" and measured. I once presented a paper on the Hispano view of *vergüenza* and was asked what steps were to be taken to develop it into a "shame" scale. Similar questions were asked of a paper on mortification. Why had a survey not been conducted to situate the concept? The *mortificación* paper, as it was judged, needed not only an operational definition of the concept showing how one was going to measure it, but also a survey and a statistical analysis to "prove" the existence of the concept. The paper was rejected for publication because it failed to meet "scientific exactitude." Another bone of contention stems from the predilection in mental health for defining a concept in terms of its remediation. A tendency exists among human services professionals to "medicalize" social problems and to define some issues in terms of their remediation. People suffer gravely from *mortificación* because it involves a social interaction in which one family member vexes another. I once received a telephone call from a state mental hospital employee saying that a recently admitted woman was suffering from *mortificaciones* (as the lady described her situation). Someone knew that I had written a paper on the topic, so I was asked, "What do you do about it?" But the vexer was obviously no longer vexing the mortified person, as she had been admitted to the mental hospital. The social worker could not see the interaction between the vexer and the vexed person as the source of the described mortifications. Thus, the social worker wanted to "treat" the individual at the mental hospital, away from the social interaction that had created the concern.

Social Science and the Phenomenological Method

Norman Denzin contrasts empirical social science based on the logical-positivist perspective and social science based on the phenomenological method:

> The human experience does not present itself to the researcher in terms of variables, causal paths, tests of significance, or answers to fixed choice questionnaires. Rather that experience comes to the researcher in terms of lived experience, thickly embedded in the historical, interactional, temporal, emotional and relational worlds of everyday life. Accordingly our concerns should be with how to uncover and disclose meaning and meaningful experience, as that meaning is grounded in the lives of those we study. A preoccupation with the study of meaning, and not the study of the method, should occupy the attention of the human disciplines. (Denzin 1984a, 1)

He continues:

> The structures of human experience are woven through a logic that is dialectical, not analytical, linear or causal. To impose analytical, linear, sequential logic on human experience is to violate the very structures of the conduct we wish to interpret and understand. Dialectical reason, as it is stitched into the fabrics of human group life, thus becomes the subject matter of phenomenological inquiry.
>
> Dialectical reason is historical, conflictual, pragmatic, emotional, and temporal. That is, it is embedded in the historical structures that confront the human as she interacts with her fellow humans through the legal, linguistic, kinship, economical, political, cultural and ideological categories given by her society. A conflict of negation, affirmation, thesis and antithesis, and synthesis is grounded in the pragmatic, practical structure of action she undertakes on a daily basis. (Denzin 1984a, 1)

People create meanings—or, according to Alfred Schutz, *typifications*—about the lived experience. These meanings are the social stock of knowledge that is passed from one generation to another through families, groups, or cultures. We learn names for events, situations, attitudes, things, and people (*consociates*, as Schutz refers to fellow human beings) (Schutz 1971). The goal of this book is to consider these typifications and define them in emotional, historical, dialectical, and social-interactional terms. Phenomenology is an attempt to bracket what we think we know about an experience; more important, it is a "study of the structures that govern the instances of particular manifestations of the essence of those phenomena. In other words, phenomenology is the systematic attempt to uncover and describe the structures, the internal meanings structures of lived experience" (van Manen 1990, 10). An example of a lived experience comes from the term *mancornadora*, which will be examined in chapter 5. The term is heard in many Mexican songs, most of them about the killing of women. Does this mean that Hispanos and Mexicans are violent? What is the original social-interactional meaning of this typified term? What is the essence of it root meaning? What do the roots *mano* and *cuerno* ("hand" and "horn") imply in the word? How is it indicative of types (typal categories) of social interactions? What is the experience of being a *mancornado(a)* like? What are the cultural-historical roots of these interactions? The dictionary can give us a concise definition, but it does not take us far enough into the social world to understand the historical, dialectical, temporal, and interactional nuances of the term. Van Manen opines that phenomenological analysis is

> the study of lived or existential meanings; it attempts to describe and interpret these meanings to a certain degree of depth and richness. In this focus upon meaning, phenomenology differs from some other social or human sciences which may focus not on meanings but on statistical relationships among variables, on the predominance of social opinions, or on the occurrence or frequency of certain behaviors, etc. (van Manen 1990, 11)

Typifying Experience

We can use the theory of typifications from the phenomenology of Alfred Schutz to describe the consciousness of feelings, emotions, attitudes, values, and social relations of Hispanos. To begin, it is necessary to describe the term *Hispano/a*. I use the term Hispanos to refer to both genders (except as noted with an *a* or an *o*, as in *Hispana/o*). Spanish-speaking persons in northern New Mexico and southern Colorado use Hispanos to refer to themselves. It is not meant to disparage any other Spanish-speaking peoples in the country, but rather is a self-referencing term with a long historical usage. Mexico and other Spanish-speaking countries, as well as the United States, influence the everyday life of New Mexico's Hispanos. For example, the chapter on *despedidas* underscores the great influence of the Mexican corrido and its Spanish precursor, the *romance*, in the writing of local recuerdos (remembrances) in the newspapers of northern New Mexico. There is no pure culture because Hispanos, like other peoples in this country, migrate from one language identity to another.

In this book, I attempt to answer such questions as these: What is the experience of misery in *mortificación* or in *desmadre* like? What are the rules in *carría* games? What are the assumptions of life behind bars in a southwestern prison? What views do Hispanos have of life and death, and how do they demonstrate these views? In grappling with these and other questions, I will attempt to peel back the layers of the reality of everyday life to expose core ideas. The whole of social reality obviously cannot be tackled, but I offer a methodology that could be extended to study other aspects of social life. I offer a sampling of some typifications found in social life. By typifications, I mean the ability to abstract and name various aspects of social reality. Indeed, "to typify is to abstract" (Natanson 1974, 69). It is the naming of social events, social situations, persons, and types of interactions. *Mitote* (gossip) is one such typification. Some kinds of verbal experiences are of the genre *mitote*, others are not. What qualifies as *mitote*? Where does the word come from? Under what conditions does *mitote* flourish? The topics in this book have been selected largely by what has struck me as important over the years.

Although other tantalizingly interesting areas are part of everyday life in New Mexico, I do not tackle them in this book. For example, how do Hispanos as individuals or families develop spiritual devotions? How (or why) do some Hispanos latch on to particular saints? One person told me that when her nephew was in the Vietnam War, she would pray diligently to San Martín (1579–1639), a ubiquitous saint in New Mexico homes and churches. For example, he is depicted on the main wall of the Villanueva, New Mexico, village church. He was the mulatto son of an African woman and a white man and suffered much discrimination from his fellow Dominican friars in seventeenth-century Peru. *Es el santo de la escoba* (San Martín is usually shown with a broom as he feeds his little animals). When this woman's nephew returned from the war, he showed slides of Vietnam to his aunt. The soldier testified that he had a particular guardian, a fellow soldier who had saved his life on a number of occasions. When shown the picture of this war buddy and guardian, she knew that her prayers to San Martín had been answered. The guardian proved to be an African American soldier.

When personal trouble started for her, one woman usually said, "Es tiempo de rezarle al santo" (It's time to pray to the saint). San Antonio has a particular import to Hispanos because they believe he finds lost objects when one makes an ardent appeal. Taking the *Santo Niño* away from him is particularly motivating to this *santo* (saint) because he wants his "charge" returned to him: hence the *santo's* motivation to recover lost objects. A prayer to San Antonio might present other needs: "San Antonio bendito, tres cosas te pido, salud, dinero y un buen marido" (Blessed Saint Anthony, three things I ask of thee, health, money, and a good husband). Another prayer says, "Tony, Tony, something has been lost." Once we turn our attention to these aspects of daily life, we begin the process of wondering about these beliefs and behaviors. These observations become the grist for phenomenological analysis. To begin in wonder is the first step in any phenomenological inquiry, as Natanson (1974) said, in order to unearth the richness of everyday life.

Commonsense Reasoning

Kenneth Leiter's *A Primer on Ethnomethodology*, based on Alfred Schutz's theory of phenomenology, lists three major themes of the phenomenology of everyday life: (1) the social stock of knowledge at hand, (2) the natural attitude, and (3) commonsense reasoning (Leiter 1980). Schutz refers to the social stock of knowledge at hand as recipes, general ways of doing things, such as the presentation of self to others, rules of thumb, social types, maxims, and definitions (1971, 8). The social stock of knowledge is handed down via family teachings, formal schooling, religious instruction, and other types of instruction. Only a small portion of the social stock of knowledge comes out of one's personal experience (Schutz 1971, 13). This knowledge is expressed in terms of everyday terminology. "The vernacular of everyday life is primarily a language of named things and events, and any name includes a typification and generalization referring to the relevant system prevailing in the linguistic in-group which found the named thing significant enough to provide a separate term for it" (Schutz, quoted in Leiter 1980, 6). For example, the prison stock of knowledge covered in chapters 6 and 7 is the naming of various kinds of convicts by Hispano men in a southwestern prison. Named social types found in barrios, work environments, universities, and prisons all participate in their own social stock of knowledge.

The natural attitude forms another basis for phenomenology. The natural attitude is an intersubjective world defined through the stock of knowledge and is taken for granted—until something disrupts the social understanding of this knowledge. In fact, the world is taken for granted until unanticipated events cause us to question our social stock of knowledge and our understanding of social reality. The natural attitude is a depiction of the structure of the social world as it is encountered and experienced by members of our social grouping. In order to study many of the concepts presented in this book, I had to suspend my prior understanding of the reality they denote for the reality to become manifest to me. For example, the idea of the chapter on *mortificación* came from a student's (an older Anglo man) question in one of my classes. He asked me if what I was talking about was an example of *mortificación*. He was married to a Mexican woman who probably complained of the mortifications she was experiencing in living with him. She used a typification from her social stock of knowledge to describe what she was experiencing. This question caused me to suspend my own ideas about *mortificación*, a term I had often heard at home concerning the doings of a mentally ill sister. I began to "bracket" what I knew about the term until I could begin a reasoned inquiry into the term. The student had laid bare for me the idea of mortification. It seemed even stranger coming as it did from an older Anglo student. Natanson talks about rendering reality "strange," or entering into a

> radical stance, a remarkable way of looking at things. That experience cannot be taken straightforwardly, that it is to-be-understood, introduces a mode of reversal into ordinary and unreflective acceptance of the mundane course of affairs: a philosophical turn of mind signifies a shifting perspective from simple placement in the world to wonder aslant about it. Philosophy begins with the critique of mundanity. The narrow sense of transformation of familiarity into strangeness involves the phenomenological attitude. (Natanson 1974, 8)

The facticity of social reality is taken as real and commonsense reasoning forms the basis for this understanding. Schutz states that although one experiences social reality from within one's own spatial-temporal perspective, one also experiences the world as known in common with social others (Schutz 1971). Our position in relation to another person is that we take it for granted that he or she thinks the same way we do; "until counter evidence [occurs] I take it for granted—and assume my fellow man does the same—that the different perspectives originating in our unique biological situations are irrelevant for the purpose at hand" (Leiter 1980, 10).

People use these two forms of commonsense reasoning daily to deal with the problematic features of everyday life. An interesting study of the Martinez family from Ormiga, Colorado, in trouble with the authorities, provides us with an understanding of how one family dealt with a problematic situation. Mrs. Martinez was supposed to appear in court to deal with problems related to her children's connection to a number of state and local social agencies. Mrs. Martinez worked in a turkey factory that the Immigration and Naturalization Service (INS) had previously raided to apprehend undocumented workers. The officials from the various social agencies expected that Mrs. Martinez would not show up for the court hearing, believing that she was a "bad" parent and would not comply with the court order. Mrs. Martinez, in her commonsense reasoning, had indeed decided not to attend the court hearing, not because she was a "bad" parent, but because she was a good worker and the factory was shorthanded after the INS raid—"and everybody knows that" (Ramos 1973, 915). Reyes Ramos convinced her to appear in court, creating disbelief when she showed up. Ramos was at the time working for the schools and had been sent by the principal to evaluate the situation in Mrs. Martinez's home.

Mrs. Martinez's "here" was that "everybody" (the "there" in Schutz's reciprocity-of-perspectives theory of "here" and "there")—that is, all reasonable people—would understand her absence from the court hearing. In commonsense thinking, two idealizations operate: the "interchangeability of standpoints" and the "congruency of a system of relevances" (Natanson 1974, 85–86). In the first, as Natanson explains,

> I take it for granted and assume that my *alter ego* [the other person] does the same that were an exchange effected we would both be at the same distance from objects and in essentially the same relation to them which pertained in each case before the transposition. In the second idealization, I take it for granted along with my alter ego that considerations unique to my and his biographical situation may be set aside in the perception and even, within certain limits, the interpretation of common objects. (Natanson 1974, 86)

Schutz takes the theory further:

> By the operation of those constructs of common sense thinking it is assumed that the sector of the world taken for granted by me is also taken for granted by you, my individual fellow-man, even more, that it is taken for granted by "Us." But this "We" does not merely include you and me but "everyone who is one of us," i.e. everyone whose system of relevances is substantially (sufficiently) in conformity with yours and mine. Thus, the general thesis of reciprocal perspectives leads to the apprehension of objects and their aspects actually known by me and potentially known by you as everyone's knowledge. (Schutz 1971, 12)

This idea is given a practical perspective in chapter 7, in which the definition of the meaning of the term "convict" is discussed in a men's group in a penitentiary.

The Problem of Methodology

In this section various issues are presented dealing with a descriptive methodology. It is not a strict methodology like that found in most social science research texts but instead presents some considerations that affect descriptive analysis.

A BASIC DESCRIPTION OF PHENOMENOLOGY

Phenomenology offers a means to study the natural stance. The term "phenomenology" is derived from two Greek words: *phainomenon* (an appearance), and *logos* (reason or word), hence we have the definition of a "reasoned inquiry."

Phenomenology concerns the essence of appearances. Appearances are anything of which one is conscious, and hence phenomenology begins with an analysis of one's own consciousness of the world (Stewart and Mickunas 1974, 3). Consciousness is analyzed in different ways by different phenomenologists. Phenomenology is a loose-knit collection of problems, philosophers, and philosophies brought together with a first-person description, but without the theoretical bias of one's own consciousness of the world (Solomon 1979, 3).

Alfred Schutz questions whether "behavior should be studied in the same manner in which the natural scientist studies his object or whether the goal of the social sciences is the explanation of 'social reality' as experienced by man living his everyday life within the social world." He goes on to posit that

> the social sciences have to deal with human conduct and its commonsense interpretations in the social reality involving the analysis of the whole system of projects and motives, of relevances and constructs. . . . Such an analysis refers by necessity to the subjective points of view, namely to the interpretation of the action and its settings in terms of the actor. (Schutz 1971, 34)

This quotation opens up the entire social world for analysis. It opens up the subjective world of actors, the meanings that people in everyday life—whether in a barrio, a prison, or a university—use to make sense of their social situation. The analysis is descriptive, interpretive, and subjective. Common sense and its interpretation are what people use in managing and coping with the problems of everyday life (Ramos 1973, 915).

Geertz favors a "thick description" approach to the study of culture and society in terms of everyday life. What we call our "data" he suggests "are really our own constructions of other people's constructions of what they and their compatriots are up to," and these constructions are "obscured because most of what we need to comprehend a particular event, ritual, custom, idea, or whatever is situated as background information before the thing itself is directly examined" (Geertz 1973, 9). This task [thick description] must be anchored to the reality of everyday life or to the culture under study. It is a double task "to uncover the conceptual structures that inform our subject's acts, the 'said' of social discourse, and to construct a system of analysis in whose terms what is generic to those structures, what belongs to them because they are what they are, will stand out against other determinants of human behavior" (Geertz 1973, 27).

Finding and developing an analysis for a term such as *mancornadora* moves us toward identifying the original cultural-historical meaning of the term. This term is used in a number of Mexican songs and in more recent songs in northern New

Mexico. We must also describe the term, concept, or symbol (i.e., its typification) within a nexus of social interaction (i.e., settings with other human beings). This is the meaning of "intersubjectivity": the linking of the symbol within a social-interactional context. In analytical work, it is also necessary to generalize the findings. After locating the root meanings of a typification or concept, one may want to extend it in a Jungian sense to other cultures and groups dealing with the same conceptual issues, but perhaps in different forms. This amplification finds what is "human" across a variety of cultures. In the case of *la mancornadora*, once one reaches the essence of this typification, one can apply the concept to themes in country-and-western music or to the major theme in the opera *Carmen*.

SCHUTZIAN TYPIFICATION

A typification captures a whole system of meanings. For example, to say that one is giving the other guy *carría* is to invoke whole systems of meaning that members of the in-group readily grasp. One need only refer to the term to get the idea across, as in saying, "I was only giving you *carría*, man!"—a type of joking exchange. Likewise, other words (e.g., *desmadre*) are quickly apprehended when used in everyday talk among an Hispano in-group. These and other terms exist as typifications, and are readily grasped and understood. Other terms may be arcane and not used much in everyday life today (e.g., *mortificación* or *mancornadora*), but once the meanings are abstracted, one can quickly grasp their application to human situations. We need to move beyond a simple dictionary definition to an understanding of the social-interactional and cultural-historical roots of the term and, once we have situated it socially, to an understanding of its broader implications.

A BECKERIAN ANALYSIS

Those who follow the work of Ernest Becker refer to a "Beckerian" analysis. It is concerned not only with linking philosophy and psychiatry, as Becker advocated, but also with the use of poetry, music, text, literature, artistic images, and folk psychology in order to achieve a better understanding of the phenomena one is studying (Becker 1964). As van Manen states,

> Phenomenological understanding is distinctively existential, emotive, enactive, embodied, situational, and non-theoretic; a powerful phenomenological text thrives on a certain irrevocable tension between what is unique and what is shared, between particular and transcendental meaning, and between the reflective and the pre-reflective spheres of the lifeworld. (van Manen 1977, 346)

I take up some of the thematic material suggested by Stewart and Mickunas (1974) below and begin with the intentionality of consciousness as a collective of ideas.

CONSCIOUSNESS OF WORDS AND FEELINGS

Phenomenologists state that consciousness must necessarily be consciousness of something toward which it is intentionally directed. Thus, one can ascribe meaning to that which is in consciousness. Consciousness "is not considered an 'interiority', an imaginary space with certain contents and processes, interacting with the physical being and with a sensorially appearing outer world." Buytendijk, influenced by the phenomenology of Husserl, believes that a return to the "things themselves"—an inspection of knowledge itself unfettered by theories or formalized conceptions, as given to us directly—reveals the intentionality of "act-character of all behavior" (Buytendijk 1960, 128). Feeling and emotions, as an example, "are the affirmations of our attitudes toward situations, and the pure phenomena of feeling reveals the human being in his well-defined attitude toward a situation." Thus, feeling is an act in which there is reference to an object that is intentionally present. This leads Buytendijk to assert that there are as many feelings as there are situations (1960, 130). For example, the consciousness of shame as an experience occurs in the presence of other people. Consciousness is always of something, whether that something is an external object, a relationship, or a part of one's own consciousness (Stewart and Mickunas 1974, 9). Consciousness can also be of real or of unreal objects (a proposition as an ideal object, e.g., a number) (Solomon 1979, 8).

Each situation in social life evokes its share of feelings. Because experience is captured in words, one can appreciate the range of feelings reflected in the Spanish words that describe types of depression: for example, *aguitado(a)*, *deprimido(a)*, *agotado(a)*, *acongojado(a)*, *aburrido(a)*, *desanimado(a)*, *desesperado(a)*. What is missing is the object of these words. *¿De que esta usted desanimado(a), desesperado(a), agüitado(a)?* (What is making you depressed, agitated, or distressed?) The problem is to link these emotive terms to the social interaction experience.

THE UNCONSCIOUS MIND

R. D. Laing objects to any vocabulary, technical or otherwise, used to describe psychiatric patients in that such terms split humans into dichotomous realities, for example, inner/outer, mind/body, psyche/soma, physical/psychic. These designations, according to Laing, serve to separate humans from each other (Laing 1976, 24–26). Finding these problems "inside" the person or "in his or her mind" has far-reaching implications in the sense that the problem is inaccessible to others.

The analyst (social worker, psychologist, or other mind doctor) implies that the person's behavior has "meaning" to which the other is blind, and in that sense the other cannot "see" or "realize" the person's actions (Laing 1969, 20). The concept of the unconscious asserts that the implications of the person's inner experience consists of processes that, if interpreted correctly (by a mind expert), can be used to explain the person's actions or inner experiences. Persons are basically unaware of the reasons for their behaviors in the intrapsychic battlefield because unconscious processes keep these behaviors from consciousness.

C. Wright Mills suggests there is no need to delve into "unconscious mongering" because the avowal and imputation of motives is concomitant with the question asked. "Motives are imputed or avowed as answers to questions interrupting acts or programs. Motives are words . . . They do not denote elements 'in' individuals. They stand for anticipated situational consequences of questioned conduct" (Mills 1970, 473). In other words, one can keep asking questions of an individual, who will provide his or her motives until the questioner is satisfied with the reason (i.e., the motive) given by the individual. It is important to note this point of disagreement by Mills because it marks the delineation between those who deal with unconscious motivations, depth psychology, or the psychoanalytic school, and those who follow the phenomenological or sociological—and hence intentionality-of-consciousness—perspective. Those who follow the unconsciousness school of thought assert that the person is unaware of psychic mechanisms and processes and requires a mind specialist to be able to impute their meaning.

Those who follow the phenomenological position on the emotions, however, assert that consciousness and motivation is always available to the person. For Schutz, motives can be described in terms of a person's response as a "because" motive or an "in order to" motive. The "because" motive is the project of the person's life action for satisfying a need. "I am in graduate school because I want to become a sociologist" is a "because" motive. The "in order to" motive refers to the carrying out of some future action (Schutz 1971, 21–22). "In order for me to become an electrician I have to know the State of New Mexico building codes" is an example of an "in order to" motive. In effect, a person can give either a "because" motive or an "in order to" motive to satisfactorily explain the motivation or reasons behind his or her actions. In short, motives are social and accessible to the person and to others.

A PROPOSED EXISTENTIAL PHENOMENOLOGICAL MODEL

A methodology can be developed from the ideas found in Stewart and Mickunas's introductory book on phenomenology. The authors identify several concepts that, as presented, are to be found across a number of phenomenologies. To present these concepts as important ideas for a methodology means that one has some degree of confidence in them. One can use these categories as "guidelines" or as a map to guide a descriptive analysis. Even though at first glance these categories seem simplistic there is a wealth of philosophical thought beyond them. The categories overlap considerably and therefore are not "crisp" and distinct. As found in Stewart and Mickunas (1974), the elements of a model are the natural attitude, intentionality of consciousness, intersubjectivity, reflecting, bracketing, the lived body, freedom and choice, language, and meaning. These topics are covered in the pages to follow, but not all of them are given the same amount of attention.

These categories support an existential phenomenology. "Existential phenomenology is primarily concerned with meaning and value. The modes by which we become conscious of meaning must be examined: feeling, perceiving, remembering, imaging, willing, reflecting" (Lawrence and O'Connor 1967, 10). One might add relating, seeing, and interacting with the elements of one's social environment. These "ing" terms reflect the lifeworld of experience. Experience is reflected as fleeting and of the moment. When one reflects on the meaning of these fleeting experiences then they become sedimented as meaning. We typify these experiences as we dress them with words. They can be further typified as felt meanings, as they are emotions and meanings. Gendlin puts it thus: "It is when we explicate a meaning and focus on it that this meaning is felt or experienced while it is being explicated. A meaning is explicated in terms of symbols whose meanings are felt or experienced. It is this feeling or experiencing that constitutes the 'having' of an explicated meaning" (1997, 66–67). The experiences of losing land still generates intense feelings of rage, anger, frustration, and depression, as Zantelle (2005) discovered when she asked her respondents about this in their family histories. One man remembered the loss of his grandparents' lands because an uncle and a grandmother could not agree on how to divide them among descendants. He stated, "My uncle got Speer, my dad got Catron [territorial attorneys], and she got herself another lawyer. They contested the case for two or three years until the lawyers kept everything. They had to sell the land to pay the lawyers" (Baca ca. 1973).

In addition, when considering Hispanos in particular, one must deal with the cultural-historical meanings of terms and concepts. Specifically, one needs to recognize the cultural-traditional perspective of how language forms the world of everyday life. A fundamental idea is that any description ought to lead to the core or essence of the concept. It should be describable in a few words. For example, what lies at the core of the experience of envy? Sandoval answers, "*Envidia* is an emotion with many faces. It makes you desire what you see in others or what they have that you wished you could possess" (Sandoval 1996, 37).

INTENTIONALITY OF CONSCIOUSNESS

The phrase "intentionality of consciousness" means that consciousness is always directed toward an object. One's consciousness is never empty because it is always weighing the importance of objects, events, emotions, attitudes, situations, or anything to which we attend. The intentionality of consciousness points to the absurdity of dividing reality into mutually exclusive categories of minds and bodies or the subject and object of the Cartesian duality. For Stewart and Mickunas, the intentionality of consciousness shifts the emphasis from the question of the reality of the world to the meaning presented to consciousness (Stewart and Mickunas 1974, 8–9).

Rollo May makes the intentionality of consciousness central to a perspective for psychotherapy. He traces the etymology of the term "intentionality" from the root term "intention"—a stretching outward to the thing to be understood. It is also the process of knowing that "we are in-formed by the thing understood and in the same act, our intellect simultaneously *gives* form to the thing understood." To "in-form" someone is to change him or her from within: a captivating idea in psychotherapy. Likewise, our interaction with the world forms us by giving meaning to consciousness. "Consciousness is defined by the fact that it *intends* something, points toward something outside itself—specifically that it *intends the object*," creating meaningful contents to consciousness (May 1969, 225–26). All of these terms come from the Latin *intendere*, which is a product of *in-* with *tendere* and *tensum*, both compounds meaning "a stretching toward something." A stretching toward something is the active nature of all consciousnesses. From *tendere* emerges the word "tend," as in "care for," "attend to," "take into account," and "lean toward something." May makes an important distinction here, underscoring that "tend" involves caring—we care about the world and ourselves in it. We have an investment in elements of social life, and hence consciousness is about being involved with the world (May 1969, 228–29; van Manen 1990).

Meaning carries a commitment with it. It is of a human being intending something, an act of will or conation. Each act of consciousness tends toward something and, no matter how latent, a direction for action (May 1969, 230).

Atender, the Spanish word for "attention," means "caring," as in attending to our parents' needs in their old age. We may say, *Voy atender a mis padres*. An "attendant" used to be a job title for persons who worked in the old "state hospital"—a mental health facility—in Las Vegas, New Mexico. Such a term reflected the job of a person who literally "waited on" (i.e., tended to) the patients' needs. In time, this job title became "psychiatric technician," with a different job description and a totally different corpus of work. What a difference is implied in social service philosophy when one attends to people's needs rather than deals with "offenders," "perpetrators," "schizophrenics," "the ill," and other invidiously labeled persons who "have a condition" that needs our remediation. Sands argues that this kind of labeling is done by persons in human services who, in taking a history of patients, attest to patterns consistent with diagnostic categories. "Once labeled, the patient becomes socialized into a sick role that he or she may continue to play throughout life" (Sands 1983, 81). When psychiatric patients have been successfully labeled, they are rewarded for playing the sick role and "punished when they try to resume conventional lives" (Scheff 1984, 66). Sands and others have questioned the reliability and validity of the *Diagnostic and Statistical Manual* (*DSM*), a classification manual for assigning a diagnostic mental health category to a human being. She also believes that certain groups in society are more likely than others to be given psychiatric labels, which is in essence a political act (Szasz 1961; Halleck 1971).

In Spanish the word *entender* has the dual meaning of "comprehension" (a cognitive act) and "conation," as in *ponerse de entender o un entendimiento*, committing to an act. *Ponerse de entender* or *de acuerdo* means that two persons have come to an understanding, as in an *entendimiento* (cognition), or an agreement, as when two persons reach an understanding that defines their *entendimiento* when they elect to follow certain actions (conation). Love and will are one and the same; cognition joins with conation (May 1969). The combination forms an understanding that parents' need for their own well-being means that they are *en acuerdo con . . .* , already implying the consciousness to carry out a *comportamiento*, a "commitment," or more specifically, an "action." There is knowledge that the need will be met—the requisite action will be taken to carry out the intention, and so the consciousness of understanding joins the carrying out of acts to meet the need. Our intentionality of consciousness is the will to meet a person's need.

INTERSUBJECTIVITY

Laing's existential phenomenology proposes that only existential thought has attempted to match the original experience of the patient or person in his being-in-the-world. In effect, psychiatry and by extension other human sciences

> cannot give an undistorted account of "a person" without giving an account of his relations with others. Even an account of one person cannot afford to forget that each person is always *acting* upon others and *acted upon* by others. The others are there also. No one acts or experiences in a vacuum. The person whom we describe, and over whom we theorize *is not the only agent in his "world."* How he perceives and acts toward the others, how they perceive and act toward him, how he perceives them as perceiving him, how they

perceive them are all aspects of the "situation." They are all pertinent to understanding one person's participation in it. (Laing 1976, 66)

For example, this view is exemplified in a *dicho* that tells us, *Dime con quien andas y te dire quien eres* (Tell me who you hang around with, and I will tell you who you are). Laing's statement has all the elements for a phenomenological frame of reference. First, Laing shows us that all social meaning is derived from our social interactions with others or from what Stewart and Mickunas (1974) call "intersubjectivity." Our reflective stance as we perceive others and our perception of them perceiving us form another tenet of phenomenology called "reflexivity." I can also have the awareness that I can be an object of my own consciousness. Our intentionality of consciousness (our perception) extends or "reaches out" toward the other. It is a stretching toward the other in our intimate subjectivity. Existential phenomenology is concerned with meaning as we "make sense" of these experiences and further our commonsense understanding of the world.

Schutz characterizes the intersubjective world in the following way:

We live in it as men among other men, bound to them through common interest and work, understanding others and being understood by them. It is a world of culture because, from the onset, the world of everyday life is a universe of significance to us, that is, a texture of meaning which we have to interpret in order to find our bearings within it and come to terms with it. (Schutz 1971, 10)

This texture of meaning, says Schutz, originates in human action, our own and that of others. All cultural objects (e.g., tools, symbols, works of art) point back by their origin and meaning to the activities of human actors. It is important, therefore, to consider the "historicity of culture" that we encounter in traditions and customs (Schutz 1971, 10). It should force us to consider the antecedent cultural-historical meanings of that which we are investigating. Where did the typified term we are investigating come from? What was its original meaning? What is the essence of its meaning—its core understanding—in everyday life? We may look at the term *mitote* and consider its everyday meaning: "gossip." It has a contagious element because others are invited to pass on the gossip. We may further note that it is a dance of the Coros, the Nahuatl-speaking Indians of the Sierra Madre, in Nayarit, Mexico. This *danza*, called *mi'totilizli*, involves the whole community and is characterized by its rowdy and noisy behavior ("El Mitote Cora" 2007). The dictionary definition of *mitote* is "rowdiness, boisterousness." This short discussion is only to whet the intellectual appetite for the fuller analysis presented in chapter 8.

MEANING AND MAKING SENSE

That knowledge exists perceptually and conceptually is demonstrated in Robert Coles's *The Old Ones of New Mexico*. Coles, who usually works on developing the text of children's lives, interviewed many older people in New Mexico because they were the key to understanding their children's children. In the chapter on necessity (*la necesidad*, indicating the conceptual), one hears an old man talking:

> I am on the bottom, and so naturally it takes time for a poor man like me to receive much of anything. I have worked all my life, and I have no regrets. I only hope my grandchildren realize their dreams. Necessity has been my master. I have had no time to stop and ask questions. I have had no time to argue. Perhaps if I had been more like my oldest son, and if all of us my age had been like him, then we could have gained some concessions from the rich people who run businesses and run the government and decide the fate of the poor. But we did not know how to fight for ourselves then. Besides, we are proud; and we will not feel sorry for ourselves. Never do I want to go to someone with my hat in my hand or on my knees—never, never. I have kept quiet in the past when I wanted to shout at Anglos; but I have never lost my pride in my dealings with them. (Coles 1973, 52)

Necessity becomes typified in his life and is more than just a word to him. The old man gives meaning to *necesidad* by centering it as lived experience. It is the enemy of the man in *pobreza*, hunger, low wages, and poverty. For the phenomenologist of everyday life, this depiction can be typified as *la necesidad o viviendo en la necesidad*. Coles's interviewee continues:

> But we never quite lost all hope, even during the worst of times. My grandfather used to say to me when I was but a boy that our people have been living on this land here in New Mexico for a long, long, long time—many generations, back and back and back of time. Only the Indians were here before us. The Anglos came much later. So we will not leave, and we will somehow keep ourselves alive. Necessity demands it. (Coles 1973, 52)

The man's perceptions of his times and of how he is with his family at this point in time are captured in a well-known *dicho, Enseña más la necesidad, que un año de universidad* (Necessity teaches more than a year of university studies). Here the perceptual joins the conceptual. The *dicho* captures what New Mexico's Hispanos have learned over the course of many generations. This common knowledge is distilled from struggle, survival, and the social stock of knowledge handed down over time.

In a nursing home *platica* group, Patsy Andrada captured elders reminiscing about past times. She used the biographical aspect identified by Schutz. Reminiscing about working in the mines near Questa, one of the elders said, "Era muy duro hacer la vida en esos días, trabajavamos de la madrugada hasta la tarde y nos pagaban muy poco y era trabajo muy peligroso" (It was very hard to make a living in those days. We worked from sunup to sundown and got paid very little for the dangerous work we did) (Andrada and Korte 1993, 31). One can typify the experience of *trabajando duro* as the key to much of the Hispano and Mexicano experience in this country when one considers their contribution to the mining industry, ranching, railroads, and the *pisca del betabel* (the sugar beet harvest in Colorado) (McWilliams 1961). When elderly people talk about the hard times of the 1930s, they talk about how little they earned for the work they did. Anne Hartman, following the ideas of Foucault's "insurrection of subjugated knowledge" (1994, 83) notes that the principals in most political movements define themselves by telling their own story. Those

> oppressed and marginalized populations whose experiences had been described, defined, and categorized by powerful experts rose up to tell their stories, to bear witness to their own experience, and to define themselves. Through this process, through this insurrection, they have become empowered; their own truths and their own knowledges have been validated and legitimized. (Hartman 1994, 25)

The task in *Nosotros* is to liberate some of these knowledges that exist apart from "a hegemony of globalized, unitary knowledge has been the invisibility of women and of people of color in the social sciences" (Hartman 1994, 24).

Max van Manen tells us that there is no one approach, no one recipe, nor "a foolproof set of techniques and know-hows that are guaranteed to produce repeatable scientific results" (van Manen 1977, 346) in making people's meanings come alive. If anything, two or more writers working on the same topic will most likely present different facets of the same phenomena. He suggests that a good phenomenologically oriented text captures various aspects: lived thoroughness or concreteness, evocation, tone, intensity, and epiphany (van Manen 1997, 350). "Concreteness" means placing a phenomenon or appearance under study in the world so that the reader can experientially recognize it. Van Manen analyzes Linschoten's study of falling asleep and sleeplessness, which uses stanzas from poetry to help the reader consider the moment before we fall asleep and the difficulty in capturing that essence. "Evocation" means that the experience is brought vividly into conscious perception so that we can reflect on it. Evocation brings us images and sensibilities that stand out vividly such that we have an experience of nearness or presence. The images are crisp and real and help us to evoke reflective responses such as questioning and wondering, or understanding (van Manen 1997, 353–54).

"Intensification" is another of van Manen's recommended ideals for creating research. It is the process whereby key words are given their full value in the writing of texts with a phenomenological perspective. We sometimes use poetic language to reach a meaning. Translating Spanish into English can have drawbacks, but the point is to evoke images that become available for reflection. "Tone" means that the text should "speak to us." It should assist in a language that creates a "feeling understanding" (van Manen 1997, 360–61). It is as if when we are reading a text, another kind of meaning begins to fill its lines. This is the inner meaning of the poem, as compared to the purely informative outer meaning. We are transported there by the use of images and language. "Epiphany" means that the text has a transformative effect—the deeper meaning is reached by images that move us, inform us, and affect us. Language touches us in our very soul (van Manen 1997, 361–65). Van Manen's methodology is a tall order to deliver for any research on the phenomenology of everyday life. We can partially fulfill some of his requirements for a phenomenological analysis by using poetry, music, literature, art, and photography. Indeed, an image developed by an artist is sometimes more profound than many pages of text.

PERCEPTUAL AND CONCEPTUAL KNOWLEDGE

Whitehead points out that "neither common sense nor science can proceed without departing from the strict consideration of what is actual in experience" (Whitehead 1961, 105; Schutz 1971, 3). The "thought objects" of everyday life are the so-called concrete facts of commonsense perceptions that are not as concrete as they seem; an "obvious aspect of this field of actual experience is its disorderly character. It is for each person a *continuum*, fragmentary, and with elements not clearly differentiated" (Whitehead 1961, 104). Moreover, one can posit two types of knowledge, the perceptual and the conceptual. The perceptual involves direct contact with an object. Perceptual knowledge cannot be outside the conceptual, nor can conceptual knowledge be separated from the perceptual. Conceptual knowledge often guides the perceptual and is interpretive in nature, says the philosopher Chang Tung-Sun. By interpretation is meant the manipulation of concepts and the employment of categories. It is one thing to perceive a chair, yet another to define it by interpreting its utility for sitting. Interpretative knowledge, "because it contains concepts and results in concepts, is conceptual knowledge. The manipulation of concepts is for the purpose of interpreting perceived facts." Conceptual knowledge is interpretative knowledge, and interpretative knowledge is theoretical knowledge (Chang 1970,

123–24). Interpretative knowledge is meant for the handling of concepts and the empowerment of categories.

The final point refers to the social nature of conceptual knowledge. Chang notes that

> All experimental knowledge is derived from the senses, and thus is individual and private, in other words non-social. Consequently perceptual knowledge can hardly be social knowledge. Yet no knowledge can do away with its social content, the emergence and existence of which occur only in the field of interpretative knowledge. (1970, 125)

Valuations are possible only in the field of interpretative knowledge, and because perceptual knowledge is private and individual, no problem of objective valuation ensues. The problems of science, according to Whitehead, are, first, the production of a theory that agrees with experience and, second, the explanation of commonsense concepts of nature, at least in outline. Whitehead was concerned with developing devices in the physical sciences by which the thought objects of commonsense perception were superseded by the thought objects of science (Schutz 1971, 4). Schutz uses this idea to develop his sociology of second-order constructs from the thought objects of men and women living their everyday experiences.

An important question raised by Schutz is the problem of forming objective concepts and an objectively verifiable theory from subjective meaning structures. For Schutz, the concepts formed by the social scientists are "constructs of the constructs [formed in commonsense thinking] by actors on the social scene" (1971, 6). Up to this point my discussion has attempted to illustrate the social nature of concepts and how they are developed out of the observer's perceptions.

If, as Schutz suggests, the concrete elements of the everyday world are already well-formed constructs in actors' minds, then the next step would seem to be forming constructs from actors' commonsense thinking. As noted above, only a small part of knowledge of the world originates within personal experience or the perceptual. The greater part of our knowledge is socially derived, handed down by friends, parents, and teachers (Schutz 1971, 14). The commonsense knowledge of the world exists as a system of constructs notable for their typicality. This is called the "social stock of knowledge" and handed down from one generation to the next. Typification consists in the equalization of traits and the selective inattention to traits that make the individual situation, event, or thing unique and irreplaceable (Schutz 1971, 234). In effect, typification glosses over the inconsistencies and includes ways of life, "methods of coming to terms with the environment, [and] efficient recipes for the use of typical means for bringing about typical ends in typical situations" (Schutz 1971, 14).

Ethnomethodology

Ethnomethodology is derived from phenomenology and is applied to the study of everyday life. It is not concerned with "ethnic minorities" per se but with "folks" and the "methods" they use to make sense of situations, events, emotions, and a host of human activities. Indeed, Harold Garfinkel coined the word "ethnomethodology" to refer to the methods that persons on jury duty were using in their deliberations as they reached a verdict. The term was partially derived from working on the Yale cross-cultural area files, where terms such as "ethnobotany," "ethnophysiology," and "ethnophysics" are used for various cultures. (These files are now called the Human Relations Area Files [HRAF]. The files categorize all cultures in the world according to agreed-upon criteria and are available for cross-cultural and other types of research.) Ethnomethodology can also concern itself with what people "know" as part of the reality of social life (Garfinkel 1974). For example, Mehan and Wood (1975) point out that Zimmerman and Weider's illustration of "freaks" taking drugs demonstrates that freaks share a common body of knowledge surrounding the uses of dope—a kind of "freak ethnopharmacology" (Mehan and Wood 1975).

Ethnomethodology as a method of discovery was proposed by Reyes Ramos to describe the way in which Mexican Americans deal with and attend to the problematic features of everyday life. Specifically, Ramos discovered that people used commonsense knowledge, as well as their life history and the common culture in which they operated, to make sense of what they were doing. A Mexican American (like Hispanos and other folks) "knows the world of everyday life and with others takes it for granted, and . . . uses background expectancies (i.e. common knowledge of everyday scenes) as a scheme of interpretation to manage his everyday affairs" (Ramos 1973, 905). Ramos's scheme helps to uncover what people being studied are taking into account. Ramos focuses on the moments when people create conflict or make trouble for each another, which he calls "naturally occurring trouble" (Ramos 1982, 120). For the ethnomethodologist, conflict reveals the taken-for-granted assumptions (i.e., the commonsense knowledge) of those experiencing conflict with each other. The focus on family conflict is found in the work of psychotherapist Don Jackson, who advocates using ethnomethodology to study the way "dysfunctional" and "normal" families create family rules, which are often violated, leading to conflict. Only as family conflict evolves will one have the opportunity to learn what social motives and family rules are being broken, which creates the conflict (Jackson 1970).

Ramos studied the interactions he calls *movidas* (hustles), discussing in particular the *movida* used by a Mr. Frausto, a Mexican American migrant worker, to deceive a field boss. An incident staged in front of the field boss involved a feigned reprimand to his girls to work harder in the field. Ramos provides us with the "contents" that Mr. Frausto, an "authoritarian father," took into account in staging the reprimand of his girls: "I thought they [the girls] were playing and not working like they should. I got after them not knowing whether or not they were playing because I didn't want the crew leader holding it up to me that my girls don't work like they should. . . . I think he is looking for an excuse to fire me" (Ramos 1979, 150). Another important point was that Mr. Frausto was involved in organizing a union in the field, so the reprimand served to throw off suspicion and thus serve a higher purpose.

Describing *movidas* provides another facet for research into the richness of everyday life. *Movidas* as interactions can be seen as first-order constructs found in social life. Indeed, Ramos gives many other examples of *movidas*. The term is well known in the barrio lexicon, with a range of meanings from putting the "moves" on a girl (or a guy) to swindling someone. It is a convenient label when considering the broader question of Mexican Americans or Hispanos as deceivers of others or as people who employ survival mechanisms particularly against those who seek their further oppression.

AN EXAMPLE OF MAKING SENSE

During an interlude in the ongoing football games on Thanksgiving Day 2004, a World War II veteran remarked that he could understand what had happened in Minnesota a few days earlier. A hunter of Hmong extraction had been accosted by six hunters who told him he was hunting on private property. Shooting broke out, and when it was all over, five men were dead, and a sixth one died later in the hospital. The Hmong hunter left the woods and was arrested. The interviewee remarked:

Yo puedo entender lo que le pasó a aquel hombre. Cuando se te amontonan muchos hombres, tienes que defenderte. Todas las peleas que yo tuve en el army, tuvo que ver con eso. Tú sabes como en el mess hall había dos mesas, estaban conectadas donde se sentaban cuatro hombres por mesa. Eramos tres [Hispanos] y hablamos juntos. Y le dije al Erminio en español, "Pásame las papas." Un hombre que estaba cerca de la mesa le pegó a Erminio en el brazo y saltaron las papas por donde quiera. "Speak English,

I can understand what happened to that man. When a bunch of men gather in front of you, you have to defend yourself. All the fights I had in the army were because of that. You know how in the mess hall there were two tables that were connected where men would sit four men to the table. There were three of us [Hispanos], and we would talk together, and I said to Ermiñio, "Pasame las papas" [Pass me the potatoes]. Another man who was on the other table hit Ermiñio's arm, and the potatoes went everywhere.

Mexican! You are in the American army," dijo él. Yo me levanté a pelearle. Pronto vino el sargento y nos dijo, "If you want to fight, go outside."

Salimos pa' afuera y se me encontraron tres más hombres. Me iban a dar una buena. Nunca se me olvidará porque este Sargento Gere, un viejo que siempre había estado en el army, me dijo, "Don't worry, kid, if you can beat this guy, the others won't touch you." Le puse uno y luego otro y cayó el cabrón. Es que yo y mis hermanos nos poníamos los guantes cuando entrábamos en el CCC. Algunos son cabronsotes pero no saben pelear. Yo sabía box y poco pronto le podría dar. Creo que eso es lo que le pasó a ese hombre. Se le arrodillaron y comenzaron a llamarle "chink," "dirty chink," y por eso pasan estas cosas. Al fin tiene uno que defenderse lo mejor que puede uno.

"Speak English, Mexican! You are in the American army," he said. I got up, and we began to fight. The sergeant came quickly and said, "If you want to fight, go outside."

We went outside, and I saw three other men. They were going to give me a good beating. I will never forget because Sergeant Gere, an old military man in the army, said to me, "Don't worry, kid, if you can beat this guy, the others won't touch you." I hit him once, then again, and he went down. My brothers and I would put on the boxing gloves when we were in the CCC camps. Some men are sons of bitches, but they don't know how to fight. I knew how to box, and pretty soon I hit that man. I think that is what happened to that man in Minnesota. They ganged up on him and began to call him "Chink, dirty chink."

This elderly veteran was attending to something in the newspapers and television and making sense of the event. His interpretation is tied closely to his biographical stance. People define situations by means of their own biographies and past experiences, and they hold any discrepancies in abeyance (Denzin 1970a). In addition, we learn something about the racism faced by one Hispano in uniform during World War II.

Second-Order Constructs and the Natural Attitude

The facts of a social science are of a different structure from those of the natural sciences. The social world is not structureless. Human beings have preselected and preinterpreted this world through a series of commonsense constructs. These constructs determine human behavior, define the goals of their action, and, as Schutz says,

help them to find their bearings within their natural and socio-cultural environment and to come to terms with it. The thought objects constructed by the social scientist refer

to and are founded upon the thought objects constructed by common-sense thought
of man living his everyday life among his fellow-men. Thus the constructs used by the
social scientist are, so to speak, constructs of the second degree, namely constructs of
the constructs made by the actors on the social scene, whose behavior the social scientist
observes and tries to explain in accordance with the procedural rules of his science.
(Schutz 1971, 5–6)

The world is presented to us as typified concepts and constructs. When I told
someone that I was writing a chapter on *desmadre* (chapter 8), my interlocutor, after
some giggly embarrassed laughter, said she knew what I was trying to describe. She
followed up with the idea that she could "dig it" because she knew disorder existed
temporarily in people's lives and sometimes over long periods of time. She knew the
general character of the concept of *desmadre* as personal disorder. She was relating
to type and not to the specifics of people's lives.

A person being studied may confirm or not confirm the general type being
presented by the phenomenologist or ethnomethodologist. As Schutz says, "If
confirmed, the content of the anticipated type will be enlarged; at the same time
the type will be split into sub-types; on the other hand the concrete real object will
prove to have its individual characteristics, which, nevertheless, have a form of
typicality" (1971, 8). Schutz provides an example about a dog. "I *may* take the typically
apperceived object as an *exemplar* of the general type and allow myself to be led to
this concept of the type, but I do not *need* by any means think of the concrete dog
as an example of the general concept of 'dog'" (1971, 8).

Some years ago I wrote *mitote* on the chalkboard. I assumed, in a class of Hispanos, that everyone knew the idea because it was part of their system of relevances.
A student raised her hand and first gave an abstract definition of *mitote* as someone
(a *mitotero/a*) who was passing gossip or lies about oneself, gossip about someone
else, and so on. The general proposition led to specifics: "Well, one time José Fulano
de Tal was telling people about Bobby and me, and I had to go out and confront
the individual who was spreading these lies about us." The idea of *mitote* exists as
a first-order or first-degree concept. It changes when one begins to search for the
commonalities in the social situation and develops second-order abstractions from
these first-order concepts.

Describing a concept from everyday life does not mean that only that perspective
will be the frame within which to consider such ideas. Someone may come up with
a different view, and the concept can be amplified and broadened. Schutz tells us
that we start understanding everyday common sense from a private perspective.
At the same time, the world is one of intersubjective culture and meaning. It is
intersubjective because we live in it as human beings among other human beings,

bound to them through common influence and work, understanding others and being understood by them. It is a world of culture because, from the outset, the world of everyday life is a universe of significance to us, that is, a texture of meaning that we have to interpret in order to find our bearings within it and come to terms with it (Schutz 1971, 10).

In this world, we can interpret symbols, images, roles, emotions, events, attitudes, courses of action, musical themes, folk poetry, and ideas because they are instituted by human action. They have a cultural-historical cast that is sometimes clear, sometimes not. They involve what Schutz called a "biographically determined" sedimentation of meanings, of previous experiences, that are organized as part of the social stock of knowledge (Schutz 1971, 9).

Identifying Background, Taken-for-Granted Features

The problem of making taken-for-granted definitions of social reality manifest is that these features of everyday life are often ignored and hence understudied. Ichheiser offers us four major reasons that researchers usually ignore these background assumptions of everyday life. First, there is the rigid ideal of scientific exactitude, which produces a bias toward selecting and emphasizing aspects of reality that lend themselves to precise quantitative investigation. Second, there is a set of assumptions rooted in the ideological or cultural background of the particular investigator. These assumptions induce the investigator to ask only those questions and to select only those problems suggested by the accepted ideology. Third, there is the natural tendency to neglect (or even to ignore) certain important facts and problems because they appear to be obvious. We tend to notice only those features of our total experience that seem *not* obvious (Ichheiser 1970, 4). Finally, as members of our own culture, we investigators may be unaware of that culture's most striking features (Ichheiser 1970, 7–8). The goal of scientific observation, description, and analysis, according to Ichheiser, is to know certain facts not in terms of immediate experience, but in terms of "full conceptual penetration," two very different forms of awareness, only the latter of which is scientific knowledge (Ichheiser 1970, 11).

Marvin Farber refers to a point free from the presuppositions that mask hidden assumptions about the nature of reality. He writes:

> What is assumed at this point? Not the spatial-temporal world; none of the scientific theories which are used to interpret the world of existence; no independent or continuous existence; no other human being, not one's own bodily existence or empirically conditioned ego; not the ideal science of pure logic, or any of the idealizations of theoretical

knowledge; in short nothing is assumed, and as [a] beginning there is only the self validating cognitive experience itself. (Quoted in Stewart and Mickunas 1974, 6)

The goal is to suspend all questions while turning to the content of consciousness itself—the essence of a phenomenon, which includes the explication of various meanings and interrelationships (Stewart and Mickunas 1974, 8). This is the process of "bracketing" social reality until it can be properly understood or defined. Natanson avows that in this process there is first "a précising of the elements of meaning necessary for the possibility of the phenomena"; second, there is recursiveness (a returning again and again to the phenomena); third, the givenness of phenomena and our conceptual closure involve a reflexive stance rendering a unitary domain defined by the intentionality of consciousness (Natanson 1974, 9).

The intentionality of consciousness is certainly a tool by which social situations penetrate our consciousness. By suspending preinterpretations, we allow ourselves to see the social reality that may be evident to someone not of the culture or in-group. For those who are part of the in-group, the problem is to suspend their belief and instead be aware of a social reality as "strange" and unstudied. In order for one to study *movidas, envidia, mitote*, or any other everyday construct, one must suspend prior beliefs about them as phenomena and attend to them as brand-new experiences. Following Natanson (1974), we need to see the elements as a precise statement of fact(s), and we need to reflect on everyday events, attitudes, values, emotions, and anything that strikes our awareness as phenomena. The intentionality of consciousness will give the phenomena closure and meaning. The purpose of our tools, therefore, is to define the phenomena within the intentionality of consciousness, within bracketing, and within intersubjectivity (social interaction) in order to attach it to the social, language, meaning, body, freedom, and a cultural historical perspective (Natanson 1974).

Roberta Sands sums up these ideas for the field of psychology:

The use of the phenomenological, descriptive language is far more accurate, more authentic, and more humane a means to explain persons than the system of type casting that is presented in the DSM III. Ordinary language is rich in adjectives, adverbs, and verbs that come close to reflecting persons' experiences. What cannot be described in this vocabulary can be suggested with symbols and figures of speech. The use of ordinary language will aid our understanding at the same time it avoids pejorative labeling and stigmatization. (1983, 85)

These are the tools, the elements that I used to create the inquiry for this book.

CHAPTER 2

The Oral Tradition:
El Saber Popular

¡El que es perico es verde y el que es cabrón, 'onde quiera duerme!

Alberto Lovato

LANGUAGE IS THE MAJOR MEANS BY WHICH PEOPLE EXPRESS THEIR EVERYDAY needs or explicate significant thoughts and feelings about the world of social relations. Naturally no study of Hispanos would be complete without considering their oral tradition. Although this chapter covers components of a phenomenological or ethnomethodological stance, strictly speaking some of the material here does not rise to either a phenomenological or ethnomethodological study. The oral tradition of Hispanos is about the use of language and creating meaning, and in this respect the oral tradition contributes significantly.

In one sense this knowledge has the characteristic of processed knowledge or shared meanings handed down from generation to generation. In many ways the material presented in the pages to follow is an epistemology, a way of looking at the social world. It is the collective wisdom of a people laid down as proverbs, riddles, folk sayings, stories, and the use of objects found in the natural world. In this sense the oral tradition is about meaning, the way in which the Spanish-speaking people in northern New Mexico have used common sense to interpret events and situations. This knowledge is replete with meaning and in that sense shares some commonality with phenomenology and ethnomethodology. One shared commonality is that these

meanings arise in social interaction in what was called intersubjectivity in the previous chapter. No doubt a lot of the collective wisdom evolved in social interaction in
the workplace and in the home, where people would gather to visit and talk. Some
of the material that follows also falls in the category of making sense of events as
they affected Hispano people and communities.

My stance is that knowledge from oral traditions can augment phenomenological and ethnomethodological studies. An example of this is Andrada and Korte's
(1993) ethnomethodological study of elderly people in a nursing home (see below).
I should add that some attention is paid to material culture in a later portion of the
chapter. By material culture I mean the use of language to name aspects of Hispano
life. For example, Antonia Baca relates living in a three-generational household prior
to 1918. She tells us that various rooms in the household compound had different
names based on the purpose for which they were used (Korte 1999b). The *granero*
room, for example, was used to store corn, beans, and wheat. The other example
is more familiar and comes from McWilliams's book *North from Mexico*, in which
he describes the various names of cowboy accoutrement derived from the Spanish
language. Similarly the names for different types of horses also derive from Spanish
(McWilliams 1961, 153–55). In this chapter some attention is given to punche, a wild
tobacco still used by Hispanos for medicinal and other purposes. This topic was
selected from a number of other possibilities primarily because it has not received
attention and ties into a story told by a couple in the foster grandparent program
in Las Vegas.

Oral traditions in New Mexico have their roots in Spain and Mexico as well
as local culture. They are a source of rich folk knowledge with a long history, the
collective wisdom of a people, their knowledge of the social world, a way of thinking
about many things, for purposes of entertainment and for the training of children and
adults in the ways of the world. Collectively, it is a folk psychology, an epistemology,
a folk knowledge like those of other folk people in other areas of the United States.
In it is a way of "making sense" of events, persons, and situations and knowledge of
the use of the natural environment.

Elements of oral culture include poetry, *dichos* and *refranes* (proverbs), *adivi-
nanzas* (riddles), *trovos* (philosophical discourse), *chistes* (jokes), folklore, corridos
(ballads), and stories. These elements can be incorporated into ethnomethodological
studies. For example, chapter 9 (on despedidas) makes use of what I call recuerdos
(remembrances)—a type of poetry used to provide condolences to families who have
lost loved ones. In chapter 11 (on *tinieblas*), I use folk poetry to study the concept
of *luz* (giving birth) in the poetry of Ricardo Sandoval. The ever-popular corrido is
the basis of a lot of folk psychology and is the basis of chapter 5 (on *mancornando*
[cuckolding]). The ever-popular folktale of *La Llorona*, where myth becomes reality,

is discussed in chapter 5. Some years ago I heard an Albuquerque psychiatrist present a case of a woman who had lost her kids to protective services. His thesis was that she considered herself living out the myth of *La Llorona*. She had lost her children because of neglect to the system of foster care. One needs to also note in passing that dichos (proverbs) have been employed by one psychologist in California in his work with mental patients in a hospital (Aviera 1996). María Zuniga (1992) has also published an article on the use of dichos in working with clients. Folk psychology is "processed" knowledge: it is lived experience and hence typified into succinct statements such as dichos.

The Oral Tradition

DICHOS AND *REFRANES*

Espinosa (1913) provides slightly over 600 single-line dichos in one of his articles. In addition he identifies a number of folk sayings imbedded in *coplas*. A *copla* is a quatrain that may incorporate dichos. The dicho is a proverb that expresses succinctly the nature of a social situation. In this sense, the dicho depicts a typical situation and is thus a typification. It presents, simply and effectively, the essence of a relationship or some aspect of social life. It is part of the social stock of knowledge passed from one generation to the next via an oral tradition. When taken as a totality it is an epistemology, that is, a worldview. One can define it within the perspective of ethnomethodology as a way in which people "make sense" of their lived experience.

Occasionally one can still hear a dicho at a meeting or in a conversation on the street. The fact that it comes from another time, when Spanish was more widely used, does not invalidate it as a source of everyday knowledge. The research question is: To what degree is this knowledge still in use and under what conditions? An allied question is: To what extent are these elements of culture used to solve moral questions? I experienced the use of dichos in a community development corporation board, where elderly board members were likely to use dichos or to present little stories to make their points.

New Mexico dichos have been captured by Rubén Cobos. Cobos cataloged 1,697 dichos (as well as creating an alphabetized appendix by type). Cobos collected "*más vale dichos*" (dichos that compare what is to be valued more). An example is "Más vale solo(a) que mal acompañado(a)" (It is better to be alone than in bad company) (Cobos 1973, 81). Clearly, this is a message from a parent, admonishing a young person to "fix" his or her choice of companions. I still remember a third-grade teacher telling us, "Dime con quién andas y te diré quién eres" (Tell me who your friends are and I will tell you who you are). Another favorite *más* is "Más vale un par de tetas que un centenar de carretas" (A woman's breasts have more pull than a hundred oxcarts)—or, to express the thought more formally, "The love instinct is so strong that the young male is deeply attached to the female and forgets or puts away all normal obligations" (Cobos 1973, 82). A variant of this dicho—probably more current—is "Más jalan un par de tetas que un par de burros."

Some dichos provide guidance. For example, one dicho gives fishing advice and more: *Agua revuelta, ganancia del pescador* (Muddy water is the fisherman's advantage). The second meaning of this dicho is a life lesson in that people often take advantage of disorder. *Dios tarda pero no olvida* (God takes his time but he always answers prayer) I also heard in childhood. One can see that these lessons fortify people in dealing with adversity. A dicho provides guides to life's problems. I remember a man in a domestic violence group who was bemoaning the lack of attention from his "sweetie," as he called her. It seems that the dictum of least interest was operative—who has the least interest in a relationship controls the relationship. Another man, a former prison inmate, told him bluntly one evening, "¡Amor pedido no es amor verdadero!" (Love that is begged for is not true love!). This statement is not listed in Cobos's book or in Espinosa's articles, suggesting that it was created for the moment.

Dichos capture many facets of "life philosophy," as Espinosa comments. "A proverb," said Espinosa, "is considered the final word on any subject, on any occasion, and in any emergency" (1913, 97). Espinosa classified them according to assonance or nonassonance, *coplas* that contain proverbs, popular comparisons, and miscellaneous. An example of a proverb with assonance (rhyme) says that "Al que da y quita—le sale una corcovita, y viene el diablo y la quita con su navajita" (He or she who gives and then takes away—will grow a small hunchback and then the devil will come and remove it with his little knife) (Espinosa 1913, 98). Imagine a child being told to be generous or else these horrible things will happen. In an organization to which the author belonged we heard a lengthy presentation by someone wishing to do business with us. An elderly board member from Peñasco remarked, "Caras vemos—corazones no sabemos" (We see their faces but do not know their hearts). This is a simple but effective caution. At another meeting we heard, "Cantando vienen y cantando se van" (They come in singing and they leave singing [or, easy come, easy go]) (Espinosa 1913, 99).

NONRHYMING DICHOS

An example of a nonrhyming dicho is "Son como los gatos—siempre caen parados" (They are like cats—they always land on their feet). Another example of this type listed by Espinosa is "Amaneció con las muelas al revés" (He woke up in a bad mood) (Espinosa 1913, 102). Another dicho proclaims, "El que nació para güey del cielo le caen las llaves" (He who is born to be a donkey, even heaven approves by sending the ears!) (Espinosa 1913, 105). Another dicho proclaims, "El muerto y el arrimado á tres días apestan" (After three days both the dead and guests stink) (Espinosa 1913, 106). "No hay peor sordo que el que no quiere oír" (There is no worse deaf person than the one who does not want to hear or understand) (Espinosa 1913, 109).

COPLAS

Espinosa distinguishes among proverbs, *coplas*, and *coplas* that contain proverbs (1913, 111). He notes the free-floating nature of the *copla*, an independent quatrain that is recited as it skips from *canción* to *canción* (Loeffler 1999, 96; in particular, see the song "Lupita divina," 96–98).

Vale más morir á palos	It is better to die of a beating
que de celos padecer.	than to be done in by jealousy.
Vale más querer á un perro	It is better to love a dog
que a una ingrata mujer,	than an ingrate woman,
que un perro es agradecido	a dog is grateful
cuando le dan de comer.	when he is given a meal.

(Espinosa 1913, 113)

In chapter 4 (on *carría*) I present some *coplas* sung in community dances from the work of Española writer Jim Sagel.

LA DÉCIMA

Espinosa describes a special form of the *décima* that he calls the "riddle-*décima*." He describes it as "a poetic composition in hendecasyllabic or octosyllabic metre in five strophic groups, the first of four verses and the last four of ten each. The popular *décima* is found in all Spanish-speaking countries and on almost any subject." Here are ten lines of this type of poetic riddle:

Yo soy padre de mi hermana	I am the father of my sister
Y me tuvo por esposo;	and she had me as her husband.
pues Dios, como poderoso	well God in His power
me la dió por desposada.	gave her to me for a spouse.
pues ella no fué engendrada,	She was not conceived,
Dios la crió con su poder	God's power created her
De mi edad la quiso hacer	the same age as mine
con su poder infinito;	in His infinite power;

y yo, por no ser solito	and my being single
Ese día pedí mujer	that day I asked for a wife

(Espinosa 1926, 149)

The subject of the *décima* is the first man (Adam) and the first woman (Eve)—hence she is both his "sister" and his spouse.

RIDDLES

Riddles were taught in my home. I realized many years afterward that this was a type of home schooling, to make us sharp in our thinking as well as to entertain. One still remembers *Redondito, redondón. Sin agujero, y sin tapón. ¿Qué es?* (It is round and does not have hole or a stopper. What is it? [An egg.]). Another one was *Lana baja lana sube, lana baja. ¿Qué es?* (Wool up, wool down. What is it? [It is a knife. We hear *lana*, wool, instead of *la navaja*]). *En el llano está Mariano tiene cruz y no es cristiano* (Mariano is out in the field. He has a cross but is not a Christian) (Arellano 1972, 72). In the old days a burro—in this case Mariano—would be prodded with a long stick with a cross at its end. In time the cross would scrape off the burro's hair and the image of a cross would appear on its hide. A riddle that was heard in childhood was *Rita, Rita en el campo grita y en la casa calladita* (Rita, Rita in the woods noisy and at home quiet). It is an ax. This riddle and many other dichos come from an agrarian past when there was more contact with animals, plants, land, water, and weather. For example:

Tres palomas volando	Three birds flying
Tres cazadores cazando	Three hunters hunting
Cad' uno mató la suya	Each one killed his own
Y las demás salieron volando.	And the rest flew off.

(Rael 1977, 1:53)

"Caduno" is the name of one of the hunters, but in Spanish we hear *Cad' uno* for "each one," hence "Each one killed his own."

COMPARISONS

There are many comparisons in Spanish folk sayings. These comparisons may be thought of one-line dichos. These examples are idiomatic expressions that are still found in abundance in today's New Mexico Spanish (Korte 2010).

Más borracho que el juisque.	Drunker than whiskey.
Más borracho que Judas.	Drunker than Judas.
Más borracho que el Diablo.	Drunker than the devil.
Más borracho que los infiernos.	Drunker than hell itself

Más pobre que las ratas.	Poorer than rats.
Más pobre que el perro.	Poorer than the dog.
Más arrancao que las mangas de un chaleco.	Poorer than torn sleeves.
Más pelau que un güevo.	Poorer [slicker] than a smooth egg.

(Espinosa 1913, 116)

Espinosa (1913) presented Spanish spoken in northern New Mexico of the time. More examples follow from his 1913 article.

Se le subío la mostaza.	He became angry.
Ni solo se aguanta.	He is so angry he can't stand himself.
Le dió la ira de mil demonios.	He is as angry as a thousand demons.
Se lo quiso llevar Judas.	Judas almost took him.
Está que hasta arde.	He is so angry he is about to burn.

(Espinosa 1913, 117)

Judas, demons, and the infernal regions come into play in many of the other comparisons offered by Espinosa and are still heard today. Some of these comparisons defy translation, such as *mostaza* as a level of anger heard often in domestic violence sessions with Hispano men. How "mustard" (*mostaza*) and anger came to be synonymous is perhaps based on a "hot" quality in both. The problem of *madera* (wood) becoming another word for b.s. may also be lost to history.

Idiomatic expressions have not received the attention they deserve. Idiomatic expressions are created by persons considered quirky, peculiar, singular, strange, unnatural, weird, and (often) outside society. "Idiosyncratic" might apply to persons who say outrageous things that, in time, enter the language. One can think of such comparisons for hunger as *Traigo la tripa clara* or *Una tripa se quiere comer a la otra* (I'm so hungry that one intestine wants to eat the other one), which I often heard from a colleague. My uncle would say "¡Se curan en salud!" of someone who did an outrageous thing and would explain his action by an equally outrageous denial. This latter expression is similar to the saying about the child who kills his parents and then asks the judge for leniency because he is now an orphan.

TROVOS

La Academia de la Nueva Raza published the *trovo* (ballad) of *café* (coffee) and *atole* (gruel). This is a poetic form in which *café* and *atole* challenge each other over their respective worth. Facundo Valdez says that *trovo* may come from troubadours, minstrels who sang or recited ballads in medieval times. He suggests that the recitation of *café* and *atole* goes back to a time in New Mexico when people did not use coffee. This *trovo* developed when coffee began to be used by "las primeras familias," as Valdez called them (the well-to-do or influential). *Atole* comes from *maíz* (corn), which Native Americans of New Mexico considered spiritual and sacred. Hence the view that *atole* provides sustenance to its people, whereas *café* is for the well-to-do. This *trovo* comes from a time of social change (Valdez 1979). I reprint a few stanzas from the twenty-four of the complete *trovo*:

CAFÉ	COFFEE
Por mi gracia y por mi nombre	Because of my name and grace
Yo me llamo Don Café	I am Don Coffee
En las tiendas más hermosas	In the best stores
Allí me hallará usted.	You will find me.
A la América he venido	I have come to America
Y es claro y evidente	and it is clear and evident
Desde mi país he venido	that I have come from my homeland
A conquistar a tu gente.	To conquer your people.

ATOLE	GRUEL
Verdad yo soy el atole	True I am *atole*
Y a Dios le pido la paz	and I ask God for peace
Café qué recio vas	Hold on Coffee, you rush
También yo te diré	I will tell you
Que muchos en el estribo	Many who are ready to leave
Se suelen quedar a pie.	Will be left on foot.

(Arellano 1972, 13)

In another piece *atole* tells coffee that those who buy coffee will be left shirtless. *Atole* wins. This *trovo* could also be interpreted as a clash of worldviews between those with a more provincial perspective and those with a more cosmopolitan view. Finally, it is worth mentioning that Espinosa found "El Trovo del Viejo Vilmas y el Negrito Poeta" (The ballad of the elder Vilmas and the Black Poet) in Puerto de Luna, Jarales, Carrumpa, and Barelas, New Mexico (1914). Finding these stories in various parts of the state testifies to the distribution of the oral transmission of this *trovo*.

Dorothy Pacheco, from a small village near Ocate (2008), learned from her mother the following dialogue between a pearl and a diamond.

Dijo la perla al diamante	The pearl said to the diamond
"Valgo mucho más que tú.	"I am worth more than you.
De negro carbón naciste,	You were born of the black coal
Y yo del mar azul."	And I from the blue sea."
Y le respondió el diamante	The diamond responds
"Tu mérito es muy común,	"Your value is very common,
Siempre fuiste y serás blanca	You are, and will always be white
Yo soy negro y vierto la luz."	I am black but give off light."

(Pacheco 2008)

Poetry: *El Verso Popular*

There is a considerable amount of poetry based on the quatrain. The *cuartetas* (quatrains) are four verses of eight syllables each, whereas the *verso* of its ancient predecessor, the *romance* from Spain, had sixteen syllables in each *verso* (Loeffler 1999, 49). In general, the last words in the second and fourth lines rhyme. Poetry needs to be considered in terms of how it is used. For example, one narration depicts an old custom of serenading people with the name of Manuel (including "Manuelitas," "Manuelas," "Samuel," "Manny," etc.) on New Year's Day. This day was called *Día de Los Manueles* and relates to presenting *mañanitas* (greetings) to honor those who represent Immanuel from *imman'el* (God with us). This seventeen-stanza piece was called "Dando los Días" and was composed by Ricardo Montoya in 1934.

Año del mil novecientos	The year was nineteen hundred
treinta y cuatro en que estamos;	and thirty-four in the present year;
en el día de Las Manuelitas	on the day of Las Manuelitas
al alba nos levantamos.	We arose early on this day.
A la una de la mañana	At one o'clock in the morning
se desconchifló el violín;	The violin broke down;
pero pronto pedimos otro	but soon we borrowed another
para seguir el motín.	so as to continue this riotous scene.

Muy buenos tragos de mula	The drinks were moonshine
Nunca los olvidaremos;	we shall never forget;
de lo sabroso que estaban	everything was great there
todos nos saboreamos.	we savored everything.
Todos se desempeñaron	All obligations were taken care of
ya con buenos traguitos;	with these great drinks;
como también empanadas	as well as with turnovers
pasteles y bizcochitos.	pies and Christmas cookies

(Córdova and Korte 2001, 16)

Naturally after many drinks of homemade corn whiskey (moonshine called *mula*, because it kicks like a mule) the troubadours would be intoxicated. The *bizcochitos* (a special Christmas cookie) and *empanadas* (turnovers) might counteract the effects of the *mula*. Córdova interviewed fifty-eight-year-old Salomé Sánchez, who was elated that *Los Días* was to be celebrated again in San Luis, Colorado. "Many times" she said, "I was the only female in the group, but I was asked to go along because of my ability to compose verses on the spot." She proceeded to compose some:

Ya no puedo cantar	I can no longer sing
A mí me duele la garganta	I have a sore throat
Será que yo necesito	It may be that I need
Esa aguita que ataranta	That "water" that makes one dizzy
A todos que están aquí	To everyone that is here
Las gracias le quiero dar	Today I want to give thanks
Porque han venido a mi casa	For coming to my house
Aquí a felicitar.	To honor me.

(Córdova and Korte 2001, 17)

Cobos (1974) made comments that are of interest. In *Cantares Familiares*, he noted: "El verso popular es fácil de manejar y se ha puesto a uso en el pasado, ya para criticar a una mala administración política, ya como un grito contra la discriminación social y económica; para expresar el humor del pueblo, o la gama de la expresión emotiva" (41) (Popular verse is easy to manage and has been used to criticize a political administration, as a protest against social and economic discrimination, to express humor, or to express something emotional). Three types are presented by Cobos:

Quisiera ser pajarito	I wish I was a little bird
pero no de los azules,	but not a blue one,
para estar contigo	so I could be with you
sábado, domingo y lunes.	Saturday, Sunday, and Monday.
Cuando yo tenía dinero	When I had money
me llamaban don Tomás;	I was called Don Tomás;
ahora que no tengo	Now that I am broke
me llaman Tomás no más.	I am only called Tomás.
Aunque tus padres me dieran	Even if your parents give me
la burra con to'o y carreta,	the burro with the wagon,
no me casaré contigo	I won't marry you
ojos de borrega prieta.	black sheep eyes.

Anselmo Arellano collected the work of many Hispano/a poets. The ever-versatile quatrain was used for the expression of human events such as going in the *renganche*, working at *la borrega*, going on "relief" (public welfare), leaving New Mexico as a soldier at the start of World War II, and for many recuerdos. *Renganche* refers to going with others under a contract to work in the beet fields of Colorado. An example of *renganche* was the situation of Atilano Baca. In 1924 Baca, his thirteen-member family, and 300 others boarded a train in Las Vegas to go do farmwork in Rocky Ford, Colorado. Poverty and necessity meant making this decision to leave New Mexico (Baca 2003).

LA BORREGA

Many Hispano men made their living as sheepherders in Wyoming. This work was called *la borrega* (work as a shepherd). There are many jokes and stories in reference to *borregeros* (sheepherders). There were still men leaving Mora, Taos, and other areas in 1964–65 for as long as six months at a time to work as *borregueros*. The poet Alfonso Archuleta tells about a group of men who were crowded into two buses for the trip to Wyoming to work as *enrenganchados* [we often use the word *renganche*] from Mora (Arellano 1976, 150–51). In these two stanzas the poetry captures the mechanisms by which the *enrenganchados* leave their community: Only two stanzas are presented.

Desde el día 30 de abril	From April 30, on
estábamos desesperados,	we were anxious

nos sacaron de Mora	they took us out of Mora
para Guayma enrenganchados.	to Wyoming on contract
Ya se ven venir los buses	We can see the buses coming
ya no tardan de llegar,	they will be here soon
les aconsejo a mis amigos	I tell my friends
que no vayan a llorar.	To please don't cry.

(Arellano 1976, 150)

The poem tells of the anxiety of leaving familiar surroundings and family. There are others who must leave on the buses to Wyoming. No doubt the lack of work around Mora and the need for sheepherders in Wyoming combined to expose locals to other areas. There are many families in Wyoming today who had their roots in New Mexico. One sees many cars from Wyoming at the annual Mora fiestas. The buses also picked up many men from Taos, as the poem points out. Thus the poetry found in Arellano's book provides insights into events in the 1930s and 1940s, a changing New Mexico, and its Hispano people.

A 1931 poem, also about being a *pastor* (sheepherder), decries the difficulty of the work.

Este maldito oficio	This darned work
es oficio muy pelón,	is very difficult
aquí no hay días de fiesta,	there are no days off
ni domingos de vacilón	nor Sundays to enjoy.

(Arellano 1976, 152)

This poem was composed by Max Trujillo, Elías Mondragón, Frank Trujillo, and Leandro Valerio in Matheson, Colorado in June 1930. They called their work *aburrido* (boring). Finally one *borreguero* complained of the lack of trees to find shelter from the sun and the lack of rain in Wyoming in 1931. He calls the situation "aplanó una seca," which might best be defined as a heavy, oppressive, hot spell.

Año de milnovecientos,	The year is nineteen hundred
treinta y uno, que ya pasa,	thirty and one, which is passing
se nos aplanó una seca	we have had a difficult drought
que quisiera estar en casa,	I would rather be home
y decirles en Las Vegas	and tell everyone in Las Vegas
lo que un borreguero paso.	the difficulties of one sheepherder
En el Estado de Wyoming	In the state of Wyoming

donde yo pastoreo,	where I am a shepherd
ya sido tan fuerte seca	we have had a bad drought
que yo a nadie le deseo	I wish it on no one
que se halle en este lugar	to find himself here
que se ha puesto muy feo.	because it has become bad.

(Arellano 1976, 153–54)

This poem by one "Vegueño" (from Las Vegas), as he calls himself, written at Rocky Point, Wyoming, on the Fourth of July, 1931, is also a prayer for rain and tells us what other *borregueros* say about the difficult summer. Even Villegas's horse and dog do not want to do their work because they can find no fodder or water.

"LA PRIMERA MATANZA EN MANUELITAS"

The Emergency Relief Agency (ERA) was the name of the precursor agency delivering direct "relief" antecedent to the Department of Public Welfare (DPW). The DPW was created in 1937, broadening its focus and name in 1965. The ERA began to address human needs in northern New Mexico by direct assistance, sometimes called "direct relief," such as providing clothing and food. The word "relief" became prominent in New Mexico and was still heard in the early 1960s instead of "public welfare." Arellano presents a poem by the poet Ricardo Montoya. The poem talks about direct "relief" for poor people lining up to get butchered meat in Manuelitas, New Mexico. On August 6, 1934, fifty cows were slaughtered to feed the people of the area. It was called a *matanza* (Arellano 1976, 136). *Matanza* refers to a family (or a political) gathering where a hog, cow, or goat is killed and butchered on a special day (e.g., New Year's Day or a political event) for guests. Montoya calls his poem "La Primera Matanza en Manuelitas" (The first butchering in Manuelitas, San Miguel County, north of Sapello near Las Vegas). Montoya describes some of the activity in the second, seventh, and eighth stanzas.

Hoy leo yo mi memoria	Today I search my memory
Frases de un tiempo feliz,	phrases for a happier time
Y describiré la carne	to describe the meat
Que se dio aquí de relief.	that was given as "relief."
Era un gentío tremendo	There was a huge number of people
El que el corral ocupada,	located in the corral
De más de 50 reces	there were more than 50 cows
Adentro no quedó nada.	inside the corral; nothing was left.

Por acá acarrean las piernas	Some were carrying out quarters
Otro allá con las aldillas,	another one with the groin*
Otro carga costillares	another carried off the ribs
Y otro con las espaldillas.	another the back of the cow.

The World War II Experience

The Forty-fifth Infantry Division (the Thunderbirds) was a National Guard Division composed of men from Oklahoma, Colorado, New Mexico, and Arizona. One of its companies, C Company of the 120th Engineers, left Las Vegas for service in the invasion of Anzio Beach in Italy in World War II. They cleared mines, repaired bridges, fixed roads, and provided potable water to the division.

Their commander was Lt. Col. Lewis Frantz. He returned to Las Vegas after the war to run the Agua Pure Company, the water utility for Las Vegas. In Florencio Trujillo's poem "Soldaditos del '45," two Hispano men, Sandoval and Trujillo, muster their courage for the war (Arellano 1976, 54). A beautiful despedida (parting or farewell) by Gilbert and Juan Romero on behalf of the 120th Engineers is found in a piece called "El regimiento de ingenieros 120" (The 120th Engineers) (Arellano 1976, 160–61).

The Corrido

In this section a corrido is presented in its entirety. There are many types of corridos. Some are humorous, others political. Chapter 9 also includes some Hispano corridos for the dead. It is important to note that in Arellano's 1976 book there are many corridos for the dead. The traditional corrido is composed of four verses to the stanza with the even lines rhyming. Below is a humorous corrido that does not follow these rules but is unique and important. The second corrido below is written in a more traditional style and is used for a political statement.

There is a unique anonymous poem about a drunkard who used the phrases of the El Padre Nuestro (The Our Father) for the fourth line of the quatrain. The title is "El Padre Nuestro de los Borrachos" (The Our Father of the Drunks). It was written in 1906 (Arellano 1976, 170–71). This poem, despite its sacrilegious tone illustrates the

---

*Several dictionaries were consulted, including the *Cuyas*, the *Enciclopedia Universal Ilustrada*, *Velázquez* (1928), the *Roque Barcia* (1879), and Cobos (2003). I also asked two butchers in town. None of the dictionaries carried the word *aldillas*. Galván and Teschner's (1975) study of Texas Spanish provided the above definition. Was Sandoval the poet playing a joke by substituting *aldillas* for *orillas*, the "dregs" of the animal?

creativity of a poet who connects two desperate themes, the need to drink and the need to pray the El Padre Nuestro at the same time. It is an outrageous juxtaposition of these two themes. Two stanzas follow:

Todo borracho es muy diestro	Every drunk is very astute
Para esto del aguardiente;	in the matter of hard liquor;
Es hablar insolente	it is to speak in insolence
Y no saber el "Padre Nuestro"	not to know the "Our Father"
Pasan todos sus desvelos,	They spend their time in devotion,
En cuidar del barrilito;	in caring for the little barrel;
Y si no les dan un traguito,	and if they don't get their drink,
Dicen: "Que estás en los cielos"	they say "Who art in Heaven"

(Arellano 1976, 170)

The corrido (ballad) reprinted below was given to this author and has not appeared anywhere since it was published in the 1940s. It is a political corrido written by Feliciano Casías, who was a social activist who taunted his adversaries with *versos* in the *Las Vegas (N.M.) Daily Optic.* Was Feliciano Casías a poet, an advocate, a community organizer, or a madman?

The story of Feliciano Casías is derived from two items printed in the mid-1940s. One item is the fifty-two-stanza work by Casías simply called *Corrido* in which he tells of his travails in keeping water rates from being raised in the early 1940s in Las Vegas, New Mexico. Casías alleges that in his struggles some persons in concert against him threw him in jail, where he was drugged and then taken into the *asilo* (the old term used to refer to the mental hospital in Las Vegas). A record at the hospital shows that he was a patient there in the 1950s but little else. Casías wrote his corrido to prove he was sane. Casías's corrido illustrates some of the unpublished material that is still available in the community. Several northern New Mexico scholars have set out to collect and publish this type of material. The work of Arellano and Vigil (1985) is a case in point, as is Adelicia Gallegos's work (Gallegos, 1996). Tomás Atencio called his work "el oro del barrio" and published under the auspices of the Academia de la Nueva Raza, which he created in the early 1970s (Atencio 1988). The purpose of the Academia was to develop a body of knowledge that could be used in two ways: "one, to develop a base for education and action, and, two to confront ourselves with existential reality" (Atencio 1972, 9).

Szasz, Scheff, and Lemert all advocate sociological perspectives in the study of mental illness and the deviant in particular. The antipsychiatry gadfly Thomas Szasz argues that psychiatry is used to jail (or take out of the public view) the nonconformist, the agitator, or the person who fails to follow the norms of society (1961). Thomas Scheff proposes that a "societal reaction" creates sanctions for the removal of these types of troublemakers from the community (Scheff 1984). Sociologist Edwin Lemert, in his study of the paranoid person, shows that a "pseudo-community" is generated in the paranoid person's mind, making him fearful that others are "out there" and plot to "get him" or silence him. Lemert focuses on processes that exclude the individual from information and from interaction with others in the organization or in work groups. This is done by various processes of exclusion, sanctions, lowering voices when the paranoid person is present, or preparing structured and preplanned communication. The person's behavior may be exaggerated, so that distortion of his image and anecdotes of his outrages become topics of the exclusionists (Lemert 1970, 660–61).

Becker, like Lemert, rejects psychodynamic or early trauma theories of paranoia. Instead the two scientists focus on the social relationships of paranoid persons and their exclusionists. Paranoia, wrote Ernest Becker, "is . . . mind *alone*, trying to make sense out of experience for an impoverished, weak, and frightened organism, [human being] an organism that can't allow itself to relax, laugh, and be careless." Paranoia seems easiest to those open to the "fine shades of experience, to the lopsidedness of the world, the miscarriages of events, the undercurrents of hopelessness of the human condition" (Becker 1969, 123–24). Becker identifies what is at the "heart of paranoia for the sensitive soul: he can't stand the impersonality of evil. He wants motives and living power behind the fateful events" (139–40). Thus paranoia motivates a cause that must be fought, a "dramatistic performance, a symbolic edifice that gives him his sense of value" (Becker 1969, 142). A human being is then caught in this fictional staging of enemies, of plots, and a discordant sense of what he or she feels is true and what the world reflects. The person has to be as great as the plot he or she has woven, and this is the tragedy of trying to prove the symbolic frame of enemies real in its details (Becker 1969, 147). In evaluating Becker's theories, one has to remember what Lemert argued: that there may be real enemies plotting and scheming.

Thus, perhaps Casías really did have significant political enemies. After all, if 1,482 *ciudadanos* (citizens) responded to the call to sign a petition against the Enron of his time, *la Compañía* (the water company) would have had cause to silence him in order to impose higher water rates. Moreover, one has only to consider the Enrons of today and ask, "What happened to the *reyes del dinero* (kings of money) in our own time? Aren't they in jail yet?" It is difficult to determine Casías's mental state without some study of the social, economic, and political conditions in the Las Vegas of the mid-1940s. It has been difficult to find local sources that could confirm Casías's charges or his state of mind. Despite this, the corrido he wrote is interesting local history. It is presented as it was found, without editing for accent marks or spelling errors. First, however, we turn to a segment of a later corrido published June 15, 1944, in *La Estrella*, a Mora newspaper of the time, as it gives some insight into Casías himself.

In this corrido, Casías assails the outgoing sheriff of Mora County, don Francisco Delgado, who has lost his position to Ceferino Quintana.

Don Ceferino Quintana	Don Ceferino Quintana
Democrata muy afamado	A well-known democrat
El le quito la estrella	Took away the star
A Don Francisco Delgado	From Don Francisco

In the fourth stanza we learn more about the event as well as something about Casías himself.

A Demócratas y comisionados	To Democrats and commissioners
los deshechos por malquiados	the misdeeds done by miscreants
es el que le quito la estrella	caused the loss of the star
de alguacil en el condado.	of the sheriff of the county.

Casías castigates the Democrats and commissioners for their *deshechos* (misdeeds). It is interesting that he used the term *malquiados*, which sounds very close to *malcriados* (poorly or badly raised—a terribly insulting term). To call them *malcriados* insults their mothers and fathers.

In the third to the last stanza Casías again takes aim:

Tengo certificado demente	I am certified demented
no es crimen como robar	it is not a crime like stealing
a los que han refraudados	from those who you have defrauded
los tienen que castigar.	they should be punished.

Casías refers to himself with the old term "demented," meaning insane. In Hispano New Mexico the phrase would typically have been *perder la mente* or *perder el sentido* (to lose one's mind). Being "demented" gave Casías a platform from which to point to social issues. He is the outsider who makes a commentary on the irregularities and injustices of a society. Clearly it was dangerous to take on an established power like the water company. Casías wrote this corrido as a *grito* (an admonition to action) to mobilize the community. This is a good example of a corrido used to fight a political battle.

CORRIDO	CORRIDO: *TRANSLATED*
1	1
1482 cuidadanos	1482 citizens
La Petitition la firmaron	signed the petition
Que se envestigaron los hechos	to investigate misdeeds
Que los han descriminado.	against those discriminated against.
2	2
Ano del novecientos	The year was nineteen hundred
Cuarenta y uno el contado	forty one, the date
Se descubrieron los hechos	the misdeeds were discovered
De uno de los condados	in one of the counties.
3	3
El Condado de San Miguel	The County of San Miguel
Esta todo controlado	is under the control of
Por el poder del dinero	the power of money
Y el que gobierna el condado.	and one who governs the county.
4	4
Politicos y abogados	Politicians and lawyers
Pucieron imperador	put in a special master
Y las regulas que tienen	and their rules
Ejicuta con rigor.	were applied with vigor.
5	5
La compañía las hiso	The company implemented
A sus propia convenencia	them to benefit themselves
Para subir las tarifas	they raised the rates
A los que no tienen defensa.	against those who could not pay
6	6
Colectaron el dinero	Money was collected
Para hacer la defensa	to mount a defense
Y poner los medidores	and put in measures
Para engrandecer la cuesta.	to increase the debt.
7	7
Noble y dos abogados	Noble and two lawyers
Convinieron a cambiar	made a pact
En un punto singular	on a singular point
Que pueden discriminar	so they can discriminate.
8	8
El pobre pueblo los sufre	Poor communities suffer
En pagar altas tarifas	in paying higher rates

Y los beneficiados
Dan carcajadas de risa.

9
El pueblo no esta organizado
Y se lo pueden llevar
Con papelitos falsos
Los pueblos engañar.

10
A las Mejicanitas
Charles Keene las va a cuidar
Un peso por cubeta de agua
Que el las mira llevar.

11
Y con orgullo des dicen
El dinero es el manda
El pueblo tiene que hacer
Lo que los oficiales mandan.

12
Si tienen mucho dinero
Y el dinero es el poder
Pero no lo figuraron
En que modo les iba a hacer

13
Un ley se introducio
Para regular las tarifas
La majoria del pueblo
Hasta soltaba la risa.

14
Una coperacion poderosa
Me jugo una traición
Y por su cobardia
Yo le subiré un million.

15
El dia 5 de julio
Rogers no hiso discusion
Le tenia figurado
De jugarme una traición.

16
No protocolaron pleito

those who benefit
are laughing at us.

9
The community is not organized
and can be taken
with false papers
to deceive us.

10
To the Mexican women
Clarence Keene will take care
to charge you a dollar for
a bucket of water.

11
And with pride
money is power
and the community must do
what officials demand.

12
If you have a lot of money
and money is power
but they don't figure
by what means it was done.

13
A law was introduced
to regulate the rates
the majority of the community
laughed out loud.

14
A powerful corporation
betrayed me
and because of their cowardice
I will raise a million.

15
On the 5th of July
Rogers said nothing
he had it figured
To betray me.

16
They left no record for which

Ni siguiera contestar	they could be accountable
Le tenia figurado	they had it figured
El modo de traicionar.	how they would deceive.

17	17
Tambien los que coperan	Also those who cooperate
Seran hombres de poder	are men of power
Prestaron sus servicios	they gave their services
Para poderme venser.	to do me in.

18	18
Oficiales y abogados	Officials and lawyers
Ellos también coperaron	they also cooperated
Y yo le pidi a la Corte	I asked the Court
Que sean descalificados.	they be disqualified.

19	19
Politicos y abogados	Politicians and lawyers
Seran competentes	may be competent
Y por traicionar al pueblo	and to betray the community
Tendran que ser delinquentes.	they must be guilty.

20	20
Teniente gobernador	The lieutenant governor
Es un hombre muy abusado	is a very astute man
Para salvar la compañía	to save the company
Uso la Institution del Estado	and the institution of the State.

21	21
En el Hospital del Estado	At the State Hospital
Usaron combinacion	they used a combination
Porque la compania	because the company
Hisiera descusion.	Had already discussed it.

22	22
Amigos pongan cuidado	Friends take care
Y también buena atención	and pay attention
Oficiales y abogados	officials and lawyers
Violaron la Constitucion.	violated the Constitution.

23	23
El hombre que descubrió	The man who uncovered
Ni tienen ni educación	has no education
Pero pudo descubrile	but he could uncover
A una Corporacion.	a corporation's deeds.

24

El dia 22 de julio
Se presento la demanda
Al Concilio de la Plaza
Pero el Concilio no manda.

24

On the 22nd of July
the demand was made
to the Town Council
But the Council did not rule.

25

El Concilio de la plaza
El convenio esta sustenido
Para que la Compania le siga
Y el pobre pueblo sufriendo.

25

The Town Council
sustained the measure
to let the company continue
and the community suffered.

26

La cachucha colorada
Tenia que señalar
Que un ignorante oficial
Me tenia que arestar.

26

The red hat
had to signal
that an ignorant official
had to have me arrested.

27

Un Diputado encontre
Le dije soy criminal
Para saber se era amigo
O era enemigo formal.

27

I encountered a deputy
and told him I was a criminal
to know if he was a friend
Or a formal enemy.

28

A la cárcel me llevo
A nadie dejaron entrar
Y yo se lo maliciaba
Que me iban a traicionar.

28

I was taken to jail
no one was allowed in
but as I suspected
they wanted to do me in.

29

Los carceleros cobardes
A nadie dejaron entrar
Sus intenciones eran
Que me querían dopiar.

29

The cowardly jailers
they let no one in
their intentions were
they wanted to dope me.

30

En la cárcel me dieron
Con que poderme desturbiar
Para llevarme al asilo
Para poderme mutilar.

30

In the jail they gave me
something to make me disturbed
to take me to the State Hospital
so I would be mutilated.

31

Al asilo me llevaron
En donde fui lastimado

31

I was taken to the Asilo
where I was injured

Para tenerme encerrado
Y querada todo tapado.

32
Seran hombres ignorantes
O de mal proceder
Para usar de traiciones
Para poder vencer.

33
Si el Presidente lo apruebe
Y pone buen atencion
Seremos beneficiados
En todita la nación.

34
El Gobierno tiene un freno
Es un freno mular
Para darele buena rienda
A los queren triacionar.

35
Este freno se compone
Con evillas de coral
Para abrochar a los hombres
Que se prestan a dopiar.

36
Y tiene muy largas riendas
Y sirven para cuatiar
A todos los atendientes
Que se prestan a mutilar,

37
Si el pueblo se organisara
Con buena formalidad
Sus derechos que pidiera
Todos los consiguiera.

38
Al pobre pueblo le encargo
Cuando van a votar
Hay muchos Convenecieros
Los podemos desechar.

39
Al Gobierno se los tengo
El tiene que investigar

and keep me locked up
to keep everything quiet.

32
They are ignorant men
or of bad intentions
to use the means of betrayal
to overcome me.

33
If the President approves
and attends to it
we will all benefit
in all the nation.

34
The government has long reins
like a muleteer's reins
to use them to rein in
the ones to be deceived.

35
The rein is composed
of coral buckles
to tie up men
to be doped.

36
They have long reins
used to whip
those attendants [at the hospital]
who do their dirty work.

37
If the community organizes
with good procedures
those rights they ask for
shall be attained.

38
To the poor people I say
when you go to vote
there are many plotters
that must be replaced.

39
The government is responsible
it has to investigate

En el corrido les digo	in this corrido I tell all
Lo que yo puedo probar.	that I can prove.

40

Este corrido lo compuse	This corrido was composed
En el Hospital del Estado	While at the State Hospital
Se les da todos los puntos	I present all the points
De lo que me han maltratado.	Of my mistreatment.

41

No se vallan a engañar	Do not be fooled
Por que no tengo educación	because I am not educated
En un solo corrido	in this lone corrido
Hay les doy esplicacion.	I give my explication.

42

Ya he usado del valor	I used courage
Sin rodeo y sin temor	and being straight
De abrir al pueblo los ojos	to open people's eyes
A quien tienen con tapaojos.	who have been blindsided.

43

Ya con esta me despido	With this I take my leave
Lo pueden considerar	you may want to consider
Por lo mucho que he sufrido	all that I have suffered
Para poderlos salvar.	to save you all.

44

Feliciano es mi nombre	Feliciano is my name
Y me appelido Casias	and my last name Casias
Yo tengo toda las pruebas	I have all the proofs
Para probar como lo hacían.	to prove how it was done.

45

En 1943	In 1943
El dia 7 de mayo	on the 7th of May
Puse la queja del pueblo	I put forth the community's concern
En la Comision del Estado.	to the State Commission.

46

El dia 20 de agosto	On the 20th of August
Aumento de agua pidieron	a rate increase was requested
El los biles fue aumentada	showing up in people's bills
Y en los depósitos nada.	and nothing in the reservoirs.

47

Y el 20 de Agosto	On the 20th of August
La Coperacion presentaron	the corporations presented

Y yo presente las pruebas	I presented the proofs
En la forma que fue refradado	To show how they defrauded.

48	48
Dicen que estoy disturbiado	They say I am disturbed
Y mi juramento no fue estorbado	my testimony was not hindered
Y yo le pregunte al Optic	and I asked the *Optic*
Porque se quedo callado.	why it was kept secret.

49	49
Las autoridades des municipales	Municipal authorities
Protejen las corporaciones	protect the corporation
De que se pagan licencias	why pay for licenses
Y usen nuestras propiedades.	when they use our property.

50	50
En lo que el corrido dice	What this corrido says
Si creen que los he injuriados	if you think I have offended you
Si las preubas no lo ensenian	if the proofs do not show
Por libelo sere juzgado.	I will be judged for libel.

51	51
A los Hispanos les pido	I tell the Hispanos
Debemos organizarrnos	we have to be organized
Estamos menospreciados	we are unappreciated
Por no estar organizados.	because we are not organized.

52	52
Si se sienten injuriados	If you feel offended
No usen de traición	don't use deceit
Las autoridades investigan	authorities investigate
Y las pruebas dan decisión.	and proofs give decision.

(Nobel was an attorney who represented the Agua Pura Company.
The *Las Vegas Daily Optic*, a local newspaper.)

The Knowledge of Everyday Things

In this final section the knowledge of everyday life is used to explore how Hispanos make use of this knowledge. This is the knowledge of the *lebenswelt*, the "lifeworld" of the lived experience of a people. The naming and use of everyday things also falls within the realm of meaning, much as dichos, poetry, and corridos reflect the oral history of a people.

The foregoing pages explored the traditional knowledge of Hispanos. Some of it was oral, some written down, and some collected in more recent years. In this section an example of the historical use of items is taken up to show how knowledge of everyday things guided reminiscing in a nursing home. Most guided reminiscence studies use oral history or other oral modalities such as stories or poetry. In this example actual items were used to guide reminiscing in a nursing home in which elderly and disabled persons lived. One could have chosen any number of objects to conduct the reminiscing, such as farm implements. The point here is that everyday things also have meaning. We end this section by considering the use of punche, a type of tobacco, by Hispanos.

GUIDED REMINISCING

Andrada's work in a state facility for disabled and elderly persons used visual, touch, taste, smell, seeing, and hearing stimuli to increase reminiscing and to regenerate old memories (Andrada and Korte 1993). Items from the person's past were used as stimuli. For example, a picture of Jack Johnson and his wife who were in Las Vegas in 1912 for the Johnson-Flynn fight generated a discussion about boxing in one of the sessions. This picture and another one with Johnson and some local Hispanos at his training camp near El Porvenir in the mountains near Las Vegas were of particular interest to a patient, now a quadriplegic, who used to box when younger.

Reflecting on the past—a *lebenswelt*, a lived world that had long disappeared—is important in recapturing meaning for the elderly, who oftentimes have little else to do in a nursing home. In my work with Andrada we were exploring the epistemology of a rural people in terms of what they knew best. We used artifacts from the local culture: handling an ancient *chapa*, a type of door lock; an antique radio; and *planchas* (stove irons) for pressing clothing. This work is like the life-review conducted with penitentiary inmates by this author and others in 1983 and reported in later chapters. What inmates know or have learned in the penitentiary forms part of a prison epistemology, a knowledge that can be transmitted orally. In one discussion a female resident of the nursing home talked about taking homemade mattresses apart and resewing them after washing the *lana* (cotton) in the river in Questa, New Mexico. Our bringing fresh bread into the facility led to a discussion about baking bread in a *horno* (a beehive-shaped, outdoor oven made of *adobe*). Men talked about engaging in *trabajo duro* (hard work) in the Terrero mining area near Pecos. One elderly man talked about the use of the whole deer to make clothing or leather goods. One day in the reminiscing group a Don Cacahuate (Mr. Peanut) story was told: One day Don Cacahuate went to work. He came back a year later, and Mrs. Cacahuate asked, "¿Va, don Cacahuate, que un año pasó y no más un peso trujo?" (Don Cacahuate, you have been away a year and you brought back only a dollar?). Don Cacahuate replied: "¿Y qué te hace poco? ¿Qué te parece, si me he esta'o mil años, te hubiera traido mil pesos?" (What of it? What do you think, if I had been out there a thousand years, I would have brought a thousand dollars?) More Cacahuate stories can be found in Rael (1977, 1:357–58). In another time Hispanos would entertain themselves with Don Cacahuate and Mrs. Cacahuate (sometimes called Doña Cebolla, Mrs. Onion) stories. Some stories were risqué. In some stories, their son Sanamagán would also play a part.

A CULTURAL HISTORY OF TOBACCO USE BY HISPANOS

Part of the natural taken-for-granted attitude is our relationship with material items found in the *lebenswelt*, the lifeworld. At the beginning of this chapter reference was made to the naming of the buildings and rooms in a three-generation family living in Tecolotito prior to 1924 (Baca ca. 1977). Similarly McWilliams (1961) describes the naming of cowboy accoutrements, types of horses, and ranch work. More recently Arellano has turned his attention to the use of wild *quelites* ("Mr. Kelly," otherwise wild spinach) and *verdolagas* (purslane) (Arellano 2010). This is knowledge useful in the lifeworld. It is part of the cultural, historical dimension described in chapter 1. In this section I present a cultural, historical analysis of punche, a type of wild New Mexico tobacco. In order to do such a cultural analysis, one has to suspend one's belief and presuppositions. My natural attitude (what I knew) about punche was that it was supposed to be very powerful stuff. Some of this can be attributed to a preteen experience and common knowledge.

What prompted the inquiry into punche was a presentation I made to foster grandparents about tobacco use in the presence of grandchildren. One elderly grandparent called one of the plants identified in an overhead projection *punchón de ratones* (the tobacco of mice/the poor). When asked what he meant, he smiled but would not elaborate. This was one of those phenomenological moments that causes one to suspend belief and begin an inquiry. It peaked my interest in punche and punchón. What were the cultural historical origins of these two products as used by Hispanos?

In the presentation I thought it necessary to talk about tobacco and tobacco-like plants used by Hispanos in the past. I had always wondered about a plant called "mullein" and whether it was punche. Punche is a type of tobacco, but, as White (1943) wondered, where did the term come from? As part of the project, I went to a local drug store and was surprised to find that punche was still being sold in the medicinal plants section. It was cheaper than a pack of cigarettes. I was interested in what the elderly know about tobacco use. What was the person's commonsense knowledge of the use of tobacco or punche?

TOBACCO IN NEW MEXICO

According to White (1943), Pueblo peoples smoked a number of wild plants in prehistoric times, including wild tobacco, but there is no evidence that they cultivated tobacco before 1540. White says that in 1934 he collected a specimen of tobacco at Ranchitos, near the present Pueblo of Santa Ana. The sample was identified as a species of *Nicotiana rustica.* Tobacco was cultivated between 1925 and 1931 when seeds of *N. rustica* were given to the Pueblos and Hispanos (called "Mexicans" by White) for cultivation (White 1943, 386–87).

"Before the first quarter of the seventeenth century had expired," according to White, "Spanish colonists were cultivating tobacco." According to the *Relación* of Fray Gerónimo de Zárate Salmerón, "The Spaniards who are there [New Mexico] . . . have a good crop of tobacco to smoke" (quoted in White 1943, 388). Another early reference comes from Fray Alonso de Benavides (1630): "They [Spaniards] gave him [an Indian] the embassy of peace according to the usage. This was . . . a reed full of tobacco (*un cañuto lleno de tabaco*) [that had already] begun to be smoked" (White 1943, 388). These reed cigarettes, White points out, were used for ritual and spiritual purposes and if the reed had tobacco, the Spaniards may have provided it.

The next reference to tobacco is in a document from 1767. Juan Bautista Pino, governor of New Mexico, "objected to the viceroy's proposition to enforce the tobacco *estanco* (taxes), as very little real tobacco was used in New Mexico, only *punche,* and by the Indians a leaf called *mata;* yet in '76 the *estanco* was ordered to be enforced and the planting of *punche* prohibited" (White 1943, 389). White notes the differences between real tobacco and punche. Punche was called an inferior species of tobacco in a note from 1881. Captain John G. Bourke visited the Taos Indians in 1881 and said, "They smoked bunchi—called To-je, a plant gathered on mountain top. They are likewise very fond of tobacco" (White 1943, 389–90).

White did not find any Native American words among the New Mexico Pueblo or Navajo Nations that resembled the word "punche." He looked at several important references but could not find a connection to any known word. Finally, he contacted Dr. Aurelio Espinosa, who offered the following. Writing in 1917, Espinosa pointed out that the word is a "speech mixture" (today we would call it "Spanglish"), as in *ponchi* for "punch," *bonchi* for "bunch," and *lonchi* for "lunch." Espinosa also noted that "punche" is derived from "*pumila: pumila > pumla, > pumbla* or *pumpla; pumpla > puncha > punche*" (White 1943, 392). So where does that leave us? T. H. Goodspeed, an authority on tobaccos, called *N. rustica* "pumila" (White 1943, 392–93). Perhaps someone in the future will connect pumila with *N. rustica* or punche. Other types of punche include *N. torreyan* and *N. attenuate* (Curtin 1965, 165). They are members of the nightshade family.

PUNCHÓN

There is a common New Mexico plant called *punchón* that has a variety of names. First, it is known as *tabaco cimarón* or *tabaco silvestre* (wild tobacco), but it is not tobacco. Its scientific name is *Verbasco thapsus L.* It is commonly known as *gordolobo* (California Spanish), *Verbasco* (modern Castilian), *candelaris* (modern Castillian), mullein, velvet dock, velvet plant, flannel leaf, wood blade, and torch weed (Curtin 1965, 166). The reference to velvet or flannel describes its large, soft leaves. One lady in the foster grandparent presentation called it "cow's tongue" because of its size and soft texture. I prefer the name "mullein," as I learned this word in a biology class. Mullein develops a large, woody stalk reaching some six feet in height. This wooden stalk was dipped in tallow and used as a lamp wick. Both Greeks and Romans used the hard dried stems to make candles, hence *candelaria* from the Spaniards (Curtin 1965). Antonio Romero (2003) told me that the hard dried stalk was dipped in oil and used by Hispanos to provide light in the mines. Mullein had always interested me because I thought it was wild tobacco. No doubt it was dried and used as tobacco when there was nothing else to smoke. Where I used to work, one of the secretaries brewed up some of its leaves and drank it. I was curious about the brew, so I asked if I could taste it. It was smooth to the taste and went down easily. The secretary used it to quell a queasy stomach. Like smoking cigarettes of punche, drinking mullein is not recommended, as one does not know what other chemical properties it harbors. The early Spanish (Curtin's word) people of California used *punchón* for pulmonary diseases and sprains. Spanish New Mexicans (her word), according to Curtin, say that the inhaled smoke was good as an asthma cure. Mullein leaves were soaked in *mula* (homemade corn whiskey) and drunk for the same purpose (Curtin 1965). I noticed recently that at a local organic store dried mullein was sold as *punchón*.

EL ROL

My grandmother kept a meticulous house. In the middle of the round kitchen table was a tin of George Washington tobacco at the ready should a neighbor drop in to talk. They would use the tin's tobacco to make homemade cigarettes and talk about events in the barrio. *El rol* was the name given to these homemade cigarettes, and probably came from the advertisement from the Bull Durham Company, which advertised ⅝ ounce of cut leaf, bright tobacco in a bag from which, they advertised, you could "roll your own." More generally Bull Durham tobacco bags were known as *el toro* because their logo was a bull. Other tobaccos used included Kite, Velvet, Prince Albert, and Duke. Brown paper was preferred and was called *papel acafetado.* Other types of cigarette paper included LLF, Tip Top, Bull Durham, and R. J. Reynolds, with its distinctive wrapper in black with yellow border and letters. Both the empty tin of Prince Albert and Golden Grain bags are now considered collectibles.

Golden Grain came in a white, cotton sack with the logo letters in orange on a white paper label. On this label was an orange sheaf of tobacco. It also carried the lettering "Smoking Tobacco." There were two yellow drawstrings to close the bag. A round tab was attached to one of the strings for ease of taking it out from one's shirt or vest pocket; if the tab hung outside the shirt pocket, it announced, "I have Golden Grain." A blue tobacco stamp sealed the top of the bag. The stamp said that the tax was 1.75 cents, and a likeness of John Adams, second president of the United States, graced the stamp. Once the tobacco was smoked, Hispanos used the small tobacco bag to preserve dried herbs or to keep buttons or coins. The cotton bags were sometimes opened and sewn together to make dish towels or even the backing of quilts. One foster grandparent said her mother would embroider the edges of the cloth to make a more attractive towel. One application was to put the bag on a child's hand to discourage thumb sucking or scratching in the case of chicken pox. The glue of the aromatic tobacco stamp could be licked and the stamp put on the temples or on the side of the nose. Doing this was called *poner un parche* or *poner un parche en las sienes* (to put a patch on the temples). Why a tobacco stamp? In terms of traditional Hispano views of health and illness a person who got *un mal aire* (a bad wind; *aire* is often times mispronounced "aigre") would develop a chest pain or headache. The "hot-cold" symptomatology was developed by the Greeks and later adopted by the Romans and then the Spaniards. The body was seen as "hot," but if exposed to a "cold" air, the person could develop an illness. Remedies of "opposites" had to be initiated. Thus a "hot" person would have to eat something cold in order to restore the body balance. The aromatic fragrance of the tobacco stamp was also considered "hot"; it was thought that it would nullify a cold (*resfrió*). According to Clark, pregnancy was considered "hot"; therefore "cold" foods (e.g., Jell-O) reduced the effect of the "hot" pregnancy (1970, 164–65). A home cure for a fever involved putting a poultice of potatoes or cucumbers doused in vinegar and wrapped with a white cloth across the forehead and head (Foster 1978, 199). I remember being admonished as a child to pat the top of the head (*la mollera*) with cold water if I was going to go swimming, else an imbalance would occur.

Powdered punche was applied to the chest for colds. A direct application was thought to relieve the pain of arthritis, bursitis, and muscle pain. Moistened leaves were used to treat snake and insect bites and to disinfect and stop bleeding. The smoke was blown under a baby's clothes to relieve colic and into the ear to relieve an earache (Montaño 2001). One of the foster grandparents in the aforementioned meeting offered the idea of blowing smoke onto an *ombligo* (belly button) to relieve stomach pain of a newborn. My grandfather lost his hearing. The doctor examined him and found tobacco in his ear. He cleaned out his ears and miraculously his hearing was restored. My grandfather had used an old folk remedy for treating a *garrapata* (tick or mite) that had found its way into his ear. No mention was made if the doctor found a *garrapata.* One lady in the foster grandparent program offered that she suffered a lot from earaches and headaches in her childhood. When she got older she went to a doctor who found mattress cotton (the type used in the old days) inside her ear.

The mystery of the *punchón de ratones* was solved when the spouse of one of the foster grandparents thought about what her husband had said, and decided to provide the answer. *Ratones voladores* (flying rats) she said, is the local name for bats. The man's wife said that as kids they would catch *ratones voladores.* A punche cigarette was lit and the poor animal forced to "suck" on the cigarette. Sometimes they blew the smoke on the bat. The animal was released and after a short and dizzy flight, the bat plunged to the ground! Naturally this brought peals of youthful laughter when these elders were young.

Conclusion

The study of oral traditions can tell us much about what Hispanos believe. What survives is an incredible amount of social knowledge about the lifeworld in general. Some of the folk knowledge is incredibly old, having its origin in an agrarian past; some of the folk knowledge descends from Spain and Mexico. The distribution of dichos and oral history ideas is interesting in its own right. One also has to appreciate the vast amount of work collected by Aurelio Espinosa, Juan B. Rael, Estevan Arellano, Anselmo Arellano, Julián Vigil, Tomás Atencio, and the collaborative work of Roberto Mondragón and Georgia Roybal. There is a vast amount of incredible knowledge of everyday life and the knowledge of a people. Often one finds dichos that have a more modern origin. Some dichos are used in work with persons in mental health settings or, as pointed out above, in a nursing home or a foster grandparent training class because they speak to the human condition in a language that is syntonic with the person's culture. The culture is not dead if one can remember or access the oral history. If we forget our language or are unable to access the knowledge of everyday life, then truly the oral culture has died and we are poorer for it.

CHAPTER 3

Mortification, an Interactional Perspective: *La Mortificación*

YO TENGO MORTIFICACIONES; TU TIENES MORTIFICACIONES; TODOS TENEMOS mortificaciones! We all have minor and major troubles that beset us. This chapter discusses a single concept, *mortificación*, but the method of examination can be used to clarify other terms relating to people's well-being. What is taken up in these pages is the intentionality of consciousness of the emotion called *mortificación*, the experience of being mortified. The consciousness of mortification is experienced in the consciousness of body and in social interaction, what the phenomenologists call intersubjectivity. What is presented in these pages is not new, since it is well known in the mental health literature. This literature, however, does not connect experiences of being mortified to phenomenology, which provides yet another perspective. I hope that making these connections will typify and elevate the concept, which is the intent of phenomenological research.

La mortificación is a term used by middle- and older-generation Spanish-speaking people to refer to "mortification," or troubles that disturb their well-being and peace of mind. In various social strata and cultures, some individuals create disquietude or distress in people they vex. These vexing interactions are known among Hispanos as *mortificaciones.* In addition, *mortificación* can be any situation for which one cannot muster a response. *Mortificación* has to be considered within the value system of *platica*, *respeto*, and *vergüenza*. *Platica* is warm, friendly conversation, while *respeto* translates directly to respect and the dignity of the individual. *Vergüenza* is a more complex concept and needs to be defined beyond the simple definition of shame. It also means innocence and can involve the valuations made by society upon one's character and family upbringing.

Denzin has argued that in researching the development of concepts from everyday life, the investigator must first learn the specific meanings attached to the processes represented by the concepts. This approach "permits the researcher to discover what is unique about each empirical instance of the concept while he uncovers what it displays in common, across many different settings. Such a concept forces (in fact allows) the sociologist to pursue the interactionist view of reality to the empirical extreme" (Denzin 1970a, 455–56). Denzin, who is a sociologist, has argued that concepts and symbols must ultimately be located and linked to interactions with others in the social world. In this chapter *Mortificación* is explored through its roots in religious history and through its presence in relationships where one person causes another to have thoughts and feelings that destroy self-esteem.

Definitions and Etymology

The earliest references to *mortificación* are found in *El libro de San Cipriano*, a medieval treatise on the invocation of spells, pacts, incantations, and exorcisms, written around 1000 C.E. by Jonas Sufurino. In chapter 13, Sufurino provides a procedure to determine if a person is suffering from natural sickness or is *mortificado* (tormented) by an evil spirit. This exorcism calls on the archangel Michael for help in enchaining and humiliating the demon. Sufurino writes about San Cipriano (Saint Cyprian), who learned the use of spells, hexes, and incantations. San Cipriano is known as the patron saint of magicians, at one time using spells, hexes, and incantation against another saint (Butler 1962, 652–53). A special prayer to San Cipriano is said when people believe a spell has been cast on them, or to deal with mental illness in the family.

This linking of *mortificación* with a malevolent spirit was also common among Spanish-speaking people in northern New Mexico. When an adult son had been drinking too much, parents identified his drinking as a *maleficio* (evil) and their torment by it as their particular mortification. There are several definitions of mortification: (1) mortification of the body by hardships and macerations, (2) gangrene, and (3) vexation or trouble. Definitions of the term *mortificar* are even more revealing and direct in their implications: (1) to mortify, to destroy vital qualities; (2) to subdue inordinate passions; (3) to afflict, disgust, or vex; and (4) to practice religious severities to conquer one's passions (*Velázquez* 1973). In addition, the *New Catholic Encyclopedia* defines mortification as

> the deliberate restraining that one places on natural impulses in order to make them increasingly subject to sanctification through obedience to reason illuminated by faith. Jesus Christ required such renunciation of anyone who wished to come after him ([Luke] 9:29). And so mortification, or what St. Paul calls the crucifixion of the flesh with its vices and concupiscences ([Galatians] 5:24), has become a distinguishing mark of those who are Christ's. (*New Catholic Encyclopedia* 1967, 1153)

In this conception, mortification is seen as necessary for salvation because human beings are strongly inclined to evil by the threefold concupiscence of the world, the flesh, and the devil, which will lead to grievous sin if not restrained. Those who seek to advance themselves in Christian perfection must mortify themselves more than ordinary believers do because "Christ made the bearing of a cross the price of being his close followers" (*New Catholic Encyclopedia* 1967, 1153).

Another historical and etymological aspect of mortification is its relationship to death, which can be traced to the Greek root word *thnētos*, meaning "subject or liable to death; mortal" found in Romans 6:12 where the body is called "mortal," not simply because it is subject to death, but because it is the medium in and through which death carries on its activity (Vine 1996, 412). Likewise, *mortify*, from *thanatoō*, "to put to death" (from *thanatos*, "death"), is translated as "to put to death" in Romans 8:13: "through the Death of Christ; here in 8:13 it is the act of the believer himself, as being responsible to answer to God's act, and to put to death the 'deeds of the body'" (Vine 1996, 412). The lay religious order *los Penitentes* (formally *La Cofradía de Nuestro Padre Jesús Nazareno*) in northern New Mexico was known to mortify the body (*mortificar el cuerpo*) through special penances, for example, flagellating themselves with whips made of cactus thorns and walking on their knees for long stretches during Holy Week.

In an etymological tracing of the *mr* consonants for a study of the significance of the nightmare, Ernest Jones argues that many *mr* root words signify sadistic and brutal action, as "to pound, grind, crush, injure, bite, beat, gall, oppress" (1951, 332–33). A person who is mortifying another via oppressive behaviors is said to be *pesado* (an oppressive person). The Spanish term for nightmare is *pesadilla*, a word that connotes heaviness and weightiness, but which can also refer to a difficult problem typically accompanied by strong feelings of anxiety, grief, and emotional oppression. We also say of persons that they are *pesados* (heavy, oppressive individuals). In other places, the term *sangrón* is used to refer to a "heavy-blooded" person similar to the *pesado*. Its opposite is an individual who is *sangre liviana* (light-blooded).

Many words, Jones says, have as their core the *mr* root. One aspect of the *mr* root means "to die; to be ruined." Another root, *mortal* or *mortify*, also means "to vex another" (Jones 1951, 332–33). Below I will discuss the question of vexing and oppressing another through *mortificación* (i.e., of causing a person to want to die). One woman I knew qualified her experience with the welfare system as "Pasé tantas vergüenzas y mortificaciones que me quise morir" (I felt so ashamed and humiliated I wanted to die).

Likewise, words with the *ml* root apply to evil. Sometimes both occur in the same sentence, as is shown at the end of this paragraph. A combination of *m* and *l* is found in such Spanish words as *mal* (evil). This root term occurs in a variety of related words. *Maldición* is literally "a curse" and can also refer to the person cursed (*un maldecido*) as well as to being saddled with an unending, unendurable problem. A *maleficio* is a curse, spell, or bewitchment. An elderly parent experienced chagrin concerning a daughter newly released from a state hospital. This father remarked, "Esta muchacha es una mortificación. Parece que nos pucieron un maleficio" (This girl is a mortification. It seems as though we have been cursed).

Loss of the Self

The relationship between *mortificación* and malevolence is of interest because it refers specifically to the interaction between the person being vexed and the person causing the difficulties. A typical example is the parental complaint from Questa, New Mexico, "La borrachera de mi hijo el Junior, es pura mortificación" (My son Junior's drinking is pure mortification).

Considered from a social interactionist perspective, a variety of *mortificaciones*— such as a husband who drinks too much or is abusive, a delinquent son who doesn't listen to parental reason, an unemployed adult son living off the elderly mother's Social Security check, or an adult daughter having difficulties with her husband—are all subject to the same analysis.

According to Lewis, mortification and chagrin belong to several variants of the "shame family" of feeling states. *Chagrin* originally came from the French, in which the word that meant "rough and granular skin employed to rub, polish or file, became by metaphor, the expression for gnawing trouble." Now, says Lewis, the word means "that which worries or frets the mind; fretting trouble, care, anxiety, melancholia." It adds an additional dimension to the varieties of shame, emphasizing the hostility accompanying shame and its "mental disquietude" (Lewis 1971, 71). Schneider also correlates shame and mortification and notes that the connections are multifaceted. Being exposed, which causes embarrassment or shame, leads to the feeling of wanting

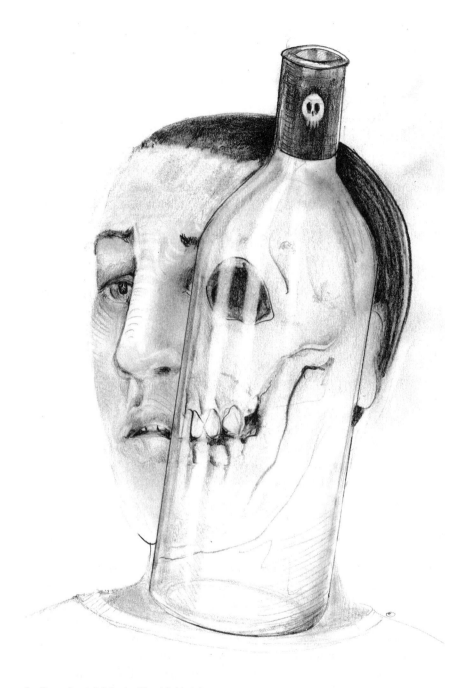

La Borrachera del Junior (Carol Baldwin)

to die. Paraphrasing Lewis, Schneider speaks of the feeling of dying in shame as an experience of the momentary loss of the self (Schneider 1979, 78–79).

Aspects of Mortification

Common to all *mortificaciones* is the onset of profound embarrassment, a change in self-esteem, self-image, and, in some cases, a kind of paralysis on the part of the vexed individual. The wish to die and the paralysis also imply the "death" of the self that characterizes these particular types of situations. In order to develop this thesis further, we must consider the common, everyday Hispano values related to saving face: *platica*, *respeto*, and *confianza*. The violation of these values causes humiliation, *vergüenza* (shame), and hence, devaluations of the self.

I have not found many references to mortificaciones in the literature. Rubel (1960) mentions the travails of "Mrs. Benites." Mrs. Benites feared beatings from her husband and altercations with her son-in-law, which she described as her many *mortificaciones*. Mrs. Benites described her situation as living *asustada*, in which part of her self, the *espiritu*, is caused to leave the body. This has been described as "soul loss." The person suffering long, continuous periods of languor, listlessness, and a lack of appetite is presumed to be *asustada/o*. Rubel (1960) indicates that the people he studied used various forms of the verb *mortificar* to describe a traumatic personal reaction to an upsetting situation. The *asustado* condition, as described by Hispanos, can be thought to fit into the "loss of self" mentioned above. The current *DSM IV* takes seriously such maladies as *susto* (*DSM-IV* 2000, 903).

Mrs. Benites in the Rubel chapter provided her own vocabulary of how she was feeling (bodily) as she experienced the threats from an out of control son-in-law. One acts in the world via the lived body; in the case of *mortificación*, the effect of these situations on the body is reflected in listlessness and an inability to muster an action to deal with these concerns (Rubel 1960). When I first gathered material for this chapter, an elderly lady in the local foster grandparent program complained about being *mortificada*. Upon meeting with her at her home, I learned of the violent nature of her boarder, an older man who once chased her with an axe. Her perception was of being *mortificada* because of living with her boarder. She would complain to her co-grandparents and to her supervisor. More than anything the above discussion makes clear the importance that phenomenology places on "being bodily." We also have to note that the body is the vehicle by which we experience social relations with others. Both Mrs. Benitez and the foster grandmother were in dire interactions with their special vexers. The nature of intersubjectivity (social interactions) can be "toxic." As emotional states, they are well known to mental health workers.

Saving Face

In face-to-face interactions with another, a person wonders if his or her presentation of self will be respected and upheld. Erving Goffman describes "face" as the sense of self and positive social valuations a person claims for himself or herself by the "line" (or "tack") others assume he or she has taken during a particular interaction (1967, 54–55). The line represents the position the person has taken in revealing aspects of his or her personal self. In presenting the self to others, the Hispano(a) assesses a variety of significant considerations in the interaction. How much should he or she reveal? How will the "contents" (i.e., the "line") be evaluated and upheld?

As a value manifested in social interaction, *respeto* (respect) means a quality of self presented in all interpersonal relations. *Respeto*, as Anthony Lauria points out, means proper attention to the requisites of the ceremonial order of behavior and the moral aspects of human activities. It involves proper demeanor. Lauria suggests that *un hombre* (or any person) *de respeto* is "a proper interactant, committed to, and capable of, maintaining another man's image of himself" (Lauria 1964, 54–55). This person is said to be *una persona de consideración* (a man or woman who has consideration for the self-image of others), but such an individual might more correctly be termed *una persona de respeto* because *respeto* involves proper demeanor for both sexes.

An individual's proper attention to another person's "line" means that the individual allows the interacting other to save or maintain his or her proper face. If face is maintained, the individual is said to have *consideración* (to be considerate) or to be respectful of the presentation of the other's self. Such a *persona de consideración* is someone in whom one can have *confianza* (trust), for he or she maintains and protects the valued self-image of another. These expectations are the routine grounds of everyday social interactions. What highlights the existence of these taken-for-granted norms for interaction is their violation, that is, when an individual knowingly disregards them. Just as one can say that a person is respectful in terms of the definitions given, other social types are suggested by the violation of these norms. I once inquired about a person from whom I wanted to buy a truck. My father said, "No lo hagas, es un sinvergüenza" (Don't buy from that man; he is shameless, without respect). The *sinvergüenza* is known for his or her bad dealings, in business or otherwise. Social types may emerge in social interactions based on how they manipulate the norm of respect (Luquin 1961).

Several other considerations are important. Among Hispanos, *platica* (warm, friendly conversation) is considered a viable means of understanding the "otherness" of the person with whom one is interacting. *Platica* manifests itself in such statements as *Platicando se entienden las cosas* (By conversing, people can under-stand each other's situation). Understood in this sense, *platica* may mean that true *confianza* can be built into a relationship. Santistevan states that *estar de acuerdo* (to be in accord) may mean that two interactants understand each other's position and have confidence that face will not be destroyed in future interactions (Santistevan 1979). Thus, both interactants can now maintain poise and develop *confianza* in each other. In everyday terms, to be *de acuerdo con otro* means that interactants have negotiated an accord. This accord is based on shared meanings and will motivate future actions as well as provide the foundation upon which a closer relationship of *confianza* may be planted, grow, and flourish.

An elderly man on welfare invited me into his house with the following state-ments: "Vamos a platicar. Platicando se entienden las cosas" (Let's talk. By talking we can understand each other). In effect, the invitation to share aspects of him and his family meant that he wanted me to understand his situation. If I did so, he assumed that I would represent him fairly and honestly with those who administered and supervised the welfare program in the county. My failure to do so would mean a normative violation, causing him *vergüenza*, that is, what he had shared would create exposure for him. It would also mean that I had become a shameless person, a *sinvergüenza*, and a *descarado* (*des-*, "without"; *cara*, "face")—literally a person without face, because I was unable (or did not care) to maintain and preserve his face or "line" before others. The social situation is always fraught with these possibilities of social interaction gone awry.

Thus, *platica* serves as a means by which two interactants present various facets of their organized and valued selves to each other. To violate norms related to this perspective is to become a heartless person. Goffman states that "in the dominant culture a person who can witness another's humiliation and unfeelingly retain a cool countenance is said to be 'heartless,' just as he who can unfeelingly participate in his own defacement is thought to be 'shameless'" (Goffman 1967, 10–11). The chart "The Staging of Self Esteem" illustrates many of the ideas in the above pages.

In the *Birth and Death of Meaning* Ernest Becker presents a simple diagram that is fraught with meaning. In the diagram, following on the work of Ervin Goffman, Becker proposes a "fundamental task" in each society, namely that it develops rituals to handle and protect what each member exposes for public scrutiny and possible undermining. Protecting self-valuations, or the idea of "face" in Goffman, is funda-mental in any social encounter. Face is vital self-esteem exposed to the interacting other or more broadly society, to be handled gently. Face is, of course, tied into the private self. "Face is society's window to the core of the self," the "body private" of one's separateness from others (Becker 1971a, 88–89). It is the self-esteem that one has fashioned over a lifetime and must be handled delicately by others.

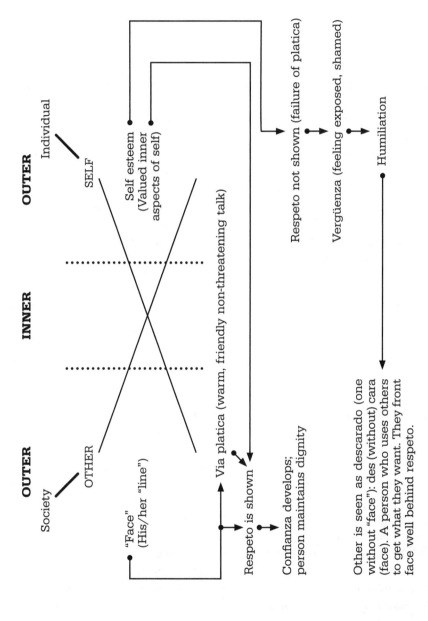

The staging of self-esteem (adapted by Alvin O. Korte from E. Becker's "Social Encounters and the Staging of Self-Esteem" in *Birth and Death of Meaning*, 1971a)

The chart "The Staging of Self Esteem" is an attempt to move beyond Ernest Becker and provide an Hispano version of the interaction between self and the other. Notably there are aspects that are public or "Outer" for both self and other. There are aspects that are private, as illustrated in the section called "Inner" and in the intersecting triangles. The self presents aspects of him- or herself that are concerned with personal information and are identified as "valued inner aspects of self" in the diagram. These are the aspects of "face" that the other has to maintain and respect. In the balance is whether one will feel respected (from which *confianza* [trust] will occur) or suffer *vergüenza* and humiliation (which will lead to a fouled interaction).

The uncertainties of human interaction mean that breakdowns can occur; an accord may not be reached. Identity claims may be made that are not met with deference and respect; *confianza* may not develop. Worse, in interactions that cause one of the participants to feel humiliated (e.g., those encounters are being called *mortificaciones*), profound embarrassment and a desire to retreat quickly from the situation may ensue. Failure of a "face" ritual may mean that the person will be called a *descarado(a)*, one without face or one who destroys the other's presentation of self (the other's self-esteem).

The Gorgon

The Gorgon was a monstrous female creature from Greek mythology. Those that looked upon her would be turned to stone (Edelman 1998). In the interview material that follows, the Gorgon turns out to be the major parent, or in the case of domestic violence, the Gorgon is the abuser. In either case there is a need to confront one's Gorgon. This is magnificently portrayed in the film *Like Water for Chocolate*. In the film Tita must confront the internalized and authoritarian mother. Once she confronts this demonic force, she is able to find freedom.

The two interviews presented here involve attacks on the self-system of two women. One woman noted:

> It [the process] is finding the little girl inside. I grew up in a very abusive environment. My mother was abusive. In time you take on the victim role. The emotional abuse takes the form of "You're too fat! Who would love you? You are not good enough." We grow up to be Mrs. Clever or the girl who had to have a career. Society is as much to blame. It is the Cinderella story of being a slave to everyone. Then one day you meet someone you really love. Love is in the picture. You begin to experience both hate and love. Love is here [top of hand, then turns it over and says], this is the hate that is

generated. One loves him and also hates him for what he is saying. He says, "You don't know how to cook." A wise person said to me, "You don't hate him, you love him but you can't live without him."

We grow up with too many things from our parents. He tells me, "You are stupid. Nobody will ever love you." Our parents tell us, "If you are out with too many men, you will be tarnished." I grew up with all this shit. "If you have a baby out of wedlock," you are told, "you asked for it."

Another woman said:

In front of the children he says, "You're just a tramp." "You are a whore and a slut." I don't care if he says those things. But I don't want my children hearing that because they will grow up to expect that from a man. I try to communicate that to him, but he won't listen. I say to him, "You are setting a bad example for our little girls." One is three, and it may not make any difference, but the other is eight. They shouldn't have to hear that abuse from him in front of the school.

Both examples provide grist for psychotherapists. In the first instance, the psychic wounding is called creating a "shame-based personality." It is learned in childhood from assaults on the developing ego. It is the internalization of the victim role. Thus, even without the mother, the first woman continues to abuse herself or seeks out others who will abuse her. The locus of control continues to be external: others will define who she is and what she will become. With the mentality of a victim, she is in essence saying, "I'm at the mercy of others." She may have trouble with intimacy, closeness, and relationships. She replays the internalized-mother tapes because this is what is expected of her. Fundamentally, she does not believe in herself, and the men in her life reaffirm that notion. It is a struggle to get beyond these internalized voices and this kind of wounding. As one female reader of the abused woman's story put it,

This [the analogy to the reversible hand] is the ultimate codependent line, as her focus is so much outside herself that she cannot imagine living without him. It's not love that keeps her there; it's fear of challenging her own internal dialogue, growing beyond her limitations, and taking responsibility for her own life, and demanding respect from those around her.

One *norteña* (a northern New Mexican woman) called this type of entrapment the process of becoming *copendeja* for the created codependency. She would say the abused woman is a *pendeja* (a pejorative term for a female who is stupid) for staying in these abusive relationships. The woman is also codependent, which was a term coined some years back in psychotherapeutic literature to describe these types of relationships. *La norteña* applied what she had learned in her readings and coined the term *copendeja*.

It is easy to read another text in these interviews, one having to do with the term *defilement*. The term and its history are ancient. *Defilement* refers to being soiled, profaned in some way; one may even say "shit upon" or, as Ricoeur writes, to come in contact with "a sort of filth, that harms by invisible properties" (1967, 25). He finds a direct link to the sexual, just as in the mother's condemnation mentioned in the first woman's story. In Ricoeur's words, sexual relations at forbidden times "are so fundamental that the inflation of the sexual is characteristic of the whole system of defilement, so that an indissoluble complicity between sexuality and defilement seems to have been formed from time immemorial" (1967, 28).

Sandra Edelman has another take that seems apropos here:

> The sense of defilement in such a case is brutally amplified by confusion; one cannot say it constitutes a twin defilement: the child is at once subjected to literal defilement and forced into a defiling encounter with the daemonic; and because the trauma is caused by the parent-qua-god, the unspoken message is that the child is inherently unworthy *before god* or she would not be subjected to (chosen for) this experience. Moreover, there is nowhere for the child to go with her pain, no one to turn to for comfort and reassurance because the defilement has been chosen by the supreme authority in her life, or with the collusion of the supreme authority. (1998, 85–86)

The second interview example given earlier is about assault in front of children. The woman moves to curtail the hurt. This experience is also mortifying, full of humiliation and defilement—a ceremony of harassment and emotional abuse.

Penetrability of the Self

What is it about the penetrability of the self that allows it to be wounded and humiliated in those forms of interaction called *mortificaciones*? A partial answer can be found in the work of Josef Nuttin, who believes that the sense of shame is connected with one of the most characteristic features of psychological life, the combination of privacy and penetrability in human life. Psychological life is not purely interior and cannot be considered impenetrable by others. This penetrability of the private self is what may cause shame. Nuttin calls this private interiority and the possibility of its exposure "the functional conditions for the origin of shame" (1950, 344–45).

Humiliating experiences, according to Helen M. Lynd, threaten the very basis for the presentation of the self to others. One's core identity is endangered and can in effect be damaged or destroyed.

> The characteristics that have been suggested as central in experiences of shame—the sudden exposure of unanticipated incongruity, the seemingly trivial incident that arouses overwhelming and almost unbearable painful emotion, the threat to the core of identity, the loss of trust in expectations of oneself, of other persons, of one's society, and a reluctantly recognized question of meaning in the world—all these things combine to make experiences of shame almost impossible to communicate. (Lynd 1958, 64)

Situations that cause embarrassment also incapacitate people in terms of role performance (Gross and Stone 1970, 190). Embarrassing situations leave the individual exposed and incapable of continuing to perform the role at hand. The person may break into tears, take flight, or, in extreme situations, commit suicide—not to save face, but because face has been damaged beyond repair. Face saving is most difficult in situations involving emotional abuse.

Role Taking

Natanson in his phenomenological analysis of role performance, differentiates various aspects of social roles as "the complex of societally formed requirements for understanding and performing patterned action in social roles." He defines *role taking* as "the dynamics for effecting and carrying out such roles in actual practice," and, relevant to this analysis, *role action* as "the intentional dimension underlying role-taking" (Natanson 1974, 177). Natanson considers the intentionality of role taking as occurring prior to role action and outlines five assumptions that underlie role action:

- *Openness.* There is a "role to be taken." The social space is open for action, and the actor has the power to take the role.
- *Repeatability.* The role taker has played the role previously and may reassume it as a prior role.
- *Familiarity.* The role taker knows what to do in the role. It is regainable in familiar form.

- *Recognition.* The role taker puts a personal stamp on the role. The actor's idiosyncratic aspect is merged with the role taking.
- *Release.* The role is completed. The social action has a discernible end. (Natanson 1974, 179–81)*

These conditions allow the role taker to assume roles within a given segment of intervals available for role taking (Natanson 1974, 182–85). Natanson uses these five assumptions in his analysis of the effects of alienation on the inability to mobilize action. The abstract capacity involved in each of the elements of role action and in their synthetic operation is deformed in experiences of alienation or mortification. In effect, the taken-for-granted cultural values that prescribe the behavior between interactants are not present in interactions termed *mortificaciones*, and the steps needed in order to act are frustrated. The person mortified is in an interactive situation in which the normally familiar grounds for interaction are unfamiliar, frustrated, altered, or destroyed. For Hispanos, elements of *respeto* and *vergüenza*, which guide interaction, no longer seem to hold true. *Platica* becomes impossible. Small wonder that the mortified person feels caught in an unfamiliar or threatening situation from which he or she wishes to flee. A parent can no longer provide Junior with wise *consejos* (counseling), as he is too busy drinking.

Inability to Act

Goffman (1967) and Gross and Stone (1970) have pointed to people's inability to implement role functions in embarrassing social situations. Because mortification has much in common with the family of shaming experiences, Goffman's thoughts are apropos. For Goffman, the flustered or embarrassed individual is "one who cannot for the time being mobilize his muscular and intellectual resources for the task at hand, although he would like to; he cannot volunteer a response to those around him that will allow them to sustain the conversation smoothly. He and his flustered actions block the line of activity the others have been pursuing. He is present with them, but he is not in play" (Goffman 1967, 100–101).

Because of this immobility, the vexed person is unable to maintain his or her poise in interactions in which vexing, obnoxious, haranguing, or brutal physical or emotional exchanges occur. For example, a vexed person who is assuming the role of father or mother toward an alcoholic son or a mentally ill daughter may find that

---

*I have put into my own words the definition of Natanson's concepts as I understand them.

the social components available for action are deformed. In other words, the familiar assumptions of the parental role are no longer in effect. The vexed individual cannot assume the parental role (or any other role) because the assumptions underlying role action and role taking (identified by Natanson, above) no longer apply. He or she tries to maintain poise and identity as a parent toward someone whose identity and behavior have become unknown. Mental anguish and *mortificación* ensue.

Embarrassment occurs when the flustered individual is considered to exhibit weakness, inferiority, low status, moral guilt, defeat, and other unenviable attributes (Goffman 1972, 72). In the Hispano lexicon, one's perceived failure as a parent translates into a family *vergüenza*, which is not necessarily a private affair that affects only the individual who experiences it. Rather, *vergüenza* is felt by family members, significant others, and the community. I was recently told by one man, "How can I assist you with the domestic violators or guys who are having problems with drinking when I have a son who is out of control? *Me va a cai mal, sabes*" (It will look bad for me, you know). Vexed parents, for example, may feel that they are no longer *respetados* (respected), that their *consejos* are not accepted, and that they are thus unable to perform their parental role.

Becker argues that the self is largely a locus of word possibilities. We become uncomfortable in strange groups and subcultures largely because we cannot frame an easy verbal transition to sustain action. Self-esteem is threatened because "words enable us to protect ourselves by confidently manipulating the interpersonal situation; also, by verbally setting the tone for action by proper ritual formulas, we permit complementary action by our interlocutor" (Becker 1975, 59).

Moreover, Becker maintains that words not only "sustain us by outlining a context of action in which we can be meaningfully motivated," but also, in a sense, "create" us "by infusing our action with meaning." "As we act meaningfully we exercise our powers and create our identity" (1975, 62). Thus, if *mortificación* leads to an inability to act (i.e., a freezing of action), then identity presentation becomes impossible. We have no words to describe our chagrin and humiliation. Small wonder the importance of the statement "Pase tantas vergüenzas y mortificaciones que me quise morir" (I felt so ashamed and humiliated that I wanted to die). The vocabulary of victimization is indicative of a self unable to create or traffic an identity. Thus, *mortificación* is experienced as a death of the self.

In summary, *mortificación* is only one term in Hispanos' everyday dictionary of emotions. One elderly person I interviewed observed, "La paciencia retira la mortificación" (Patience alleviates mortification). This statement indicates that Hispanos may have practical strategies for dealing with *mortificaciones.* However, social scientists and mental health practitioners have not paid much attention to the study of these cultural coping mechanisms. As noted in chapter 1, researchers should use the troubles people create for each other in their day-to-day existence for a study of their coping and managing strategies. We might learn not only how Hispanos and Mexican Americans symbolize their social reality, but also how they understand, cope, and manage everyday problem situations.

CHAPTER 4

Shame, Respect, and Joking Exchanges: *Vergüenza, Respeto, y la Carría*

IN 1922, JOHN DEWEY WROTE, "THESE TWO FACTS, THAT MORAL JUDGMENT AND moral responsibility are the work wrought in us by the social environment, signify that all morality is social; not because we *ought* to take into account the effect of our acts upon the welfare of others, but because of facts. Others *do* take into account what we do and they respond accordingly to our acts" (Dewey 1922, 316).

Dewey, in declaring that morality is social, points to a fundamental element: accountability for our social behavior. He made a strong argument that culture defines the social behavior of its members. Hispanos are not exempt from the social. In many ways, Spanish, as used by Hispanos in the mountains, upland villages, and small communities of northern New Mexico retains many archaic terms that reveal the culture and its morality. Hispanos have retained some folkways that have existed since the colonization of New Mexico in 1598. It is within the disappearing value framework of *respeto* and *vergüenza* that we can view various ideas regarding a particular type of joking exchange called *La carría*.

La Carría

Dando carría is a type of verbal game in which a person's social or personal characteristics or failings are made the subject of a joking exchange involving mild insults and defamation. The countering and banter give the game a reiterative and accelerating character. The idea of *dando* or *dar* (giving or to give) *carría* is that it is "brought to" (or imposed on) an individual. In some prison interviews conducted in 1983, the idea of "capping" on another man falls within this definition. Rubén Cobos defines *carría* as slang for "static" and *dar carría* as "to bother or harass" ("Ese bato me da mucha carría" [That dude gives me a lot of static]) (Cobos 2003).*

In an observed incident in a board meeting of a community development corporation in northern New Mexico in 1982, a series of questions were directed at an engineer who was presenting his and his company's capabilities in dealing with a community trash problem. One of the men from the village was subtly questioning the engineer's truthfulness. He was doing it so skillfully the subject never guessed the intent. In this case, *dando carría* was meant to reveal this person's truthfulness. If the subject had understood what was going on, he would have needed to maintain his composure, his "face," so as not to give up the "line" he had taken. If he had questioned his interrogator's intent, though, he would have "lost it" and would have come across as a common liar and con man. If he never "connected," the group would have realized how skillfully a man who sold rock for a living had "taken on this announced identity": an engineer with a solution to a community problem.

"Doing the dozens" in African American culture (Abrahams 1972) depends on a shared "stock of knowledge" (Schutz 1971), much as *carría* occurs in the informal socialization of Hispano men and women from villages and barrios. Juan Maes offers yet another view: "It is a gesture of affection between *carnales*." In this respect, *carría* exists where trust has been developed among intimates, whether brothers (*carnales*) or barrio "bros" (friends) (Maes 1998).

La carría incites individuals to break with the social value of *seriedad* (serious comportment). At its worst, *carría* can be destructive because it is a direct negation of social values and the social order. In its root meaning the word seems to be related to *cara*, face. The *Velázquez* dictionary defines the homophone *carilla* as (1) little or small face, (2) mask used by beekeepers, and (3) silver coin used in Aragón, Spain. One can discern other terms that relate to the face, for example, *carrilludo(a)* (plump or round-cheeked). Others terms include *carilucio(a)* (a shiny or glossy face) and

---

*The word can also be spelled *carilla*. In this chapter, I use Cobos's spelling in honor of his contribution to Hispano scholarship. *Cabuya* (or *cabulla*), another recognized *barrio* term, has a special definition that will be discussed later.

carinegro(a) (having a swarthy complexion) (*Velázquez* 1973). *Carrillo* refers to, among other things, the fleshy part of the face or cheeks. Woods and Alvarez-Altman say that *carrillo* is derived from one "with an unusual or prominent cheek" (Woods and Alvarez-Altman 1978, 35). It is interesting to note that the metallic chin straps in a soldier's helmet were called *carrilleras*. A person's name came from their occupation. The name "Carrillo" probably came from a person's occupation as a soldier.

Because *carría* is a defamation game, one should not lose sight of the fact that it is aimed at a person's face—it is in essence "a slap on the face" (or cheeks), the *carriles*. Thus, the game is to attack the person's "face," or social presentation. "Face" is what we are all about in the presentation of a "line" or position to others (Goffman 1967, 5). We expect and hope that others will respect our position. However, others can scrutinize or make light of our social presentation. *La carría* is an insult, a joking and embarrassment game in which participants are invited to engage in lighthearted schemes designed to incite an individual to break from the value system.

The *Velázquez* dictionary defines *cabuya* as a type of sisal hemp or, as a verb, "to tie with sisal" or, more to the point, *ponerse en la cabuya* (to grasp the trend of a topic) (*Velázquez* 1973). This last point is significant because *carría*, like other games of defamation, has a reiterative character: the target must not only understand the often obscure references being made about him or her but must be able to respond with compelling repartee to the group of detractors. *Cabuya* refers to more subtle aspects because the target never realizes he or she is the object of the fun. The engineer who was given his dose of *cabuya* (or *carría*) *nunca no se le prendio el foco* (never understood that he was the butt of some very subtle insults).

Shame, *Respeto*, and the Problem of Deference

The two cardinal values destroyed by *carría* are *vergüenza* and *respeto*. The simplest notion of *vergüenza* is the concept of shame or, more appropriately, modesty as it relates to child rearing in the villages of northern New Mexico. Margaret Mead advanced the proposition that children in New Mexico villages were admonished to have *vergüenza* (i.e., not to be forward) and not to stand out in the group (Mead 1955). This is another definition of *vergüenza*—a reticence to be too forward.

Facundo Valdez says that children are born without *vergüenza*, or shame. A child, he suggests, can be called a *sinvergüenza* (literally without shame) because he or she is obtrusive and has not learned the use of reason. A child called a *sinvergüenza* with affection is considered mischievous. Applied to an adult, however, the term names a shameless, blatant, and obtrusive person who lacks proper family socialization (Valdez 1979).

Pitt-Rivers in a study of an Andalusian village in Spain refers to *vergüenza* as a moral quality, like innocence, which it more closely resembles. "It is closely related with right and wrong, since its presence or absence is detected through an ethical evaluation of a person's behaviour which is thought, in fact, to be determined by it, but it is not synonymous with conscience" (Pitt-Rivers 1971, 112). *Vergüenza* is the overt—or sociological—counterpart of *conscience*: it may initiate moral condemnation by the community. To commit certain acts "blatantly makes a person a *sin vergüenza* (shameless one); but to have done it discreetly, would only have been wrong." "Shamelessness faces the world, faces people in particular situations. Wrong faces one's conscience" (Pitt-Rivers 1971, 113). Pitt-Rivers proposed the following definition of *vergüenza*: "Vergüenza is the regard for the morals of society, for the rules whereby social intercourse takes place, for the opinion which others have of one, but this, not purely out of calculation. True vergüenza is mode of feeling which makes one sensitive to one's reputation and thereby causes one to accept the sanction of public opinion" (Pitt-Rivers 1971, 113). A *sinvergüenza* is a person who either does not accept society's sanctions or, under the guise of respectful behavior, swindles people out of their possessions. According to many Hispanos, certain professions (e.g., law) could be performed only by *sinvergüenzas*, because taking an advocacy position meant an adversarial position opposing individuals in legal proceedings (Valdez 1979).

The theme of being sensitive to one's social reputation as embodied in the ideal of *vergüenza* is also akin to *respeto* (respect). Kenny comes close to the same theme with regard to the virtue of *simpatía* (sympathy). Among Spaniards, "In being simpatico, one is indulging in fellowship by literally completing or integrating oneself with others. But this cannot be done without developing self-insight as well as respect for the 'otherness' of one's fellow, for his uniqueness as a creature being" (Kenny 1965, 81). Thus, *respeto* is the recognition of the uniqueness of the other self, but, more important, accords dignity to others, which ensures a reciprocity of self with the other. It is this reciprocity that leads to poise and self-balance and on which the development of trust (*confianza*) can be built (Kenny 1965, 81). These values undergird the nature of trust development in social interaction for Spaniards and Hispanos.

Becker proposes that social encounters are fraught with the possibility of being bungled because they form the staging area for handling a "person-object's" most important characteristic: his or her self-esteem. In social encounters each individual "exposes for public scrutiny and possible intolerable undermining, the one thing he needs most: the positive self valuation he has so laboriously fashioned." Thus, cultures have fashioned elaborate rituals and codes of deference and demeanor to protect "face," which, in Becker's view, is equated with one's positive self-valuations. Face is therefore "public" in that it is presented to the world for scrutiny. Self-esteem is always potentially at risk to be undermined in social encounters (Becker 1964, 88) and even more so in *carría* games.

FAMILY *EDUCACIÓN*

The important and underlying premise of family education is what Dewey echoed so long ago:

> We are held accountable by others for the consequences of our acts. They visit their likes and dislikes of these consequences upon us. . . . Morals is as much a matter of interaction of a person with his social environment as walking is an interaction of legs with a physical environment. . . . If the standards of morals are low, it is because the education given by the interaction of the individuals with his social environments is defective. . . . Morals are social. (Dewey 1922, 315–19)

Poor child socialization is reflected in the concept of *educación*, which refers specifically to the family's moral education. An evaluation of a person's *falta de educación* literally implies a lack of family socialization, which is a grievous assessment of a person. Other terms reflecting the same theme can be found in the Hispano's lexicon. Thus, *no tener crianza* means "lack of social upbringing." The root *criar* means "to bring up" or "to create." A common admonishment is, *Tienes que respetar para que seas respetado* (You have to respect [others] so that [they] will respect you). One can speculate that in this culture the modal personality would be one who is *serio* (serious), *formal* (formal), and *respetable* (respectful of others). Although it is difficult to illustrate whether Hispano parents still socialize children to these values, the value system itself is still extant to the degree that a violation of the values via insult games such as *carría* illustrates its existence. Goffman sees this norm of respect as a requisite of other societies and therefore as a universal norm. Societies everywhere must socialize their members "as self-regulating participants in social encounters. One way of mobilizing the individual for this purpose is through ritual; he is taught to be perceptive, to have feelings attached to self and a self expressed through face, to have pride, honor, and dignity, to have considerateness, to have tact and a certain amount of poise." Of further sociological importance is that these characteristics do not come from "inner psychic propensities but from moral rules that are impressed upon him from without" (Goffman 1967, 44–45).

Value Theory

How do value expectations lead to social obligation and social comportment? The Mexican philosopher Jorge Portilla, analyzing the phenomenology of value and its relationship with external social obligations and duty, provides the following analysis:

> Value once understood becomes endowed with an aura of pressing need to become properly realized as behavior, as an act, as a positive and affirmative action. As a first sketch, what is apprehended and understood is reflexively called *deber*, an obligation or duty. This response, this affirmation, which corresponds to a subjective source of understanding of the nature of value, and its need to be manifested as an act, becomes then an intimate movement toward a bond. The bond becomes *la seriedad* or *el comportamiento de seriedad*, serious deportment and its social consequences. It becomes a tacit and intimate bond to take value as serious. *La seriedad* is the intimate and profound compromise or bond that sustains together value and existence in acts of deportment. (Portilla 1966, 18)

The concept of duty or obligation is similarly captured by Goffman:

> When an individual becomes involved in the maintenance of a rule, he tends also to be committed to a particular image of self. In the case of his obligations, he becomes to himself and others the sort of person who would naturally be expected to do so. In the case of his expectations, he becomes dependent upon the assumption that others will properly perform such of their obligations as affect him, for their treatment of him will express a conception of him. (1967, 50–51)

According to Dennis Wrong, a norm is "internalized" by an individual when he "both affirms it and conforms to it in his conduct" (1970, 33); thus, one's duty to *vergüenza* is to be alert to situations whereby one's family—and, by extension, one's family socialization (*educación*)—may be scrutinized by social others. Both *vergüenza* and *respeto*, as learned in family socialization, sustain *seriedad*. The duty to one's sense of *vergüenza* is therefore to reflect one's upbringing. For *respeto*, the compromise to duty is that one treats others with respect because this is what one should expect in return.

El Relajo and *La Carría*

Portilla's formal definition of *relajo* is the following:

> *El relajo* is a proposition to a group of persons to suspend reality, *la seriedad*, serious comportment. This suspension is realized or manifested by a person whose goal is to involve others in this deportment, by way of reiteration of action with the express purpose of separation of the exigencies of conduct required by value. Deportment as regulated by value is substituted by an atmosphere of disorder in which the realization of value becomes impossible. (Portilla 1966, 25)

Both *carría* and *relajo*, as "disorder," are antithetical to *seriedad* (serious comportment), to *respeto* (respect for the other), and to *vergüenza* (one's presentation as a social person). As insult, joking, and embarrassment games, *la carría* (and as it is called in Mexico, *el relaje*) calls for the suspension of proper respectful behavior. *El relajo* is a direct negation of value or, more specifically, a break in the tie or link that unites people with their values (Portilla 1966, 26). At their worst, both *relajo* and *carría* can destroy the social order and lead to disharmony in groups and the community.

Carría and *relajo* games occur in the context of group interactions. The group will define the values targeted for derision. And because individuals are embodiments of value, they must uphold their values and suffer the game. The group responds to and organizes the verbal interaction around the destruction of these values. Mills argues for the consideration of the social situation to determine the meaning and motivation of the interaction: "Rather than interpreting actions and language as external manifestations of subjective and deeper lying elements in individuals, the research task is the locating of particular courses of action with typal frames of normative actions and socially situated clusters of motive" (Mills 1970, 480). Thus, the definition of the social situation is that in which the actors give meaning to behaviors. In a *carría* or *relajo* game, what may seem absurd to an outsider (i.e., an uninvolved observer) may be appropriate to the way the interactants have defined the social situation of a *carría* game.

One interesting facet of these games is the presentation of a tractable self who can manage all types of verbal exchanges. Becker observes that the self is largely a word edifice and that fundamental to all social ceremonies is the proper use of words. The self-system is largely a locus of communication in word possibilities, "an ideational linguistic device, in a continual state of modification and creation" (Becker 1971a, 92). It is crucial to win these exchanges of insult because, as both Becker and

Goffman have noted, self-esteem maintenance is at its core (Becker 1971a; Goffman 1967). Goffman emphasizes the point:

> In aggressive interchanges, the winner not only succeeds in introducing features favorable to himself and unfavorable to others but also demonstrates that as interactant he can handle himself better than his adversaries. . . . Evidence of this capacity is often more important than all the other information the person conveys in interchange so that the introduction of "a crack" in the verbal interaction tends to imply that the initiator is better at footwork than those who must suffer his remarks. However, if they succeed in making a successful parry of the play, he must not only face the disparagement with which the others have answered him but also accept the fact that his assumption of superiority in footwork has proven false. He is made to look foolish, he loses face. (1967, 25)

In effect, in an exchange that involves mild insults and defamation, the characteristics of the banter give the game a reiterative and accelerating character. Two characteristics of *relajo* and *carría* games emerge: (1) contagion, as others are invited into the verbal melee, and (2) the reiteration of the comic theme. Concerning the latter, when the group gathers in the future, the "material" from a previous encounter can be resurrected and redeveloped. The individual who continues to be the butt of jokes should not "crack" or break, but should have learned to parry verbally in any new engagement. In Spanish, the idea is *no rajarse* (not to crack). *Si te rajas te chingan* (If you crack, you get screwed) is barrio knowledge, and it applies to verbal exchanges as well as physical encounters.

La Quemadota

La carría can be functional in limiting interactions with unwanted individuals. One might refer to the interchange described in this section as the *quemadota*, which may be loosely translated as a type of "sting" operation because the object is to severely "burn" the victim in the encounter. *Quemadotas* refers to the preparation of a "victim" over a period of time to accomplish two things: (1) to expel this unwanted intruder from the group, and (2) to bring about his or her total loss of face. In the example given below, the "preparation" of the victim was carried out over many weeks.

A group of Chicano college students used to get together and drink heavily. Each person had an earned nickname indicative of group camaraderie. One member was called "el Animal" because the group considered him to be uncivilized. "La Mosquita" acquired his moniker because of his predilection to "buzz around" like a fly when liquor was available. The joke in the group was Hay viene la Mosquita buscando el pisto (here comes the fly looking for booze). The members of the group called themselves "las Moscas" because, like flies, they would gather for the weekly binge. They also took their name from a comical song popular at the time and similar in form to "Seventy-six Bottles of Beer on the Wall."

The group had developed a shortened form of salutation when meeting each other on campus. The salutation was simply *Pareces* . . . [and after a pause and *sotto voce* so others would not hear] *puta* (You look like . . . a whore). One member of the group was from India. This particular individual, from a religious Quaker background, was well liked by the group and was quickly taught all the choice Spanish curse terms. His particular rendition of the *pareces* greeting was considered hilarious because he pronounced it in a peculiar fashion.

The Indian lost his scholarship because he attended more to *las Moscas* than to his studies. As a result, he was in danger of destitution and deportation. The local priest had provided him shelter. The Spanish priest was somewhat of an aristocrat and an intellectual; he decided to infiltrate the *las Moscas* as its "savior." He once remarked that he wanted to "save" these "almas perdidas" (lost souls). The group would kid him respectfully but wouldn't allow him to change their behaviors. The *pareces* salutation began to intrigue him. "What is this *pareces? Pareces* this and *pareces* that," he would ask. "What do you guys mean by all this? Why all the snickering about *pareces*?" Finally, the day came when, in the company of another Spanish priest and countryman, the Indian told the priest "Pareces [short pause and then the blow . . .] puta!" The priest lost his cool. The fact that the incident happened in front of another member of the clergy was particularly irritating, humiliating, and demeaning. The priest berated the group for his total defacement and for corrupting the Indian. The group *Se curaron con el cura*—that is, they "cured" themselves with the *cura* (priest). This play on words is based on the localism *Se curan en salud* (He/she/they cured themselves even though they are healthy). The group took on an announced identity as proclaimed by the priest and obliterated it. As Goffman would have it, "The person's attachment to face gives others something to aim at; they can not only make an effort to wound him unofficially, but even make an official effort to utterly destroy his face" (1967, 39).

This fundamental point of *relajo* or *carría* is central to understanding these joking exchanges. A group may devalue a person by a nickname or devise an insult that may be cause for embarrassment. An individual's personal characteristic or social deed may become the object of the group's derision. Among a group of Mexican American steelworkers at a lunch break, one man comments that Lázaro, who has a pockmarked face, needs to purchase more insurance. This suggestion perks the group's interest. Lázaro asks why he needs more insurance. The originator of the verbal prank then declares to him in front of the others, "¡Si cai un granizal te va

acabar de chingar la cara!" (If a hail storm hits, it will finish destroying your face!).
What can the poor man do? If he is quick, he can come back with a clever repartee;
if not, he can suffer the insult, leave the scene, or engage in a fistfight. It should be
noted that the Spanish word for this facial condition is *cacaraneada* (a face pitted by
the smallpox). One can speculate whether *caramiadas* (for *camaradas*—comrades)
evolved from this play on words.

These situations are defined and presented to an individual in the language of
everyday life. The situation is presented to pique interest and to see if the victim,
like a fish, will "bite." The group's interest is to see if the victim will commit him or
herself to an action that will symbolically separate him or her from his or her own
self-value, with the result of incurring shame, exposure, *vergüenza*, and the group's
laughter and derision as the person loses his or her composure. Portilla believes
that *relajo* should also be understood as "an act in reality and not an introspection,
because the individual decides his actions and takes his internal views and decisions
as objects" (1966, 26).

It is logical that a cultural group that stresses courtesy, proper demeanor,
and respect for the other would also require a social "safety valve." Some societies
have "joking relations" in which liberties can be taken with specific kin members
(Eggan 1975, 48). *Relajo* and *carría* games have not been discussed much in the
literature, so as to reveal other facets of these behaviors. Nor has there been
much of an attempt to analyze ancient traditions, for example, a dance where the
musicos (musicians) would proclaim *el valse chiquiado* (a waltz used for creating
merriment, perhaps a petulant (*chiquido*) response to a challenge at a dance). Jim
Sagel noted that many of the *versos* still survive. In *el valse*, the male would begin
to sing a verse to his intended partner before taking her out to dance. The role of
the woman was to respond in kind, "upping the ante and multiplying the mirth of
the listeners, for most of the verses were delightfully sarcastic" (Sagel 1990b, 13).
A man might start out with

Viene la luna saliendo	The moon is rising
Vestida de seda negra—	Dressed in black silk—
Anda dile a tu mamá	Go and ask your mother
Si quiere ser mi suegra.	If she'd like to be my mother-in-law.

To which the woman would reply:

Viene la luna saliendo	The moon is rising
Vestida de seda colorada—	Dressed in red silk—

Anda dile a tu mamá	Go and tell your mama
Que no te quiero pa' nada.	That I don't want you at all.

(Sagel 1990b, 13–14)

Echar versos, to compose, sing, and recite *coplas* or *versos*, was popular in the eighteenth- and nineteenth-century tradition. At almost every social gathering (e.g., baptisms, weddings, *prendorios* [betrothal parties]), and energized with some *copitas de vino* (drinks), the *cantadores* were the center of attention. Aurelio M. Espinosa traces these *cantadores* to the courts of King John II in fifteenth-century Spain, when these ancient jongleurs and troubadours sang of Spanish heroes (Espinosa 1926, 150). The New Mexico *verso*, such as the one presented above, is an octosyllabic quatrain that expresses, in four short verses, a complete judgment or idea. The verses are, as a rule, united by assonance or rhyme, with the second and fourth so joined (Espinosa 1926, 151).

Other Face Defamations and Nicknames

In his study of urban black culture, Abrahams says that playing "the dozens" (also called "mother rhyming," as in the attack on someone's mother) is a means of training the man of words. He cites H. Rap Brown as saying, "We played the dozens for recreation, like white folks play Scrabble. . . . Though the dozens is a mean game because what one tries to do is totally destroy somebody else with words. . . . Signifying is more humane. Instead of coming down on somebody's mother, you come down on them. But, before you can signify you got to be able to rap" (Abrahams 1972, 217).

Romano observed a verbal dueling game in a Mexican American south Texas community. According to him, the male Mexican American is under constant pressure to "protect" himself from verbal dueling, *envidia* (envy), and gossip. Everyday words and metaphors contain insinuations, innuendos, and outright accusations of effeminacy and lack of courage. Innocent remarks that contain the term *leche* (milk) may constitute a veiled reference to sperm (or lack thereof). In short, the intended metaphorical significance is derived from common everyday words, and one must be savvy enough to distinguish between common usage and a verbal play on such words. Thus, there are levels of refinement in verbal dueling. A competent opponent is expected to reveal neither his intentions and meanings nor his reactions during an exchange. The highest refinement in verbal dueling is achieved when the implied meaning is phrased in such a manner as to convince the victim that he has been greatly complimented and flattered (Romano 1960, 972). This is true *cabuya*. In the film *Picardía mejicana*, Mexican actor and singer Vicente Fernandez hangs around with two other n'er-do-wells (Salazar 1978). In the beginning of the film, the dialogue is full of insults that come at the viewer nonstop. Many of these insults are specific to Mexico City street talk.† (This film's *relajo* verbal interchanges are very abstract and illustrate the agility of these Mexico City barrio men to banter rapidly and nonstop.)

NICKNAMES

Nicknames often reflect the products of *carrías*. Specifically, nicknames often reflect a defamation of a person by focusing on a particular facial characteristic. Thus, a dark-complected individual may be called "Whitey" or, worse, *Huero/ Güero* (blondie). A person may receive the nickname "Kiki" for *que quijadotas* (protruding jaws). Another fellow is called *Boquinete* because, like the white sucker (*Catostomus commersoni*, a bottom-feeding fish), he has a protruding upper lip. One individual is called *Comunidad* because it is known that his father was someone from the community. I have known two "Cheetahs" (Tarzan's chimp), two "Gorillas," a *Chango* (chimp), two "Hippos," one *Boquinete*, one "Tarzan," and an assortment of other jungle types. I note that this practice has not changed much in all the years since I originally began this study. Imagine being called *Marro* (hammer), or, what is more likely, "Sledge Hammer," that is, a doltish fellow with a square head. In reading obituaries in the *Albuquerque Journal North* ("Obituaries" 1999), which covers northern New Mexico counties, I am often struck by the nicknames of the deceased, some of which were probably earned in *carrías*.

Social Identities and *La Carría*

An elemental aspect of social interaction is that social personalities are identified and catalogued for future reference. Such references may color or dictate the nature of future social interactions. Moreover, certain important social-structural elements will emerge to give social interaction a stable character. A simple example from John Dollard will suffice. According to one of Dollard's informants, the "dirty dozens" occurs after two young African American men begin to joke before a small group of peers:

> At first no obscene words or references are used. Later however, the "weak" kidder who "can't take it" will fight back by telling the other about his "mammy"; thus the dirty dozens

---

†Some of this verbal dueling was beyond this writer's ken.

begins. It is at this point also that the onlookers play an important part, as when they jump in by saying "aw, he told you about your mother. I wouldn't stand for that. Don't be a sissy. Tell him something back. I know this is a fight," etc. (1939, 12)

In this example, the group in the interaction has identified a characteristic of one of the interactants, namely the weak kidder who can't take it. Thus, the nature of interaction is one of constantly adjusting to the other person(s), negotiating new definitions of the situation, and directing action toward these meanings. As Blumer would have it,

> Human beings in interacting with one another have to take into account what each other is doing or is about to do; they are forced to direct their own conduct or handle their situation in terms of what they take into account. Thus the activities of others enter as positive factors in the formation of their own conduct; in the face of the actions of others one may abandon an intention or purpose, revise it, check it or suspend it, or replace it. (1969, 8)

We adjust and fit our activity to the action of others. Attack is what gives *la carría* its reiterative character, as one person adjusts to another's line of mild insult.

Norman K. Denzin proposed the hypothesis of "self-lodging." Group life consists of a series of social selves that are lodged in the social structure. "Through the process of *self-lodging*, humans translate crucial features of their own identity into the selves, memories and imaginations of others. . . . By lodging the self in interaction, in the selves of others, a reciprocal bond is created and the firm foundations for future relationships are established" (1970b, 262). The self-lodging hypothesis, according to Denzin, suggests that after the identification process has been negotiated (Goffman 1959) and settled, it gives rise to a recurring pattern of interactions, which rest on the reciprocal definition given to the lodged selves. The respective selves offer their own vocabularies and grounds for identification. Motivation arises out of the interactional process. The self and its interpretation by others are grounded in interaction, and as selves become lodged within the social structure, the styles and reasons for interaction become ritualized. Once identification has been established, the presentation of selves is no longer problematic (Denzin 1970b, 262).

Denzin moves beyond Goffman's (1959) presentation of self to answer the question: What happens after the self is presented? In giving a rationale for the identification of social selves within the social structure, Denzin is also viewing the problem of motivation within a social-interactional structure (Denzin 1970b). In effect, as one perceives the other's behavior, one is motivated to adjust one's behavior to the interlocutor. In other words, if I must deal with a known personality, such as

Two guys greet each other (Carol Baldwin). Translation: 'Where have you been, I thought you were dead?' Response: 'Naw man!' (Fifties pacheco argot in New Mexico)

a *sinvergüenza*, in a business venture, I will negotiate my behavior (i.e., my assents) from a different perspective. If I take the other to be a proper interactant, one whom I perceive to be trustworthy, my actions and accords will also change accordingly.

Thus, in social interactions lodged social types (i.e., personalities) will be identified, catalogued, and interacted with according to type. Edwardo Luquin, writing about Mexicans, identified a number of social personalities in terms of their misuse of *respeto*. Such social personalities as *el lambiscon, el madrugador*, and *el pistolero* are well known in the barrio (Luquin 1961). For example, *el lambiscon* or *el lambe* (the bootlicker) is an interactant who masks his true motives behind respect. Thus, says Luquin, *el lambe* "conoce perfectamente el valor y significado es su apretón de manos y de un abrazo; posee la clave de todo aquello que suele inclinar la voluntad de un hombre en favor de otro; lo único que no conoce ni quiere conocer, es el valor de la dignidad" (*el lambe* knows value and its significance with a firm handshake and a pat on the back; the one thing he does not know and does not want to recognize is the value of dignity) (Luquin 1961, 64). One definition of *respeto* is to give and recognize another person's dignity. It is owed that person, much as *deber* is the recognition that one must make the respect manifest with one's deeds. The backslapper and handshaker is a superficial person without substance and is only interested in impression management. *Deber* (obligation) is the recognition that one must make that respect manifest with one's gravitas. The backslapper lodges in the interactional network as a "flimflam man," regardless of his or her social status. *Es otro sinvergüenza en la movida* (He is another *sinvergüenza* looking for opportunities), whether that person is a local politician looking for votes or the president of a small university.

LOS PÍCAROS

In the New Mexico village and barrio, another socially lodged type is the *sin oficio*. This is a person without a social purpose. Such individuals live by following a norm of disorder, never being serious, always being disrespectful, and deliberately placing "themselves beyond the pale of social convention and law, and keep[ing] themselves alive by sheer trickery, by the fertility of an unscrupulous imagination" (Mérimée 1930, 202). They are *sinvergüenzas* because in order to make fun of people, they must do it shamelessly. They are truly *descarados* (without face) in their actions. They are known as *pícaros* (antiheros), who are also found in the picaresque literature of the Golden Age of Spain, such as *Vida de Lazarillo de Tormes*, published in 1554. New Mexico Spanish (and my grandmother's Spanish) retains the term *pícaro*, the antihero in the village and the identity Portilla calls *el relajiento* (1966, 39). My grandmother sometimes referred to my siblings and me as *pícaros*.

Sagel tells us that the *pícaro* lives on the fringes of society, constantly poking fun at its limitations and excesses. He is called lazy, but it is not out of shiftlessness that he refuses to work; he is "carefree, doing what he pleases, thumbing his nose at convention, acting perfectly outrageous and getting away with it because when his vecinos aren't too afraid to ask him to stop, they're begging him to go on, for his independence is as entertaining as it is enticing. He's a great storyteller, having honed his wit to get by." In the end the *pícaro* is "crazy in a meaningful way and meaningful in a crazy way" (1990b, 12).

Lovato relates a vignette that illustrates many of the points raised here. Lovato's study concerns an order given by a county ditch commission in New Mexico to clean up the cans and bottles from the village community irrigation ditch, but *los vatos* (the guys) had other ideas. The full Spanish version is provided to illustrate for the Spanish reader the special characteristics of rural New Mexico Spanish.

> Güeno pus, comenzamos a limpiar la acequia—cerveza tras cerveza sí, pero le entramos como hombres trabajoders que nunca *juimos*. Al echar toda las evidencias de nuestras borracheras a la *troca* del Matón, salimos rumbo al dompe. Pero, antes de irnos pa' el *dompe*, dimos una *güeltecita* pa' 'ya 'bajo nomás pa'darles una poca de carrilla a los de la comisión de la acequia.
>
> Huacha—dijía Inocencio—huacha que quemadota les doy a esos cuates—Y se empinó una botella de *Thunderbird* vacía, haciendose el que se estaba echando un tragote y luego me la pasó a mi y al *Flash*. El Matón iba delante con el Posól mientras que todos *nojotros* ibamos atrás con la jarrería, de modo que iba todo *embuma'o* porque estaba cierto a el le iba caer la carrilla porque el era de la troquita y él sería el primero que lo iban a conocer. Ya se oían los murmullos de la comisión cuando pasamos en frente de sus casas empinando el codeo con tamaña botella vacía.
>
> —A que *balbaros*—ya andan en la borrachera esos huevones sin oficio! Otros decían:—"¡Y de 'ónde cabrones tendrán tando dinero pa' andar pasiándose pa' 'rriba y pa' 'bajo todos los días! Yo creo que todos están en el *Welfare* y en las estampas! ¡Talagudos cabrones!" (Lovato 1974, 42; emphases in original)

Translation:

> Well, now, we began to clean up the ditch—beer after beer, and we began like hardworking men, which we never were. Throwing the evidence of our drinking into Matón's truck, we went to the vicinity of the dump. But before we went to the dump, we made a small run down the road to give a little *carría* to the commissioners of the ditch association.
>
> "Look," said Inocencio, "look at what a burn I'm going to give those fellows"—and he lifted the empty bottle of Thunderbird, pretending he was taking a big swig, then he

passed it on to me and to Posól while the rest of us were in the back amid the cans, while he was driving very fast because it was certain that to him would fall the *carría* (in this case the commissioner's ire) because he was the owner of the truck, and it was certain he would be the one recognized. One could already hear the mutterings of the commission members as we passed in front of their houses "drinking" from the empty bottle.

"Barbarous—they are drinking again, those lazy persons without social purpose!" others would say. "And where do those sons of bitches get the &%^@** to have such money to be drinking and driving up and down every day! I think they are on welfare and on food stamps! Talagudos cabrones!" (roughly "rotten scoundrels")

The socialization of *respeto* and *vergüenza* suggests a great deal about social behavior among Spanish-speaking persons. *La carría* and *relajo* destroy the social order imposed by value. Goffman's point is that "only the discredited individual ought to feel ashamed; but, by the standards of the little social system maintained through the interaction, the discreditor is just as guilty as the person he discredits—sometimes more so, for if he has been posing as a tactful man, in destroying another's image he destroys his own" (1967, 106).‡

Hispanos have always loved their rogues. Historically, picaresque literature begins with *Lazarillo de Tormes*, as noted above. Hispanos in the past entertained themselves by telling Don Cacahuate stories, some of which were risqué. Another rogue was Pedro de Ordemales. One version comes from *Entre Verde y Seco* (Between green and dry). In this story, Pedro is left to take care of his aged mother while his brother Juan goes to work. Pedro feeds his mother *atole* (in some stories it is *shaquegüe* [blue corn meal], in others, *sopa*). He does such a bad job of this that the old lady dies. Pedro puts her in a chair so that when Juan shows up, he will tip the chair and she will fall to the floor and he will be blamed for her death. This happens and Juan is beset with grief, so Pedro offers another scheme. In this scheme the mother is put on a burro and the animal is let loose in a garden belonging to the priest (some versions make this character a rich man). When the priest yells at the burro the mother falls off the animal. The brothers manage to get a good funeral and burial, including music by *Las Carmelitas* (a lay church group) and other *sociedades* (church societies) for the mother (Arellano 1972, 73–74). Juan B. Rael presents six stories of the Pedro saga from southern Colorado as well as three stories of *mano* and *mana Faschico*, who are village idiots. One heard these stories from one's mother in childhood. Perhaps they were used to entertain, or to teach children to be more aware of one's relationships with others (Rael 1977). Espinosa's Pedro is a study of

---

‡ It should be noted that the best work on the topic of *carría* is by the New Mexico sage Estévan Arellano (1992). His book, *Inocencio: Ni pisca ni escarda y siempre se come el mejor elote* (Inocencio: He does not clean the weeds around the plants yet he always eats the best ear of corn) (1992) won great recognition in Mexico, where it was published.

the New Mexico Spanish spoken at another time (Espinosa 1914). Arellano (1972) presents a story of a character called Juan Tonto. The tradition continues in Sagel's book in which a wife wakes up in a terrible state fearing that she is dying. She tells her husband to call the priest as she holds on to the bedpost. "Do you want to go to the hospital?" asks her husband. She makes her way to the kitchen. She sees the glass from which she had drunk a little wine. She instructs her husband, "Aquéstate y no me hagas aprecio" (Go to back to bed and never mind). "¡No tengo más que la borrachera!" (The only thing wrong with me is that I am still drunk) (Sagel 1990a, 22). Sagel's stories and poems are from an "insider" perspective, narrating the goings and doings of people in everyday life. One character that Sagel unearths is called "Rooster García." García was allegedly conceived in a chicken coop as the neighborhood children watch Rooster's mother in the primal act.

Finally, one often hears, *¡Ya no hay respeto!* (There is no longer any respect). Usually the person will proclaim that he or she heard this saying in youth. Observers of *falta de respeto* (lack of respect) have been associated with schools in their roles as teachers, aides, or foster grandparents.

What I have argued in this chapter is the derealization of value. *Carría* and *relajo* games have the potential to destroy value or, in Portilla's words, *la seriedad*, serious comportment§ (Portilla 1966). Although the game of *carría* may involve lighthearted bantering among familiar friends, taken too far *la carría* can destroy the small social order created in social interaction. There is a point reached in these interactions where finally someone "breaks" and the game is no longer light banter but an attack on a self that must be defended against or the victim leaves the social scene in utter defeat and humiliation. In this sense *la carría* is very destructive and can lead to violence. It is important to note that there are people in the community who are good at this kind of banter. Some have been memorialized in classic literature such as *Vida de Lazarillo de Tormes* (1965) and in other books dealing with the picaresque antihero. Arellano's book *Inocencio* is about a more modern *pícaro* in a northern New Mexico village (Arellano 1992). I don't believe the *pícaro* is ignorant but possesses an incredible sensitivity to the nuances of social behavior. Finally, I have been told that where men work in construction groups this kind of banter goes on all day. Some participation observation could lead to other insights on *la carría*.

---

§ The antithesis of these behaviors is to enter into *nadaísmo,* a kind of nihilism that devalues and destroys the social order. It can be said of these social types that *les importa nada* (they care about nothing, nothing is sacred to them). *Nadaísmo* is a world of total disorder and chaos, whether personal or social. This topic will be discussed further in chapter 7.

CHAPTER 5

Violence in Mexican Music: *Mancornando*

Me llaman el asesino por hay
y dicen que me anda buscando la ley.
> "El asesino," Mexican song

Les seguí los pasos y maté a los dos.
> "Veinte años," Mexican song

LA MANCORNADORA IS A THEME IN MEXICAN MUSIC THAT DEPICTS A HEAVY existential experience between men and women. The songs are filled with graphic and painful metaphors. The outcome is often tragic and violent, and often involves the killing of women. The term *mancornar* represents power and control, and the animal horn is its symbol. It is a difficult subject to broach, but its presence in a number of songs and in social life suggests certain commonalities that are worth exploring. It is important to locate these themes within a broader frame, which includes ideas from Norman Denzin, Ernest Becker, Harold Searles, and Terry Warner. Denzin's phenomenology of domestic violence provides insights into violence that involve concepts of self-deceit, uncontrolled anger, violent emotional action, negative symbolic interaction, and bad faith, all of which form the framework for this chapter. Moreover, the violent person attempts to justify his or her acts of violence by invoking a vocabulary of motives that are self-deceptive. The content of this chapter is about violent emotionality (Denzin 1984b). The lyrics support these themes.

La mancornadora is reflected in only a small segment of Mexican music. It is couched within ever-popular corridos and *rancheras* played on the radio, at dances, and often in community fiestas in New Mexico. Much of what I discuss below is about the *ejemplo* or *trágico*; both are a type of corrido that presents a tragic example as a moral lesson to the community regarding certain acts.

Violence as Loss

Denzin's phenomenological analysis of lived violence focuses on spousal abuse, child abuse, and other forms of violence. His aim was to develop a depth framework that could be used to understand the multiple forms of family violence. The empirical evidence for this framework came from a comprehensive analysis of the literature on incidents of marital rape, sadomasochistic ritual, and spouse and child abuse, inflicting out of control emotions on the other person, making threats of murder and physical torture, and indulging in acts of "playful" violence (Denzin 1984b, 484).

The nub of Denzin's definition of violence is the centrality of loss. "Violence will be defined here as the attempt to regain, through the use of emotional and physical force, something that has been lost" (Denzin 1984b, 488). If loss is the central idea, then an expansion of the ideas of loss should explain (1) the depression and depletion of self-esteem following loss, (2) the violence attached to stalking, and (3) killing as a means of holding onto the lost object, as well as illuminating the self-deceit that accompanies these violent episodes. The lyrics in the songs discussed in this chapter are related to this central concept of loss. For example, loss and stalking are the poignant theme of the song "Veinte años." The singer laments, "La mujer que quise me dejó por otro, / les seguí los pasos y maté a los dos" (The woman I loved left me for another. / I followed them and I killed them both). "Las leyes de la tierra me dieron sin clemencia, / viente años de prisión." The man is sentenced to twenty years in prison. He killed "por que estaba loco" (because I was crazy, crazy for her love).

Becker's comprehensive theory of depression remains a bold and radical view of depression as loss. Becker's idea is to keep what is "durable" in Freud's psychoanalysis (see Becker 1971a, chap. 6). Becker's view helps to draw out a deeper understanding of loss as he extends the Freudian ideas of object loss to "game loss," "self-esteem loss," and "meaning loss." Depression, in everyday interactions, comes from people's inability to create shared reality with others because a vital person in the "game" is missing. "Meaning loss" and the inability to create meaning, which occurs when action gets bogged down, saps an individual's sense of self-esteem. Becker reasons, "If the ego is the basis for action, and if a warm feeling of self-value must pervade one's acts, then it is only a step to focusing on the really crucial dynamic of a breakdown of action, namely, the undermining of the individual's sense of self-value" (Becker 1964, 110).

Becker recognizes the importance of Freud's theory of object loss whereby the ego develops by responding to social objects. Any corresponding loss of object means a corresponding depletion in the ego. Thus, to relinquish an object means massive trauma for the person (Becker 1964). In his elaboration of this theory, Becker utilizes the sociological dimension added by Thomas Szasz's theory of the loss of "game." Szasz's idea of "game" introduces the social dimension by proposing that not only are human objects important, but that "norms and rules—or more generally—games . . . are worth playing!" (quoted in Becker 1964, 112). Becker suggests that persons "suffer grievously when they can find no games worth playing, even though their object world might remain more or less intact." Broadening the concept, he expresses the entire enterprise in terms of the creation of self—one that is inseparably joined with others by social rules and norms. The game provides the person with a "staged drama of significance which is the theater of his action." Moreover, "to lose an object, then, is to lose someone to whom one has made appeal for self-validation." One can not only lose a "game," but lose "a performance part in which identity is fabricated and sustained" (Becker 1964, 112).

More to the point is the idea that when action bogs down, meaning dies. Because meaning is refined into a symbolic meaning framework, it stands to reason that individuals need to "keep verbal referents going in a self-consistent scheme . . . and life retains its meaning" (Becker 1964, 115). Action remains possible, and life retains its meanings. Words make up a consistent self-identity, so a "loss of game" means that the person will shift to another vocabulary of motives. Vocabulary of motives is nothing more than the vocalizations (words) used by persons trying to understand and make sense of the situations in which they find themselves (Becker 1964). Music is a perfect expression of the vocabulary of motives—or, more simply, of emotions—associated with situations of loss.

Vengeance, Loss, and Keeping the Object

Vengeance as a form of game loss can be seen as a way of holding on to an object. Becker reminds us that to lose an object "is to lose the possibility of undertaking a range of satisfying action," and "to hate and to seek revenge is to create a continually present object" (Becker 1964, 125–26). Searles, in his study of the dynamic of vengeance, notes that the vengeful person "has not really given up the other person toward whom his vengefulness is directed: that is, his preoccupation with vengeful fantasies about that person serves, in effect, as a way of psychologically holding on to him [her]" (1956, 31). Othello, upon suspecting Desdemona's infidelity, kills her as a means of "keeping her true." "Be thus when thou art dead, and I will kill thee, and love thee after" (Mogenson 1992, 48). Thus, incidents of stalking can be understood within this framework. In "Veinte años," the singer laments, "Les seguí los pasos y maté a los dos" (I followed them and killed them both).

The vocabularies of meaning for the vengeful person become self-deceptions about "getting even," of "showing up" the person to whom he or she is bound, or any number of other motives in dealing with the loss. It keeps the performance going even if the subject of the vengeance is no longer in play.

The Vocabularies of Meaning in Violence

Building on Horney's 1948 work, Searles maintains that the purpose of vengeance is mainly twofold—to manage repressed grief and to deal with separation anxiety. This idea ties in to Becker's expansion of the object-loss theory and specifically to the "loss of game." In quoting Karen Horney, Searles also proposes that the functions of vengeance or vindictiveness are (1) to provide a form of self-protection for the person against hostility from without and from within; (2) to restore injured pride; (3) to provide the hope for or the actual sensation of a vindictive triumph; and (4) to keep under control feelings of hopelessness about one's life (Searles 1956, 32).

Anger as Delusion

Warner wrote a useful and penetrating chapter viewing anger as a social construction. Anger and other related emotions are seen as delusions. In being angry, a person is making a mistaken judgment (the delusion) that the object of his or her anger (whoever it is), and not he or she, is responsible for his or her anger. In being angry, the person is "engaging in a form of conduct in and by which she [or he] maintains that she [or he] is not doing so at all, but is passive, [so that] angry people are systematically in error in their beliefs about how things are with them" (Warner 1986, 136). Other strong emotions (e.g., irritation, hate, embarrassment, dread, self-pity, and contempt) have this property in common, and, as Warner argues, all are "self-delusional." The song "Veinte años" also indicates the killer's vocabularies of meaning as "por que estaba loco, / loco por su amor" (because I was [went] crazy, / I was crazed for her love). This self-blaming attributes his condition to her and is called *agentive anger* because she is seen as the agent of his anger (Warner 1986).

The Typifications

Another conceptual tool used here comes from the phenomenological philosophy of Alfred Schutz and forms the basis of further analysis. Typifications in Schutzian phenomenology are abstractions from everyday life and exist in all cultures and social groupings. They arise from the intersubjective nature of social life (Schutz 1971, 73–75). *Intersubjectivity* refers to the relations between persons and the way in which cultures abstract the terms used to describe (or "typify") various kinds of social interactions out of daily experiences. To typify is to abstract the commonalities of social behavior.

Song, poetry, images, stories, parables, dichos, and narratives become the social stock of a culture's knowledge that is transmitted, often orally, from one generation to another via typifications (Schutz 1971). In time, the typification becomes a type of cultural archetype. Popular music depicts falling in love and the end of a relationship that has become a sour and bitter fruit. Music can serve as another source of "subjugated knowledges." Hartman (1994) calls for the liberation of "subjugated knowledges," which exist in many forms. The gist of Hartman's argument is that the many sources of knowledge of the minority experience include narratives, poems, and stories—or, more broadly, "the narrative." Knowledge of these frameworks is as important as the knowledge produced by empirical methods. The violent themes found in the ever popular Mexican corrido reflect what is important to the culture. The corrido as a song form covers historical events, narration, comedic themes, the *ejemplo,* and the *trágico* (the tragic example). The *ejemplo* such as a brutal killing is often used to provide a moral lesson to members of the culture. The *trágico* captures some tragic event. Mendoza separates these corridos into two types (1974). Later in the chapter some well-known Mexican corridos still commonly heard in New Mexico are provided as *mancornadora* songs.

The Symbol of the Horn

In a diary entry written in September 1863, the poet Gerard Manley Hopkins wrote:

> The various lights under which the horn may be looked at have given rise to a vast number of words in language. It may be regarded as a projection, a climax, a badge of strength, power or vigor, a tapering body, a spiral, a wavy object, a bow, a vessel to hold withal or to drink from, a smooth hard material not brittle, stony, metallic or wooden, smoothing sprouting up, something to thrust or push with, a sign of honour or pride, an instrument of music, etc. (1962, 90)

Hopkins goes on to tell us that the shape of the horn, its curving, *curvus*, is one of its forms. The Latin terms *corvus* (raven) and *cornix* (crow) are related to *cornu* (horn) and *curvus* (curved). The cornel tree derives its name from the hard hornlike nature of its wood. "Corner" is derived from its shape and its Latin root *cornu* (Hopkins 1962, 91).

One hears in daily life that someone has "turned the corner" or turned his or her life around. The phrase "turning the corner" illustrates personal power in reforming one's life or in dealing with a difficult problem. The "cornering" on a problem must be emphasized, but the antithesis is also present in other phrases, for example, "being skewered on the horns of a dilemma." In northern New Mexico one can hear the phrase *le pucieron los cuernos* (having had the horns put on one), which means having something go wrong, usually a relationship turned sour or a bad turn of events. There is a deeper and more offensive and sinister side to all this as well.

THE HORN AS STRENGTH AND POWER IN RELATIONSHIPS

The horn signifies strength and power but also has an ambivalent characteristic. Michelangelo painted Moses with horns symbolic of his spiritual power. A fascinating book by Mellinkoff attributes the horns on Moses portrayed by Michelangelo and other painters as the result of a mistake made by Jerome in his translation of the Old Testament. The Hebrew word *qeren* in Exodus (34:29) can mean "horns" or "rays of light." Jerome translated *qeren* as Latin *cornuta*, meaning "horned" (Mellinkoff 1970, 1).

In the last scene in James Clavel's *Shogun*, Toronada is wearing a helmet with horns as he begins his quest for the control of all the provinces in ancient Japan (Clavel 1975). Jacobi points to the negative aspects of this symbol: "The raging bull which gored the first Christian martyrs in the Roman arena will remain forever a symbol of blind rage, destructive intensity, death-dealing power" (1959, 151). The other feature of the symbol is the penetrating and impaling power of the horn. Impaling means "boring, piercing," or "penetrating" and is closely related to the instruments used, for example, spike, arrow, sword, spit, and dagger. But it is the horn that possesses these attributes and does the penetrating and may relate to passionate and active penetrating qualities. Jacobi offers the power of Christ's word as symbolized by a sword issuing from his mouth. This symbol is his penetrating love. Thus, "The penetrating principle can take on the most diverse forms; its action can be both destructive and fruitful; it is an 'inciter' which promotes development or it may bring death and so provide the impetus to rebirth" (Jacobi 1959, 153–54). One may also consider the impaling aspects of a relationship and of love turned angry and bitter.

THE *MANCORNAR* THEME

Cornar in the term *mancornar* can be related to the horn because *cornar* is also in the root of the term *cuerno*, "horn." The *Enciclopedia universal ilustrada* refers to *mancornar* specifically as "wrestling a steer" (*un novillo*) and affixing the horns to the ground so that they cannot move. The etymology of *mancornar* seems to come from *mano y cuerno* (hand and horn) (*Enciclopedia* 1930, 718). The song "Paso del Norte" is about dope smugglers being taken to prison. The song proclaims, "They were *mancornados*" (handcuffed). An old New Mexico meaning of *mancornar* was to place a wooden yolk across two oxen to make them pull together. The term is also in found in Rubén Cobos's *Dictionary of New Mexico and Southern Colorado Spanish* (2003). Cobos says that *mancuernar* meant the placement of the double rosary around a newly married couple in a ceremony called the *lasso*. Belarmino Baca, who at eighty-four years of age recalled that in his youth his family would employ a *carro de caballo* (horse-drawn wagon) to get from Anton Chico to Las Vegas, New Mexico, which was a distance of thirty-one miles and an overnight campout. The horses were hobbled, or, as he termed it, had *mancuernías* placed on them (Baca 2003). Another resident of rural eastern Mora County said that animals would be controlled by a leather strap connecting the horn to what he called the *manillas* (area above the hoof) so that "they won't jump the fences." All of these terms point to control and power over either persons or animals. Even the double rosary can be thought of as "control" because each person is "enchained" by or placed into each other's life—or perhaps it indicates the control that God exercises over the couple's marriage.

A definition given by a janitress is provocative because of its simplicity. Her definition is important to this thesis in that the people being studied provide these definitions from their own lived experiences. When asked about the term *mancornar*, she paused for a moment, thought, and then said two things. First, she said that it meant "one woman and two men." She had crystallized and typified into a few words the essence of these events. The second part of her definition had to do with the time when as a younger woman she had sung with her brother, and had abstracted from her knowledge these themes in these songs, wherein the term *mancuernar* was associated with women as *mancornadoras* (defined below). I will explore this second definition as a typification and a form of "negative symbolic interaction" (Denzin 1984b).

PLUMBING THE DEPTHS WHILE WEARING THE HORNS

Dennis Saleeby offered the following suggestion at a faculty training conference: "Follow the folk psychology." The "folk psychology" in this case is what Hispanos know as part of their everyday social stock of knowledge (Saleeby 1995). A talk with a young female student from the New Mexico mountain village of El Rito concerning *pucieron los cuernos* illustrates that this idea is not entirely unknown or lost in some parts of New Mexico.

In New Mexico, *pucieron los cuernos* (the wearing of the horns) smacks of the tension of being *mancornado*, an *alcahuete* (one who does not see or know what one's wife or daughter is doing), in a social setting. Someone else has woven a net of intrigue and vexing troubles and has control over the person's destiny. The impaling power of the horn is felt when the person finally realizes what is happening to him as he sees his love disappear with another man. He has been cuckolded by the new lover. The reference group in the community knows the man is wearing the horns because he did not know what was going on behind his back. This is another definition of the *alcahuete* role. The term *alcahuete* has a long history in Spanish literature (Kany 1960).

One of the interesting manifestations of "wearing the horns" is that the deceived husband or lover, and not the adulterer or panderer, becomes the object of ridicule and opprobrium. Julian Pitt-Rivers makes this point in his book *People of the Sierra* (1971) and in his chapter in Péristiany's collection *Honour and Shame* (1966) regarding his studies of the Andalusian peoples of Spain. It should not be lost on the reader that many Spanish-speaking colonists who first settled New Mexico came from this region of Spain. No doubt they brought their moral teachings and ways of thinking about these things. "Wearing the horns" was a phrase used in another generation in New Mexico and is still extant in some small villages. *Poniedo a alguien de rosa* (literally, dressing someone up) is another of these euphemisms, as is "being an *orejón*"—one who has large ears to hear yet does not hear the gossip about himself. *Pucieron los cuernos* is evocative of more fearful dimensions, especially those associated with the devil, *il Cornuto*, the horned one and the ultimate enemy of good and decency and of man.

Horned animals such as the billy goat give us such names as *cabro* for goat or *cabrón* (intruder, interloper) in everyday terms—*un entremetido* in people's affairs. One father, expressing concern for his daughter, said "Si un cabrón se arrima a mi casa . . ." He regarded any suitor for his daughter as an interloper.

Pitt-Rivers has an interesting theory about the nature of the family. He writes that male sexuality is essential to the foundation of the family as well as necessary for its defense. The woman brings to the family her *vergüenza*, which in this case is not to be translated as "shame," but the innocence and sanctity she brings to the family. She must guard against human contacts that might expose her to dishonor. If the male fails in his duty to protect the *vergüenza* of the family, then he has to wear the symbol of his failure and shame—the horns.

He has betrayed the values of the family, bringing dishonour to all the social groups who are reciprocally within his honour: his family and his community. His manliness is defiled, for he has fallen under the domination of the Devil and must wear his symbol of the stigma of his betrayal. The responsibility is his, not the adulterer's, for the latter was only acting in accordance with his male nature. (Pitt-Rivers 1966, 46)

Pitt-Rivers goes on to posit that if one sees the adulterer and the cuckold (who wears the horns of his dishonor) not in "terms of right or wrong but in terms of sanctity or defilement, we can see why the latter, the defiled one, should be the object of contempt, not the defiler" (Pitt-Rivers 1966, 47). Quoting from Evans-Pritchard's book *Nuer Religion* about the Nuer people of Africa, Pitt-Rivers points out that adultery creates a state of pollution and that "it is not the adulterer but the injured husband who is likely to be sick" (Pitt-Rivers 1966, 76).

The symbolism of defilement, according to Ricoeur, is "immersed in the cosmic, [and] the subterranean equivalences and correspondence between the defiled, the consecrated, and the sacred." The taboo "involves objects, actions or persons who are 'isolated' or 'forbidden' because of the danger of contact with them." He tells us, "Defilement adheres to everything unusual, everything terrifying in the world, attractive and repellant at the same time, that this symbolism is ultimately inexhaustible and ineradicable" (Ricoeur 1967, 11–12). Defilement "stains" or promotes a negative change in the one who has been defiled. He has the task of somehow removing the stain, of making himself "worthy" again, of setting right what has been offset because of his inability to act. The symbols of defilement are the imaginary horns he must wear. *¿Como se quitan los cuernos?* (How does one overcome wearing the horns?)

What causes the individual to develop such a rage when he is losing his beloved? Denzin's formulation is also that of certain writers of the psychoanalytic persuasion who posit that "loss equals violence" (Denzin 1984b). Mogenson suggests that violence and, specifically, the killing of the loved object are a means to fix the love relationship forever in time. The killing of Desdemona in Giuseppe Verdi's opera *Otello* is the cause célèbre (Mogenson 1992*)*. Another theory is presented in songs that reflect the *burla* (rebuffed) factor. When the man feels *desaigro*, as the Mexican song calls the defiled one, sees that his wife or lover has rejected his love, and feels *burlado* (rebuffed), he becomes rage itself. Warner calls this kind of anger "agentive anger" in which, being *desaigrado*, the man blames the woman for his anger and being rebuffed. But as Warner shows, it is delusional thinking (Warner 1986).

Poetic language often provides images for feelings that other languages fail to discern. The language of social science pales in comparison to the image generated by the poet or the musician. Eugene Gendlin refers to "felt meanings," that is, experiencing a meaning in thought, observation, action, speech, problem solving, remembering, and psychotherapy. "It is when we explicate a meaning and focus on it that this meaning is felt or experienced while it is being explicated. A meaning is explicated in terms of symbols whose meanings are felt or experienced. It is this feeling of experiencing that constitutes the 'having' of an explicated meaning" (Gendlin 1997, 66–67). We "feel," for example, that an act either is "right" or is not. Our comprehension that something feels right or wrong is the basis of experiencing. Gendlin gives the example (among many others) of our impressions of someone we have just met. We have not yet formulated an explicit thought of what our impression is. When we attempt to do so, the felt meanings in our awareness function, just as in recalling a name, to tell us that we do not have an impression, that these words do not describe it adequately, and we concentrate further on the feel of the felt meanings to obtain a more adequate explication of it (Gendlin 1997, 77). This is the reflective act in which emotions and feelings become one and the same.

This compound concept of feeling and meaning (felt meaning) provides a mechanism for understanding that feelings as emotions are also meaningful experiences of the self. Meanings are not just "mind things," cognitive stuff inseparable from emotional life. Emotions are experienced bodily, for example, in crying, laughter, and anxiety. Felt meanings are therefore also bodily expressions of emotions. We attach meaning to the body experience. To say, "I am body" is to recognize one's meaning creation in the world as a bodily act as well (Stewart and Mickunas 1974). To feel psychic pain is to recognize its effect coming from the depths of body and psychic experience.

Mexican music is incredibly expressive in giving voice to the most painful experiences. One song used in the film *Frida* (Taymor 2002) gives the musical backdrop of Frida Kahlo's sense of anguish and betrayal when she finds her husband, Diego Rivera, in bed with her prettier sister. In what is one of the most moving scenes, Frida drinks heavily from a bottle of tequila as she lops off her hair with some shears. The background music is "Paloma negra," symbolic of black despair and the daimonic.

In Mexican music, *palomas* (doves) are beautiful creatures portending peace and love—*la caridad.* "Paloma blanca" is a song reserved for the Virgin of Guadalupe. The title of "Paloma negra," therefore, is prescient of all manner of dark and negative ontic experiences, with their attendant weighty emotions. A Mexican song called "La Negra Tomasa" is not about the love of a dark-skinned woman named Tomasa. It is about a love affair and longing for black-tar heroin. It is the name given to a variety of heroin produced mainly in Mexico and prevalent in the western United States. We are introduced to the dark dread in the first lines of "Paloma negra":

Ya me canso de llora y no amanecer,	I tire of weeping without end,
Ya no se si maldecirte o por ti rezar.	I do not know whether to curse or pray for you.

Tengo miedo de buscarte y encontrate,	I fear looking for you and finding you,
Donde me aseguaran mis amigos que te vas.	Where my friends say you've gone.

In the first line, the person tires of tears that come without end. The dilemma is expressed in the next line, which proclaims the ambivalence of either cursing the lover or praying for him or her. "I am afraid to search for you and encounter you" because my friends have said that you are gone. The sense of primal abandonment is attacking the sense of self in the ensuing disquietude.

Hay momentos en que quisiera	There are times when I would like
mejor rajarme,	to give up,
Y arrancarme ya los clavos de mi penar.	And rip off the nails of my pain.
Pero mis ojos se mueren sin mirar tus ojos,	But I die to look into your eyes,
Y mi cariño hoy con la aurora te	At dawn my love waits for you.
vuelve a esperar.	

Ambivalent dread returns with the recognition of an awful moment in which the protagonist wants to collapse. The song captures this experience as a moment in which this person wants to give in and as the song says "rip off the nails of [his] pain." The antithesis shows itself in the last couplet: "But I am dying to see your eyes / and my insane love turns to seek you out." The nails are spikes that have penetrated to the core of the protagonist's being with their impaling power. Need we point out that impaling with the horn or "hornlike" items such as spikes or knives is the experience of being *mancornado.*

Ya agrarraste por tu cuenta la parranda,	You have begun drinking,
Paloma negra, paloma negra dónde,	Oh black dove, where are you.
dónde andarás.	
Ya no juegues con mi honra parrandera	Don't play with my honor,
Si tus caricias deben ser mías, de nadie más.	Your caresses should be mine
	and no one else's.

A depersonalized antiself called *la Parranda* cries out in this dark song, "Ya agarraste . . . la parranda!" Parranda grasps for meaning, but only living, fully embodied selves can make real meaning, as Laing (1976) taught us. Parranda is the derealized wounded self that has seized the individual and speaks for him. This wounded self can only ask pitifully, *¿Dónde andarás?* Where are you, *paloma negra?* But who or what is the *paloma negra?* Is it the lived experience of entry into nothingness—of darkness further clouded in a tequila haze? *La parranda* is not just drunkenness, but a dark oblivion symbolized by the blackness. The sense of embodied being has now

La Parranda (Jody Sims)

been compromised, as the cry of a depersonalized self proclaims in the dim screen of intoxication. The last line seems clearer as the self reaches for reality, imploring, "Tus caricias deben ser mias, de nadie mas."

Y aunque te amo con locura ya no vuelvas,	Even if I am a crazed lover you do not return,
Paloma negra tu eres el relaje de un penar,	Black dove you are the source of my pain,
Quiero ser libre vivir mi vida con quien yo quiera.	I want to be free and live my life as I want.
Dios dame fuerza que me estoy muriendo por irla a buscar.	Lord give me strength because I yearn to find her.

The sense of loss is intensified, but so is the dawning realization that the loved one as the *paloma negra* will not return. The chasm is now open, and one stands giddily looking into the dark, deep abyss. The *paloma negra* has now been transferred to the source of suffering. The words "I want to live my life in freedom, to live with the one I love. / And God grant me the strength as I am dying to go in search for her"—he yearns for a life free of her, but still wants to go find her—illustrate the ambivalence in the situation.

It is not too difficult to see why stalking occurs. The loved-crazed person has to fight the sense of loss, the need to connect to the love object. Within the self is darkness and emptiness. Only the presence of the other will fill the emptiness that leads to the sense of being depersonalized. The person is fighting the fear of oblivion and death that comes from this form of abandonment. This need is supplanted by the need to grab life to become real again. The other's love made one feel real, embodied in a symbolic game that gave one identity and purpose, but now it is gone. Oh, to look at her again! "Paloma negra" is insightful and frightening because it takes us to the edge of the abyss of nonbeing.

To be in despair is to be caught between two competing and equally compelling situations. Kierkegaard's work in general is about how despair also connotes the sense of dread. One is encountering and contracting dread—to die but not to die, to enter into a death trajectory but not to be able to pass through it. To enter into nothingness yet at the same time to be on this side of life. It is better that the individual die than to be in this place of darkest angst in which no movement either forward or backward is possible. This is the experience of dread and despair, panic, and uncontrollable anxiety.

Action becomes impossible because the life forces do not propel the individual forward through the morass. Becker shows that the problem of depression is the inability to create meaning, the inability to move forward. When right action is impossible, meaning dies (Becker 1964). Forward motion creates meaning for symbolic animals, but it becomes impossible for the person experiencing dread or depression. For human beings, any kind of forward movement creates meaning; depression is the inability to act and therefore the inability to create meaning. The anguished talk of the depressed person, Becker tells us, is an attempt to "unplug" the verbal referents that make life meaningful and that are important to make life go forward. Laing shows us that in the schizoid experience the divided self needs to be with people in order to feel real, alive, grounded, but, by the same token, being with people poses a threat to this weakened and vulnerable self—for example, the case of Mrs. R in *The Divided Self* (Laing 1976). The divided self finds itself always in dread—retreating from powerful others who may overwhelm him or her with their presence or returning to isolation to feel the death of the self. Jackson and Davidson remark that death images prevail in psychopathologies such as depression, schizophrenia, and anorexia (Jackson and Davidson 1986). The Mexican song and its images reflect this sense of death. Love and death have become one.

Mancornadora Songs

I discuss several types of *mancornadora* songs within the above point of view. Many of these songs are well known among Hispanos in New Mexico. One type of song refers specifically to the behavior of the *mancornadora* and spells out what being a *mancornadora* means. In this case, *la mancornadora* usually finds she is trying to juggle a relationship between two men. "La güera Chavela" is a good example of this type. Other older songs are also well-known examples, such as "Rosita Alvirez," Michaela in "24 de junio" (June 24 is the feast day of many San Juan villages in New Mexico), "La Martina," and "Rafaelita." It is interesting that even country-and-western music has dealt with these themes, and I discuss an example later in this chapter.

In these Mexican songs, the male is rebuffed, slighted, and made to feel *desairado*, often in public and usually at a dance. He often finds his girlfriend dancing with another man. The outcome is violent. Only one *mancornador* song I found portrays the woman as a coquette. In "La joven mancornadora," the woman boasts of the power and control she has over men's hearts.

Another class of *mancornadora* songs finds the man dealing with his loss. In both "La mancornadora" and "Lagunes de pesar," the focus is on the singer's feelings of loss and pain, and not on a tragic killing of the two new lovers. Another theme involves stalking and vengeful deaths, in such pieces as "El preso número nueve" (Prisoner number nine), "El asesino" (The assassin), and the aforementioned "Veinte años" (Twenty years). In "Preso número nueve," we find the protagonist confessing his sins to the prison priest. He awaits his execution in the morning. He tells of a woman's treachery and vows to follow her and her lover in the next life and kill them again. In songs with this theme, the wounded lover stalks and kills his beloved and the man who took her from him. Many more songs identify the *traidora* (treacherous woman) theme. These songs usually fit more into the *ranchera* tradition of song.

THE *TRAIDORA* THEME

María Herrera-Sobeck points out that in the corrido, "particularly those narrating the feats of Mexican fighting men, we encounter the mythical image of the hero embarking upon a tragic journey toward his death and the archetype of the destructive woman who precipitates his death" (Herrera-Sobeck 1982, 136). Herrera-Sobeck goes on to name a wide variety of treacherous women, beginning with doña Marina, "la Malinche," who betrayed her Indian people to the conquistadors for love of Hernán Cortés (Paz 1961). Others mentioned are Coatlicue, the Goddess of the Serpent Skirt, also called the Devourer of Wastes; Chicomecoatl, Seven Serpents Goddess of Corn, to whom human sacrifices were offered; and La Llorona, who for love of another man drowns her children, in the process losing his love, and ends up searching in vain as she wails for her lost children near bodies of water. A modern variant of La Llorona is South Carolina's Susan Smith, who drowned her two sons in 1994 by leaving them in a car that she plunged into a lake. The police first searched for a man Smith claimed had kidnapped the children, but if they had considered the event from a mythic perspective and understood the meaning of the myth, they would have apprehended Smith earlier. After watching Smith on national television one morning, I proclaimed, "¡Es La Llorona!" She was arrested in the afternoon. Myth becomes reality.

Octavio Paz opines that "our popular songs and sayings and our everyday behavior treat love as a falsehood and betrayal" (Paz 1961, 41). It is the theme of the *traición* so often heard in the *ranchera. La traición* is the old theme of betraying someone or having the tables turned on oneself, becoming trapped or "cornered" or "having the horns" put to oneself.

Paz writes that the Mexican male is a hermetic being, closed in about himself, stoic about suffering and danger. History has given the Mexican much about which to be suspicious and distrustful. Manliness is judged according to one's invulnerability. To give into the other is to "lessen . . . our manliness." "Our relations with other men," says Paz, are "tinged with suspicion." Thus, "Every time a Mexican confides in a friend or acquaintance, every time he opens himself up, it is an abdication." "Therefore confidences result in dishonor, and they are as dangerous for the person to whom they are made as they are for the person who makes them" (Paz 1961, 30). In relations, the *mala mujer* (bad woman) is like the *macho* himself. She comes and goes; "activity and immodesty unite to petrify her soul. The *mala* is hard and impious and independent like the *macho*. In her own way she also transcends her physiological weaknesses [her "open physiology," as Paz calls it] and closes herself off from the world" (Paz 1961, 39). Paz also writes about love as a contest, a conquest, in which it "is an attempt to penetrate another being, but it can only be realized if the surrender is mutual" (Paz 1961, 42). It is this penetrability that leads to the impaling of the heart and gives birth to tragedy.

"LA GÜERA CHAVELA" AND "ROSITA ALVIREZ"

The corrido called "La güera Chavela" is a fine *ejemplo trágico* (tragic example) (Mendoza 1974) of the *mancornadora* theme. The name Chavela is the common variant of Isabela, and *güera* tells us she was a blonde. The singer tells us he is going to give us twenty stanzas (*una veintela*) to remember a man named Jesús Cárdenas. The corrido begins with a dire warning of the events that are to occur. Jesús Cárdenas invites José to the dancehall to sing some songs. José tells Jesús that because of the lateness of the hour, he has decided to stay home and that he has a foreboding of bad events (all translations of songs are the author's):

Jesús le decía a José	Jesús tells José
"Vamos a bailar a La Parra	"Let's go to the dance at La Parra,
A cantar una canción	Let's sing some songs
al compás de mi guitarra."	to the tune of my guitar."
José le decía a Jesús,	José told Jesús,
"Pues hombre aquí me quedo	"Well. I think I will stay here.
son las doce de la noche	It is midnight
y la verdad yo tengo miedo."	And the truth is I am afraid."

The setting for the event is a *baile*, a dance with much fanfare and excitement ("un baile se celebraba de mucha gracia"). At that moment, Jesús's intended, Chavela, is dancing in the arms of another, "un hombre desconocido," we are told.

Chavela andaba en los brazos	Chavela was dancing
de un hombre desconocido	with a stranger.
cuando Jesús llegó al baile	When Jesús came to the dance
apenas se dirigió.	he directed himself to her.

Como era las más bonita	But as she was the prettiest
Chavela lo desairó	she shunned him.

Jesús does not take to the *desaire*. The song tells us:

Yo desairado no quedo	I won't be rebuffed
porque yo nunca a quedado	because this has never happened.
pues, ¿qué piensa Chavela,	Well, what is Chavela thinking,
que soy un desdichado?	That I am a wretch?

Jesús rejects the shunning (*desaire*) as intolerable. "What does Chavela think? That I am just a nobody?" Meanwhile, the stranger is promising Chavela many things.

El hombre desconocido	The stranger
con quien bailaba Chavela	with whom Chavela danced
le prometía muchas cosas	promised her many things
para que con él se fuera.	so that she would go with him.

The foreboding theme at the beginning is again reiterated by Chavela's *comadre* (friend).

Decía doña Manuelita	Doña Manuelita warns Chavela,
"Comadre, no ande bailando	"Comadre, please don't dance
por aquí pasó Jesús	Because Jesús passed by here
y dice que anda tanteando."	and says he is scheming."

Y le contestó Chavela	And Chavela replies
con una fuerte risada,	with a strong laugh,
"No tenga miedo, comadre,	"Don't be afraid, *comadre*,
si al cabo no me hace nada."	because he won't hurt me."

The *Velázquez* dictionary gives the meaning of *tanteando* as (1) to measure, to proportion; (2) to mark the game with counters; (3) to consider carefully, to scrutinize; and (4) to sketch the outlines of a design (*Velázquez* 1973). Jesús's morbid plan is built on his assessment of the situation. Chavela is unconcerned, as she relates to her *comadre* with a strong laugh, "Don't worry, *comadre*, nothing will happen."

The next phrases are telling as Chavela invites Jesús back into her confidence ("Véngase, prieto, a mis brazos"). But Jesús, already inflamed, rejects her advances.

Y le contesta Jesús,	Jesús replies,
"Quítate de aquí Chavela	"Get away from me, Chavela,
No creas que tú estás tratando	Don't be mistaken, you are
con un muchacho de escuela."	not dealing with a schoolboy!"

Chavela takes him back into La Parra, the bar, inviting him for a drink to dissuade him from his intentions; in Spanish, the phrase used is more graphic: "para borrarle el intento" (literally to erase or change his intentions).

Chavela lo agarró del brazo	Chavela takes him by the arm,
metiéndolo para adentro	leads him indoors,
Brindándole una cerveza	Offering him a beer
para borrarle el intento.	to change his intentions.

But Jesús and the situation are not to be mitigated. Jesús warns her that he will not holster his pistol.

Y le contesta Jesús	Jesús tells her,
"Mi pistola no la enfundo	"I will not holster my gun.
ahora se hacen a mi ley	Either you stop or I will
o los separo del mundo."	separate you from this world."

Con su pistola en la mano	With a pistol in his hand
tres tiros le disparó	he fires three shots.
Dos se fueron por el veinto	Two miss her
y uno fue el que le pegó.	and the other one hits her.

The moral example from the *ejemplo trágico* tradition is brought to the fore as Chavela lies dying:

Decía la güera Chavela	The *güera* Chavela,
cuando estaba mal herida,	badly wounded, says,
"Esto de querer a dos,	"This loving two men, *comadre*,
comadre, cuesta la vida."	has cost me my life."

Decía la güera Chavela	As the *güera* Chavela
cuando estaba agonizando	was in agony, she said,
"Mucho cuidado, muchachas,	"Be careful, girls,
con andar mancornando."	when you are *mancornando*."

The singer ends the tale with these tragic lines:

Con una bala sola tenía	With a single bullet
al lado del corazón	lodged near her heart
entre todas sus amigas	All her women friends
la llevaron al panteón	Took her to the cemetery.
Ya con esta me despido	With this one I take my leave,
abrochándome una espuela	as I tie up my spur
ya les canté los versitos	I have sung you the stanzas
de la traidora Chavela.	of the *traidora* Chavela.

The same theme of two men and one woman is repeated in "Rosita Alvirez," "Rafaelita," and the very violent "La Martina." These other corridos do not mention the term *mancornadora* per se, but the *traición* and the involvement of two men are clear in them. The well-known "Rosita Alvirez," a corrido of 1900 from Saltillo, Mexico, involves a daughter's disobedience. Her mother warns her against going to the dance. The daughter protests, saying she likes to dance.

Su mamá se lo decía	Her mother would tell her,
"Hija, esta noche no sales";	"Daughter, don't go out tonight";
"Mamá, no tengo la culpa	"Mother, don't blame me
que a mí me gustan los bailes."	Because I like dances."

At the dance, Rosita, like Chavela, shuns a man named Hipólito, who protests his treatment:

"Rosita, no me desaires,	"Rosita, please don't do this,
La gente lo va a notar."	people will take notice."
"Pues que digan lo que quieran	"Well, let them say what they want
contigo no he de bailar."	I won't dance with you."

Rosita Alvirez fares no better than Chavela in one version of this well-known corrido: as the singer says, the dancehall had recently been painted red, and with Rosita's blood they gave it another coat. It is to be noted that the well-known Mexican singer and actor Antonio Aguilar in his rendition of this famous corrido mocks Rosita's impending death with a titanic *grito* that cries out, "¡Ay, Rosita, por desairgrista te van a matar!" (Hey, Rosita, because you shunned men, you are going to die). Rosita's advice to her friend Irene is, "No te olvides de mi nombre. / Cuando vayas a los bailes, / no desprecies a los hombres" (Don't forget me. / When you go to dances / don't disparage men).

"MICAELA"

"El 24 del junio" (June 24, feast day of San Juan) is a song about a dance on this date. Micaela tells Juan that because this day is his patron saint's day, he should take her to the dance. He balks and replies that he does not want to give her the *desaire* (snub) and shares a premonition with her that something bad will happen. He says, "De que esta noche en el baile, / se te amargue la función" (Tonight's dance will turn out bitter for you). He further warns her about Simón:

"Mira, Micaela, que te hablo	"Listen, Micaela,
no le hagas mucho calor	don't attend to Simón
que está tentando el diablo	because the devil
de echarme en el plato a Simón."	is tempting me to put Simón in his place."

The use of *calor* (heat) metaphorically and powerfully denotes that Micaela has the power to incite love (a fire) in Simón. Juan emphasizes the metaphor by saying that the devil is tempting him to "put Simón in his place." Micaela does not heed the warning and begins to dance with Simón, "el mero rival de Juan" (Juan's major rival).

Llegó Micaela primero	Micaela arrived at the dance
se puso luego a bailar	and began to dance
Se encontró de compañero,	with her partner,
al mero rival de Juan.	Juan's main rival.

The song continues in a lively, joyous mood to reflect the next event.

Alegres pasan las horas,	The hours passed by happily,
las doce marca el reloj	it was twelve midnight
Cuando un tiro de pistola	when a shot rang out
dos cuerpos atravesó.	that hit two bodies.

Vuela, vuela, palomita,	Fly, fly, little dove,
pasa por ese panteón	pass over that cemetery
pasa por ese panteón	pass over that cemetery
donde ha de estar Micaelita	where Micaelita is
con su querido Simón.	With her beloved Simón.

What is so compelling about this song is the beauty and festive nature of the music, a beautiful waltz, which belies this macabre and sinister project.

"LA MARTINA"

"La Martina" is probably the most horrid tragedy of this tetrad. Sangre Joven, a local Las Vegas musical group, played this song in a Fourth of July Parade in Las Vegas, New Mexico, some years back. In "Martina," a husband comes home and begins to ask his sixteen-year-old wife a series of questions. "¿De quién es esa pistola?" (Whose is that pistol?) "¿De quién es ese reloj?" (Whose is that watch?) "¿De quién es ese caballo en el corral que relinchó?" (Whose is that horse in the corral?) She responds by saying that his father gave the horse to him so that he can go to the wedding of his younger sister ("Tu papá te lo mandó para que fueras a la boda de tu hermana menor"). He asks, "Who has been sleeping in my bed?" She responds, "En tu cama nadie duerme cuando tú no estás aquí. Dime si tienes desconfianza no te separes de mí." (Nobody slept in your bed. Tell me if you distrust me, do not pull away from me.) In the final scene, Martina is taken to her parents as the husband says, "¡Suegros, aquí está Martina que una traición me jugó!" (In-laws, here is Martina, who has done me wrong). They tell him, "Llévatela a ti, mi yerno que la iglesia te la entregó y si te la traicionó la culpa no tengo yo" (Take her, son-in-law, the church has turned her over to you, we are no longer responsible for her). In the last scene, her husband has her kneel as he puts six bullets into her from the back ("Hincadita de rodillas nomás seis tiros le dio"). It ends with, "El amigo del caballo ni por la silla llegó" (The owner of the horse never returned for the saddle).

The intruder in these songs is mentioned only as a rival. In "La Martina," the husband is unable to confront the intruder directly. In the song "El Coyote" by the legendary José Alfredo Jiménez, an intruder is called simply "el Coyote." The singer tells us that he gave "las cuarto al coyote y me fui para la sierra" (I gave the coyote what he deserves and I fled to the mountains).

"RAFAELITA"

In "Raefaelita," two men find out they love the same woman. Her behavior is labeled that of a *mancornadora* because, as the song has it, "dos buenos gallos" (two good men) have lost their lives. I mention "Rafaelita" primarily because the feelings of one of the antagonists, Cecilio, are said to be *encendido* (inflamed), which is in keeping with the deep penetrating power of the horn and its incitement of feelings. In the sections to follow, I pay more attention to the emotionality involved in these incidents.

Emotionality and the Theme

In both the "El asesino" and "El preso número nueve," the victims are blamed for their own demise. Both songs denote the killer's self-deceit in justifying the act to himself and the high level of emotion attached to the deed. In "El asesino,"

Me llaman el asesino por hay	I'm called an assassin
y dicen que me anda buscando la ley	and I am a fugitive from the law
porque mate de manera legal	because I justifiably killed
la que burló mi querer.	the one who negated my love.
En un momento de celos mate	I killed in a fit of jealousy,
volando de sentimiento y dolor	in uncontrolled hurt and pain,
la que burlaba mi honor y mi ser	the one who mocked my honor,
mi vida y mi corazón.	my being, and my heart.

The last lines underscore the motive behind the crime. The term *volando* ("volatile," like the wind flying in all directions) connotes the out-of-control passion, with a deep *sentimiento* and *dolor* (hurt). In the present case, the term *burlando* incites the attack. *Burlando* (*burlaba* in the song) is a strong term suggesting the mocking of the person's honor, his being, his heart, and his love, as the song has it. This last line is indicative of the self-deceit involved in the assassin's angry justification of the act. We are told also at the beginning of the song that the killing was "de manera legal," justifying the awful act.

Ya está en el cielo jusgada por dios	She is in heaven judged by God,
ya ella del alto si a caso me ve	and if from high she should see,
sabrá la ingrata que tuve razon	the ingrate will know my cause,
sabrá cuanto la adore.	she will know how much I loved her.

The anger does not subside in the next lines, as the assassin vows further revenge by killing the one who made him commit the original heinous crime; clearly she is the agent of his anger. Ironically this song and the previous ones presented have a great beat for playing at a dance.

Veinte años que de sentencia me den	Twenty years I will get;
con gusto voy mi delito a pagar	I will happily serve my time,
pero antes quiero vengar me también	but I want vengeance
del que me hizo criminal.	against the one who made me a criminal.

In "El preso número nueve," the killer is not repentant even though he faces execution at daybreak. The theme is the same, a disloyal friend who takes away the protagonist's love.

Al preso número nueve	Prisoner number nine
ya lo van a confesar	is saying his confession,
está rezando en la celda	he is praying in his cell
con le cura del penal	with the priest of the prison,
Porque antes de amanecer,	because before daybreak
la vida le han de quitar	he will forfeit his life
Porque mató a su mujer	because he killed his wife
y a un amigo desleal.	and a disloyal friend.
Dice así al confessor	He tells his confessor,
"los mató, si señor,	"Yes, sir, I killed them,
Y si vuelvo a nacer	and if born again (in the hereafter),
Yo los vuelvo a matar."	I will kill them again."

Even though confession should prepare him for the hereafter, prisoner number 9 vows that he will seek his vengeance once again in the afterlife.

Less Violent Themes

Two other *mancornadora* songs also focus on the pain of separation and loss, but no violence ensues in them. If loss leads to violence, as per the Denzin thesis, then these two *mancornadora* songs present a protagonist who has elected to let go of the relationship, grieve for his loss, if he must, and move on. These behaviors are different from the *desaigre* song described earlier because these two songs represent what is called "sacrificing love" (see below). The goal in these two songs is to get on with one's life, and to let go of the pain of the relationship. María y Archie Garduño of Las Vegas as well as the Mariachi Rio Grande from the area sing this well-known *mancornadora* song called "La mancornadora." The words are from the Garduños.

Ando ausente del bien que adoré	I wander absent from the one I loved,
y apasionado por una mujer.	filled with passion for another woman.
Solo cantando dicipio mis penas	Now only singing can dissolve my pain,
Con las copas llenas voy a divagar.	with my cups full will I wander.
Si lo hiciste de mala intención	If you did it with bad intentions
o con el fin de hacerme padecer,	or for the purpose of making me suffer,

tú bien sabes que vivo entre flores	you know that I live among flowers
y nuevos amores me deben querer.	and new loves will surely desire me.
Si tú fueras legal con mi amor,	If you were faithful with my love,
Tú gozarías de mi protección	you would enjoy my protection,
pero en el mundo tú fuiste traidora,	but in this world you were a traitress,
la mancornadora de mi corazón.	the two-timer of my heart.
La despedida yo no se las doy	Farewell I will not bid you
la despedida será mi canción	my farewell shall be a song.
la despedida yo se las daré	I will only bid farewell
cuando yo me vaya de esta población.	when I leave this town.

(Loeffler 1999, 98–99)

In this song, the singer tries to understand what has happened to him. He is *ausente* (away) from the one he loved but is still passionate for her. He finds release in drinking ("sólo tomando") because it dissipates his pain ("disipo las penas"). His concern is the reason why she has left him. Two questions are asked in the song. Was it "si lo hiciste con mala intención" (with a bad intention toward him), or was it "con el fin de hacerme padecer" (or with the motive to betray him)? In the song, the lover takes no revenge, but reminds her that she was a *traidora*, the *mancornadora* of his heart. Even the normative and traditional despedida (good-bye) is not offered.

In "Lagunas de pesar," the singer presents his concern in simple phrases. Essentially the singer has given up on his love for this *mancornadora*. As with the previous song, there is no revenge theme, only a giving up on the lost love. *Lagunas de pesar* is metaphorical, a dark, deep oppressive lake of foreboding thoughts. *Pesar* comes from *pesadilla*, the word for "nightmare," with its connotations of heavy and weighty feelings.

Por mis canciones sabrás	With my song you will know
cómo me la ando pasando	Of my doings,
Rumbos y amores distintos	Different loves and directions
ando en el mundo 'probando;	I am experiencing.
ya ves, mancornadora,	Now see here, *mancornadora*,
a qué te supo este trago.	See what drinking will do.
¿Con quién te quejas?	Why are you complaining?
Si tu mal tú lo buscaste;	You found your own evil.

¿A quien le importa	Who should care about you
tus lagunas de pesares?	and your pain?
Haz de entender	You should know that love
qué el amor debémos ser pares.	should be reciprocated.
Ahorrame el sentimiento	Save your sentiments and
de verte llorando por mi.	your crying for me.

In the later lines, the singer is taking leave of the relationship by proclaiming that this woman has created her own *mal* (bad situation). "Who cares about your *lagunas de pesares* (pain)?" he asks. Continuing, he proclaims that love must be two-sided ("Haz de entender qué el amor debémos ser pares"). Finally, the singer tells her, in effect, to "save your tears and don't waste them crying over me."

"La joven mancornadora" (The young *mancornadora*) is the only song I found in which the narrative is given from the *mancornadora*'s point of view. The song boasts of her ability to destroy men's hearts. She calls herself a provocateur and a coquette.

Por hay dicen que soy	People say that I am
la joven mancornadora	a youthful *mancornadora*
por quien muchos hombres lloran,	for whom men yearn [cry],
Pero soy inocente en el amor	But I am innocent in love
Pero soy inocente en el amor.	But I am innocent in love.
También dicen que yo soy	They say of me
coqueta y provocativa	I am a coquette and a provocateur
Si tus miradas fueron puñales	If your looks were blows
me matarían solo al mirar.	I would be dead from them.
Si tus palabras fueron fatales	If your words were fatal
me matarian solo al hablar	I would be dead from them as well.
También dicen que nací para	They also say I was born to fill
llenar las cantinas con hombres	the bars with men
que causan penas,	whom I have hurt,
Pero soy inocente en el amor,	But I am innocent in love,
Pero soy inocente en el amor	But I am innocent in love.
Me dicen el mal de amores	They call me dangerous
porque yo vivo cantando	Because I live singing
Y a todos ando volando	And blowing all of them away,

| Pero soy inocente en le amor | But I am innocent in love, |
| Pero soy inocente en el amor. | But I am innocent in love. |

Breaking Up Is Hard to Do

This section will illustrate that these events are not just the content of ancient corridos, with their incredible lyrics and beautiful music undergirding vile acts. There is no intent to glorify events whose ultimate harsh reality is violent death. Nor is this section intended to identify or malign anyone as a *mancornadora*, but to illustrate with real material that these events instantly produce raw, violent emotionality and often death.

A *Journal North* story reported an awful event in a northern New Mexico community. The case involved a mother of two ("G") who was killed by a jealous man ("U") from whom she had been separated for the last two months. On a Saturday, before attending a dance with a new man at the community of Las Palomas (fictive place), she called an acquaintance and told her that U was waiting at the end of the road to get her. G went to the dance anyway and did not return till the next morning. U was present when her grandfather discovered that G had been wounded. U wrapped G and took her to a nearby clinic where she died. She had received wounds to her left side of her breast and her head. U reportedly told police he had made a grave mistake "and was going away for a long time" ("Affidavits Filed" 2005). Reality becomes myth.

According to a 1992 newspaper article, a Guachupange man was jailed in Santa Fe, where he was apprehended following an incident in which he allegedly shot into his former girlfriend's mobile home, where seven children were having a slumber party. Alberto Madelino (a fictive name), thirty-five, was held on two counts of aggravated battery, two counts of aggravated assault, and one count of shooting a weapon into an occupied building at Running Water Mobile Home Park in Guachupange. Robert Santiago, fifty-eight, the new boyfriend, was stabbed once in the back and twice in the chest and remained in intensive care at St. Vincent's Hospital in Santa Fe. Robert N., twenty-two, son of Madelino's former girlfriend, Katarina Petra, had his left hand slashed and was treated and released from the hospital late Friday. Sheriff Montaño said that according to reports given at the scene, Madelino used to date Katarina Petra of Guachupange, but she recently started dating Robert Santiago. About eleven o'clock Friday night, Madelino drove by Petra's mobile home, where she and Robert Santiago were sitting on the porch, and fired once at the couple with a rifle from his car, Montaño said. Katarina and Robert Santiago ran into the home, while Madelino ran to the porch and fired two more shots into the home.

None of these three shots hurt anyone, though seven children, ages seven to fifteen, were having a slumber party inside the house at the time. Robert Santiago and Robert N. were able to "jump" Madelino on the porch and disarm him, but he pulled a twelve-inch butcher knife and injured them both, then fled in his car, Montaño said. According to the sheriff, Santa Fe police were waiting for Madelino and arrested him when he arrived at the home of relatives in Santa Fe later that evening ("Ex-Boyfriend" 1992).

The *Rio Grande Sun* reported that the court sentenced Madelino to seven and a half years in prison, suspended three of those years, and ordered him to serve four and a half years, with two years probation upon release. The defense attorney presented several witnesses, as well as a psychiatrist, who testified to Madelino's being a good candidate for therapy. It was noted also that he had no prior criminal history. Madelino stated, "I made a huge mistake," and "I just hope it doesn't ruin my life." The judge took exception to the violation of a restraining order that Katarina had obtained. "I've heard judges say that these court orders are just pieces of paper, they can't stop bullets," the judge remarked. "That's because of people like you." The judge took into account Mr. Madelino's good work history and his being a good father in the past. "But you [have] sentenced Ms. Petra to a life of fear and your children to a life that is almost certain to be lived in emotional problems," said the judge, "And that needs to be punished" ("Rage Earns" 1992).

This story of uncontrolled rage, possible violent death, and the emotional scars they leave behind is presented primarily to illustrate the basic themes of this chapter. Although the law dealt with the breaking of the restraining order, aggravated assault, battery with a deadly weapon, and shooting into an inhabited building, questions remain about motives. It is interesting to note that, according to the newspaper article, Madelino's attorney argued that Madelino's son had informed him that his mother intended to sleep with Robert Santiago and that the estranged wife said to Madelino, "I'm going to sleep with Robert Santiago, and I'm going to enjoy it." Because the law deals only with the legal infractions, one can merely speculate about the unleashed raw emotionality involved in this situation.

If this incident had resulted in multiple deaths, the story might easily have become the stuff of a corrido. All the elements are there. It would provide an *ejemplo trágico* that, in effect, would warn the community, *Cuidado cuando se parte una pareja, si la partida no es completa* (Take care when a couple breaks up and the break is not complete). The incident reflects Denzin's theory that loss leads to violence and violent emotionality. It also indicates that the one suffering the loss needs to deal with it because it and the accompanying grief might work themselves out in a violent way. Most important, these tragic incidents are common, and offer the moral lesson of corridos. They raise a further question regarding peaceful resolution of love affairs and expectations between men and women.

Violence in American Music

As noted in the beginning of this chapter, the material from popular songs cannot be viewed as reflecting solely a violent Mexican culture. The theme of "one woman, two men" can be found in other cultures, and the theme of violence and loss after the breakup of a relationship is not a "Mexican problem" per se. "La güera Chavela," "Rosita Alvirez," "El asesino," "Veinte años," and "El preso número nueve" all have the theme of stalking and killing the loved one out of vengeance. But so does a country-and-western song titled "L.A. County" sung by Lyle Lovett (1990). His protagonist straps on his "friend," a black Colt .45, in Houston as he heads out to Los Angeles to find his sweetheart, who is marrying another man. The coda in which "the lights of L.A. are like diamonds in the sky" distracts us. As he arrives at the church wedding, the narrative identifies the bride "in her dress of white" at the altar. The song continues, "I stood standing in the aisle," "I said nothing," and then, "My friend bid them good-bye." The coda leads us away from the terrible event by a reiteration, "The lights of L.A. are like diamonds in the sky."

In "Papa Loved Mama," with words and music by Kim Williams and Garth Brooks (1992), the killer, "Papa," kills "Mama" by driving a "rig" into a motel where "Mama" is with another man. Mama, a "trucker's wife," gets tired of being alone because Papa is always on the road. Papa loved Mama, Mama loved other men. "Mama is in the graveyard and Papa's in the pen," ends the song. A song by Jimi Hendrix (1966) asks the question, "Hey, Joe, Where you goin' with that gun in your hand?" The response is equally chilling, "I'm goin' down to shoot my old lady, / you know I caught her messin' round with another man." The Sparx, a New Mexico women's musical group, have a song called "El corrido de Juanito" about a young woman who goes to a dance with a cousin. The woman's boyfriend shoots the cousin, thinking that his girlfriend is out with a new fellow (The Sparx 2007).

The killing of women in the above songs is not a characteristic of any one culture or geographic group. This theme is found in Georges Bizet's opera *Carmen*, as don José falls in love with the coquette Carmen. Don José deserts the army and becomes a smuggler for Carmen. In the meantime, Carmen has fallen in love with a bullfighter. Finally, don José, finding himself *apasionado por una mujer*, in front of the bullring encounters his beloved Carmen while the strains of "toreador, toreador" can be heard in the background. Because she will not go with him and leave her new love, don José kills her. It is ironic that Carmen dies by the power of the impaling instrument, a knife. She dies in front of a place where being impaled or gored by a bull's horn is always a possibility.

Graver Issues: Getting Out of the Mess

How then should the breakup of a relationship be handled? The person has the choice of renouncing the relationship or continuing in a stalking violence-prone modality. One choice involves, as some *mancornadora* songs suggest, giving up the relationship, the love object, and the "game," and moving forward. Mogenson put the matter succinctly as he contrasts the sacrificial lover and the romantic murderer. His reference to Desdemona is from Giuseppe Verdi's *Otello*.

> While the sacrificial lover renounces attitudes or relationships out of a recognition that they have become anomalous to life, the romantic murderer views life as the anomaly and puts it to the sword. Unable to manage loss, the amorous murderer construes his beloved to be unfaithful whenever she fails to act in accordance with his idealized image of her. At bottom, of course, the problem is an inability to mourn. Devastated by early losses, the narcissistic lover is unable to live with his Desdemona because he is unable to live without his idealization of her. Again and again, the changes which are an inevitable part of life threaten the lover's relationship ideal and arouse his jealousy. Even if there is no actual third party, the lover feels cuckolded by life itself whenever his beloved responds more faithfully to its realities than to his need for object-constancy and stasis. Any change that the lover is unable to mournfully embrace and work through afflicts his consciousness in the form of paranoid suspicions. For when a lover's eros is unable to "die and rise the same, and prove / Mysterious by this love" it is vulnerable to the insinuations of an Iago. Sexual indiscretion with a Cassio becomes the explanation of every vicissitude and letdown. By killing his Desdemona the Romantic murderer endeavors to take out of the arms of life and restore her to the fidelity of the *Liebestod.* In death he attempts to secure the static, loss-free relationship he could not secure in life. (Mogenson 1992, 48–49)

Mogenson's view is that the inability to mourn one's loss leads to the violence of killing the love object. It is a way to keep the object, to "freeze the relationship" in time, as it was before in the relationship. The murderer cannot leave the idealized view of the woman he loves. The problem is also fundamental in that the romantic lover must turn the loss into a sacrifice. Mogenson leads us to the idea that sacrifice is essentially a life-affirming action. "It is an attempt to disidentify our lives and love from attitudes and/or relationships in which they have become stagnant. Appreciating that change and death are an inherent part of life, we agree to let go of one style of loving *in order to affirm another*" (Mogenson 1992, 48). The loss is real; otherwise it is not a sacrifice, but we affirm the new life through the sacrifice, which also is real. The next vignette, taken from another actual event, illustrates this idea.

Carlitos's Way

A twenty-one-year-old Hispano man whom I will call Carlitos was sent to domestic violence counseling because he had assaulted his girlfriend. Toward the end of the mandated sessions, he broke up with his girlfriend. During the breakup, he saw her hugging and kissing a new boyfriend. He had trouble sleeping and became agitated, finding himself crying openly. He became angry with his supervisors at work. He developed a plan in which he went to a friend to get a gun. He was planning a double homicide and his own suicide. Fortunately for Carlitos, his employer kept referring him to the agency for follow-up. He was counseled and referred to a community mental health clinic for depression medication. In a subsequent session of the domestic violence anger-management group, the instructor made it a point to talk about the role of loss in the creation of violence. The notion of "sacrifice" as a means of letting go of a relationship was central to the discussion that night. Carlitos acknowledged, "You were talking to me tonight." He revealed later that evening that he had returned the gun. He said he had talked about homicide for the new couple and suicide for himself. He had planned to leave a note to his mother. Under medication for depression, he began to take on a more ontologically secure position, which seems elemental now, but was a crucial turning point as he found himself reaching out to life. "After all, I am young and I can build my life again. I am going to save my money and buy a good car. I may go to Denver to work. Look at who she is with now. He doesn't even have a job. I have my car paid off and have an apartment and better than that guy who doesn't work." All of these self-affirmations in his newly found vocabulary of motives that evening were a means of securing his sense of ontological wellness. By these vocabularies he was "unplugging" his action as Becker postulated. This young man had courted the *paloma negra* to the very brink and found himself letting go of the relationship, mourning his loss, and affirming life.

"Renunciación"

A beautiful Mexican song called "Renunciación" as sung by the late Javier Solis will end this section. In the song, the protagonist tells of his love for one from whom he is about to take his leave. He blesses her and begs forgiveness for any hurt brought to her. Renunciation, says Mogenson, by itself is not enough. It has to be accompanied by sacrifice. Sacrifice restores a sense of sacredness to life. *La renunciación* (renunciation) must make life richer. "After a relationship or an *overly personal attitude toward a relationship* has been sacrificed, the ongoing life of the lovers must clearly show that it was indeed better to have loved than never to have loved at all" (Mogenson 1992, 47). Mogenson says that mourning is elegiac:

> We can never fall victim to the shadows of love *through the same life redundancies.* Inasmuch as a renunciation has truly been a sacrifice—its loss imagined and new life affirmed in the process of detachment—our compulsion to repeat its specific erotic process will cease. The allure of the living and the halo of the dead are one. (Mogenson 1992, 48)

The protagonist in "Renunciación" knows this as he sings, "Si esa es vida yo quiero vivir, / si es muerte yo quiero murir" (If this is life I want to live, / if it is death I want to die).

In Verdi's opera, Otello kills Desdemona because he believes she has been unfaithful to him. The romantic murderer is unable to mourn and unable to live his idealization of her. This is the anger delusion. Mogenson offers us a quote from Nietzsche: "You must be ready to burn yourself in your own flame: how could you become new, if you had not first become ashes?" (Mogenson 1992, 55).

Afterthoughts

This material on the *la mancornadora* was written over many years. During this time, certain events have caused me to think about the broader ramifications of what I have written here. As a "mental health" worker, I have been trained to work for solutions to these problems. But, in a way, I want to resist offering "solutions" or prescriptions because the chapter is meant mainly to be descriptive, not prescriptive. However, in recent months, both print and television in Albuquerque and northern New Mexico have carried stories of violent death of women victims of domestic violence. Most of these stories describe a killing after a woman attempts to leave a destructive, psychologically battering situation. These stories add further weight to Denzin's thesis that loss leads to violence. Those of us who work with domestic violence offenders and in women's shelters know the calculus of violence: when the woman decides to leave an abusive situation, her husband or boyfriend often becomes more dangerous. Needless to say, a good safety plan and competent help should be in place prior to the act of leaving the abuser.

In the Madelino account told earlier, as well as other stories of the same ilk, the problem for Madelino was that he had not let go of the "love object," to use a Freudian term. He had not grieved for his loss, and "love had turned angry," as conceptualized in object relations theory. This loss triggered a strong, violent, and condemnable act and a threat to others. Part of the "remedy" for these acts is for the man or woman to "let go" of the relationship. Vengeance bonds the abuser to his victim. The potential abuser/killer needs to recognize his loss, get help, enter into the grief process, and in time let go of the relationship. This type of loss has to be recognized as "love turned angry," is abusive, violent, and dangerous.

If what I have described here is reality, then it is appropriate to think about this chapter not so much in terms of *la mancornadora*, which focuses on the acts of such women as la Güera Chavela, Rosita Alvirez, and Carmen, but in terms of the process of *mancornando*. When in this situation, one must come to the realization that this kind of wounding has extreme consequences. The realization will lead to the "letting go." One must sacrifice the relationship and establish control over one's extreme feelings after another man or woman has entered the picture and taken away one's lover. Alcohol and drugs during this period prevent the "getting well" and exacerbate the situation.

These *mancornadora* songs, including those of Lyle Lovett, Jimmy Hendrix, and Garth Brooks, point to the problem, but offer no solutions except violence. Focusing on *mancornando*, however—the hurt, the flooding by pain and anger, and the violent explosion—puts the problem where it should be. Now it is up to the wounded person to do something constructive. Should it be therapy? If violence is possible because of loss, should the individual engage in appropriate professional counseling to get help in grieving? Few have dealt with these issues except as a tragedy after the fact or, more regrettably, as a postmortem in a newspaper. The operas *Carmen* and *Otello* tell us that the problem of loss is not a "Mexican" or an Hispano "thing." Hispanos are no more violent than other groups. Murder is not the answer, nor should being *mancornado*, as a temporary state of mental insanity, be used as a legal defense.

CHAPTER 6

Being in Prison: *En la Pinta*

Y los reyos protestan el chingaderismo
dentro those leaden labyrinths where the soul
dries as it dies and love is a four letter word
countering plastic celluloid dreams and playboy
fold-outs and muted memories haunt a sleep
that knows no sanctuary.

Ricardo Sánchez, *Canto y grito mi liberación*

HISPANO LIFE IN PRISON IS POORLY DOCUMENTED. THIS IS DUE IN PART TO LACK of access and in part to the fact that men in prison as brothers, husbands, or sweethearts are often forgotten by society. The work reported in this chapter is partly drawn from a study conducted many years ago in a southwestern state. Other material was collected at a correctional facility in another state. I refer to these institutions as CF I and CF II. For purposes of continued confidentiality I do not identify the facilities further and I have given the men fictitious names in this chapter and in chapter 7. The offenses committed by the men—drug dealing, burglary, rape, and armed robbery—are also not specifically connected to each man.

Some of the men who were part of the study group have probably since been released from prison in the intervening years. Most of what is presented here is drawn from interviews conducted in CF II over a period of one year by three mental health professionals. Other interviews were conducted in 1983 at CF I but are largely not reported here. We generally visited a group of men monthly for the better part of a day over an eight-month period. We ate with them and were locked in a secure area where we talked. Sometimes we met for two straight days. We tape-recorded

Hands and bars (Jeremy Herrera)

and transcribed everything. We had the men evaluate what was written, thereby providing some reliability to the material as it was being processed.

The study was geared to learning more about how Hispanos/Chicanos do time, how they maintain their identity as men and Hispanos, and how they manage and cope with conflicts among themselves and between them and the correctional officers. Prison life is complex, so it is difficult to make generalizations beyond what is presented here. The reader should not assume that the chapter describes the way all Hispano men do time in all prisons. The details here are applicable to the men interviewed in CF II during this period in the history of this particular maximum-security institution. In other words, the findings are not generalizable beyond this institution, at the time, or for this group of men.

The Research Problem

According to Polsky, successful field research with career criminals is conducted with "trained abilities to look at people, listen to them, think and feel with them, talk to them rather than at them" (Polsky 1969, 119). Polsky also makes an important distinction between criminologists who would be scientists and social workers interested in reforming the criminal.

For our study, we needed to develop knowledge that would be useful in working with Chicanos in prison. What can one learn about how Hispanos make their lives in prison, to the extent they are able to do so? These questions and others were important as we began our study of Chicanos in prison (their term in this context), whose value systems may not be easily understood by outsiders. We wanted to examine the structure of their actions, which may be different from outsiders' actions. Certain questions guided the study. How is identity presentation possible in a prison? How do leaders lead in a system designed to control and maintain order? How do men do "time"? What can we learn that will be useful to others in our profession?

In both institutions, some of the men had long histories of involvement with programs offered in the prisons. The education program in CF I was important as a place where men could earn diplomas and degrees. A psychotherapeutic group in CF II led to discussions about a variety of topics. The topic was often dealt with further in individual therapy sessions. There were also interviews with men at lesser levels of confinement in CF II. Perhaps the men became involved as a way of dealing with the ennui of prison life. The group setting provided an avenue for discourse and time away from the cells. We, all male interviewers, were trained social workers, each of whom had at least a master's degree. This is an important point because each member had to confront his attitudes about criminal behavior and deviance as learned in university classes, to put aside the mental health classification system of the *Diagnostic and Statistical Manual* III (*DSM-III*, being used at the time), to deal with one's fears, and, in one case, to make a bridge from the knowledge gained from working with groups of middle-class Anglo families to the knowledge useful in the world of imprisoned Hispano men. We also had to suspend our own fears of being locked up with these men in the total environment of a prison where we conducted our interviews.

We had to enter the prisoners' world on their terms. In order to explore their worldview—and, ultimately, to involve them as co-researchers—we had to suspend our presuppositions about them regarding class, appearance, reasons for incarceration, previous criminal behavior, and their adjustment to the basic prison culture. Because underlying assumptions and frames of reference determine the particular interpretations social scientists make of data, it is critical that attempts at understanding the Chicano way of coping with prison life be embedded in a suppositionless approach to knowing and knowledge building. We often had to "bracket" (i.e., place in temporary abeyance) what we thought we knew about prisoners, about older Chicanos doing time, and the "sociopathic personality."

The Classification System and the Facility

One of the ways of looking at men in prison is via classification systems invented by the men themselves and passed down from one group of prisoners to others. These systems of inmate classifications have been known since the Schrag study (1961) of a prison in Washington State and Gersham Sykes's book *The Society of Captives* (1966). The notion of classifying others in a social system is nothing new. The prison system classifies men according to type of offense, length of sentence, danger to others, and required level of restraint.

CF II was designed to provide maximum control through isolation, administrative grouping, and surveillance. Living units, or the men's "houses," as they called them, are single cells, with sixteen cells to a pod and three pods in each of seven cell blocks. The capacity is 336 inmates. The prison was built for maximum control (a "mind bender," as one inmate called it). Each cell block is controlled by an officer in a control room, including the opening and closing of all cell doors in and out of the pod. The inmate is totally dependent on this officer for any and all movement. One hour a day is available for exercise in a wired enclosure close to the pod. An inmate can spend his entire time in this facility without coming in contact with any inmates other than the fifteen in his pod.

Functional unit one (FU1) is administrative segregation, also called "the hole." The inmates in this unit are considered extremely dangerous and have been convicted of assault behaviors toward other inmates or correctional officers. FU2 is made up of inmates who are serving long sentences, are considered escape risks, or are in transition from administrative segregation status to a less-secure correctional facility. FU3 is composed of protective custody inmates, those who are not able to live in the general prison population without being killed or severely injured. The men in the study were seasoned convicts from FU2 who were serving long sentences and had been "state raised"—that is, they had come through foster care, state reformatories, and, later, adult prisons, for example, Soledad and San Quentin (*San Quilmas* as the men called it) in California. One inmate said that being in this facility (FU2) was like being in a kennel:

> Facility X is like a kennel. You ever been to one? You see some dogs that sit back quietly, eat their food alone, and wait patiently, because they know their masters will be around for them eventually. Then you get your lap dogs, your ass-kissing dogs, which is most of the dogs, running up to the fence, barking, carrying on, and nipping at the other dogs, stealing food. They're always causing trouble. And then you got your pissed-off dogs who just glare at you when you walk by.

Prison Roles

The men called themselves "convicts," and the system called them "inmates." There were "convict" ways of doing things as well as expectations regarding convict behavior. Chicano convicts, like other convicts, have a system of expected behavior that they take for granted, norms and rules that govern behavior among them. This typified system makes it possible for Chicano *pintos* (a common term used to describe Chicanos in prison, from the word *penitenciaría* [penitentiary]) to develop a knowledge and awareness of their everyday world. Awareness becomes possible because typified concepts already exist at a conceptual, abstract level. Typifications are systems of relevancies—the socially shared and developed meanings ascribed by members of an in-group (Schutz 1971). Living in prison, new inductees ("youngsters") enter into a dictionary of meanings of identified types such as *ratas* (rats), convicts, "punks," "meatheads," *veteranos*, "sissies," and *chotas* (cops). The *rata* is well known in history. According to the men, Judas Iscariot was a betrayer and hence a *rata* because he told the "cops" where to find Jesus. In this scenario, Jesus was a convict like the men in prison because he was also in "rebellion"—a different take on the figure of Jesus. Wilmer tells us that the first man, Adam, "snitched" to God on Eve, and then she snitched on the snake who beguiled her. As first informers in the history of criminal life, they also were beguiled by the snake, which created the first lie (Wilmer 1965).

Concrete interactional activities lead to the typifications of such behaviors as "snitching," "jiving," "ratting," "having heart," "bringing lightweight games," and "boning." These behavioral meanings are for the inductee a way of understanding prison culture on top of the numerous official regulations and routines. A more important consideration is the "convict code": a series of norms about a convict's conduct. If anything, it differentiates convicts from being just inmates. In the *Santa Fe Prison News* article titled "What's a Convict?" from June 3, 1983, the author states that even though the code exists "only in the minds of those doing time, [it] is more real than a Supreme Court decision, and has probably been around much longer." The author goes on to identify what a convict is:

- A man who does his own time.
- A man who does not steal from another prisoner, regardless of the circumstances.
- A man who does all he can to help his fellow prisoners, without asking payment of any kind.
- A man who is not afraid to speak out when he thinks he or his fellow prisoners are being mistreated.

- A man who keeps his head in times of stress and tries to help those around him to hold on to theirs.
- A man who keeps his word and pays his debts.
- A man who does not snitch or do anything to advance himself at the cost of another prisoner.
- A man who will go out of his way to help and protect the weak and inexperienced, for no other reason than the fact that he can remember that he wore their shoes.
- A man who does not cry and whine about the injustices of his case or the excessive amount of time he received, but instead goes about his business in trying to resolve the issues in a more positive manner.
- A man who thinks all men are equal. He does not think he is higher than any man alive, nor does he think he is lower than any man alive. Nor is he swayed by the opinion of others.
- A man who does not care what others may think of him as long as he knows he's doing the right thing, for he has learned that it is utterly impossible to please all men.
- A man who is not afraid to be kind to others, because some might mistake his kindness for weakness. He treats the next guy like he would like to be treated, knowing that what goes around comes around. ("What's a Convict?" 1983)

I quote the code in full in the interest of presenting it as a moral code, some of whose tenets might be as worthy outside the prison walls as they are inside. Lawrence Weider presents yet another version of "the code" in a halfway house for former prison inmates, but his examples are far different from what is presented here. In Weider's study, the code is used to draw a line of demarcation between the persons running the halfway house and the former prison inmates (Weider 1974b). Here, though, the code is used to delineate behaviors for certain inmate roles, in particular the *veterano*, or the experienced, wiser convict. The *veterano* role appeared early in our first interview and became the focus of the second and many other interviews.

Berger and Luckmann present a schema for analyzing a role in interactional terms and within the social construction of meaning perspective. They propose that

language objectivates the shared experience and makes them [these experiences] available to all within the linguistic community, thus becoming both the basis and the instrument of the collective stock of knowledge. Furthermore, language provides the means for objectifying new experiences, allowing their incorporation into the already existing stock of knowledge, and it is the most important means by which the objectivated and objectified sedimentations are transmitted in the traditions of the collectivity in question. (Berger and Luckmann 1966, 68)

To explain "objectivated," Berger and Luckmann use the idea of the sign that stands for or serves as an index of subjective meanings. Signs are means by which the self and the other recognize the commonality of meaning and are available to their producer as objective "reminders" of the original intention in making them (Berger and Luckmann 1966, 35–36). We traffic in signs and symbols all the time. The signs I cover in the next sections depict a reality of meaning not necessarily available to others, but one that could be made explicit by those we were interviewing.

It is important to tackle the notion of a role from an interactional perspective. We can note that in the prisoners' observations of their own behavior or in reflections of their or others' experience, they become distanced from this role. As noted by Berger and Luckmann, "This distance between the actor and his action can be retained in consciousness and projected to future repetitions of the action. In this way both the acting self and the acting others are apprehended not as unique individuals but as *types*. By definition, these types are interchangeable" (Berger and Luckmann 1966, 73). Roles thus defined are types of actors in such typal social contexts. A simple example might be what one of the men reported one evening. He noted that while a certain individual was watching television, another man, described as a "creeper," came from behind and struck the first individual on the head with a broom handle because he did not like what this individual was watching. Now one can say that a "creeper" is a social type in prison defined by the attacks on men from behind with objects. The actor is the "creeper," and the action is that of "creeping from behind." This objectivation of an observed act in a pod may or may not take on more signification and enter the prisoners' vocabulary if more acts of this general type are observed in future times in other pods and if the signification (sign) "creeper" takes hold among the men.

Roles are dependent on the concrete social context in which they appear. An individual may be described as "squealing to the cops" (correctional officers) and engaging in "*rata*-like" behaviors, informing on fellow inmates. The behavior in question, "squealing to the cops," can be performed by any actor and thus is the type-x action (i.e., a role performance). As Berger and Luckmann propose, a vocabulary exists that refers to these forms of action (e.g., "squealing to the cops"). An action can thus be apprehended apart from the individual performance of it and the variable subjective, individual, or idiographic processes (i.e., performances) associated with it. Establishing labels for types of individuals or behaviors is one method for the study of the stock of knowledge possessed by inmates and others with whom the prisoner interacts. Berger and Luckmann thus view roles as typifications of one's own or another person's performances. Not only specific actions but forms of action are typified (Berger and Luckmann 1966, 68). One person may in effect approach another person as a type (e.g., a meathead con, a cop, a sissy, a punk) and interact with him in a situation that is itself typical.

The *Veterano*

Prisoners at CF II identified eight sets of behaviors associated with the *veterano* role: (1) projecting passive and active leadership, (2) helping others, (3) mediating conflict, (4) giving advice and counseling, (5) supporting, (6) setting up social exchanges, (7) being a role player or role model, and (8) taking care of "youngsters." In addition, in terms of Hispano values, one finds elements of food sharing, familism, *carnalismo* (from the word *carnal* [brother]), and ethnic loyalty that sustain the men above and beyond the convict code. Indeed, in a study of Chicanos in San Quentin, Davidson attends to the nature of "familism" and *carnalismo* of Chicanos there. He was hired to study the nature of familism for the institution (Davidson 1983). In doing so, he discovered the nature of the Mexican Mafia, *la Eme*, "M," which was also known to two of the men in our group because they had served time in San Quentin.

Social Exchange

Social exchange can be defined as the sharing of goods (e.g., matches, cigarettes, or food). Such exchanges can be equated with cultural values of sharing among Chicanos. As one person observed,

> One of the things I noticed in our pod, of our cultural thing, is any time you go to a Chicano family, a home, as soon as you walk in, "Hay comida hay" (there's food there), it's there, "You're invited." We do that same thing here. Like the Chicano, we save our dinner, okay? Then we bring it out at night. There's only three or four of us that do that, save our food. There's no arguments who is gonna cook. One guy starts cookin', gets the pot out and starts making the chili, the other guy is cutting the meat; the other guy is toasting the bread. And everybody is invited. We see somebody over there, "Orale! Venganse! Aqui esta!" (Hello! Come! Here it is!)
>
> There it is: *Es familia*, man! Everybody in this unit is *familia*. (We started doing this) before we got into that class. The guys would go to the commissary and buy their cheese over there and sit there and eat it in their room (cell), or they'd come out to watch TV, and they'd get their bag and sit there. But then they seen us—we get our potato chips or

whatever, throw them on the table and make our cheese spread and it's for everybody that's there. So everybody's starting to do that now. That's one of our cultural things.

The exchange in the pod began because three individuals who helped serve food in the cafeteria were also hoarding it. As one prisoner remarked,

> They would bring it out at night for them! For the three guys! They would sit up on the tier and eat like a bunch of pigs, and the rest they would throw out the window what they couldn't eat. When we started doing what we do, that killed all that. We tell them, "Bring it down here to the table for everybody!" So now at a certain hour between 7:00 and 7:30 P.M. everybody just starts going to their cells, and see one guy come and put cookies out there; another guy comes out, and he's got some lunch meat left; some other guy's got the cheese, some other guy saved the bread. We just make a good spread, and we all sit there and eat.

The food exchange led to other activities and ideas, such as having a pod for compatible peers and for mutual self-help. According to one prisoner, "At nighttime I see this, and it makes me feel good because it's a unity thing. The Chicanos are staying together. . . . It's a pride thing. 'Orale ese, mi casa es tu casa.' The men refer to their cells as their 'houses.'" They asked permission so that one could visit their *casas*, in the pods. There was a certain pride in maintaining an orderly cell. The food exchange can also generalize to an exchange of favors. "We look and see on Sunday, some guy making out his canteen slip. '¿Tienes feria?' (Do you have money?) 'Si, orale. ¿Que necesitas?' (What do you need?) You order for him. You see that guy smokes, but he don't have money. Orale, I pass the cigarettes over to him, and he comes over. 'Orale, hay te va carnal!' (Here you are brother!)."

Reciprocity is not expected. In the words of one of the *pintos*, "It's not *que me debes* (that you owe me)—a couple of weeks from now he sees that you don't have any money—no *feria*—and he'll talk to you on canteen day. 'Pues, orale, hay te van unas cigaros y unas galletas' (Here are some cigarettes and some cookies)." Sharing in the pod involves sharing whatever personal items one may have. For example, an inmate who has his own coffeepot often invites his *camaradas* (friends) over. "Llega a mi canton. ¿Quieres café?" (Come to my house [cell], do you want some coffee?)

Exchange systems serve to maintain and reinforce cultural value systems of sharing. "It's for everybody—it's all *familia*, man. *Son camaradas y carnales hay dentro* (They are comrades and brothers in prison)." Sharing with others was one of the eight maxims of the convict code identified earlier and by Weider, who goes on to point out that the sociological literature on the code does not focus on explaining observed patterns of behavior in terms of rules (Weider 1974b, 115–18).

The *veteranos* are interested in developing these social-exchange systems to maintain a sense of tranquility, quiet, and equilibrium in the pod. Hans Toch writes about inmates' need to have security while in prison (Toch 1977). As one individual remarked:

> The time ain't nothing. I'll do a life sentence here. I don't care. While I'm doing it, I would like to have my living conditions as best as they can be, where I have something to do with my mind, some kind of projects to work with, things like that. In a pod like this it is better for us to have this kind of feeling amongst everybody in there that to have this guy sittin' over here looking at this guy and looking for something to set him up to run over there and stab each other. That upsets everybody, that kind of feeling in this place. Besides, man, you can feel them vibes; you know that the guy is waiting for them to stab this guy over here or whatever. It makes everybody uncomfortable. If you get a meathead in there that's gonna be that kind of person, that's gonna bring in those feelings, man, get out, get your stuff and book! We don't need those feeling in here. We are doing too much time, man, to be living like that.

By contrast, other pods do not experience the amount of equilibrium and harmony and social exchange that the *veteranos* are trying to establish. A statement from one of the men in another pod reflects this difference.

> This little Chicano—he don't speak English too good, but he watches TV all the time. This black dude walk up there and hit this dude on the back of the head with a broom because he was watching a program he didn't like. This guy was a creeper—he's done it before. In that pod, there's a lot of disorganization. It's mostly blacks in there. There's tension here, tension there. I go over there to talk to a few people in there. The first thing I tell them, "How's everything in here?" And right away it's "Sssh, man! It's torture! It's torment!" Most of them guys I talk to wanna move over here with us because they hear how mellow it is. There's no tension.

If social exchange, cooperation, and regard for each other's feelings lead to a "mellowing out," the antithesis is the correctional officer's attempts to sabotage such activities. As one inmate said,

> These people [the cops] don't like that—that everybody gets along because getting along when they come and try to cause a distraction with one guy, try to roll there. They don't like that. I know they're already scheming again on how to break us up. We're not doing anything wrong. We're not conspiring to hurt nobody. We're not conspiring to escape. The only conspiracy we're doing is how to keep ourselves mellow.

Exchange involves making things for each other during what they call their "arts and crafts hour." It illustrates their ingenuity in occupying themselves in activities to manage time and kill boredom. One prisoner explained:

> I was gonna bring up an instance where this guy made this real nice lamp shade. You know another guy is making doilies, so we call it our arts-and-crafts hour. You go out here and see guys making these out of papers; he's not making it just for himself. He makes one for everybody. It's our unity thing. We're doing this to keep occupied. Anybody comes in and he don't have nothing—none of us have anything—anything we have is made out of boxes and paper and stuff. When we make our little "coffee tables" and "little shelves" for our goodies and whatever, and we'll make one for that guy or show him how's it's made. Then he starts making one. They like how he makes it, so he'll make one for this guy and this other guy, and this guy does something different, so pretty soon everybody's busy helping somebody do something.

Another prisoner states:

> The cops don't like that [prisoners being quiet]. We're not conspiring to hurt nobody or nothing. We're not doing the hard time they want us to do. I think that's probably what it is. 'Cause they look in all these other pods and see the hate and bad vibes in there, and that's what they're used to. They look in our pod and see us making something here—some guys playing dominos. We don't make a lot of noise. . . . Every once in a while one of us will bring our box down and put on some tapes and listen to music. It's an open joke and everybody be happy. They look down on us [from the control area]. Pretty soon they call the goon squad [a special team of officers trained to quell rebellion and outbreaks] and [say], "How come all you guys are so happy?" Everybody's supposed to be drunk or something just because we're not there fighting. They come in, and the whole atmosphere just goes *whoosh*! Everything just tears apart. We all just shangle on.

According to the guards' expectations, the men should be fighting each other all the time—after all, they are "animals." It should also be noted that the inmates retrieved all scraps of paper, even a handkerchief I tossed, out of the wastebasket, no doubt for *paño* art (a type of art in which prisoners use handkerchiefs as their canvas). One inmate gave me a drawing of Zapata painted on some discarded cardboard from a large box. The cover for the drawing was Saran wrap (no doubt appropriated from the kitchen). And it was interesting to see one man's "piano" in his cell, its black and white keys drawn on cardboard box material. The former musician also had a "guitar" neck made from a long piece of styrofoam; its "strings" were cotton string.

Setting the Example

At one point, CF II implemented a policy whereby no pictures could be hung or displayed on the walls of assigned cells. Initially there was "open rebellion" by inmates over this policy because it meant that family pictures, personal mementos, and religious artifacts could not be displayed. The "youngsters" asked, "What should we do? Strike?" "This and that. Striking is dead!" replied one of the *veteranos*. According to one well-seasoned *veterano*, everyone was waiting to see what he was

> gonna do. I said, "Okay, all right, this is what I'll do. When they come in to inspect, I'll take them [the pictures] down. As soon as they leave, I'll put them back up." At first it was a big rebellious thing—even I was against it. I thought about it and thought, regardless of what I do, they still gonna come in and grade me, so I'll take them down, and when they leave, I'll put 'em back up when they leave.

By taking the pictures down and returning them to the walls after inspection, the prisoners were able to avoid a confrontation and still maintain some level of control over their one area of privacy—the cell. As one prisoner remarked afterwards, "We can beat them at their own game by being cool."

Advice Giving

A younger inmate asked a *veterano* what he should do with another inmate, a "sissy," who had borrowed two or three packages of cigarettes and failed to repay them. A "sissy" is a person who can be made to back down in a face-to-face interaction. The *veterano*'s counsel was,

> Look, man, you can drop him, [and] you can get another assault case on you. When you go to court for this one, they're going to throw this one on you. You won't get any action from the judge. [Or] you can let this one slide. What's two or three packs [of cigarettes]? That's for nothing. Don't ever loan him anything. Just shine him on. What's more important to you?

Advice giving extends to new inmates who must face the prospect of losing a wife or girlfriend. As one noted,

A lot of times we build up things in your minds, problems, advice on how to do it or what's happening. We had a few incidents—guys that are doing life that are married and they don't want to cope with the fact that their old lady's gonna be out there playing on them and stuff. I rap to them about it—it's only to be expected man. Be thankful, man, that she writes to you, sends you money, comes and visits you. You gotta realize she's got her own needs too. I had a couple of guys going on a big mental trip on that. That's one of the big problems. Once they understand that regardless how bad a head trip you gotta make yourself go through, the people out there still have to fulfill their life, too. They can't put themselves in prison with you, too.

Others noted that they had lost girlfriends every time they were resentenced. One concluded, "We know from experience what it's like to go through that and how to deal with it—how we deal with it."

Protection of "Youngsters"

How do the *pintos* support and protect new inductees, the "youngsters"? The question we asked was, "How is it different from the treatment of youngsters in other groups like the black group, the white group? Do they have the same structure?" One *veterano* answered,

No, I don't think they do. First, the blacks are all by themselves. They don't care, don't worry about anything else. They get a young black dude and they "bone" him. They're gonna try to turn him on. . . . They bone each other. They have no moral[s] about helping their own people, where[as] the Chicano, the *veterano*, a "youngster" comes in [and is looked after]; a young black dude, they're gonna turn him out.

The term "bone" means the rape of new inmates.

Mediating Situations

There is always tension between the inmate system and the authority system. How do convicts provide leadership in situation between themselves and the guards? How do they manage a situation where taking a leadership role will identify the convict to the authority system? A partial answer is provided below. This topic is taken up in a larger sense in the next chapter.

Correctional officers may perceive instances of tension in the pod as a situation that might be developing. According to a *veterano*,

> The cops, they come in and [think] something is coming down in there, they'll pull one of us out, wanting to know what's happening, telling us they know what's happening and if there's anything we can do to stop it. They know that in our pod if anything is going to happen, they have us, the *veteranos*. We can either be the ringleaders, or we can avoid the hassle or start the hassle. We've been through all the strikes and the riots and all that.

These incidents may be handled by the *veteranos* themselves by working directly with an individual. It is important that these potential incidents be handled openly in front of the other men so that the *veterano* is not seen as a rat or a snitch. As one convict expressed it,

> I don't like no cop coming to my cell or take me outside to talk to me. If they want to ask me something or find out something, tell me in front of everybody. It's something that can be answered without jeopardizing anybody or anything. I'll answer them, anything I'll answer them. If not, I'll tell them, "That's your job. That's your job to find out." But even the cops have enough respect for us so that they know better than to come and ask us anything about anybody or anything.

Having experience with many types of problems, the *veteranos* can be a focal point for redirecting problems or quelling disquietude an individual may be facing as he adjusts to personal losses or faces the prospect of long incarceration. It is worth noting that the men indicated that one does not have to be Chicano in order to be a *veterano*. Certain white inmates were also identified as being *veteranos*.

It should be noted that some Hispanic values seem to parallel those of the convict code, for example, the sharing of food and the respect norm. *Carnalismo* (brotherhood) is used by these *camaradas* (comrades) and extended to a partner (a "crime partner"). Thus, the violation of the *respeto* norm of never "copping to the Man" is illustrated in a discussion the men had when they read in the newspapers about an individual who had "ratted on his partner" to get an easier sentence. This individual was already typed and known to the men inside the prison even before he began serving his formal sentence. He carried the *rata* label into the joint.

"The 'convict' is a 'criminal failure' and the 'rat' is a 'convict failure' of the prison system" (Wilmer 1965, 44–45). Prison is characterized by a system of continual conflict between custodians and prisoners. This conflict is open warfare for men whose every move is regulated by rules, regulations, orders, restraints, and punishment. The inmates follow a system of values that has as its goal group cohesion and solidarity. They extol a system of values around group integrity, loyalty to the in-group, respect, and opposition to the out-group of guards and keepers. Sykes and Messinger present a theory as to why the inmate social system and its code and argot of description of prison types are similar from prison to prison. For example, what has been said here about the *veterano pinto* is similar to the person Sykes and Messinger describe as the *right guy*, the *real con*, the *real man*. He is someone loyal to his fellow prisoners, who never lets them down no matter how difficult things get. He keeps his promises and does not welsh on a deal. He is trustworthy. He is not nosy about another man's business and does not shoot off his mouth about his own (1960).

> The right guy never interferes with other inmates who are conniving against officials. He doesn't go around looking for a fight, but he never runs away from one when he is in the right. Anybody who starts a fight with a right guy has to be ready to go all the way. What he's got or can get of the extras in the prison—like cigarettes, food stolen from the mess hall, and so on—he shares with his friends. He doesn't take advantage of those who don't have much. He doesn't strong-arm other inmates into punking or fagging for him; instead, he acts like a man. (Sykes and Messinger 1960, 10)

Sykes and Messinger's theory recognizes that the inmate social system responds to the harsh conditions of custody, which in many cases involve profound attacks on a prisoner's sense of personal worth and self-esteem. The degradation and isolation that prison communicates are further implemented by the fact that society has condemned the prisoner as an outlaw, a deviant so dangerous that he must be kept behind closely guarded walls and watched day and night. He cannot be trusted, and his every act is viewed with suspicion by the guards. In the free society, a person is closely linked to concepts of personal worth by numerous cultural definitions. Coming to prison strips these definitions. The person is reduced to a level of bare subsistence, to being merely a number in the "man's" world. The numerous rules and regulations govern the inmate's life, ranging from the hours of sleeping to the routine of work and the job itself. The remaining significant feature of the prisonization experience is being thrown in with murderers, thieves, confidence men, rapists, and sexual deviants (Sykes and Messinger 1960). The inmate is deprived of a sense of security by others who may prey on weaker men: "The problems of self-protection in a society composed exclusively of criminals constitute one of the inadvertent rigors of confinement," point out Sykes and Messinger (1960, 15). "In short, imprisonment 'punishes' the offender in a variety of ways extending far beyond the simple fact of imprisonment." The inmate must respond and adapt. Sykes and Messinger suggest that the adaptive need is met by the requisites of the convict code as a system of values (1960, 13–15).

Conditions of mutual mistrust between guards and captives create untold tension, fear, antagonism, and anxiety for both populations. The consequences of "prisonization" can be ameliorated when inmates observe the tenets of solidarity demanded by the convict code. A cohesive group provides the prisoner with a meaningful social group with which to identify. Group cohesion helps the prisoner escape isolation, at least in part. It helps to solve the problem of personal security posed by the involuntary intimacy of men noted for their seriously antisocial behavior. Group cohesion in the form of reciprocity of favors undermines one of the most potent sources of aggression, the drive for personal aggrandizement through exploitation by force and fraud. An additional benefit is the maintenance of self-esteem through dignity, composure, courage ("having heart"), and the ability to "take it" and "hand it out" as necessary (the "get down" as the men identified it), which means that the inmate can regain the male role as defined by the inmate population (Sykes 1966, 16–17). Regarding confrontation, one of the men said, "Yo soy el Águila y el Águila no se chorrear" (I am the Eagle, and the Eagle does not wet his pants, back down). This comment is very similar to the Mexican song "El águila negra," which leads off with the lines, "Hola, buitres del infierno, ya llego el Águila Negra, y viene para apuntar cuentas. Nos se pongan a tiemblar" (Hola, vultures from hell, here is the Black Eagle, and I am here to settle scores. Don't start getting scared).

The Special Place of the Rat

Types exist because their behaviors are identified or "typed out," and typal actors are defined in the matrix of social interaction. If the *veterano* exists, so does the *veterano*'s antipode: the *rata*. The social matrix of interaction is sometimes irrelevant in the creation of "rats." Rats can be found in middle schools, in jails, and in small colleges, such as where I worked, where they were sometimes called "*lambe* faculty." I heard the television news about a man who was turning in his "crime partners." This CEO-nista gave "testimony" before Congress and was "ratting" on the heads involved in the ENRON-ia scandal (the Spanish term *enronia* means that one will "dirty" him-/herself by an act of spreading gossip, snitching, being a *lambe*).

Wilmer quotes an inmate who said about rats, "When I was arrested, the other guy was frightened by the police. They told him that if he didn't answer truthfully they would file charges against me. So this guy told a 'story' on me" (Wilmer 1965, 47). This is the essential element in "ratting": it is used to gain advantage over another person and make oneself look good or to lessen an upcoming jail sentence. Wilmer points out that the corrections system needs all manner of rats to maintain order in the prison. Men who will broker information about their brother inmates in order to get a favor from "the Man" are the rats in a prison (or at the university). In prison, the rat, if caught, may be the subject of a "stabbing" and pay for his act with his life, or he may have to check into "PC" (the protective custody cell block). Real men and women do not snitch.

As a psychiatrist, Wilmer was concerned with the problem of snitching and the creation of a therapeutic community. It can be said that psychotherapy is snitching on oneself, as one prisoner pointed out. In Wilmer's view, "authority" and security depend on and foster snitching, perpetuating the warfare between police and criminals. It is almost axiomatic that the "tighter the security the more potentially dangerous is the 'rat' to the captives and the greater the need of custody to have informers from the very world they have closed off tightly" (1965, 49).

Earning One's Bones: It Takes the Years

Developing into a *veterano* or a convict takes years. In order to gain respect and develop a reputation, one has to be able to hold one's own. One convict, el Águila, told us:

> Okay, it happens gradually over a period of time. You come in say, twelve, thirteen years old. Okay, now you walk in there, man, and you know, number one, they got to be able to hold your own, okay. And with your limited perspective, the limited awareness, especially at that age, okay, they don't look into beyond to principles and values. Not that that gets you any more toward being at that. All you know, man, is you get to hold your money. So what you do is you start developing a rep. Okay? Riddler [fictitious name] and I went into this one day. And man, we're going to make sure that we establish ourselves amongst what people were around. Okay? And that's other fuckups that we happen to be there with, Okay? Now just so happen that among our kind of people, all right, we have to get down and bone [fight], okay, at that particular level. When you get up this level here, then more than likely it gonna be okay, but starting from that level, man, you fight because you have to survive. Why are you surviving? Because you are not going to be a punk for nothing, okay? Unless you are a punk, then it doesn't matter, okay. You're not going to let anybody badmouth [you], okay, 'cause that's the same as being a punk, all right? You're not going to be disrespected, that's what it comes down to, all right?

> One man in CFI said that when he first went to prison and was accosted, he picked up a metal chair and beat the other person senseless. He spent time in solitary confinement, but he was never bothered again. Not being able to hold one's own can also get one labeled a punk, as indicated in the previous comments. A "punk" is an inmate who is disrespected by others.

These comments are instructive in that they point out what the *veteranos* were teaching. El Águila tells us that these values become "a principle" epitomized in the words "No te rajes" (Don't crack). This is a hardening process that takes many years. It becomes a way of dealing with the inter-inmate violence. In the film *American Me* (Olmos 1992), one of the "wannabes" is given an order to kill another inmate, and the older cons set up the play for him. If he violates the order, then he becomes the one who gets it next because *se rajo*, he broke with the group. It is serious business.

Riddler had a different idea about adjusting to prison:

> When I was in a California prison . . . I went to the gym for three days, and I watched the guys in my weight boxing, working out. I'd watch, I'd see who was who, and then on about the third day, I went out and told this dude everyone seemed to respect and weigh my weight, and I told him, "Can I put the gloves on with you?" So we put the gloves and I dropped him. That took care of anybody messing with me. I got rid of that problem quick. But that's what I would do to these joints. Even in G [Soledad Prison] was the same thing. But I always made it a point to get in with the guys that everybody respected. I made it a point to always do that in all the joints that in all that time I've been here.

Finally

As noted earlier, some of the values espoused by the *veteranos* also have their correlates in the Hispano home. Values such as sharing of foods or goods are part of family life or of recognizing others as *familia*, those who belong to the in-group, a "crime partner," or others in the pod. A study of a sampling of Hispanos from various southwestern geographic areas and social strata found that the most important enduring values revolved around preserving language, food, family gatherings, ceremonial visits, and widespread myth, such as that of *La Llorona* (Sisneros 2000). Family becomes a buffer against the realities of the outer world. Food, language preservation, and family gatherings for funerals, baptismals, and marriages cement these bonds. In the prison, the value of *carnalismo* bonds men together as crime partners and prison mates. Perhaps these Hispanic values confirm the need for cohesiveness and control over a hostile environment and magnify social interaction among prisoners. The *veterano* attempts to lend humanness to a hostile environment.

CHAPTER 7

Multiple Realities:
Múltiples Realidades

The degree to which society is civilized can be judged by entering its prisons.

Fyodor Dostoyevsky, *The House of the Dead*

IN THIS CHAPTER, I CONTINUE TO EXPLORE THE QUESTION OF WHAT CONSTITUTES a convict, a *veterano*, as defined by a group of Chicanos in a maximum-security prison in the Southwest. This chapter shows, more than anything, some of the tensions that arise in the prison. How do men deal with the tensions that build up between them? The larger question is, How do *veteranos* exercise leadership in a prison? To take a leadership role is to take a position that pits one against the guards and prison security. Other questions include: How do men do time? And how do they handle conflict? Finally, this chapter takes up the analysis of talk, that is, a consideration of what meanings are being expressed in a discussion between several convicts in a group session.

In prison, taking an up-front position, by circulating petitions and writing complaints, is not tolerated by those in charge. Some days prior to a group session we conducted in 1983, a petition had been circulating. It had received support from some of the men and no support from others. A level of anxiety and uneasiness was evident as the men were brought to the room where the group interview was to be held. As the men were collected from the different pods, one man was complaining about "*rata*-like" behavior by those who had not signed the petition. The complaint was a clear alert that threats and physical violence were possible that night if this man were to confront another man as a "rat." We had learned in previous sessions and from work in another prison that calling another inmate a rat had serious consequences, including the possibility of being killed. Ross and Richards, one an academic and the other a convict, tell us that "snitching, no matter the reason for it, may result in a potential death sentence for he who tells tales to the authorities" (Ross and Richards 2002, 73). As we collected individuals for the group session, we noticed the tension and a difference in the inmates' composure. As they sat down, we were already aware that two men, with opposing positions regarding the petition, were sitting opposite each other at the long foldout table. Nonverbal behavior involved taking off their shirts and posturing by flexing their muscles, which only added to the tension. And adding to the tensions inside the room were four guards in their "response squad" uniforms walking outside in the yard. The response squad—the "goon squad," as the men referred to it—was a special unit used to quell fights and deal with unruly prisoners.

Of Lions and Tigers and Bears

Omni* was an older con who had spent many years in prison. He had tremendous presence due to his years in several systems. Like his crime partner, Orbis, his overall prisonization experience included foster care in his younger years. Orbis had often backed up Omni in crimes they concocted on the outside and had done time in California prisons. Sometimes Orbis was the "eyes" for Omni. Both had come through the reformatory system in the state where the group interview took place. Both had been involved in major criminal activities and at the time of the interviews still had ten years of their original sentences to serve. Opie was a young man serving a sentence for drug distribution. The group saw him as a "wannabe," a young convict who associated with the older convicts, but had yet to make his mark and do the "hard time" the others had seen. During the study, he had been transferred to a lower level of incarceration. He had been called a "rat" at the other locality and had to be sent back to the maximum-security prison for his own protection. Opus was the man who started the petition. He reminded me of the college students I taught. He was intelligent, personable, and had been an honor student in high school. He had been caught selling drugs to help his mother and her children on welfare. He was serving a long sentence. Opus, like a work in progress, was reading books such as Marquez's *One Hundred Years of Solitude.* Omar was an African American, but was accepted

---

*In the interest of confidentiality and convenience I have changed the names to ones beginning with *O*.

in the Chicano group. One might say that Onus was "onerous," or ornery, and given to strong-man positions, negativity, and antisocial behavior. Opus and Orbis were the other protagonists in the debate that follows. Several other men were part of the group, but they came and went at different points. I identify my colleagues as Researcher 1, Researcher 2, and Researcher 3.

A Bit of Theory

From a theoretical perspective, Ramos considers that ethnomethodology provides a methodology when

> attention is given to the discovery of the commonsense knowledge that the people under study use to make sense out of what they are doing. . . . the common sense knowledge that the people under study use to cope with their practical circumstances is seen as the link between the way they structure and manage a particular situation and the way they structure and manage their other activities. . . . The other basic feature of an ethnomethodological perspective is the use of conflict or trouble. . . . people naturally create conflict or make trouble for one another. . . . the function of conflict is that when it is created for the people under study these individuals tend to reveal what they take into account. (Ramos 1982, 120)

Trouble reveals what Mexican Americans—or members of any other group such as Hispanos—being studied must take into account as they deal with the various facets of their lives in the varied environments in which they find themselves. As people create problems for each other, they must seek, develop, and implement solutions or strategies to deal with these problems. In essence, the study of managing and interpreting the daily affairs of Mexican Americans, whether they are middle class, live on welfare, or are in prison involves the recognition that they "use background knowledge . . . as interpretative schemes to cope with the problematic features of their daily lives" (Ramos 1973, 906).

Garfinkel notes that background expectancies are seen but go unnoticed. One must "either be a stranger to the 'life as usual' character of everyday scenes, or become estranged from them." The task then is of "treating a societal member's practical circumstances, which include from the member's point of view the morally necessary character of many of its background features, as matters of theoretic interest" (Garfinkel 1967, 37). Members of society (i.e., any group with whom one shares relevances or shared meanings) use background expectations as schemes of interpretation. The social philosophy of Schutz serves as a guide for the study of these background commonsense interpretations that people make in dealing with their situations. Schutzian philosophy proposes that the lifeworld is simply "taken for granted as reality by the ordinary members of society in the subjectively meaningful conduct of their lives" (Berger and Luckmann 1966, 19–20). The taken-for-granted nature of social reality is difficult to grasp because it demands that we suspend what we know about the world. This suspension of belief allows us to look at the world from a fresh perspective. In the present study this means that whatever preconceptions one had about incarcerated men had to be held in abeyance so that one could be a spectator in the world of imprisoned men.

Multiple Realities

The idea of multiple realities comes from the work of Alfred Schutz, who states that the taken-for-granted nature of social reality does not give us much concern unless something happens to make us question our assumptions about the nature of that reality. We hardly notice the comings and goings of social life, which Schutz refers to as the "natural attitude." We simply take these things for granted as we go about the business of daily life. One way to pay attention to daily life, suggests Schutz, is to observe the changing nature of social life as if we were at a theater. As we watch the changing scenes, they affect us as changing multiple realities. Social life also has its share of multiple realities as we are thrown in with others who do not share our perspective on social reality. Their realities clash and collide with our own (Schutz 1971). The crash creates disarray, and one task of social life is to reconcile these ruptures. Of course, we can elect not to deal or interact with people whose political or religious orientations we do not share.

Analyzing conflict can be seen as an investigative device for uncovering what two or more persons are taking into account in their interactions with each other. Conflict in this sense helps to unravel the implicitly stated "rules" that people assume to be governing behavior. Like Ramos, family therapist Don Jackson suggests that analyzing conflict in families (or groups) is a good investigative device for uncovering taken-for-granted assumptions. The reiterative nature of group processes means that if we do not capture these assumptions the first time around, we can always get at them on the second and third passes (Jackson 1970).

But what happens when we think a set of rules is being violated by others with whom we share a small, cramped environment? In this chapter, I look at one particular set of rules: "the convict code." This code often appears in its most idealized form, but in reality it is not that clear cut, as shown in the analysis of group "talk" that follows.

The Convict Code

I presented one version of the convict code in chapter 5. In this chapter I discuss another version, which was presented as a list of dos and don'ts.

Do	*Do NOT*
Mind your own business.	Snitch on another convict.
Watch what you say.	Pressure another convict.
Be loyal to the convicts as a group.	Lose your head.
Play it cool.	Attract attention.
Be sharp.	Exploit other convicts.
Be honorable.	
Do your own time.	
Be tough.	
Be a man.	
Pay your debts.	

(Ross and Richards 2002, 71–72)

Ross and Richards define the edict "Do your own time" as keeping to yourself as much as possible, but being sure not to look as if you are afraid of others. Be cool; project a self-possessed confidence and be prepared to back it up. If someone messes with you, be prepared to move quickly and decisively to defend your rights. Your response may get you time in the "hole" (i.e., solitary confinement), but when you get out, it will work to your advantage among the rest of the prison population, but watch out for the guy you hammered because his clique may try to get revenge (Ross and Richards 2002, 72). As a set of rules the code can also be used to evaluate another person's behavior. The simplest example is when a fellow prisoner who snitches to "the Man" and therefore has violated the code is known thereafter as a "rat." In one vignette, presented below, a man is called a "meathead con." "Meathead cons" are convicts who have never violated the code, but are not known as thinkers, like the *veteranos.*

Following Davidson, the term "prisoners" is preferred over "inmates." The inmate ideology, says Davidson, grew out of rehabilitation philosophy when guards became "correctional officers" and, by extension, the prisoners became "inmates" to be "programmed" through rehabilitation. Convicts, however, know that they are being punished and that the guards are instrumental in that punishment. Convicts keep a code that is separate from official prison rules, according to which they do not do anything detrimental to the group, do not "snitch" on other prisoners, and never give in to "the Man" (Davidson 1983, 46). Both Latino and Anglo subjects in the study I conducted with two other researchers preferred the term "convict." Latinos also preferred the terms *pinto* and *veterano*. Other names for one who has been convicted include *preso*, "prisoner," which is often used in Mexican songs, and *reo*, also a prisoner. Although the Hispanos preferred the term *veterano*, they often used the term "convict" in the group discussion.

The Meeting

The meeting I focus on here started by covering some of the topics from the previous session. Some talk between Omni and Orbis had evidently already occurred in the pod where these two men resided. "You can be submissive without being obedient" was the general subject of the conversation, which focused on the signing of the petition I mentioned earlier. The language is raw:

ORBIS: The Apostles and Jesus, they were submissive but they weren't obedient. They got beat up and everything, man, you know what I mean. They didn't get rebellious toward the people who told them not to preach and blah, blah, blah. They didn't stand up and say, "Ah, fuck you" and start blowing their tops at them. They didn't say nothing. They submitted! They didn't say nothing. They submitted to the beatings and the treatment they got. But as soon as they got away from it, they went out and did the same things.

OMNI: That's not like being a *veterano*. I wouldn't submit to getting heat.

ORBIS: Well, yeah, but you're doing it in the sense that when they open your door for you to get to your house [cell], you go into your house and all that kind of stuff. That's being submissive.

OMNI: Yeah, but that's part of the program. But getting heat and taking this bullshit, man, isn't part of it.

ORBIS: Yeah, but it goes around the same trip. You still, you got things you don't dig, rules and regulations that you don't like, you're totally against, man, but you still have to do them.

OMNI: Not really, man, you know. Sometimes you rebel against them, you know. To show them you don't care about their rules, you know. And you have to pay the consequences for them, you know. You're not being submissive about it. Brother here, man [pointing to Opus], man, got fucked around 'cause he's a convict, a *veterano*, you know.

ONUS: But is being a convict getting into trouble, man, and getting fucked around by the man? Putting yourself into a position to be fucked around by the Man?

ORBIS: Yeah. That's right, man.

OMNI: Well, sometimes, man, you think there's people behind you, man, you know, that are going to back your play, you and the convict, man. . . . If another convict goes against the system, regardless if it's right or wrong, you know, and you're asked to sign your name, you're supposed to sign your name to it. You don't dig the motherfucker either [the petition against the correctional officer in question], you know. Not letting Opus [the petitioner] take the heat. Some didn't sign it 'cause we don't like them cops. This guy's a good guy. No fucking cop's a good guy.

For Omni, being a convict meant continued resistance to the rules and regulations of the system. So when the petition came around, he thought that other convicts would support the petition as a sign of continued rebellion and, in his words, would "back the man's play." Omni, according to his "natural attitude," assumed that other convicts, as members of the penitentiary, would sign automatically. His natural attitude—his "reciprocity of perspectives," as Schutz (1971) calls it—meant that all who thought like him would sign the petition. Failing that, the incident became "trouble" that he had to deal with as a convict. Moreover, he would now also have to take into account the "others'" perspectives because they differed from his. His natural attitude led to anger at an event that challenged his way of thinking. Omni was not going to challenge Onus directly because that would lead to more conflict and a possible violent confrontation. Nevertheless, he had to support the idea that convicts should continue with further conflict against the correctional officers.

OPUS: Soon as that petition went out, and not everybody signed it, they held court and that was the major reason why I was sent down to "A" [isolation, or "the hole"].

RESEARCHER 1: How did you respond to them in order to make them put that move on you?

OPUS: How did I respond? The next day I went in and told the man. I says, "Look, uh, I need your help. I'm having problems with one of your officers. I'd like to move!" And he says, "All right, tell me about it." So I told him about this meathead, man, and the next morning I was in seein' the doctor, an old [correctional officer] comes in and, says, starts griping like a dog at your heels, you know how he is early in the morning. So I was so bummed out I was staying in from work anyway, you know. The doc was talking to me and he was talking to me at the same time which fitted [the correctional officer] perfectly. He mentioned something moving me to Block [X] or else moving to Block [Y]. I told him to do whatever he wanted, make any move he wanted. That's where I'll stay.

ORBIS: I heard you had threatened him. That's what I heard.

OPUS: I've been doing time a long time, man. I don't be threatening anybody, let alone a guard who has the key.

OMNI: I have never heard this from anybody about you. It wasn't behind what those people said. That he went in there and threatened him and all that. That ain't you. I know.

RESEARCHER 1: But that's what I heard Orbis saying. That one way of getting by is exactly what you said, "not to threaten a person who's got the key." But you don't, you don't obey that person either. You submit. You alter what you would like to do. I'm sure what you like to do . . . I guess what you'd like to do is to threaten.

OPUS: I don't want to threaten anybody, man.

QUESTION ABOUT A LITTLE FREEDOM

RESEARCHER 1: Yeah, that's what I hear you saying but . . . how much do you alter what you would like to do in order to maintain some freedom to move around? You don't lose yourself. You don't obey. You don't say, "Well, okay, your rules are right, and I'll go with your rules." Okay, you say, "I've got to survive so I'll submit, but I'm not going to obey."

OMAR: I see what we got to go with these changes with these officers. 'Cause they have a book and they have laws and rules and regulations. Every intelligent guy in here should read this thing. I knew for myself what happened to Opus, I knew it was bunk. That's the same way I was railroaded. Next thing you know, I know I was all stabbed all up [in a knife attack by cell mates]. That's how it is, you know.

OMNI: But you see, Opus, man thought he was doing the right thing to do by filing a grievance against the cop.

OMAR: That was good. That was good. I mean, I liked his play. I signed it because I thought it was good.

Opus gives his assessment of the situation. Omni continues with his idea that submission to authority is as abhorrent to him as it was to the Apostles. The core idea is that challenging the system (in the guise of a complaint against one correction officer) can put you "up front." It is a basic theme that a challenge can also lead to loss of privileges, namely when the convict is put in "the hole."

CHALLENGING THE NONSIGNERS

OMNI: But there was a lot of people, man, that supposed to be convicts that *didn't* sign it, motherfucker, because they like the cop. The cop is a good cop. You know what I mean."

[Several enter into the conversation: "Hold it, hold it." "Wait a minute! I didn't sign it." "I didn't sign it either."]

ONUS: Hold it! Hold it! [Angrily] Are you saying I like the cop?

OMNI: I don't know! Why didn't you sign it?

ONUS: Hey! Because I didn't feel like it! But don't say I like the man, okay? I'd appreciate it. I don't dig the man!

ORBIS: What is all this?

ONUS: I'd just appreciate it, if you would . . . just saying—

OMNI: (Interrupts) I'm saying what I feel.

OMNI: The brother asked for help, man, by saying . . . I'm talking about convicts, man.

ONUS: I consider myself a convict, man.

OMNI: The brother put up a thing [the petition], man! I need support. I need a signature just saying we don't dig this man.

ONUS: How many other times? How many other times has this fucking asshole, man, and other people tried to get him [the correctional officer] outta here? It don't do no good!

OMNI: Listen, it doesn't matter that it don't do no good, man. Just being a convict and showing support, man.

ORBIS: I don't agree, man.

OMNI: Now, man, I don't agree, man!

OMNI: If you came to me, man, and say, "Omni, look, man, I don't dig this cop. This is what's happening, man! The man's fucking over me and I'm making this [petition]—"

ONUS: [Interrupting) You've had a lot of fucking hassles here lately too, man! So dig where you're coming from, dude!

OMNI: I don't have any hassles with nobody.

ONUS: Well, like I said: you dig where you're coming from, man! Don't be saying that people who didn't sign it dig the man. [Indignantly and emphatically] *I don't dig no man!"*

OMNI: Then why didn't you sign it?

ONUS: Because I didn't feel like it! [Name omitted], I don't have to live for you! I don't have to live for that man! I don't have to live for nobody! *I live for me!*

OMNI: I understand that. I understand that. I understand all that.

RESEARCHER 1: Could you [addressing Onus] explain one thing to me? Could you explain what you experienced when the petition was put before you?

ONUS: Hey, I looked at it and knowing that this man over here [emphasizing the correctional officer], okay, is, his position of power. Ain't nothing going to be done to him. Because it's been tried already, I can dig where he's [Opus] coming from. Okay, I can dig all right, but I didn't sign it because I know that nothing is gonna be done to that man. At all!

RESEARCHER 1: So it was a fruitless kind of thing?

ONUS: Yes, it was.

ORBIS: I signed too, before.

OMNI: Even though it was all fruitless, man, the thing what I can't understand is . . . a brother, a fellow convict, you know, just asked for your support, man, you know? You know regardless of whether it was gonna do any good or not no good, . . . you sign it. This is what I feel. I said, "Hey, man, here's a petition." I looked at it. It's against a cop, you know; it's against the system.

ORBIS: Well, if you'd go so far as to do that, here's the way I figure it, man. If you don't like a cop, okay. You don't dig this cop and you wanna jump on him and bust him up that, it don't mean I'm gonna jump in and bust him up, man. I'm not gonna follow . . . I'm not stupid, man.

RESEARCHER 1: What does it mean if you don't?

ORBIS: It don't mean nothing! It means that, see . . . The reason I didn't sign, see, because I'd signed twice on the same man. I signed two petitions and it don't do no good. All you're doing there is setting yourself up, man! That if anything ever happens to that man, if he was to get stabbed or somethin', the first people they're going to jack up are the ones who signed the petition. I'm not stupid!

RESEARCHER 1: Okay, but I'm trying to get it out of a personal realm. I'm trying to get into . . . more a cultural realm. What does it mean to the people that are important to you if you decide not to sign it? What does it mean to them? What does it mean to you?

OPUS: Nothing. I didn't get enough support on it, and I couldn't push it through and enter it in his state file. That's the only . . .

SHOWING SUPPORT FOR THE CODE

Omni identifies a particular tenet of the convict code, "Show support for fellow convicts," and mirrors this principle back to the group. But the men continue to proclaim their convict status and to relate to their own individual perspectives, saying, "I live for me!" or "If the man gets busted, we all get it." There is also a level of hopelessness because previous petitions have gone nowhere. This experience is part of being in prison, of being stripped of one's center of control and being subject to the prison rules and prevailing regulations.

RESEARCHER 1: Does it lower him or raise him up any or just stays the same?

OPUS: His signature, all it counts for is that there is forty-eight men in a pod, in a unit, and his would be just one of the forty-eight. See, so . . .

ONUS: So [directing himself to Opus], let me ask you this: Because I didn't sign it, would that indicate that I dig the man? That I like the man?

OPUS: No, no.

ONUS: Thank you!

OMAR: But you took that personally.

ONUS: Yeah, I did. Yes, I did because this is what the man [pointing to Omni] said. He said the people that didn't sign it like the man. I don't dig no fucking pig! I don't dig the man.

OPUS: He didn't say everybody or, or. . . .

ONUS: Well, I took it personally.

OMNI: I didn't say that.

ONUS: I don't dig the man!

OPIE: [Trying to get in] Some of the people—

OPUS: He didn't say everybody or—

ONUS: [Angrily] Well, I took it personally. I'll admit it, I did. You damn straight I did.

RESEARCHER 1: What did it mean to you [Opie] for Orbis not to sign it?

OPIE: Well, see, what I heard him saying that he already did twice [signing two previous petitions] and it didn't do no good. That's why he didn't do it, okay? If it would have came to me right . . . The kind of experience that I've had in this kind of like a following trip, the old convict code, I would have probably, uh, knowing that I know [Opus], I probably would have signed it knowing that I was going to get in trouble.

RESEARCHER 1: Okay, I want us moving one step over from there, though. Not what you would have done, but when you learned that [Orbis] didn't sign it. What did that mean to you?

OPIE: Nothing. You know, I didn't sign it. . . . I would have looked at it in the terms of, uh, he liked or disliked the man. I would have just looked at it: Well, I got a personal problem with this dude, with this man. And really whether I liked him or not liked him, I wasn't signing it for that. I was signing for the favoritism I got for my friend. I would have missed the whole issue. It would have meant me going into [indecipherable]. I'd a been quote "stupid" because it would have been both other there saying, "Well, brother, we didn't get nothing done. Now we have to fight the Man."

ORBIS: That's happened with food strikes, everything else that I've been in, man. You know, 'cause I've been through that. "Let's don't eat, then. *Food strike!*" And blah blah blah blah. And nothing happens. And the ones that, the incidents that I've been in, the ones that instigated are the ones that had canned food in their cells and all that stuff, man! And us like the dummies, man, we're starving to death! Naw, man! Dead action!

ORBIS: That's the same trip with this place here. This place, the leaders that instigated the move, that complaining about the cells, "And we need a cell with so much room, blah, blah, blah." Man, they made a big stink about it, and "We'll sign petitions to get a new prison built." The ones that done all the instigating, they're not even here! They're at [another prison with a lower level of security]. All the other dummies are here.

OMAR: You know, I understand what everybody's position everybody take. See, you know, a unified effort, man, would accomplish a lot of things because, see, when the Man put strains on this man [Opus], I got to live in the pod with him and that puts strains on me. Don't know what's gonna be his reaction because tension builds up, and it can be over a table top game where I might do somethin' or say somethin,' and it's not me really me, you know, but it's the tension in there levels off for me. I think everybody, whether they work or not, should show their support when a convict is trying gettin' something accomplished around here. Because like the ole saying says: "Eat shit: A million flies can't be wrong." Forty-eight people can't be wrong either.

Are a million flies wrong? Opus does not want to confront the nonsigners. Orbis believes that similar efforts in the past, food strikes in particular, did not accomplish much, so why should this particular petition?

RESEARCHER 1: Forty-eight people could be wrong.

VARIOUS: No, they can't!

OPIE: See, narrowing it down to your thing is like it means that I know people like Orbis, Omni, Onus, and Opus. Now if I would have made this petition and I would had their signatures on it probably for self-gratification, I would have felt a lot of power, but then I would have missed my whole reason for filing this. 'Cause if I was doing it on a personal basis, but I needed other people's opinions to be with me to say, "Hey, man, this man's no good." People like that, experienced, that have been through the hassles with these kinds of things, I would have probably felt power.

ORBIS: That's right.

ORBIS: If I don't like somebody, whether it's a cop or a convict or what, man. If I don't like them, and you're my friend, and I don't like these people or this particular dude or whatever, man, you know. And I expect you not to like him because you're my friend. Naw, naw, man, that's dead. Is the friend of my enemy my friend?

OMAR: No, no, see, what you have to understand, see, is not practicing racism or nothing.

ORBIS: See, that's what it amounts to . . .

OMAR: When a guy who discriminated against, you know, a convict and guys who eat shit out of his ass every day, they're trying to conversate [have a conversation] with, it's a different thing. See, I understand exactly the position he's taking. It's not the man that Onus don't like; it's his attitude with his actions toward this man [points to Opus] because I sit at my door and watch this man [the correctional officer] personally intimidate this man for nothing. See, let me say this to get back to original where this all derive from. You's was talking about the rules and the values of Chicanos, right, and you said when you got to talking about how they maintain the dignity, right, respect, and stability. See man, that's why I say, "Locking a man up, you know," whatever a person can do or may do, is necessary because human necessity is a need, right? For when you confine a man is an offense to his integrity. And see, this an insult to a man's dignity, his character and everything else because this institution is designed to psychologically and physically destroy a man. This one particularly right? And you can see the forces in this institution in terms of rules and regulations. They are beginning to shape our lives, and, see, you can submit to them. You can be obedient to 'em if you wanna, but whatever you do, if you go against them, it's gonna hurt you, and if you try to go with the current, it's gonna hurt. So anythin' I can say for an individual is basically to be his self, right. But, see, when a convict take a stand . . .

BREAKING WITH ANONYMITY

RESEARCHER 1: [Interrupting] That's not where we are, though. Let me break in because what we're talking about is anonymity. What we're talking about is keeping a low profile, and what I see happening is that the group of convicts have power. They have a way of fighting this dehumanizing process. What Opus decided to do was that he was gonna break the anonymity, and he was gonna say, "I'm gonna take a stand," and I think that's what we're trying to look at.

ONUS: Let me interject right here. I'd like to say something. Now, I can dig where both these men [Omni and Opus] are coming from. Okay, now here's what I'd got to say, man. If I claim myself to be this man's [Opus's] friend or this man's [Omni's] friend [with whom he had argued earlier, a signer], and these guys claim to be my friend, all right, be on a convict level, be on a personal level, or what have you, okay. Now since I didn't sign that petition, is this man and this man, he gonna be friend enough to me to turn around and say, "Well, hey, man, you didn't sign this, *Fuck you!*" What kinda friend is that? I mean, don't they, don't they have the respect for me, man, to appreciate the way I feel, and the way that I think. Just because I didn't sign it, now I'm a lowlife or some kinda fucking morsel? No, all I'm saying is, just a minute [someone wants to interrupt]. Uh-uh, hey, if they're my friends as they say they are, then have enough respect for me to appreciate and respect my feelings, okay. Then you can be my friends. Otherwise, I don't need friends like you, man. That's what it comes down to.

OPUS: That's right.

ONUS: Okay, but if we are friends, then it doesn't matter if I signed or not—one phony signature, man. Know what I mean?

OPUS: Yeah, this was, this meant to not get anybody on a personal level. If they signed, fine. If they didn't, that's cool, too, because either way it wouldn't hurt me. What it was used for, as a means for a defense against the accusations that this guy brought against me. Plus it would have went into his state file. That's where he gets hurt, not his institutional file or his job in question and all that.

Orbis poses the question, "Is the friend of my enemy my friend?" He sees the direction of the question as leading to "dead action," a point he proclaims repeatedly in this session. One man points to the problem of how locking up men leads to an attack on "human integrity," so anything that is being proposed to change things is therefore worth doing. The prisonization experience and its rules and regulations shape the men in the institution. Does that mean that the convict code cannot protect them from the dehumanizing experience of prison life? For some men, one way to cope with prison life is anonymity. Not to stand out contradicts the tenet in the code that stipulates that you should show your support and be loyal to other convicts.

RESEARCHER 1: What are the rules? What are the set rules?

OPUS: There are no set rules for filing petitions!

RESEARCHER 1: There are no set rules. What I'm trying to get at is to get it away from the personal thing and to look at it in terms of, here we have a group of people who are convicts. One of the convicts decides that he is gonna do something that's gonna set the spotlight on him, and he asks other people to join into that. What are the rules? I mean, is there a rule that if he's a convict, that he backs your play?

OPUS: *No.*

RESEARCHER 1: Is there a rule that you're taking a step out and you're on your own hook?

OPUS: Definitely on my hook! 'Cause . . .

RESEARCHER 1: That's not what Omni was saying. Omni was saying, "If a convict makes a play, then it's the responsibility of all the other convicts to back that play."

OPUS: It would turn into something other than a petition because in DOC [Department of Corrections] in [names a western state], we've all sat through hunger strikes, we've all sat through work strikes, through every other kind of strike you can think of to call attention to the inadequate treatment that we were getting. Okay, none of it worked!

ONUS: What you're trying to get into is how convicts function in here. What unspoken rules do we live by? Do you guys understand what they're asking for?

OMNI: And, man, for there to be bullshit like this here or the way that we started to express ourselves, that's not needed 'cause that not the way that convicts function.

SOMEONE: Right.

OMNI: The only thing I was trying to say was like my signature protects the other guy. That if each guy thought that way, you know what I mean? It's just a protection thing all the way down the line.

ONUS: Yes, yes, Omni. But it's not that way, especially here in this state system.

RESEARCHER 3: But, Onus, that's not true because, or I wonder if that's the—

OMAR: You don't know if it's true. Okay, yes, I know I've been in other penal systems besides this state system, so has this man.

RESEARCHER 3: Has the system always been that people back each other regardless of what the specific thing is? It's almost like whether it's here or out in the streets. The thing is if you have a cause that you want to try to get accomplished, you take out the personal feelings, you take out your personal self. You say, "Look it, I don't know if I agree with this or I don't know if this is right because this person is my friend or is on the same side." It may not even be a friend but on the same side, he's trying to. . . If you want to look at it from the convict . . .

ONUS: I understand what you're saying. What you're asking, so please . . .

RESEARCHER 3: So doesn't that . . . isn't that . . .

ONUS: That doesn't apply here in this state!

RESEARCHER 3: Why not?

ONUS: Because you don't have the same caliber of people like you have out on the [West] Coast. You don't have them, man! The unity that you speak of, okay, or want to have here does not exist!

RESEARCHER 3: Is it because of [name omitted]? You're personalizing it, and all you're saying is . . .

ONUS: It could very well be. It could very well fucking be! Okay, but that's because I don't see the people here, man, that are out on the Coast. Okay, people out there are together, man. They stand together! Meatheads here don't do that.

RESEARCHER 3: I thought that was the purpose of the petition or the things that Omni was saying. You don't personalize. It's not that you like or don't like the guy. You don't do that.

ONUS: We're not looking at it like a microcosm. We're looking at it like this [puts arms overhead to illustrate global view with emphasis]! On a large scale.

OMNI: Okay, let me break in here. But this thing was . . . Dudes, convicts, from California, from other joints you know . . . like . . . [drowned out]

ONUS: [Interrupting] We know people, man. We know people!

OMNI: . . . don't stick together. But my feeling was when I signed this thing was I'm that kind of people. I don't care . . .

ONUS: I consider myself that.

RESEARCHER 1: But listen to what he's saying. He's not saying you're not that kind of people. He's not saying, "He's not that kind of people."

OMNI: I know that. I know that. What I'm trying to get to him, even though there's not that many of us . . . the one that there is, man, you know, support it.

OMAR: That's right.

RESEARCHER 1: What he's saying is, he's talking about the system. He's saying that in some systems he would have signed that because the system was there and it was strong and it was in place, and he knew it would jell. He's saying here you don't have any assurance that it is going to jell.

OMNI: I know it. I know it.

RESEARCHER 3: But, Omni, where does that start? Where does it start? It starts with everybody believing that. Because if you're doing this to go along with the mass, with most of the people. I mean, if you're comparing this with California, saying, "Everybody does it over there. Nobody does it here," where does that start? I mean, somehow individual things, [name omitted] was saying that . . .

ONUS: [Interrupting, standing up and hitting the wall] Hey, you know what? I beat my fucking head [pounds on wall] on this fucking wall so many times it ain't even funny, man. Okay, you've never been in the penitentiary! You have not done and been through what we had to do. Okay, I been there, man. I taken shit and I've eaten shit! You haven't! *Okay?*

RESEARCHER 3: Now what does that have to do with what we're talking about?

ONUS: Because you don't know what unity is, man! True unity in a prison situation, where it is a life and death situation. *That's what it is in here.*

RESEARCHER 1 TO RESEARCHER 3: He's talking about the stance you've taken.

ONUS: *We live it!* You can talk about it, but we live it, okay? I've been there. I've backed up people's plays in this penitentiary, okay, behind the walls, and nothing has happened!

RESEARCHER 1: That's the reason this penitentiary was built the way it was built.

Prisoners line up (Nacho Jaramillo)

There is much emphasis in the conversation about the men in prisons on the West Coast, where some of these men have done time. Some convicts in the group realized that out on the Coast the men had much more unity than in the Southwestern prison where they are now incarcerated. The question is also posed if it was the caliber of convicts on the Coast that made the difference, if the Coast prisons created a different kind of convict, one who would support a petition or risk his anonymity for the sake of conflict with the system. The question of the prison environment brings up a different factor. It may be that in earlier times on the West Coast the men were in prison environments that were not as restrictive as the present system. This Southwestern prison does not have a "yard" where men can interact freely with others. They are restricted to interacting with the same persons all day long. On the West Coast, they were allowed daily exercise. It is likely, too, that they were in prison for a lesser level of control for offenses that they committed when younger. All these questions cannot be answered here. In the maximum-security prison in which these men find themselves, it is difficult to organize, hence the reference to the construction of this particular prison and the limited contact between inmates.

RESEARCHER 1: This penitentiary was built the way it was built to break up that unity!
SEVERAL: Yeah, Yeah! Exactly!
RESEARCHER 1: The whole purpose of this penitentiary was to break up unity, and

what he is saying is that he's talking of what the gamble is. He's saying, "On this petition maybe I shouldn't gamble because maybe the risks are greater than any hope of getting anything done. So I'm not gonna do it. I'm not gonna run the risk here, but I'll run it some place else."

ORBIS: Let me give an example. Now say you guys as psychiatrists for the institutional for this state. You say today you and this man here, you say, okay, "Let's make a petition that we're gonna demand that these guys have a pod of where they're gonna be. And we're gonna sign our names on it." Now, knowing that if you make that petition and everybody that signs that petition is gonna get some heat from upstairs, your jobs are on the line. You're not gonna sign that pile of shit!

RESEARCHER 1: That's a value question. I think we might sign it if we know if we had enough backing to make the run.

ORBIS: You won't sign it because there's time we're in a meeting with that little speaker [pointing to a wall speaker that is also a microphone]. Then, you don't even want to talk about certain things. So I know you won't sign it.

RESEARCHER 1: I hadn't been aware of that [the speaker].

OMAR: I see where you're coming from, but still just like there but a few of us in here, right. And so the few of us are gonna have to stick together. We gonna have to be strong until the bitter end. You know what I'm saying?

OMAR: There ain't no doing foolish things. I know that Opus ain't gonna beat up no cop. He knows no cop is worth no twenty years. You know. I know y'all ain't gonna do nothing stupid like that. But I'm saying we utilize the tool of communication to get somethin', something across, right, and so we utilize this instrument. This thing, physical force, we're using, we use a mental force, we use all that we have because we can't go out there and fight these folk. We're not trying to do that, right. We trying to put it on paper because the paper is more effective than the feds, right?

ONUS: And talking about being more effective, okay. You bring up a good point there. Why? [addresses Omni] In a given situation . . . okay, let's say, man, back out at the Coast, we know what's it like out there. We've been out there, man. We know the people. Out there, we can be effective. We can make the *movidas* [hustles] we want to move and accomplish. Here you can't do that. I've seen that, okay. Now I'm not gonna sit and catch no cases and get buried in this motherfucking state, okay? Without ever hoping to have the opportunity to get back out and be in a place where I can be more effective, as this man says.

OMAR: Yeah!

ORBIS: Here you can't do that, Omni.

OMNI: I mean this was just a piece of paper, man, you know, and we just [haltingly], you know, that this is me, man, I mean, a convict, a brother, you know, wants a signature, man. Regardless if it's right or wrong. He's not saying, well, we're gonna have a food strike or we're gonna . . . a food strike, I ain't gonna go for that, you know. It ain't gonna accomplish nothing, man. I'm not gonna go for jumping on the man, you know. But if a brother comes to me and says, "Hey, man, I got this petition on this man and he's been fucking over me, man." I know this ain't gonna do no good, man, but I know in me that I got to sign this thing, man, because of the old ways.

RESEARCHER 1: But that's just in you.

OMNI: Yes, but I'm doing it! I'm me.

ONUS: Let me ask you this question, Omni. Then it's your own personal ethics. It's what you believe in. And I can dig that, all right, and it's respected. Man, my ethics might not correlate with yours. It might not parallel with yours. In this instance it does not . . . it doesn't, man. Because I see that nothing can happen.

OMNI: But it doesn't matter if nothing can happen, you know, if the self "do it," saying, well, man . . .

ONUS: The belief in the self!

ORBIS: Yeah, you know.

ONUS: Let me give you a parallel on this. This happened since I've been down there. Another petition went around, and these guys been getting fucked around for so long for yard [an hour out in the yard], for being out for an hour a day, they are on a rotating basis. One guy, they, uh, one guy an hour. And sometimes you don't get out of your cell at all. And a petition comes around, it was really strongly worded, and it used words of threat and methods of threat and throwing shit on the cops, throwing piss on the cops and stuff like that. I had just gotten down there, and these guys had been fucked around for so long, even shot at, hit, and spit at and stuff, and this petition comes around saying they wanted socks, and T-shirts, toothpaste, toothbrushes . . . the essentials.

OPUS: Yeah, and I says, "Man, the first thing this is gonna do if I sign this sucker is it's gonna open my house [cell] to inspection. What do I have that I can't have?" That was my first thought. I say, "Well, I don't have anything that I can't have because they would have kept it when I first came in, which they did." They took about half my stuff. So I signed it because these guys had gotten fucked around. Not me, 'cause I had just gotten down there. I didn't know beans from tortillas. So I signed it. The first thing they do is *pop*—my door comes open and man, there's sixteen cops standing there.

OMAR: Now, what you've just done describing, this is understood. Now, let's open up our minds here, all right, and let's absorb a little bit more than just the superficial things. Now, the convict ethics that we live by in here, which Omni clearly described for us here, we all are aware of that. Everybody sitting in here, convict wise. Okay? Maybe these gentlemen sitting here are also aware of this, but we are definitely aware of it. Now we have seen, man, what that ethic belief can do. It can get us jammed up the way it got you jammed up and locked down, or it can do more for us. And what more can that do for us? Man, why don't we elevate ourselves, that ethical belief that we have, man, and place ourselves in a position where we can do something, man? Throwing shit, throwing piss on the man, sure that's airing our frustrations, okay, and showing them, hey, you're wrong, and they are wrong, I agree. They should be giving them men [the exercise] yard, giving them their socks, their toothpaste, whatever. They should have that, but they're not getting it. What can we do to change it? We've got to do something. Why not place ourselves in a position where we can do something about it more effectively, man? I have seen, hey man, what we've been put through here, like he said, is this degradation process. Being torn apart, stripped down. We can allow that to happen, through that ethical belief that we cling to, all right. But what happens if we modify that ethical belief, and we start saying, "Well, wait a minute, man, we've been going up against the Man, fighting him, throwing shit on him, and what have you. Has it accomplished much of anything?" What happens? What happens, man, when we see, hey, if they're in a position to do their manipulation and they're manipulating us and moving us this way they want to move us? Why don't we put ourselves in a position to do the same thing? Still live by the convict code. Yeah, and have the ethical beliefs. But, man, be in a far superior position.

OPUS: I think that happened with this, my incident . . .

OMAR: Okay, maybe it did happen.

OPUS: We'll take the sacrificial lamb syndrome, okay. I get down to "A" [the isolation unit] but, man, all my brothers were still out here, man, sending me smokes, sending this, that, and the other. It doesn't matter if I'm knocked down. That thought has not even entered my mind because I stay in my house [cell] just as much there as I do over here.

RESEARCHER 1: He's talking about a different level, though, Opus.

OMAR: That's what I'm saying. You're looking at it from this perspective, joint perspective. I'm saying go beyond that, Opus.

ONUS: Don't look at it short range. Don't look at the cigarette you can get or the canteen you can get. That's looking short range, man. Look *long range*. Isn't that what our purpose is? Is to get ourselves out of this penitentiary and stay out of this penitentiary [raps on the table repeatedly]?

OPUS: For some people. I don't have those thoughts, man. I'm doing, you know . . . a lot of years, a lot of years.

ONUS: [Pleading] I know what you're doing, Opus. I know what you're doing. I know what all of you guys are doing. But still you got to forward to the time when you get out of this penitentiary. . . . And how are you going to keep yourself out? How are you going to adapt to this system, man?

OPUS: I don't trip out . . . I can't see it.

ONUS: I do. I know, hey, one of these days my turn is coming, and man, I have got to figure out a way myself, by the beliefs I have, which are convict. I still have to make them mesh with society out there because I want to stay out this time. I'm already a three-time loser. I can't take another fall, and this is what I'm doing. I'm going through some big changes, man. And I'm seeing how I can be more effective, at the same time help my people.

One of the men calls for disobedience and a strong commitment to the convict code, what he calls "ethics." Are "ethics" (i.e., personal behavioral beliefs) different from the convict code? Onus reveals that even in lockdown he had support from others (e.g., getting cigarettes). Staying in his cell prepared him for the more difficult stay in lockdown—the "hole," also officially called "administrative segregation." Opus's perspective about being anonymous is based to some degree on the perspective that he is doing a long, long sentence. Onus, in contrast, has to think about the time he will be released and, he hopes, go through the "heavy changes" necessary to "make it" out there and stay out this time.

RESEARCHER 1: What happened when convicts disagree on strategy? How do you change? How does he get people to look at things differently? You know, I see you kinda holding the line. How do you work together to go a little bit in his direction and little bit in your direction? How does that happen?

OPIE: That's where that survey he's doing. This is an old convict right here [referring to Omni]. He's molded in his ways, and when he speaks, it affects your younger convicts that have that same heart but different parallel. See the differences?

ONUS: We been beating our heads against that wall, like I've said, and for all these years. And what has changed? Not much of anything. Now, man, let's come up with something new. Let's see how we can approach this thing from a different angle, man. Okay, let's use new juice, man. Sure, he comes out of the old school, I might come out of the newer school, but I've got what I believe in and I know it is going to work. Because I've seen certain things that I've done within this system.

SOMEONE IN THE GROUP: How would you handle that situation?

ONUS: That situation with meathead in there?

ANSWER: Um huh.

OMNI: I don't respond like that. I used to. I'm not saying I never have [referring to "going off" on the cop].

ONUS: I have. But I seen there was a change needed. There was a change needed and I changed that, man. I did. And now that's what I say, the *chotas*, they leave me alone. They don't fuck with me, man, at all anymore. That's why I can sit back and I just do my time, okay, and these motherfuckers look, man, and they stay away.

OMAR: I want to ask you something. What position can a person elevate to in here? Be all right now in "A" Block.

ONUS: That what's occurred to me, man. If we can see ourselves as convicts together, if we are supposed to be so together all right as to . . .

OMAR: [Interrupting] See, I live for my possibles, right? So when my possibles are violated, I'm willing to put my life up on the line for my possibles, that's what I'm saying.

ONUS: Okay, let me clarify.

OMAR: And so, I'm not gonna change, you know. If he cusses me out one day, I was so high above that I thought about that all weekend. I could've gotten my shank and wait till he come to pee or wait till the yard and kill him. Before I done that, man, I say, "Well, look, man, I can reason with that and I got nothing in the world to prove." So that ain't never hurt nobody . . .

ONUS: So that's what we are talking about, man. These guys are approaching it from a different angle. That's the whole purpose of this discussion.

OMAR: I've said we could. We could intelligently and reasonably work things out. Me and Opus could, me and this buddy. But if you got something to prove to the world . . . You never hurt nobody, you've never done nothing, you've never been fucked around all your life, then you got everything to prove. I don't have to prove to nobody that I would kill somebody. I ain't got to prove to nobody that I could bust them up. I'm so scared 'cause the law come and tear me all apart. I done all these things. I don't need anything . . .

ONUS: I'm sure, Omar, we've all had been shot, stabbed, beat up, all up, and what have you.

OMAR: Beat up all up and we've done all these things.

ONUS: Now there's got to be a change. There's got to be a change, man. I mean, I know I'm tired of being shot, I'm tired of being stabbed, you know. I've never been stabbed in the joint, but on the streets I have. But, man, there's got to be a change. It's got to start with us. Myself, that's where it's got to start.

OMAR: You're right, but what if I have something to prove and you stepped on my toes? And you stayed out of line with me. [Raising his voice] I stepped outta line with you, right, I got something to prove, let me clear this up. This is what goes on when down there. I got something to prove that I ain't no faggot no more, that I'm trying to be [unintelligible]. You see what I'm trying to say. See, they put me on a cross when I was down there, brothers that was in there trying to knock these guys off, you know. And they put me right up in there, and they come to the door, "Omar" everyday, and these dudes say, "Why this dude's with them? We got to get them outta here." That's what was happening, right?

SOMEONE IN THE GROUP: Why'd you let them come to your room?

OMAR: No, they come to the door hollering at me 'cause they want me to say things.

ONUS: Because most people . . .

ONUS: Most people look at it this way. Association brings on assimilation.

OMAR: That's what happen, that's what happen.

ONUS: Watch who you associate with. Watch how you come off with people, man. If you come off like a tough guy, or you are known to associate with other "booty bandits," then you are considered the same. Don't set yourself up!

OMAR: I didn't. But see, you're right, but that's what happened, right? When they got outta line down there, I stood my ground. I wasn't worried about what you feel, whether you behind me or not or none of this. I'm not living for that right because there's so much things going on down there. Because they, man, say, "You're not trying to get outta here." And they come to my door and tell me, "Throw my trash out on the tier." "What, man? Get the fuck away from my door." Throw no trash on the tier, it don't make no sense. If they're trying to get something accomplished, there are better ways of doing it besides. I never participated in that. I'm not that stupid. I've been around convicts that put the steel in their hand, and what they dehumanizing theirselves and be lowering their morals and all this stuff that was going on. I totally disagree with that, and they would have done some reasonable like write a petition, I would have signed it. But, see, everybody down there and most of these dudes around here be a whole bunch of homosexuals trying to be down [unintelligible]. They be wanting to live other people's lives. They be trying to tell other people what to do. There's only a few people around here I can say I honestly listen to, you know. And a lot of these brothers be running here talking that brother shit. I don't want to hear that shit.

ONUS: What it comes down to, Omar, is the way a person conducts himself. The way he carries himself. The way he feels, the way he . . .

OMAR: That's personality. That don't mean nothing.

ONUS: That's means everything . . .

OMAR: I deal in principles 'cause the guy that . . .

ONUS: That's what we are talking about . . . principles and values. I tell you, I carry myself because I don't have anybody trying to fuck me up. I don't have convicts trying to fuck me up. I don't have the Man trying to fuck me up. I'm left alone. Why is that, Omar?

Onus states that a convict's taking a stand for other convicts is the old way. He espouses a smarter, brighter, and, according to him, more up-to-date way of dealing with authority in the prison. But his message is one of avoidance, anonymity, and not "playing their game." The *chotas* (cops), he says, leave him alone, and in part of the discussion I have omitted, they even put a "mister" in front of his name. He just shines them on. Omar, in contrast, talks in very figurative language of what he calls his "possibilities," which means having to make a decision not to use his shank to "take out" one of his detractors. At one point, he had to prove his mettle and demonstrate that he could be dangerous because the common element was being "fucked over." That's "rep," he tells us. We will learn more about reputation later. He says that taking this position is a way to prove that he is not a "faggot." He is instructed by Onus to watch his associations (e.g., the "booty bandits") in prison because they can lead one astray. We did not inquire about this interesting typification—"booty bandits"—but it seems to refer to tougher men who steal from less-secure inmates—whatever "booty" they can take.

Omar answers Onus's question, "Why is that, Omar?"

OMAR: Why is that? You're just a lucky guy, man.
ONUS: Luck? Is that all? Just luck? Doesn't it have nothing to do with the way I believe and the way I carry myself?
OMAR: You have a lot to believe in the position you take.
OMAR: Okay, and what I believe and how I apply myself.
OMAR: That's the same way now.
RESEARCHER 1: That is, for the therapy session.
OMAR: Can I clear up one thing, then go on?
RESEARCHER 1: No. Let's get back to the culture thing and pick this thing up on Friday.

DEVELOPMENT OF REPUTATION

OMAR: That's fine with me.
RESEARCHER 1: I think what we have to do is, I felt that section was real good on the *veterano*, but I think we need to move on and try to look at some of . . . I don't know what your background is, but most people in this room have been raised in institutions and have been raised by the state. Well, what I'd try to get into is try to look at that in terms of you know, how did, what developed in terms of giving you some kind of map to live by?
ONUS: That's what we're talking about, behavior. Principles and values and the way that convicts apply themselves.

RESEARCHER 1: But how did it develop? What happened when you came of age twelve, age nine, or whatever, you came into a state—

OMNI: I think when you come to jail, you know, when you first come to jail, you're not aware of those things, you know, don't back him down. *No te rajes*, you know, to back down or to be a pussy about anything, a man, you know. Once, like somebody's come when you're small [young], man, when you first go to the pen, and they, this guy says, "Man, well, this guy wants to fight you, you know." And they tell you, *No te vayas a rajar*, you know. Because if you don't, you know, his value is that you start getting for yourself and that starts getting to you, man, you know . . . getting in your mind *que no te vas a rajar*, you know. And that don't just mean in fighting or starting becoming your beliefs.

RESEARCHER 1: How? What's the difference in that and what you experience when you were in the streets? How does it change?

RESEARCHER 2: Could the same thing happen in the streets?

Several: Yeah, I say so, oh yes. You're right. Yeah.

OMNI: Yeah, but you are not fully aware of it.

ONUS: Not to a degree, not to a degree.

RESEARCHER 1: It's a difference in degree?

ONUS: Yeah, because in here everything is magnified, okay? It's more intense, feelings are more intense. Inside it's more intense.

OMNI: Yeah, and it's a different method, too, because the same thing we're talking about here, about being told what to do, you know, when you're little [young] the same thing here, the same thing applies to signing the petition, man! And the same way is that someone is sending you a petition, then you sign it.

RESEARCHER 1: So you gotta do it?

OMNI: That's it.

ONUS: Now on the streets, man, you are able to take the source. . . . I'm not packed into a small little area like you are a penal institution, okay? If something starts to come down, man, either you can go ahead and confront it and get down [get into a fight] or you can go and get jerked off [makes a slapping motion]. Now in the instance that you do get down, even on the streets, after it's over with, you're still floating up, into other areas. . . . In here that don't happen. You can't go on because you're surrounded with this constantly even though you get into the hassle. After the hassle is over, the dudes are in the same place. You don't go anywhere.

The influence of the peer group is critical in developing a self that will not back down. In the penitentiary the problem of living in a crowded and tense environment becomes even more critical. One is in the same cell block, and is goaded into actions that one may not want to engage in—but you are forced by the edict *No te rajes.* One must deal with all types of inmates. In the previous chapter, the idea of "taking care of business" was seen as an important tenet of the convict code.

RESEARCHER 2: Is it possible that some of these incidents [fights] could flare up five, six years later . . . ?

ONUS: Yes, it can.

RESEARCHER 2: And that continues to agitate or . . .

ONUS: Yes, yes, it can.

INFLUENCE OF FAMILY

RESEARCHER 1: When on the streets, though, before you go into the state raising, you have aunts, uncles, you have parents. So what difference do they make? How does that change you?

ORBIS: I wouldn't know. I never had that.

ONUS: I don't think it changes much because I think your reputation beats you to the institution. The guys that you beat up while you were in the streets are in the institution with you. You know, they're there before you get there. They hear that you're coming up. And you're expected to act in a certain way whether you act that way or not.

RESEARCHER 1: What differences do parents make?

ONUS: Right, that's what you're asking. How do people have an effect upon your life? What's the difference?

RESEARCHER 1: Yeah, it sounds like before you get into the state raising, your parents are your teachers. I mean, you don't have any parents around, right?

ONUS: You're deprived of what's happening with your family, your relations, because they're no longer there.

RESEARCHER 1: Right.

ONUS: So whatever effect they might have had prior to you coming to the institution, that's cut off.

RESEARCHER 1: OK, whatever effect they could, they have had, prior, that's what I'm understanding. What effect did your parents or your uncles or your aunts or whoever you look up to, your adults, before you go, what effect did they have on you?

ONUS: If they would have had a strong enough effect upon you, you would've never went to the penitentiary to begin with. But because they didn't have an effect upon you or your life, something happened that made you go to the joint. So whatever bond that your *familia* placed before you was not substantial enough to sustain you, to keep you together out there. It evolves into something that brought you to prison or take you to Reformatory A, man. It grabs on you.

ONUS: I think that having a family or having people around you—relatives—that care about you has a lot to with what gonna happen in your life. Because Orbis and I talked about it one day, and we come from similar backgrounds. In respect to family life, we never really knew our mothers or father, or we never really had anybody that cared that much about us. So we were on the streets doing what we wanted to do. And while we were out there, it seemed that the only way, at that particular time, we'd gain any type of affection—it wasn't affection, but in our own mixed-up way of thinking it was—it was that we went out and gained reps, we got down. We tried to see who could be the toughest of guys, who could come through, and who could drink the most, who could shoot the most dope, and what have you. And that's where I think the root of it is. We didn't have that, man. And the only way we could get any type of attention at all [was] to [be] one of those people who got down. And this is the cause.

RESEARCHER 1: Where did the culture come in?

ONUS: I think that possibly the culture was denied us. Maybe if the culture itself was exposed to us a lot more than what it was, maybe this wouldn't have happened.

RESEARCHER 2: You keep talking about a convict code. Do you think you could articulate some of the ideas in one-line sentences?

OMNI: That all starts, you know, the first time you come to jail, or before you can come. Because before you came, you met somebody that had been to reform school already, and he's already doing time. [He says,] "It ain't nothing, man." And you're not scared to get here, you know, and once you're in the place and you learn how to jail, and how to adapt yourself to it, it becomes a routine.

OPUS: It seems like culture shock to me, because the first time I came to jail was when I met you in the fish tank [county lockup]. I had been to jail for traffic tickets, that was the extent of it. I was twenty-four years old, nine or ten years ago. And I didn't know nothing. I knew a lot of people that were in jail, and I knew a lot people that had been to Reformatory B, like Opie, or Reformatory A—and guys that were in the fish tank that I knew that I had met in jail. And the first thing somebody told me that I knew previously when I was a youngster was OPIE: "What the hell you doing here?" I'm the guy who was carrying the books, going to school, not missing a day of school, getting straight A's in school. Singing in choirs, doing everything that a straight-A student would do. Plus, I took care of my brothers and sisters because my parents were alcoholics.

ONUS: What he's asking was where does this convict code or how does the convict code apply itself?

RESEARCHER 2: I guess I caught something that Omni was saying, the idea of *No te rajes* is also the idea of don't back down.

ONUS: That's where it all starts. It all starts right there. Like I was saying, about knowing people prior to going into the joints—you have seen people come out of there and you see them as being very strong, very down individuals. That where it all starts in that.

RESEARCHER 2: You can talk about "getting down" and handling those kinds of things. On the *raza* side, you can also talk about being *macho, hombre.*

OMNI: *Un Chicano, to rajarte*, to back down, you know, it's a shame, man! It's a disgrace. So then you try always never to do anything, to back down from anything regardless of the consequences.

RESEARCHER 2: But this also gives you visibility.

ONUS: Yes, it does.

RESEARCHER 2: And it destroys autonomy, or the other word I was trying . . . anonymity.

OMNI: It destroys—from once you get out of here, man, and you go get involved in something else, go robbing a bank or whatever you gonna go do. You know, once you're committed yourself to doing it, say, "Yeah, let's go." But it might give me a feeling in your heart: "Well, man, I really don't want to." *Pero no me voy a rajar.* I can't back down. I can't do stage[?] now. I've already [done that], you know. "All right, let's go man." *Te los pones* [i.e., you put on the role of bank robber or other criminal role].

ONUS: I think what you're saying, too, is that when you hang on this type of attitudes like you standing out, you lose that cover you might have had before you stand up in life. You attract that attention, man.

ORBIS: Well, you know, now that you say, that's what happened to me! I think I got that attitude I have now about things, I acquired in the family drug program, in that type therapy program, and that's being able to say no. Before I could never say no, man. Like you just said, the guys would say, "Let's go, man. I know this grocery store." You know that there's a shotgun in the back or whatever, and know that it's stupid, but you can't do it, you know? But for me, before, I would say, "Ah, well!" Before, I would tell them guys, "Nah, man, I ain't gonna go, man, we can't get away with it," whatever. I would, "Ooh man, let's go," because I didn't want them to think that I have no balls, you know what I mean? So we would go and get busted! I'd go knowing that we were gonna get busted. Where now, the difference with me now is that I can say *no*, man. "You want it, you do it, but I ain't going."

ONUS: And knowing that you're not showing your balls.

SEVERAL: Yeah.

CONCLUSIONS

The session ends with the question, What constitutes a "state-raised con"? The reformatory is a place in which one can develop a "rep." The "rep" is critical for survival; it is that basic. One establishes that one can "get down and bone." Older *veteranos* will test a new guy's mettle when they look him over and tell him, *No te vas a rajar.* For Omni, the "rep" is codified in this simple statement, not to back down. As he said, the "dudes" are looking over the new men and saying to them, *No te vas a rajar*, because the alternative is to be shamed. Part of this training comes from the streets, part of it is learned in the reformatory and in the "fish tanks" (i.e., county lockups) prior to prison.

Being in prison means living in cramped quarters with all kinds of noxious individuals. If a convict has to fight someone, he may have to face that person again because both are in the same compacted environment over a period of time. Feelings are intensified, and it is as Omar said earlier: if one man is getting heat, the rest are upset by that. In the streets after a fight, an individual has more degrees of freedom and lateral movement to avoid some other distasteful person, but not in the intensity of prison life. The ability to manage tensions seems to be an important quality of personal leadership. In the group session, an interesting contrast is made between the convict code, on the one hand, and personal ethics, individual qualities, and personal beliefs and attitudes, on the other.

Parental guidance or family life was either nonexistent or had minimal effect on the men we talked to in the prison. Most of their learning came from the acceptance of significant others in a reference group in the streets or the reformatory. This learning is expressed as determining who can shoot up more dope, take more chances, and impress the peer group more thoroughly. Opie observed his uncle's family, but he was an outsider to it and it was alien to him. He sees that authority in the prison is not his "father" or his "mother," as he calls them. His own upbringing was materialistic and nonnourishing for him. The group in prison has become more important, a result that can be called a confused view of "affection." In another session not reported here, Omni sees the foster-care experience as part of his prisonization experience. The majority of the men in the session were state-raised cons. They reflected more of a "street culture" than an Hispano culture. Omni was determined to base his call on the tenets of the convict code but was largely unsuccessful given the overwhelming nature of the prison experience. In short, each man weighed the impact and looked out for his own interests on the decision to support or not support the petition. In the tension of the prison, ethnicity and any group loyalty are dissipated. Researcher 1 tries unsuccessfully to bring the discussion back to ethnicity and values. What we get instead in this analysis of "talk" is the language of oppressed men trying to "make sense" of a difficult and challenging situation.

◆　　◆　　◆

Two distinct worlds are significant here. One is that of the correctional officers, who have the difficult task of keeping order in an entire institution. It is what Goffman called "trimming," "the shaping and coding into an object that can be fed into the administrative machinery of the establishment, to be worked on smoothly by routine operations" (1961, 16). Thus institutions have to maintain order and control within the environment. As part of the programming process, organizations stress obedience to rules. Organizations often resort to withdrawal of privileges to get compliance to rules. The world of the correctional officers is a world of control, rules, regulations, and authoritarianism. The world of the prisoners is a world dictated by the code of the street, of growing up in a culture of crime, and of being influenced by one's peers, which continues into the mature phase of the prisonization experience. The two epistemologies are in conflict with each other, and so prisoners and guards are suspicious of each other, leading to further stress for each group. It would be interesting to do a study of the guards' worldview. We were told that high rates of alcoholism, stress, divorce, and physical ailments exist. Do guards develop a classification of inmate and behavioral types? How do they use and manage "snitches," "rats," and others seeking favor? How do they cope with the verbal and physical assaults? Hans Toch (1977) advocated a kind of life review in prison settings. The kind of "life review" conducted with these men might be applied in other prison settings. Does the life-review method have limitations?

For Hispanos, the veteran role also rises as a principle in the preceding pages. The environment and fear of further punishments overshadow whatever decisions these men are able to make. There are few options except to "mellow out" with each other before they get escorted back to different pods. Several had a very poor understanding of Hispano culture per se. Only one man had deep roots in the southern part of the state, as he still had family members there and called it home, providing himself with some grounding in the family. So the discussion of personal "ethics" as a moral compass was really identification with such street gang "values" as *No te rajes*: having to show "heart" when fighting another man or in "doing a job" with a crime partner.

CHAPTER 8

Curse and Disorder: *El Desmadre*

Battles in academia are so fierce because the stakes are so small.

Common saying

THIS CHAPTER TAKES THE WORD *DESMADRE* AS USED IN EVERYDAY LIFE AND subjects it to a descriptive analysis. To conduct a phenomenological analysis is to bracket what we think we know about an experience. More important, it is to "study . . . the structures that govern the instances of particular manifestations of the essence of that phenomenon. Phenomenology is the systematic attempt to uncover and describe the structures, the internal meaning structures of lived experience" (van Manen 1990, 10). In a book on the argot of the California prisons, Patricia Gutiérrez (n.d.) called *desmadre* "disorder." This chapter is concerned with the social interactional nexus under which *desmadre* develops. Ultimately we would like to arrive at the core meaning(s) of *desmadre*, its *essence*, to use a term from phenomenology. First, we must deal with a number of instances of *desmadre* as heard in daily life.

Origins

A newly installed garbage can in historic West Las Vegas had the word *desmadre* written on it in gang graffiti style, with its overemphasized iconography. Perhaps the author was making a statement of his or her own condition or his or her disapproval of the sprucing up of this section of town for the hordes of summer tourists.

The term *desmadre* is heard in youth. Some of its usages stand out as memories of a group of preteen youths chasing a lizard, pelting it with rocks, and yelling "¡Desmadralo, desmadralo!" (Kill it, kill it!). A fight breaks out during a National Guard drill. The aggressor lands a number of punches. Onlookers egg him on with "¡Desmadralo!"—encouraging the assailant to give the victim the same fate as the lizard. A fellow who worked in a maintenance department used to deal with all manner of situations by making a fist and proclaiming "¡Yo los desmadro!" An elderly man in Santa Fe once told me, "Tienes que cuaidar todo tus biles cada mes, por que si no, te desmadran" (You have to watch your bills every month to make sure they are correct; if not, they will bill you twice for the same thing). The key to understanding the intent of the garbage can image is to amplify the term's meanings from many sources and find a structure in which we can place the above examples.

A CORE DEFINITION

The prefix *des-* means "without"; *madre* refers to the mother. The *Velázquez Dictionary* has seven pages of words in Spanish with the prefix *des-*. For example, the word for lacing one's shoes is *abrochar;* to undo the lacing is *desabrochar* or *desatar* (to untie). Does the term *desmadre* mean a dysfunctional family life or intolerable social situations? The sociology of violence and aggression, imbued with ideas from existential phenomenology, yields rich results. Much of what follows is offensive to life, but one must recognize that it comes from the existential hell in which some people find themselves. The study of this kind of violence can only be captured by a dictionary of disparaging actions and feeling states.*

ENVIDIA Y CHISME

Envy is an all-too-common behavior connected with spreading gossip (Schoeck 1969). *Envidia, mentiras, mitote, desmadre* (envy, lies, gossip, and disorder) are all aspects of the microenvironment connected with linguistic behaviors—for example, the naming of things, events, and social happenings. As the simple calculus in James 3:16 has it, "For where jealousy and selfish ambition exist, there is disorder and every foul practice." This cause-effect relationship points to the havoc the tongue is capable of wreaking. Frederick Sandoval tells us that the seeds of *envidia* occur

---

*When some people find themselves in intolerable situations, they adopt the language of *desmadre*. This would be a study in its own right.

when someone is "experiencing success, fame, power, affluence, popularity, beauty, intelligence, talent, achievement, athleticism or materialism" (1996, 37). To deal with the anxiety or bad feelings aroused by the other's good fortune, one begins a covetous verbal attack on the other. These elements are the basis of *mitote* (gossip) and, more generally, to *desmadrar* another person. St. James serves sociology by crystallizing the effects of bad talk and the creation of social disorder. The "epistle" presented here is about the social havoc and discord of *desmadre* created in the social interactional setting. In this sense, St. James may help at the beginning, but we have to do more with *desmadre* as a generic term that defines all manner of social and lingual events. We shall start small with *mitote*, then consider lying and the intentionality of consciousness, and build a case for *desmadre*.

MITOTE

Mitote, as known to Hispanos, can be found in a three-party interaction. In a senior center, a board member spreads *chisme* (gossip or *mitote*) about the qualifications of one of the secretaries. The director of the program brings the *chisme* to the secretary, who repudiates the claim. Later, in the staff meeting the secretary "calls out" all the parties in the interaction. She confronts the board member by calling her a *mitotera* (gossip mongerer). She calls the center director a *pendejo* (stupid fool) for not verifying for himself the quality of her work rather than bringing the complaint to her without checking its veracity and thus pitting her against the board member. A dicho (folk saying) holds, *Para ser pendejo no se requiere maestro* (To be stupid does not require a teacher). Who is the victim in this three-party interaction? A near perfect term is suggested next.

MORALITY IS SOCIAL

In barrio Spanish, the brute term *joder* reflects the feelings invoked in the senior center example: to "fuck around with" or to "fuck up" (*American Heritage Spanish Dictionary* 1986). This term is applicable across a variety of situations. In the betrayal experience, one might say, *Me jodió* , or *Me jodieron* if it is the act of a group. When an event or situation goes bad in northern New Mexico, one exclaims, *¡Que joda!*, without thinking of the deeper meaning. In other words, one is always in a position to judge the other's action and its effects on oneself. Reasons must be found "not to explain but to justify, to legitimize, that is, to appeal to a right" (Ricoeur 1974, 298).

In reflecting on a motive behind an assessment of an act against oneself, one raises "the motive to the level of a judged value, [and] also make[s] it an occasion of contact between myself and the other" (Ricoeur 1974, 298). I learn to evaluate my acts in evaluating those of others. As Ricoeur says, "It is the nature of the will to seek reasons: in terms of them it moves beyond social valuation and finds roots and context in them. Thus the reflective character of valuation gives to the value judgment a significance comparable to judgments of responsibility." One has feelings "in the project," and "it is the project which has value" (Ricoeur 1974, 298). One indulges in a further act of consciousness. As "I reflect on the value of the project, I partially set aside its thrust. Thus valuation is a drawing back to question the legitimacy of my project and my own value because the project is myself" (Ricoeur 1974, 298). The event has affected one directly, for one has a stake in what happened. One's evaluation of another person's action toward oneself can be benign or hostile. If hostile, the need to make a valuation develops. Generally confronting the other about perceived malice results in a name, some "vocabulary of motive" (Mills 1970), to help one understand that what the other did is unjustifiable. The other's vocabulary of motive may take the form of "I didn't mean it" or "It was not intentional." A dicho says, *Cae mas pronto un hablador que un cojo* (The liar will fall down before the lame will). One thinks that the other's action was intentional, therefore a conscious act, leaving one in an ugly rage.

THE LIE

A dicho says *La mentira dura mientras que la verdad llega* (Lies exist only until uncovered by truth). According to Sartre, each person has the capability of self-negation in many forms. Take irony.

> In irony a man nihilates what he posits within one and the same act; he leads us to believe in order not to be believed; he affirms to deny and denies to affirm; he creates a positive object but it has no being other than its nothingness. Thus attitudes toward the self permit us to raise a new question: What are we to say is the being of man who has the possibility of denying himself? (Sartre 1965, 137–38)

This is "self-negation" in the general sense. In Spanish, it is sometimes said of a liar *se desnegaron*—the act of self-negation that creates a lie to cover another lie, therefore first lying to the interlocutor and second to oneself to cover the first lie.

According to Sartre, the lie has a transcendent character. It is a cynical act in which the liar affirms a truth within himself, denying it in his words, and denying the denial to himself. This double negation refers to the transcendent because it does not exist, and the original negation refers to a truth that Sartre calls "facticity" (1965, 138). It is important that the lie must affect the consciousness itself because the liar has it in mind (i.e., in his consciousness) to deny the denial to himself and to the other. He must know the "facts" of the situation (i.e., its facticity), but also finds that he must cover up the original negation of truth. The second step is to make the lie transcendent, for example, in the weak excuse "It was not intentional." It is plausible to say that the lie as it exists in consciousness and in the liar's intentions must also take the next step—that is, to will itself or its "manifestations" (which are transcendent in the statement, "It was not intentional") into action. One aspect of the lie is in consciousness, the liar's knowledge that what he or she is about to launch into action as "truth" is a new construction. Rollo May (1969) tells that cognition and conation (i.e., thinking and willing) are one and the same. Lying is intentional in that it is intended to distort, and hence make the lie transcendent.

BAD FAITH

The person who says, "It was not intentional," means by his action that *it* was intentional in the sense that an intelligent being has already designed to confuse, obfuscate, and negate his participation in his truth—in short, to lie; otherwise, he is not a conscious being. He is the person of "bad faith," as Sartre has called it, or *una persona de mala fe.* Sartre calls bad faith *mauvaise foi,* which is a wonderful analogue to *mala fe* in Spanish. People sometimes act *con mal intento, con malas intenciónes o fe* (with bad intents or out of bad faith). As children sometimes act, we act out of *mala voluntad (de mala fe)*—an act done or conducted literally in "bad will" or in bad faith. It is an intentionality of consciousness dedicated to obfuscate, lie, and deceive.

In "Saber adivinar no es difícil," Roberto Mondragón tells us, "Los árboles y los hombres por sus frutos se conocen. Un árbol que da manzana, ha de ser un manzano. ¡Igual que si un árbol da pera, debe de ser un peral!" (Trees like men are known by their fruits. An apple tree produces apples. Equally, a pear tree produces pears) (Mondragón 2000, 5). People are known by their acts (fruits). *Mitote* and its *entrañas* (like briars full of thorns) exemplify the social disorder and chaos of *desmadre.* It can refer to historical time periods that reflect social disorder for a people, such as those years when the Santa Fe Ring operated in the late nineteenth century to take away, by all manner of schemes, the common lands of Hispanos. In the sociology of the microenvironment, any situation that leads to pain and disrelationship (i.e., strain) can be seen as *desmadre* or what St. James's letter calls disorder. *Desmadre* is implicated in human acts. Some acts are recognized as *desmadrando* (doing someone in).

A biology instructor in a small school is surprised that a faculty meeting is taking place. Why was he not invited to the meeting? He eavesdrops. He is horrified and dismayed that he is the object of discussion. His character and capabilities are under attack! His assessment of the situation is later given in Spanish: "¿Y sabes que?" he asks. "¡Me estaban desmadrando!" As the old dicho says, *El que escucha, mierda enbucha* (He who eavesdrops gets his feelings hurt by what he hears). The point to note is that *desmadre* language is not restricted to the streets, middle schools, jails, and prisons, but can be found in all walks of life, including university departments.

EL HOMBRE COMO JODIDO

"What *Homo sapiens* needed as much as the air he breathes," wrote Becker, was "the symbolically contrived meanings that keep his action moving forward and gave him an imagined sense of his own worth," which are opposed to "the chaos of undependable and immoral behavior in his fellow men, the chaos of unregulated, irresponsible social life" (Becker 1971b, 62, 111). We come now to a species of man we call *Homo jodidus*, a playful take on the term *jodido*. These are the men and women who perpetrate the violence of lies, *mitotes*, envy, and other social maladies. This species is known by its acts much in the manner of Mondragón's trees. This involves people's behaviors and not some psychic condition. It is a pessimistic view, but according to Nikolai Berdyaev, pessimism at least recognizes that people suffer at the hands of others: "Pessimism is more noble than optimism, because it is more sensitive to the evil, sin and suffering involved in the depths of life" (1965, 325). It is a relative pessimism because absolute pessimism is not permitted in Christianity. The intent here is to consider the social acts of *desmadre* as intentional and their victims' experiences as misery.

El jodido (*el hombre como jodido*) is known by his acts. *El que jode es de mala fe* (He is a person of bad faith). *Jode a otros y los dejan jodidos* (He messes with others and leaves them in bad shape). *El que jode "es de mala voluntad"* (He who messes with others is of bad faith). Our parents used to say that he or she is a person with bad intentions toward others, or worse, toward us. The acts remain as hidden bad intentions, but definitely evil in their implications and in their consequences, that is, causing the suffering of others. They create social schisms among individuals, producing what Ricoeur (1986) calls "fallibility." In Ricoeur's philosophy, *fault*—as in a geological line in the earth that indicates where an earthquake may occur—points to the schisms and their attendant miseries. Social schisms are recognized in the psychotherapeutic literature and in the literature on violence. Denzin's concept of schizmogenesis refers to interactions that generate schisms, conflicts, and contradictions between two interacting units (which can be individuals, groups, or cultures). A second point is that the process of schizmogenesis is at "once temporal, historical, dialectical and self referencing, while based on emergent, spurious and fearful spontaneous interactions. Such interactions turn on, multiply and elaborate reciprocal, interactional, and exchange expectations that do not tend toward equilibrium and distributive justice" (Denzin 1984b, 483). This process applies to the phenomenology of violence, called "negative symbolic interaction," which destroys the very values on which interaction is initially built (Denzin 1984b, 485–86). Persons are victimized and suffer the consequences of such acts whether they are in violent families, prisons, or disordered organizations.

JODIENDO

According to Rubén Cobos, *jodido* means "to be badly off." For example, "Está bien jodido; perdió todo lo que tenía" (He is really bad off; he lost everything he had) (Cobos 2003). He does provide us another New Mexican usage as in "Hicieron un baile pero jódon" (They provided a first rate dance) (Cobos 2003). Cobos does not deal with the term's sexual connotation. In another dictionary, *joder* is defined as "to annoy," "to bother," and "to have sexual intercourse." The *American Heritage Spanish Dictionary* (1986) gives its vulgar meaning, which refers to the act of being "fucked up," or, we may add, "fucked over." The allied term is *chingado.*† *Jodido* and all its implications seem easier to speak about. All have vulgar connotations, and yet some people commonly use them in everyday life. The *joder* family of words is a different approach that does not use the *chingado* family of words to deal with interactions where someone is hurt by another's nefarious interaction.

The term *jodido* forces us to look at an interaction turned foul, whereas the talk about *nos jodieron* is about the way we were done in by someone. One can look at a class of historical events, for example, *Nos jodieron con la tierra y el agua* (They stole off our land and water) or, more intimately, the way a colleague spreads rumor and innuendo to gain a "step up" with a "boss." The focus is on the perpetrator when he is declared a "real *vato jodido.*" Because the perpetrator can also be female, we can speak about her by changing the *o* to an *a*. We know him or her in daily life when others warn us, *Cuidate con ese/esa, es muy jodido/a* (Watch out for that one, she'll/he'll do you in). We sometimes are forewarned about a person's reputation for treasonous and duplicitous behavior. It is only post hoc that the words sink in, that we have been "done in" or someone has "put it to us." It is a violent act! He (or she) is one to watch for, but because such people gravitate toward power, it is too late, and we feel our feelings darkening toward the *jodido(a).*

Social identities arise in interaction. A simple example is that of prison "rats" (*ratas*) who snitch on other convicts. In the convict code, prohibitions against snitching are paramount. It should be noted that "rats" exist in junior high schools,

---

† Octavio Paz (1961) covers this latter term extensively.

social organizations, and all manner of other departments. The *rata* is also sometimes called a *lambe*—the proverbial bootlicker. *Lambes* in the university do not maintain faith with their colleagues, but "maneuver" for their own benefit at the cost of the group, just like *ratas* in prison. The view must be post hoc as *los hombres jodidos* engage in acts that create pain and misery for others. It is a passive violence that occurs behind the scenes, not openly, and not in front of oneself where one can at least defend one's honor. The *hombre jodido* can be found in all strata of social life—landlords, university colleagues, politicians, commanders in the military, businesspersons, husbands, fathers, and lovers. The Mexican singer Yolanda del Rio sings passionately and painfully about several types of men—sexual philanderers and drunks—who neglect their families and ignore the misery wrought on others. In one song, "Tus maletas en la puerta" (Your suitcases are at the door), del Río is throwing out an alcoholic, abusive husband. She sings:

Que creias que toda la vida	Did you think that all my life
te iba estar aguantando	I would continue to tolerate your abuse
no creias que ya decedida	you did not think that once decided
te mandara al Diablo	I would send you to the devil
pero segues llegando borracho	but you continue coming in drunk
y hasta sin el gasto	and having spent all the money
a mis hijos no mas asustando	my children are frightened
que oyen que me insultas	to hear your insults
y me das malos tratos	and your ill treatment of me

(del Río 2007)

The same can be said about abusive men on this side of the border.

We say *Ese me jodió* once we realize that the interaction has turned foul or that someone has spoken badly (i.e., enviously) about us. It has just gotten back to us, and it creates psychic pain. The problem of *desmadre* is the inability to carry out one's personal role in a relationship. How can one be a more effective parent or spouse if the husband or wife is always drunk or abusive? The perpetrator cannot be trusted to fulfill his or her proper role. He or she is unpredictable. The social situation prevents the victim from becoming a better human being, from realizing his or her potential. It is "viviendo suspendida con susto" (living suspended with fright), as one domestic violence survivor proclaimed. Ernest Becker noted that it is the kind of depression that leaves people with the inability to act in order to change their circumstances. To act is to create meaning in life (Becker 1964). In some domestic violence situations, the inability to act means the individual will remain in these venomous interactions.

BARRIO MEANINGS

The elemental idea of the menacing *Te voy a partir de tu madre* (I will tear you from your mother) is the etymology of the *desmadre* term. *Partir* (to part) is related to *parting* and to give birth; the term *parientes* refers to relatives; and a *partera* is a midwife. The latter role involves the literal parting of the child from the mother. The nontoxic definition of *desmadrar* is "to separate animals from their mothers" (*American Heritage Spanish Dictionary* 1986). Specifically, *partir de la madre* is a neutral phrase until one realizes that it can refer to a violent act, that is, the killing of newborn animals. To threaten a child or another person with *Te voy a partir la [de tu] madre* is ominous because it represents being deprived of one's mother, her love, nurturance, and, worse, life itself. Barrio-speak shortens it to *¡Tu madre!*, often with accompanying gestures. In this sense, *desmadre* becomes the horrific representative of a threat, a deep, menacing, gnawing fear of being swallowed up by unknown dangers.

THE PSYCHIATRIZATION OF PRIVATE TROUBLES

To perceive why Mexicans, Mexican Americans, and Hispanos devalue and curse in the name of the mother, consider Santiago Ramírez's syndrome of *importamadrismo*. It postulates three basic components of the Mexican psyche derived from childhood: (1) an intense relationship between mother and infant; (2) a weak father-son bond; and (3) a traumatic experience from early weaning with consequent feelings of abandonment by the mother (Ramirez, cited in Herrera-Sobek 1990, 83). The devaluation of the mother in popular expressions involves a denial type of defense mechanism that states the opposite of what the person really feels (Herrera-Sobek 1990, 14). As Ramírez puts it,

> If anything is valuable to him, the Mexican, it is precisely that—his mother. In some of his articulations and his popular expressions he is denying the object to whom he is profoundly attached. In other forms of expression the truth and the bond with the mother is [*sic*] more clearly manifested such as in songs or when and individual states "they hit me in the mother" [equivalent to the English expression "they kicked my ass"] or "they broke my mother" [a poor English equivalent: "they beat me up badly"]. He is expressing that it is precisely that early bond with the mother that is important; without it he loses all contact and all strength. (Quoted in Herrera-Sobek 1990, 14–15)

The concept of *importamadrismo* "medicalizes" a supposed syndrome from common language. The term, as heard in New Mexico and elsewhere, must be considered from the existential-phenomenological perspective as a social interactional frame of action within the intentionality-of-consciousness model and not a malady of national character based on faulty families.

Montiel's point about the psychiatrization of experience and about not making the family the problem remains a valid criticism when we allow national characterizations to become the basis of understanding (Montiel 1970). The compressed word *importamadrismo* is evaluative of a consciousness of a social situation, for example, when we say of an individual (or he or she says) *Le* [or *Me*] *importamadre* (I don't care anymore), referring to the social circumstance in which the individual finds him- or herself.

Phenomenology holds that language and words are used to dress our actions. Moreover, we are word edifices, the means by which we as social beings traffic, create, and derive meaning in the world (Becker 1971a). Schutz's theory of typifications proposes that the lifeworld is presented in language that explicates our situations in the world (1971). For the Mexicano, Chicano, and Hispano, the language of *desmadre* is an existential explication of one's being-in-the-world, of feeling *desmadrado* in a world with others. Psychoanalytically derived theory about the son, a weak father figure, and a rejecting mother captures but a small portion of the whole. Only when we put these psychoanalytical perspectives into a broadened view of the person in his or her lived experience can we achieve Becker's larger insights. Becker notes that it is the loss of "game"—that is, the loss of significant social interactions and meaning structures and the inability to keep forward motion going, getting bogged down in the loss of meaning and in depression—that is significant to social life (Becker 1971a). The social interactional components of game form the basis of Becker's comprehensive theory of depression (Becker 1964). Game is any satisfying social interaction that makes life meaningful and predictable. Accordingly, the language of *desmadre* as a disparagement of meaning is crucial. We need to remember that words create worlds. Meaning structures are socially constructed in the social process of the lifeworld (Becker 1971a).

LOS DESMADRAZGOS DE RICARDO SÁNCHEZ

In *Canto y grito mi liberción y lloro mis desmadrazgos*, Ricardo Sánchez writes about his life prior to becoming incarcerated, about life in the penitentiary, the support of his wife and children, and his subsequent liberation by the Chicano movement (Sánchez 1995). He served time in "La Tejana"—the Ramsey Prison Farm in Texas. The depiction of this life is *viviendo desmadrado* (a lived existential condition). Sánchez's penetrating "consciousness" of insights is alarming in its anger and rage at the brutality of "prisonization" (imprisonment).

I was encloistered in a prison of inculcated hates; hates that reached out and in to kill me and mock me; hates designed to shred my humanity so that ameriKa could have shredded human-ness for breakfast—a blood pudding kind of feast, and i realized it not. Time frames exploded like expletives bent on carnage, and i came to for the nth time. *Muerto sin saberlo*, and refuge has stone walls, iron bars . . . refuge was *grifa* and mordant isolation leading to total self-abnegation. Brown . . . brown . . . brown and the mirror shattered. I stared it down—it capitulated. Rant and rave, you bastard conscience . . . it is no joy being the sum total of the Chicano experience . . . merged you are in the *desmadrazgo* of *hispano* father and Indian mother, half-breed son-of-a-bitch whelping in your wilderness with a cross for a banner and *crujías* for a crutch . . . there twixt *el gran putismo* of life in the u.s.a. coalescing with *desmadrazgo* and *espiritualismo*, and my manhood shrivels when I view my self-flagellation promenading like the great paradox, and sometimes my questions are rhetorically answered by *patronismo* . . . and do I recoil? Once in a while.

> el hijo de la chingada
> es un vato que es muy loco,
> su vida muy desmadrada,
> del mundo le importa poco.
> (Sánchez 1995, 152–53)

One aspect of Sánchez's work is its expression of hatred of all kinds, hatred designed to inculcate self-negation that "shreds" the protagonist's basic humanity. Another emerges as livid, pure, unadulterated rage. The man is totally *encabronado*, a term some men in a domestic violence group used to mean "angered," but this translation falls short. Sánchez typifies part of his rage as a product of an Indian mother and an "hispano father," "a half-breed son-of-a-bitch whelping in your wilderness." This is another *desmadrazgo*—the sum total of the (his) Chicano experience. His rage is that of "death and havoc cohabitating," "un duelo angustioso" (an anxious hurt), painful wounds distorting all perception. He became "una bestia sin corazón," a beast without heart (Sánchez 1995, 152–53).

The brutal prisonization produces a *grito* (cry) of pain, despair, anger, and hate without bottom—*sin fondo*. It is the outcry of the downtrodden, the oppressed, and of those without hope. *Del mundo les importa poco* (the world matters not to them). It is the meaning of the compressed (concatenated) word *importamadrismo*. The world has ceased to be of importance. This compressed word inculcates the elements of not caring, not giving a damn about anything. What does this mean? Is it a complete break with responsibility? If one does not care, one will take all manner of risks, engage danger, and challenge others to encounters, for example, fistfights or the more serious "get downs," as the men in the prisons told us in 1983. There is no restraint; chaos and the daimonic (May 1969) win out over prudence and good judgment. The daimonic will be fully developed below.

YOU MISERABLE BASTARD

An Hispano *dicho* tells us, *Cuando se muere el perro se acaba la rabia* (When the dog dies, so does the rage [rabies]). For some men, who rage all their lives, making their wives, girlfriends, sweethearts, and children feel frightened and threatened, the rage will end only when they die. The domestic violence is an epidemic, as is all too commonly reported in the press.

In the domestic violence story line, he is the cause of her unhappiness and discomfort, the source of fear in the family. The emotional outburst may give way to a hideous truth. She calls him a "miserable bastard," laying bare his *desmadrazgo*, which is an intolerable situation. "You miserable bastard" typifies her venting of all she has seen of his behavior and what the family has been living through. In her "psychological autopsy," she comes to identify the "pathology" in him rather than in herself or in the family. She "calls him out." One might go further and identify "authoritarian bastards" and other species of "miserable bastards" who make life intolerable for others, for example, administrators, faculty, employers, military commanders, and petty bureaucrats. Their narrow, authoritarian, and stingy perspective gives them many invidious labels. Denzin provides an example of the emotional outburst:

> I went up to the sonnafabitch and told him I hated him. He was standing there so smug and calm in front of a group of people at the party. I said, You really screwed up my life. I've hated you for a long time. Now I just have pity. You miserable bastard. I hope you die and go to Hell. You've f——d up everybody's life you've ever touched. You're a miserable excuse for a human being. I don't see how anybody can stand to talk to you, let alone be seen with you. (Denzin 1984b, 502–3)

One thing seen in work with groups of male domestic violators is the "*hombrecito* [little man] thing," that is, the child making an oath that once he gets older and stronger he will avenge his mother's suffering. One presenter at a domestic violence conference said he made a pact with his brother that they would get even when they got older. When they came of age physically, they tried giving their abusive father antifreeze in his bottle. "Know what?" said the presenter. "He didn't die!" Regrettably, some *hombrecitos* learn all too well how to become abusers themselves.

SUMMARY

Ricoeur uses the metaphor of a geographic fault for fallibility. Fallibility is not about finding fault in persons, but about considering fault as a rift between people (Ricoeur 1986). The rift-gap-fault metaphor points to that which creates pain and hurt between individuals, and within and between groups. Fallibility can be connected to bad faith, for example, the person of bad faith (*de mala fe*). Some people operate in bad faith. *Hacen todo no por lo bien pero de mala fe* (All they do is not for good, but in bad faith). It is will gone asunder. In Spanish, it resonates within the term *mala voluntad*. People of goodwill are understood to be assistive of others. Persons of *mala voluntad* create schisms, pitting groups against one another for personal gain or amusement.

May, Kazantzakis, Becker: A Possible Synthesis

In this section, I examine the broader meaning of what has been presented thus far. It is an attempt to "make sense" of the negative splitting forces that tear individuals or groups apart. We are concerned with the broader meanings of dealing with our antagonists and with the schizmogenesis we experience in daily life.

In *Love and Will*, Rollo May proposes a number of interesting ideas emanating from Greek thought:

- "The daimonic is any natural function that has the power to take over the whole person" (May 1969, 123).
- "If the daimonic is shown particularly in creativity, we should find the clearest testimonies to its presence in poets and artists. Poets often have a conscious awareness that they are working something through from the depths which push the self to a new plane" (May 1969, 127).
- Violence is the daimonic gone awry. It is "demon possession in its starkest form. Our age is one of transition, in which the normal channels for utilizing the daimonic are denied; and such ages tend to be times when the daimonic is expressed in its most destructive form" (May 1969, 130).
- "Thus the destructive side of the daimonic is deplored; but we turn a deaf ear, indeed play ostrich, to the fact that the destructive side can be met only be transforming that very power into constructive activities" (May 1969, 130).

Any obsession—envy, jealousy, power, sex, money, authority, work, alcohol and drugs, perfection—has the power to take over men's and women's lives and destroy them. We can add the rage, anger, and violence as additional parts of the daimonic force gone awry.

In a discussion of human types based on the ideas of Kierkegaard, Becker identifies the weak man who "asserts himself out of defiance of his own weakness, who tries to be a god unto himself, the master of his fate, a self-created man." "He will not be a weak man, a passive sufferer, he will plunge into life, a restless spirit . . . which wants to forget. Or he will seek forgetfulness in sensuality, perhaps in debauchery" (Becker 1973, 84). One is reminded of Samuel Ramos's discussion of the *pelado*, a lowlife in Mexican society who deals with his insecurity by engaging in "gross and aggressive" language behaviors. "Es un animal que se entriega a pantomomias de ferocidad para asustar a los demás, haciéndole creer que es más fuerte y decidido" (He is an animal, pantomiming a ferociousness to frighten others, making others believe that he is strong and decisive) (Ramos 1965, 84). Ramos suggests that it is all "camouflage," that is, a self-delusional weakness that the *pelado* tries to cover up in front of others. The *pelado* lives in his own vital lie about his being, an abnormal fear of others as well as an uncertainty of the other, or what Ramos calls "desconfía de todo hombre que se acerca" (a man mistrustful of everyone) (Ramos 1965, 56). He is *el borracho terco* (the stubborn drunk) who creates havoc at the bar or at home. This short digression about an insecure man illustrates the idea that any self-defensive mechanism is a characterological lie, that is, a camouflage for weakness. Becker's *Angel in Armor* (1969) is a study of these Freudian "defense mechanisms" (e.g., paranoia, repression, suppression, denial) that hide a weak ego. A point needs to be made regarding defense mechanisms. Becker's treatment of defense mechanisms locates them within the nexus of social life so that they are seen as defenses against intolerable situations and not as an intrapsychic battlefield.

Kierkegaard defines a "demoniac rage" as an inability to take help from another person or even from the "highest source" (1954, 205). It is the sufferer whose self is in despair because of an unwillingness to be who he should be. Becker joins Kierkegaard and calls this a demonic passion, an attack or revolt against life/existence itself, manifested as living for the moment, defiance against tomorrow, an immersion in the body, its sensations, its intensity of touch and smell. The aim of this passion is to deny one's lack of control over events, one's powerlessness, and one's vagueness in a mechanical world "spinning into decay and death" (Becker 1973, 84). Becker does not necessarily see this passion as bad because it is a rediscovery of one's basic vitality as a symbolic animal. The modern world wants to deny one's personhood, even one's own body, to make it a depersonalized abstraction. Becker calls this passion or rage a defiant "Prometheanism." It is a confident view that our power can catapult man into space. It is an empty-headed immersion in materialism and the "delights of technics with no thought to goals or meaning" (Becker 1973, 85).

> On more ominous levels, modern man's defiance of accident, evil and death takes the form of skyrocketing production of consumer and military goods. Carried to its demonic extreme this defiance gave us Hitler and Vietnam: a rage against our impotence, a defiance of our animal condition, our pathetic creature limitations. If we don't have the omnipotence of gods, we can at least destroy like gods. (85)

The daimonic works for both good and evil, for positive and negative, and with constructive and destructive outcomes. As a positive force, it allows propulsion, assertiveness, perpetuation, and augmentation. The daimonic

> becomes evil when it usurps the total self without regard to the integration of that self, or to the unique forms and desires of others and their need for integration. It then appears as excessive aggression, hostility, cruelty—the things about ourselves that horrify us most, and which we repress whenever we can, or more likely, project on others. But these are the reverse side of the same assertion which empowers our creativity. (May 1969, 123)

We can wage war in Iraq as well as provide sustenance, water, and shelter for the victims of earthquakes, hurricanes, and tsunami.

"Daimonic" is also spelled "demonic" or "daemonic," as used by poets, and is derived from the Greek *daimon*. It is the creativity of the poet (i.e., the artist) as well as that of the dedicated ethical and religious leader (May 1969, 123). Its translation into Latin gives us *genii* (or *jinni*). The word *genius* comes from these roots and originally meant a spirit presiding over the destiny of a person. It later came to refer to a particular mental endowment or talent. Like *genius* (from the root *genere*, meaning "to beget, to generate"), the daimonic is the "voice of the generative processes of the individual. The daimonic is the unique pattern of sensibilities and powers which constitutes the individual as a self in relation to his world" (May 1969, 125). The Spanish *genio* means not only "temperament" (as in *Tiene mal genio o es de mal genio* [He or she has a bad disposition] or *buen genio* [a good disposition]), but also "genius," as in the special talents possessed by persons. *Haciendo genios* means "putting on a scowl," that is, manifesting explosive tendencies—hence the reference back to that which drives and takes over the person, such as the obsessions identified above.

Greek thought provides opposites, such as "to tear apart" from *diabollein*, from which *diabolic* derives. Its antonym is *symbollein*, meaning "to throw together," "to unite" (May 1969, 138). The symbolic is critical to "building" society, family life, and individuals. Celebrating family events, such as a child's birthday, going out to eat with one's family, enjoying family trips, or going to the movies, a baseball game, or the zoo are all events that build up family life and are examples of the symbolic, that is, the *symbollein*. The opposite also applies when the father's (or mother's) infidelity, drunkenness, or drug use tears the family apart. These events create schizmogenesis (i.e., *desmadre* fault lines) in groups and families. All issues of morality are basically social, as John Dewey (1922) reminds us.

The concept of the daimonic is objected to because we don't want to be seen as motivated by base instincts (May 1969). The daimonic cannot be boiled down to little demons and angels constituting our nature or motivating our behaviors. It is difficult to accept. Yet when we read in the newspaper about a cruel atrocity, we wonder about our more savage impulses. "Violence is the daimonic gone awry. It is 'demon possession' in its starkest forms. . . . Not to recognize the daimonic itself turns out to be daimonic; it makes us accomplices on the side of destructive powers" (May 1969, 130–31). Indeed, as Rilke says, in thinking about psychoanalysis, if we chase away our devils, our better angels will also flee, which is to say that we need to face our "demons," those aspects of ourselves that frighten us (1948, 51). Perhaps Rilke understood that if the analysis was successful, his devils, the daimonic source of both his creativity and destructiveness, would be destroyed.

In Hispano men's domestic violence groups, one often hears the term *endia-blado*, as if the person is motivated by some *diablo* (devil). Another term for this level of angry violence is *encabronado*. Both terms seem to indicate that a power greater than oneself has taken over. The upshot is that only as we conquer these aspects of ourselves that sometimes dominate us can we be freed from them. That denied part of you "is the source of hostility and aggression, but when you can, through consciousness, integrate it into your self-system, it becomes the source of energy and spirit which enlivens you" (May 1969, 133). May takes from Jungian psychology the concept of the shadow side of the self that represents the opposite sex (*anima* in the case of men; *animus* in the case of women). *Animus* means both a feeling of hostility (a violent, malevolent intention, i.e., animosity) and "to animate, to give spirit, to enliven" (May 1969, 133). Here again Spanish is helpful when we speak of someone whose consciousness is *desanimado/a*: *des-* (without) and *ánima* (spirit), that is, a soulless and depressed person. Contrast that with a person who proclaims that he or she is *animado/a* (animated and motivated). One needs this "possession" or vitality to create art, music, poetry, to build things, to procreate.

May is clear about the confrontation of our demons, the taking in of the daimonic:

> You take in the daimonic which would possess you if you didn't. The one way to get over daimon possession is to possess it, by frankly confronting it, coming to terms with it, integrating it into the self system. This process yields several benefits. It strengthens the self because it integrates that which has been left out. It overcomes the "split," the paralyzing ambivalence in the self. And it renders the person more "human" by breaking

down the self-righteousness and aloof detachment which are the usual defenses of the human being who denies the daimonic. (May 1969, 133–34)

Nikos Kazantzakis is aware of the daimonic, as a passage from his book *Saint Francis* illustrates. Brother Leo addresses St. Francis: "The militant Christian's greatest worth is not his virtue, but his struggle to transform into virtue the impudence, dishonor, unfaithfulness, and malice within him. One day Lucifer will be the most glorious archangel standing next to God; not Michael, Gabriel, or Raphael—but Lucifer, after he has finally transubstantiated his terrible darkness into light" (Kazantzakis 1962, 21).

A longer passage makes clearer the internal struggle to reconcile the *symbollein* and the *diabollein*, and shows Kazantzakis's understanding of the nature of suffering and the "split" referred to earlier.

Francis recalled his parents and signed: "Alas, I still have not managed to reconcile them." "Who? Who are you talking about, Brother Francis?" "About my mother and father, Brother Leo. The two of them have been wrestling inside me for ages. The struggle has lasted my whole life—I want you to realize that. They may take on different names—God and Satan, spirit and flesh, good and bad, light and darkness—but they always remain my mother and father. My father cries within me: 'Earn money, get rich, use your gold to buy a coat of arms, become a nobleman. Only the rich and the nobility deserve to live in the world. Don't be good; once good, you're finished! If someone chips a tooth, break his whole jaw in return. Do not try to make people love you; try to make them fear you. Do not forgive: strike!' . . . And my mother, her voice trembling within me, says to me softly, fearfully, lest my father hear her: 'Be good, dear Francis, and you shall have my blessing. You must love the poor, the humble, the oppressed. If someone injures you, forgive him!' My mother and father wrestle with me, and all my life I have been struggling to reconcile them. But they refuse to become reconciled; they refuse to become reconciled, Brother Leo, and because of that, I suffer." (Kazantzakis 1962, 31)

Of course, the internalized "father" and "mother" are metaphors of the larger struggle. In the case of St. Francis, the two opposing internal dialogues contradict one another. It is this "split" within that is the source of misery.

Another part of the *pinto* (penitentiary convict) dialogue is about the power of the reference group and its demands. One *pinto* was aware of his source of misery as he proclaimed:

Where I was at, man, was misery, man. On a mental level it was misery. I was on that level of misery, and, man, I didn't like it. The peer pressure that I had coming at me . . . it was too much. Oh, I had to do some really fucked-up things, in opposition to my nature. Just to prove to these assholes, man, that I was a man, and I thought these motherfuckers were my friends. But they wasn't my friends because friends wouldn't demand that.

Becker said much about human finitude, finding man living a characterological lie. This vital lie comes out of the terror of the Oedipus stage of development, where defense mechanisms are born to protect the child against anxiety. To deal with the world, we develop stratagems for facing anxiety, maintaining self-esteem, and living and working with self-confidence. "In the prison of one's character one can pretend and feel that he is *somebody*, that the world is manageable, there is a reason for one's life, a ready justification for one's actions" (Becker 1973, 87). We build up a characterology to deny one thing and one thing only, our "creatureliness":

> The creatureliness is the terror. Once admit that you are a defecating creature and you invite the primeval ocean of creature anxiety to flood over you. But it is more than creature anxiety; it is also man's anxiety, that anxiety that results from the human paradox that man is an animal conscious of his animal limitations. Anxiety is the result of the perception of the truth of one's condition. What does it mean to be a self-conscious animal? The idea is ludicrous, if it is not monstrous. It means to know that one is food for worms. This is terror: to have emerged from nothing, to have a name, consciousness of self, deep inner feelings, an excruciating inner yearning for life and self-expression—and with this yet to die. (Becker 1973, 87)

In *The Denial of Death* (1973), Becker invokes Kierkegaard's characterological anxiety to point the way out of the dilemma: facing the reality of who we truly are in order to transcend it. To confront the vital characterological lie is to open up the possibility of unlearning repression, denial, or some other of our defense mechanisms. According to William James, "This is the salvation through self-despair, the dying to be truly born, of Lutheran theology, the passage into nothing of which Jacob Behmen [Böhme] writes. To get to it, a critical point must usually be passed, a corner turned within one. Something must give way, a native hardness must break down and liquefy" (qtd. in Becker 1973, 88). And from Ortega y Gassett: "He who does not really feel himself lost, is without remission; that is to say, he never finds himself, never comes up against his own reality" (quoted in Becker 1973, 89).

The purpose of this "death" of the self is to be

> brought to nothing, in order for self-transcendence to begin. Then the self can begin to relate to powers beyond itself. It has to thrash around in its finitude; it has to "die" in order to question that finitude, in order to see beyond that. To what? Kierkegaard answers: to

infinitude, to absolute transcendence, to the Ultimate Power of Creation which made finite creatures. (Becker 1973, 89)

What a prospect: to shed our character armor, our defense mechanisms, our denial about our drinking, drug taking, or whatever daimonic force has taken over our being and our lives. To be between the finitude of our limitations and the possibility that anxiety brings—that of the infinite—and to find faith, to know powers beyond our own limitations.

Berdyaev's ethic sums up how we should deal with evil:

Act as though you had heard God's voice and are called to participate in His work by free and creative deeds; reveal in yourself a clean and original conscience, discipline your personality, struggle against evil within you and about you, but not in a way to crowd evil and evil men into hell, and set up a realm of hell, but rather really to conquer evil and forward the illumination and transfiguration of evil men. (1965, 190–91)

Finally, Becker concludes, "In Kierkegaard, psychology and religion, philosophy and science, poetry and truth merge indistinguishably together in the yearning of the creature" (1973, 92). From the book of Sirach 3:9 comes this enigmatic statement: "For a father's blessing gives the family roots, but a mother's curse uproots the growing plant."

CHAPTER 9

Leave Taking: *Despedidas*

En Dios descanses Lencho.

> A. Korte remembering a friend

The idea of death haunts the human animal.

> Ernest Becker, *The Denial of Death*

HISPANOS IN NORTHERN NEW MEXICO COMMEMORATE THE DEATH OF A LOVED one with a written narrative referred to as a recuerdo (a remembrance). These narratives (or ballads) share many characteristics of the corrido and its forerunner, the Spanish romance. The romance, a popular form of epic poetry, and the corrido depict events in the lives of heroic, historical, and common folk. Both reflect historical events, describe injustices, depict social values, and present moral teachings elicited from catastrophic social events, for example, a tragic murder, a sentence of death, or imprisonment for a heinous act. An important and fundamental aspect of both the corrido and the romance is that they both come from the common people, *desde abajo* (from below) (Rodríguez-Puértolas 1975) and are meant to be recited or sung in public.

The recuerdo as a form of corrido has the important task of recounting a person's life in an epic, lyric, and heroic manner. The recuerdo is a normative farewell on behalf of the deceased. The ballad, directed to the community, usually tells how the person met his or her death. It serves the added purpose of supplying the survivors with communal support for their loss. These written narratives provide insight into the cultural beliefs and behaviors surrounding Hispanos and death in northern New Mexico.

Many corridos end with a refrain in which the singer takes leave of the audience. This leave taking is called *la despedida* and is normative in the sense that as a social rule one usually takes one's leave in a social interaction. The corrido often ends by identifying the singer with the words *Ya con esta me despido* (I now take my leave). Loeffler writes that the despedida as a poetic convention in the romance dates to medieval times (1999, 2). In Mérimée is found this despedida from the thirteenth century.

Sy queredes sabe quien fiso esti ditado, If you want to know the writer
Gonçalo de Berçeo es por nombre clamado. Gonzalo de Berçeo is the acclaimed name.

(1930, 42)

Newspapers are a favorite outlet for despedidas on behalf of the deceased or by the family of the deceased. A family will place a picture of the deceased in the classified section of a newspaper and often a message seemingly written by the deceased describing a better life in the hereafter. This serves to console the survivors. Other messages from family members express how much they miss the deceased. A despedida is also published on the anniversary of the death. The public nature of these remembrances is related to the Spanish recuerdo. One of my purposes in this chapter is to show how the romance form has been retained in recuerdos from newspapers as part of the family life and folklore of northern New Mexico. Thus, my analysis attempts to account for the cultural-historical genesis that created these concepts—as reflected in the language and thoughts of ordinary people—as well as grounding these concepts in the everyday life of people.

The Romance and Corrido

The romance dates back to the epic poems of eleventh- and twelfth-century France and Spain. Some, like the *Seven Infants of Lara*, may date back to the tenth century (Mérimée 1930). Another predecessor is *Le chanson de Roland*, written by a French cleric between 1096 and 1100 C.E. Perhaps the best known of these epic poems is *El cantar de mio Cid*, which commemorates the epic deeds of Rodrigo de Vivar (ca. 1030–1099), who united Spain against the Moors (Tuck 1977).

The similarities between the corrido and the romance are not casual. Both are characterized by realism and are lyrical in their presentation. A chronological format is used to present the message and the event, and both the corrido and the romance are designed to be sung in public in a sober and simple descriptive manner (Rodríguez-Puértolas 1975). In general, romances and corridos break the verse of an epic poem at the pause (i.e., caesura) in the middle of a verse. Such a break results in four verses from two, creating eight syllabic verses, with four verses to the stanza and the even lines rhyming. Tuck provides an example from *El Cid*:

El Cid a Doña Ximena ivala Abrasar	The Cid was going to embrace Lady Ximena
Doña Ximena al Cid la mano va a besar.	Lady Ximena was going to kiss the hand of the Cid.

(Tuck 1977, 21)

Most scholars agree that the romance's octosyllabic form is the hemistich of the old epic line of sixteen syllables. Mérimée developed classifications of romances, noting that some were traditional (*viejos*) from the fifteenth century and earlier, whereas others were lyrical and *artísticos* (polished in form from the fifteenth, sixteenth, and seventeenth centuries). Then there were those of street origins (*vulgares*), which are "crude in subject and form" (Mérimée 1930, 171).

The predecessors of the romance were the *cantares de gesta* (long chants) that were used to celebrate national heroes or great events (Mérimée 1930, 26). Thirteenth-century authors referred to them as *cantares* (*chants*). It has been speculated that French minstrels earned a living by reciting these verses, either from memory or from copies they owned. Spanish minstrels probably borrowed these *cantares* from neighboring regions in France. These were the *mester de joglaría* (ministers of jonglery) with their origin in the popular poetry of common people and *mester de clerecía* belonging to the more erudite and clerical classes, which developed during the thirteenth and fourteen centuries along with a parallel development of universities. *Mester de clerecía* themes were often religious, liturgical, mystical, romantic, biblical, and even epic (Mérimée 1930, 26–38, 171–72).

Another source for dating the romance comes from the time of the expulsion of the Jews from Spain in 1492 or earlier. Mendoza claimed that the Jews were the best "propagators and conservators of the romance, taking it to North Africa, Greece, the Balkans, Turkey and Tangier" (Mendoza 1974, 21). Campa found in New Mexico an early and well-known romance, "Delgadina," which deals with a father's incest. In the romance, when Delgadina refuses her father's advances, she is forced to die of thirst and hunger (Campa 1946). Campa wrote in 1946 that fifty-four versions of Delgadina ballads were found in "Spanish America," nine of which came from New Mexico, seven from Chile, eight from Puerto Rico, twelve from Mexico, two from California, eight from Cuba, seven from La Plata, and one from Santo Domingo (1946, 30–31). A version of "Delgadina" was sung by Cresencio M. García from Mimbres, New Mexico (Loeffler 1999, 3–4).

As noted in chapter 4, the corrido has different types, just like the romance. Mendoza identifies the corrido by such diverse names as *romance, historia, narración, ejemplo, tragedia, mañanitas,* recuerdos, and *versos y coplas* (romance, history, narration, tragic moral examples, serenades or morning greetings, memorials, and verses and responses) (Mendoza 1974, ix–x). The corrido, like the romance, sings of social values, cultural customs, and injustices.

Some corridos are humorous, critically poking fun at institutions. Others depict the particular beauty of a city, say good-bye to a pleasant region, or describe unusual and rare happenings, like the coming of the railroad. Other themes include military victories, religious events, love affairs, disappointments, jealousies, rivalries, and tragedies (Mendoza 1974, 149–50). A case in point involves the first use of the gas chamber at the penitentiary at Florence, Arizona, on July 6, 1934. It was used to execute two brothers, Manuel and Federico Hernández, for the killing of an old *Americano* miner named Washburn (Sifuentes 1982). A corrido written about this event ends by warning the community against such acts.

The corrido is well known in Mexico and the American Southwest. In its simple form, it can clearly and effectively communicate about events that evoke public sentiments. Thus, like the romance, it effectively depicts a people's heritage, culture, and history. Mérimée's thoughts about the romance are equally applicable to corridos:

> The romance still remains today one of the people's favorite form of narrative verse, because it is easy to write and because its meter is readily adaptable to the average thought of the people, and the average musical phrase. It has never ceased to live and to be cultivated: refranes [refrains] and romances are the two most rustic and most enduring products of Spanish soil. (Mérimée 1930, 172)

Recuerdos and Death

Arellano and Vigil state that the oldest recorded corrido in New Mexico was written in 1832 (1985, 8). It is called "El condenado a muerte" (One condemned to death). The singer of this ballad says that he will soon be led to his death, and so he says his good-byes to his wife and begs forgiveness from all present. Another of these early recuerdos was translated by John D. Robb. This ballad, titled "El Corrido de le Muerte de Antonio Mestes," tells of the death of Antonio Mestas, who fell off his horse in July 1889 near a ridge called El Mogote in New Mexico (Dorson 1964). This recuerdo, like many, serves the deceased by having someone say his or her farewells through the words of the writer-singer.

Many corridos start by proclaiming the date of the event and, in the case of a number of New Mexican recuerdos, God's decision to take a life. Thus, in the Antonio Mestas recuerdo the singer opens with these lines:

In the year of eighteen hundred
and eighty nine in July
On the fifth day God determined
Antonio Mestas must die
That he should be thrown from the saddle
And meet his death on the ground,
Near the ridge of El Mogote
And there his body was found.

(Dorson 1964, 485)

The recuerdo tells us that the cowboy Mestas worked for an Englishman, that Mestas dreamed of his death, how the search party was organized, and finally how a bird directed the searchers to the site where he fell. The ballad ends with Mestas's wife, Martinita, lamenting, "I shall never see my dear husband returning home again."

Another old despedida was published in *El Independiente*, a Las Vegas, New Mexico, newspaper on April, 1, 1930. In this despedida Alegario Baca laments the passing of his wife, Julianita L. Baca. He apologizes for his lack of education. The despedida is presented as published, with spelling errors uncorrected. This corrido is written not only to express Baca's grief but also to say good-bye on behalf of his wife.

La dijo en mi despedida	I say within me my departure.
Pues Tambien Eufelia Baca	Also Eufelia Baca
Demannanita benta	Early morn came
Pues junti con la Virjinia	And with you, Virginia
Tambien Ignacio Trujillo	Also Ignacio Trujillo
Pues junto con la Selina	Also with Selina
Rafaelita y la Gabina	Rafaelita and Gabina
Las dejo con gran dolor	I leave with great pain
Tres hermanos que me quedan	I have three brothers
Del estado de Colorado	Who are in Colorado
Adios Hermano Damacio	Good-bye Damacio
Y mi hermana Trinidad	And my sister Trinidad
Pues adios hermano Antonio	Well good-bye brother Antonio
ya la Julianita se ba	Julianita is departing
Adios mi esposa Querida	Good-bye my dear wife
Ya te fuiste de este mundo	You have left this world

Y me dejates llorando	And left me crying
Aqui solito en el mundo	Alone in the world
Adios Julianita L. Baca	Good-bye Julianita L. Baca
Adios para siempre adios	Good-bye forever good-bye
Lla te fuiste al sepulcro	You have left for the grave
Porque te llamo Dios	Because God called you
Pues pido Indulgencia	I ask forgiveness
A todos en general	From all in general
Amigos Pues lla seba	Friends you all know
El corzon de mi casa	The heart of my home
Mi corazón Despedosado	My heart is departing
En tan profundo dolor	In such profound pain
Lla no Puedo conducer	I can no longer continue
Esta triste Despedida	This sad farewell
Lla Julianita seba	Julianita is leaving
Porque lla esta de partida	Because she is on her way
Alla ba la despedida	This is farewell
Como mi Dios me lo dicta	As God dictated
Adios para siempre Adios	Good-bye forever good-bye
Pues mi esposa Julianita	Well my wife Julianita
El que hizo esta despedida	The one who wrote this farewell
Es de poca educación	Has little education
y de grande Corazón	but a great heart
Para todos sus amigos	For all his friends
y aqui squedo solido	He is now alone
Nomas pegando suspiros	and only sighing
Su nombre	His name
Lo boy a poner	I am going to tell you
Con tinta y papel de plata	With pen and silver paper
Por la boluntad de Dios	By the will of God
Y soy	I am
Alegario Baca	Alegario Baca

(April 1, 1930)

A Philosophy of Everyday Life

Denzin's sociological methodology consists of finding a number of specific social examples of the concept under study (here, the despedida in connection to the recuerdo and the corrido) to show what they have in common across a variety of contexts, linking these symbols to social interaction, and relating these structures to cultural meanings as rules of conduct for everyday life (Denzin 1970a, 452–54). The method is to "sensitize the concept" and find many examples of despedidas to determine what they have in common and to connect them to social interaction. From this commonality comes an understanding of their meaning in everyday life (Denzin 1970a, 455). They are not operational definitions in the sense described in the first chapter; that is, defining the concept in terms or how it will be measured, selecting measuring instruments, collecting a sample, and then subjecting the data to statistical analysis. Despedidas as behaviors in everyday life are implicitly understood by actors as background information. Despedidas are not given much thought and are simply enacted and seen as routine, taken-for-granted activity. Goffman shows how interaction rituals facilitate the presentation of self to others. Thus, deference and demeanor govern the presentation of "face" in an interaction between two persons (Goffman 1967). And Becker observes that one cannot just part from the other, but must watch the person leave while holding one's "face" (1971a).

For Garfinkel, following the phenomenological philosophy of Alfred Schutz, the world consists of rule-governed activities of everyday life. Societal members encounter and know the social order as "perceived normal courses of action—familiar scenes of everyday affairs, the world of daily life known in common with others and with others taken for granted." Garfinkel goes on to point out that despite an immense literature, there are "few methods by which the essential features of socially recognized 'familiar scenes' may be detected and related to dimensions of social organization" (Garfinkel 1973, 21). Moreover, it would seem that the task is to identify "constitutive rules," that is, rules of which one is not aware until they are broken (23). When these norm violations occur in small groups, someone will "invoke the rule" and point to the violation, thus providing a natural methodology for discovering these rules (Jackson 1970).

It is assumed that the formal leave taking (the despedida) is a part of the Hispano's familiar taken-for-granted background knowledge and expectation. When a violation of this norm occurs, the routine grounds of everyday life are disrupted. Death is the one event that ruptures these expectations for normative leave taking. As Hispanos make sense of these events, they abstract meanings from these experiences. Hispanos have assigned the term *despedidas* to a number of experiences related to forms of leave taking. In a broader sense, one might point out that despedidas are the refractive images of death in everyday life.

Various Forms of Despedidas as Leave Taking

Valle and Mendoza developed some of the early work on the forming of social interactions and their terminations in their book *The Latino Elder*. The despedida is the disengagement stage of the *platica* interview. For Valle and Mendoza, *platica* is a form of interview that begins with friendly conversation (*amistad*) that leads to a more serious and deeper level of discourse marked by trust and mutuality. Valle and Mendoza were the first to describe the despedida as a "sometimes lengthy parting conversation" (Valle and Mendoza 1978, 28). In addition, the despedidas between an elderly person and a visitor may involve several notable features, including agreements and mutual assurances of future exchanges of help, thanks to the visitor for time spent together, a tour through a garden, displays of family memorabilia, and gifts of cut flowers, fruit, or food.

In García's study of an English-dominant, second-generation, working-class family, leave taking is seen as consisting of four overlapping interactional levels: the initiation of the leave taking, preparation for it, final joking interaction, and final leave taking (García 1978). These levels are intertwined with Mexican American and Hispano ethnicity as it is modified by familial themes.

Other forms of despedidas manifested in daily life can be cited. Some are associated with death and dying and reflect a sense of the tragic. Thus, the wedding *entrega* is a form of despedida. In this chapter I shall look at various points of leave taking in the funeral process, such as the *entrega de difuntos* (words spoken at the eulogy) and the final *descanso* (resting place). Finally, I present the recuerdo in its classic and modern form.

ENTREGA DE NOVIOS

The *entrega de novios* is a ceremony in which the newlyweds (*novios*) are "given over" (*entregados*) to each other by the marriage godparents (*padrinos*). The newlyweds kneel before the assemblage at the reception or wedding dance. A singer will engage in a long chant, reminding the happy newlyweds of the seriousness and difficulties to be encountered in life. Thus, two four-line stanzas state:

No crean, los esposados,	Please don't believe, newlyweds,
Que aquí se van a engañar	That you will be fooled,

| El estado no es un día | Marriage is not for a day, |
| Es por eternidad | It is for eternity. |

Yo me derijo a la novia	I now address the bride
Con todo mi buen sentido	With my goodly sense,
Ya no hay padre y ya no hay madre	There is no longer father or mother,
Ahora lo que hay es marido	All that you have is a husband.

Adiós, mis queridos padres	Good-bye, my loving parents,
Dueños de mi corazón	owners of my heart,
Ya me voy con mi marido	I leave with my husband,
Echeme su bendición.	Give me your blessing.

The parents, too, express their own sad point of view:

Adiós ya se van	Good-bye, they are going,
Adiós, adiós ya se van	Good-bye, Good-bye, they are going
Dios sabrá si volveran	God only knows if they will return
O nos hechen en olvido.	Or they will forget us.

Needless to say, these forms of *despedidas* at weddings have a profound effect on the sets of parents, the newlyweds, and the guests. The *entrega* links the tragic to what is otherwise a festive occasion. The wedding guests are reminded of the tragic side of life. Octavio Paz maintains that the fiesta is both festive and tragic: "Our fiestas are explosions," he said. "Life and death, joy and sorrow, music and mere noise are united, not to re-create or recognize themselves, but to swallow each other up. There is nothing so joyous as a Mexican fiesta, but there is also nothing so sorrowful. Fiesta night is also a night of mourning" (Paz 1961, 53). Life, marriage, birth, and rejoicing are but one facet of endings, parting, death, and finality.

THE FUNERAL TRAJECTORY

Important forms of leave taking also occur around the death trajectory. Specifically, a number of terminal points exist in which acquaintances can take their leave from a person who is about to die. First, the person known to be terminally ill is visited at home or in the hospital. This practice is called *vísperas* (vespers) and in the past consisted of praying before the terminally ill person or providing a vigil (*velando al enfermo*). One religious and social association that has been in existence for more than a century still provides an *enfermero* (nurse) as well as a person from the association to assist the family with the dying member (Vigil 1984). It is not unusual to see entire families *vigilar al enfermo* (provide a round-the-clock vigil) at a hospital for an older terminally ill person. These visits to the sick and dying are forms of despedidas intended to recognize what the person has meant as a friend and community member.

Once the person dies, the *acompañamiento* (accompaniment) requires that the family of the deceased be visited and given support before and during the funerary process. In Anton Chico, New Mexico, the coffin is lifted and carried on community members' shoulders from the village church to the graveside. Each member is replaced after a short interval so that every person in the community has a chance to accompany the body. Condolences (*el pésame*) are offered to the family of the bereaved at the *velorio*, which is a watching over, a nightlong vigil or wake (Lucero-White 1945, 255). In the past, people did not take death out of the house, but conducted the vigil at home (Medina 1983). Today, the *velorio* for Catholics is actually a rosary in a funeral chapel or at a church. What is noteworthy is that attendees give condolences before and after the rosary. It is another form of the *acompañamiento* and despedida at the *velorio*. Before and during the funeral mass, persons will walk to the front of the church to view the body and to offer *el pésame* to the family on the side pews. The eulogy at the graveside is more a form of thanksgiving (*dar las gracias*) to those in the community *por el acompañamiento*, to those who led the religious services at the *velorio*, and to those who offered support. It is a way to offer thanks for a life that was "on loan" (*prestada*) and to give thanks for one's own family and life. The person giving the eulogy will often thank the community on behalf of the family. In some communities, the people at the graveside service are invited to the family's home for one more repast.

Antonio Medina, from Mora, New Mexico, describes the eulogy, *dar gracias* (the giving of thanks), as a healing and expiating process. He states, "Thus, when a child is born, the community rejoices; when an individual dies, others experience their own death. Life and death are communal experiences. So also is the perception of an unalterable cycle of change that is simply stated, 'Dentro de las vida hay muerte y dentro de la muerte hay vida'" (Within life there is death, and within death there is life) (Medina 1983).

If life is on loan, then it is a duty to "return" life to God. The eulogy, aside from its expiating role of giving thanks (*dar gracias*), becomes another point where communally one can take leave of the deceased with good thoughts about him or her. The *entrega de muertos*, if I may use such a term, is a "returning" of the deceased to the Creator. An unsolicited "eulogy" from a colleague provided the following lines:

Queridos hermanos y hermanas	Beloved brothers and sisters,
estamos aquí para entregar	We are gathered here to

a este hombre que encuentro la	return this man who
mano de Dios.	encountered God's hand.

(Sánchez 1991)

The rest of the eulogy would extol the man's virtues during his life in a long recitation of positive attributes.

Writing in 1941, Jaramillo stated that in the past a black-bordered card would invite individuals to an eight-day mass after the funeral (Jaramillo 1941). A modern version of this *misa de ocho días* was recently published in a Santa Fe newspaper. More often, Hispanos will offer a mass at the anniversary of the death. This mass is called *la misa del cabo del año* (the mass at the end of the year). It is interesting that, in more traditional times, the *cabo del año* mass ended the period of bereavement (*luto*). The practice comes from *luto* ordinances, codified in sixteenth-century Spain, which set the period of time the community should mourn royal personages and common folk (*Enciclopedia* 1930, 881). One article in the *Taos News* provided a firsthand account of the events during a *cabo del año mass.* In general, after mass the relatives gather at the home of one of the survivors for food, reminiscing, and an opportunity to reunite after the tragedy (Mares 1986).

To summarize, the wisdom of the culture has provided many *termini* where family, friends, and community may take their leave from a deceased person and offer support, condolences, food, and other forms of help. It is critical that persons become involved in the process so that the final letting go (*despedida*) can be accomplished with ease and lack of guilt. Reynolds caps this idea by noting that much of the work that goes on in Mexican American funerals functions to end one's relationship with the deceased on a positive note. Thus, comments on "how well the deceased looked," "how much at peace she seemed," and "how good she was in life" are all a part of this ritualized behavior (Reynolds 1970, 261).

STATIONS OF THE LOST

A common sight in New Mexico is a homemade cross, located along a highway which marks where an Hispano(a) died. These crosses are made of various materials, including wood or steel slats. Some people use automobile parts or motorcycle chains, probably from the vehicle that took the victim's life. These *descansos* (resting places) are made and maintained by the family. After Memorial Day or on the anniversary of a death, the *descanso* may have a fresh coat of paint or be adorned with a new plastic wreath from Wal-Mart. In the New Mexico of the past, *descansos* were resting places on the way to the *camposanto* ("holy camp," or, more properly, a consecrated graveyard). In the 1700s the governor had to issue an order forbidding people from

A road despedida (Nacho Jaramillo)

stopping and offering *sudarios* (prayers) at *descansos* due to the possibility of attacks from Indians (Arellano 1986).

Today the *descanso* marks the place, the point in space, where a family member left this earth. As per the requisites of the normative order, the cross or *descanso* also marks a violation of the leave-taking norm. These crosses are thus "stations of the lost."

RECUERDOS AND THE HEROIC

Recuerdos exemplify William James's observation that "mankind's common instinct for reality . . . has always held the world to be essentially a theater for heroism" (James 1958, 281). The recuerdos described in these pages reflect ordinary people facing difficult and terrible situations, including the "ultimate horror"—the anxiety of death (Berdyaev 1959). For the people and events depicted in these recuerdos, the "theater of their action," a phrase Ernest Becker was so fond of using in his books, also reflects the human values of a culture.

Some recuerdos follow the "classic" corrido style described earlier. Some are written as prose at the one-year anniversary of the death, whereas others reflect the family's continuing pain. They provide an outlet for grief, guilt, and tender memories.

In all cases, the public presentation illustrates a characteristic of the recuerdo's relationship to the romances of old.

In "El corrido del segundo teniente Eloy Baca" (The ballad of Second Lieutenant Eloy Baca), the singer tells us early on about the courage of Lieutenant Baca, an aviator during World War II. We learn he was a bright student from Martinez Town, a barrio in Albuquerque. Baca's plane was called *La Chiquita* (Little One). The singer provides the farewell on behalf of the crew:

Adiós plaza del Albuquerque	Farewell Albuquerque
Adiós Estados Unidos	Farewell United States
Nuestro banco es Alemania	Our destiny is Germany
Todos vamos deciendo	All are saying.

(*Compendio de folklores* n.d.)

We learn of the downing of the airplane on July 26 (no year is mentioned) in Germany. Later it is learned that Teniente Baca and his companions are prisoners of war and are not injured, despite thousands of holes in *La Chiquita*. The singer uses the corrido to comfort Baca's mother and brothers.

Eloy escribe a su casa	Eloy writes home,
No lloren que es cobardía	Don't cry because it is cowardly.
Que presentandonos Dios vida	If God gives us life
Nos veremos algun día	We shall see each other again.
Madrecita yo te pido	Dearest mother, I beg you
Que no llores por mi ausencia	Do not cry over my absences,
Que por milagro estoy vivo	Because of a miracle I am alive
Pidele a Dios por paciencia	Ask God for patience.
Algun día volvere	Some day we will see each other,
A tus brazos amorosos	And in your loving arms
Me uñiré con mis hermanos	I will be with my brothers
Y viviremos gozosos	And we shall all be happy.
Vuelen, vuelen aeroplanos	Fly, fly, airplanes,
Sí Alemania nos ataca	If Germany attacks us
Aquí terminan los versos	Here ends these verses
Del Teniente Eloy Baca	from Lieutenant Eloy Baca

Points are commonly made about the Hispano's invoking of God's help in such declarations as *Si Dios nos presta vida y salud* (If God lends us life and health). *Si Dios es servido* (if it pleases God) can also be said. One well-known writer of these forms, Cleofas Vigil, expressed the following in his memorial to a *pariente* (relative):

Este mundo no es nuestro	This world is not ours,
Ni la temporaria vida	Not this temporary life.
Venimos al mundo desnudos	All we have is on loan to us,
Pues ya eso está provado	Well that is proven.
El Creador reclama lo que	The Creator reclaims that
es de él	which is His.
La muerte nos llega en	Death comes to us in
muchas formas	many forms.
pronto se llege este lance	That lance comes quickly.
Pues no somos mas que sombras	After all, we are nothing but shadows.

(Vigil 1991)

The corrido of the self-proclaimed assassin Procopio Rael offers his despedida in the first two stanzas. This particular corrido is also historical: it depicts the activities of the members of the notorious Vicente Silva gang of forty Hispano bandits in the 1880s in San Miguel County, New Mexico. It also provides the moral lesson of the *tragedia* (tragic example).

Adiós mi Padre y mi Madre	Good-bye, Father and Mother,
Echenme su bendición	Give me your blessing,
Que por andar de asesino	Because of being an assassin
Me boy [voy] para la prición [*sic*]	I am going to prison.
Adiós mi querida esposa	Good-bye, my loving wife,
En quien yo nunca pensé	Whom I always neglected,
Acuérdate de tu esposo	Remember your husband,
Que se ba pa' Santa Fé	Who is going to Santa Fe.

(Arellano and Vigil 1985, 156)

The Rael poem was published May 16, 1894, in a Las Vegas newspaper called *El Sol de Mayo*. The singer of this tale is being sent to the territorial prison in Santa Fe. As in many corridos, the singer of the tale identifies himself as he takes his final despedida:

Procopio Rael es mi nombre	Procopio Rael is my name,
Mi historia queda vigente	My story remains pending.

| Puede que en estos diez años | Perhaps in the next ten years |
| Se olvide todo a la gente | People will have forgotten all. |

The Recuerdo as Condolence

The despedida a los muertos takes on a particular form. Many recuerdos start with asking God for enlightenment to be able to write the piece. It generally tells of the good qualities of a person and what he or she meant to others. It ends by providing a spiritual thanks to community members for their recent assistance. "En Memoria de Nuestra Madre Asención Gurule" (In memory of our mother Asención Gurule) was written on February 1, 1940. Only a few stanzas are reproduced:

A Dios le pido licencia	I ask God for permission
memoria y entendimiento,	memory and understanding,
para escribir esta memoria	to write this memorial
de un triste fallecimiento.	of a sad passing.

Mil nuevecientos cuarenta	[In] Nineteen forty
el diecinueve de enero,	on the nineteenth of January,
te fuiste a darle cuenta	you went to give an account
al Juez real y verdadero.	to the real and true Judge.

Lloramos tu despedida	We weep your departure
pero estamos consolados,	but we are consoled,
que tú estas en otra vida	that you are in another life
con los Bien Aventurados	with all the chosen.

Fuiste esposa modelo	You were a model wife
y madre muy cariñosa,	and a loving mother,
debes estar en el cielo	you are in heaven
por ser una fiel esposa.	for being a faithful wife.

Viente y siete años habían pasado	Twenty-seven years have passed
de que papá se había ido,	when our father departed
y ahora se han de haber juntado	and by now you are together
en el lugar prometido.	in that promised place.

(Arellano 1976, 125–26)

We learn that Asención Gurule was eighty-seven years of age when she died. She never faltered in her religion. She was the mother of five children, two sons, and three daughters. Her burial is east of Las Vegas at a place called Trujillo, New Mexico. Finally the recuerdo generally asks for consolation to the family and a benediction from the deceased.

Many recuerdos say simply in one of the four stanza lines, "El Señor se lo (la) llevo" (God took him or her). A recuerdo from Taos puts it simply:

Año del ochenta y dos	The year was 1982
el día que Edna graduó.	The day of Edna's graduation.
Era el 22 de mayo	It was May 22
El Señor se la llevó.	God took her with him.

(Gallegos 1987)

Memoria de Janice Medina

The *memoria* (memorial or recuerdo) for Janice Medina was written by Adelecia Gallegos from Taos. Gallegos is well known for the many memorials she has written in the romance and corrido traditions, which have been published in the *Taos News*. These recuerdos echo public sentiment when someone meets a terrible end or when notable person in the community passes on.

This recuerdo illustrates many of the concepts described in the preceding pages and presents the everyday beliefs of Hispanic New Mexicans as they make sense of the most difficult times in a family's life.

The last words in the second and third stanzas rhyme in this recuerdo. The lines are kept short for clarity and ease of presentation. As in the corrido form, the date and time of the tragic event are presented early. Toward the end of the recuerdo, the deceased takes her leave, declaring her despedida.

Gallegos's purpose in writing the memorial is to console the Medina family for a loss they have suffered. She invokes God's help in lessening her own anguish so that she can write this memorial. Many memorials also invoke God's help at the beginning of the piece by asking for understanding and inspiration to write the lines that follow.

1

A Dios le pido memoria	I ask for God's help
Y aliento a mi corazón	And peace for my heart
Para escribir esta memoria	To write this memorial,
Memoria de condolación	A memorial of condolence.

2

El día once de enero	On the eleventh of February,
Muy temprano en la mañana	Early in the morning,
Allí en el Cañon de Fernandez	In Fernandez Canyon
Muy triste se oyó la campana.	The bell tolled sadly.

3

Año del ochenta y cinco	The year was '85,
Al empezar el año nuevo	At the beginning of the year
A la jovencita Janice Medina	God took the youthful
El Señor se la llevó.	Janice Medina with him.

(Gallegos 1985)

Lorin Brown (aka de Córdova) tells us that in the New Mexico of the 1940s, the bell of the village church would toll the death knell. A rock would be struck against the body of the bell, sounding a slow toll. Villagers would inquire about who had been called. This practice evidently still prevails in El Cañon (de Córdova 1972). God and Jesus Christ are referred to as "El Señor." It is important to note that El Señor came for Janice Medina, not Death, and in many of these recuerdos it is God who determines the place and time of death.

4

La escuela se vistió de luto	At school everyone was grieving,
Los estudiantes todos lloraban	Students were crying.
Cuando de la muerte de Janice	When they heard about Janice's death,
Ellos todos se enteraban.	They all became aware

It is not known how today's Hispanos *guardan el luto*, observing *luto*, the customary period of mourning, which was formerly a year, with the first six months being rigorous mourning. The custom was that family members should not go to dances, movies, or listen to music. Mirrors would be turned to the wall. The practice of lifting the *luto* for Hispanos in New Mexico occurs with the announcement of a mass—the *cabo del año misa*—or giving a newspaper notice at the end of a year of mourning, as mentioned earlier. There are parallels to the Jewish *Jahrzeit*.

The *luto* has changed over time. In other times, both men and women would in effect *vestirse en luto* (dress themselves in black to symbolize grief). In the phrase "la escuela se vistió de luto," Gallegos is in effect saying that the schoolmates went into grieving. The phrase "se enteraban" might be taken to mean how the students learned of Janice's death. Condolences are offered tenderly in the next lines as the author recognizes their pain. Persons at a rosary or funeral will offer a meaning of the event to the family, providing the bereaved family the most compelling and exquisite part of this memorial.

5

Roberto y Juanita Medina	Roberto and Juanita Medina's
Esta triste su corazón	Hearts are sad,
Pero Janice está en el cielo	But Janice is in heaven
Con Dios en una linda mansión.	With God in a lovely mansion.

6

Del Jardin de Roberto Medina	In Roberto Medina's garden
Era la flor más hermosa	She was the most lovely flower,
Pero Dios necesitaba una flor	But God needed a flower
Y de allí el cortó una rosa.	And from there he took his rose.

In the tradition of the *ejemplo trágico*, the author reminds the reader of the transitory nature of life. The notion of life being on loan (*la vida es prestada*) is introduced.

7

Esta vida Dios nos presta	This life is on loan by God
Solo por una temporada	For only a short time.
No sabemos cual es el día	We don't know the day
Que tenemos que esperar su llamada.	On which we will be called.

People will often use the notion of life being "on loan" when they offer a condolence. Thus, before and after rosaries and at funeral masses, the bereaved are consoled by being told, "Your dad [or other] was lent to you for [as many years as he had lived]." Because life is only on loan, it can be reclaimed by the giver of life, God.

In contrast to the corrido, where the story of the fallen hero is told, this memorial to Janice Medina presents minimal information on the event of the death itself. Instead, the author reminds us, using this *ejemplo trágico*, of the need to be wary. This theme is repeated twice.

8

Janice jovencita muy contenta	Youthful, happy Janice
En la nieve andaba eskiando	Had been skiing,
No sabiendo que cuando llegara	Not knowing upon her return
Ya la muerte la esta esperando.	That death was waiting.

9

Atendimos un hermoso rosario	We attended a beautiful rosary,
Muy tristes están los Medinas	The Medinas were very sad,
Muy tristes con las lindas canciónes	Sad also were the beautiful hymns
Que cantaban las Guadalupanas.	Sung by the Guadalupanas.

10

Sabemos que jóven o viejo	We know that, young and old,
Un día Dios nos ha de llamar,	One day we will be called by God,
Y el día que el Señor nos llame	and on the day of his calling
El río tenemos que cruzar.	That river we must cross.

Five virtues are symbolized by women's names. They have been identified as Amparo (light), Socorro (help), Gracia (grace), Consuelo (wise consul), and Rosario (rosary). Light, help, and grace are clear, but the other two are not as clear. "Rosario," like the rosary, is meant to connect—like a chain (*encadenar*): to link and to reinforce by means of networking. Applied to persons and caring systems, the terms signify enlightenment and the provision of help, grace, and support through linking. *Consuelo*, according to the *New Revised Velázquez Dictionary* (1985), means consolation, comfort, and relief. In everyday parlance, Hispanics will say *Me consuelo con . . .* (I console myself with the idea that . . .), meaning, "I tried everything" or "I did the best I could."

The final passages of the memorial to Janice Medina petition the power of God three times to bring to the Medina family healing and comfort, *un consuelo*. The petitions are made for Janice's sisters and parents in the exquisite statement at the end of the memorial. The *consuelo* to the sisters is that "Su hermanita esta descansando. / Ya esta con Dios en el cielo" (Your sister is at rest. / She is with God in heaven). This is the healing balsam (*el balsamo de consuelo*) that Mrs. Gallegos asks for in her prayer for this stricken family.

11

Le pido a Dios por sus hermanitas	I ask God on behalf of her sisters
Que les mande el balsamo de consuelo	That God may send his healing Grace,
Su hermanita está descansando	Your sister is at rest
Y está con Dios en el cielo.	She is with God in heaven.

12

El día catorce de enero	On the 14th of January
Muy triste estaba la gente.	Everyone was sad.
La Banda de la escuela tocó	The school band played
En su misa de cuerpo presente.	At her funeral mass.

13

Están tristes los corazones	There were many sad hearts,
Lloran mucho sus dos hermanas.	Her two sisters cried openly.
Las gracias le dan a la gente	People were being thanked,
También a las Guadalupanas.	Including the Guadalupanas.

14

Roberto y Juanita Medina	Roberto and Juanita Medina,
Su hijita está con Dios en el cielo.	Your daughter is with God in heaven.
Y a ustedes les mandará	And she will send
El Balsamo de consuelo.	A balsam of healing.

Death is experienced communally. *El acompañamiento* (the accompaniment) can be assumed to be normative because people will come together in these small communities to offer their help and prayers, and, more important, to be present with the bereaved (*vamos a acompañar*). The *acompañamiento* is reflected in the communal rosary, where the Guadalupanas sing hymns. The high school band is also present to accompany their fallen sister. The community is reciprocally thanked (*las gracias*) for their support and their *acompañamiento.* The memorial ends simply and elegantly.

15

Ya con esta me despido.	With this I take my leave.
Ella está en una mansion Hermosa.	Janice is in a lovely mansion
Cuando Dios le llame a ustedes	When God calls you,
Allí encontrarán su rosa.	There you will find your rose.

One might ask, "What does the farewell accomplish?" In terms of some of the concepts developed here, the despedida is normative. For the person who died as a result of a tragic highway accident, the normative requisite of a despedida is violated. Thus, the deceased has, in a sense, violated a norm. Likewise, the person on whose behalf the recuerdo is written was unable to say a proper farewell (*despedirse*). Thus, we find some recuerdos written for the departed because he or she was unable to perform this requisite of the social order for him- or herself.

The main focus of this chapter has been the written recuerdo as one manifestation of the despedida. Despedidas represent terminations—the termination of life, the death of the fallen hero in a corrido, and the ritualized farewell to a person. I have attempted to illustrate the various ways in which this cultural norm is exercised. In the *Santa Fe New Mexican*, an Hispano printed Tony's *adiós* in English. Only a small part of Tony's farewell is presented below:

Today I am saying Adiós to all my
family and friends. For I will no
longer be here in the physical sense,
But my spirit will be with you for always . . .
Love one another. Help each other,
And most importantly forgive one
another. In this way, my life will
live through you.
For this is not my death,
but a new beginning, for me
As it is for you.
Adiós mi familia y mis amigos.
Your kind expression of sympathy
is gratefully acknowledged and
deeply appreciated . . . From the Family of Tony E. Martinez.

("Tony's Adiós" 1992)

Tragedy and the Heroic

Tragedy and the hero are bound together. In the *Poetics*, Aristotle's universalism provides us with the elements of both. For tragedy to exist, a human experience must arouse pity and fear while purging the spectator of the unpleasantness of these emotions, a purging that Aristotle identifies as "catharsis." This catharsis of the emotions, according to Fuller, works by "transforming them from our own predicament to the sufferings of the tragic hero." This transference signifies that we can detach ourselves and momentarily be released from our individual burdens; we can experience "a nobler, all-embracing, impersonal sympathy and compassion" that raise us to a higher moral level (Fuller 1955, 226). The hero's denouement also means the creation of a thing of beauty as we learn a lesson to improve our "character." To produce the best effect, the hero's downfall must "be sudden and unlooked for." It is as important also for the writer-singer of the tale, or in the present discussion the despedida, to be able to use the meter and rhythm of the subject's language and culture to depict his or her fate (Fuller 1955, 227).

The question of what is heroic ultimately goes to the essential meaning of a person's life. Ernest Becker wrestled with this idea and approached it in the *Birth and Death of Meaning* by espousing a four-tiered level of personal and individual development, or, in his words, "four levels of power and meaning" (Becker 1971a, 186). The first is the personal, a "secret hero" of one's inner scenario of thoughts, feelings, and talents, the person one knows oneself to be. The second is the social representation of one's social extension of oneself to intimate others, and the third constitutes one's relationship to the corporation, the party, nation, science, history, and humanity. The last level of power is the person's relationship to creation, an unknown and invisible source of personal meaning. This last level provides the individual centered meaning, such that

> as you last out your life with courage, forbearance and dignity you affirm your divine calling by simply living it out. Your Creator will make good your service, whether He makes it good to you in any personal way, say, by way of spiritual immortality or by way of being initiated into still unknown dimensions of cosmic life to serve equally there, in some kind of embodiment; or whether He makes it good in His own way, by using the sacrifice of your life to glorify and aggrandize His own work, His own design on the universe, whatever that might be: at least you have served the Ultimate Master, you have lived your life truly and not foolishly if you die for good you at least die well. (Becker 1971a, 189)

What hero systems are espoused by Hispanos, as reflected by the recuerdo writers as they ponder the meaning of the end? The lines from Vigil's "En memoria de James C. Martinez" are worth repeating here: "Este mundo no es nuestro / Ni la temporaria vida / Todo lo tenemos prestado" (This world is not ours / Not this temporary life / All we have is on loan to us) (Vigil 1991, 1). There is a resignation to life because death comes to all of us. Some have called this view fatalism and have misinterpreted its meaning in the daily life of Mexican Americans and Hispanos. Their acceptance of death in their everyday life, Kalish and Reynolds propose, serves them well as mourners. Within this framework, persons can accept their feelings of loss more honestly. In order to live more fully, death must be faced effectively, and bringing it to one's family is actually liberating to the self; otherwise one would live with feelings of omniscience. These views are antithetical to those that would deny death (Kalish and Reynolds 1981).

Vigil renders this view poetically in his recuerdo:

Qué consuelo nos fuera	What a consoling thought
De enternecernos cuando nacemos	If at birth we would be moved
Y estar contentos y alegres	To be happy
El día que nos muremos	On the day of our death

(Vigil 1991)

Vigil reminds us how quickly we forget that life is on loan (*prestada*): "After all we are nothing but shadows."

Most Hispanos believe in an afterlife and in a last judgment. The recuerdo, after offering the details of a person's death, also offers the survivors a *consuelo*. A despedida offered at my *comadres'* rosary and also sung several years earlier for her departed brother illustrates this theme:

Ya tu alma esta en el cielo	Your soul is in heaven
dando cuenta al Creador	giving an account to the Creator.
tu esposo y tus hijitos	May your husband and children
consuelo les de Dios.	receive comfort from God.

(Martinez n.d.)

Heaven is often referred to as *la gloria*, a *descanso*, or, more poetically, "la Mansión Celestial" (the Celestial Mansion). Another recuerdo illustrates these points. *El reino del cielo* and *la gloria* are names for heaven.

Ahora, preciosa	Now, precious,
En el reino del cielo estaras	You are in the kingdom of heaven,
Ganado por tus esfuerzos	Won by your works [struggles]
Que a tantos supiste sanar.	In healing many.
Venimos a este mundo,	We come to this world
Y el tiempo se va pasando	As time passes
Con afanes y dolores,	With trouble and pain,
La vida se va acabando.	Life is ever ending.
Adiós Teresita	Good-bye, Teresita,
Que Dios la tenga en la gloria	May God have you in glory.
Ella se fue con su Dios,	She went with her God,
pero, nos dejo su memoria.	But she left us her memory.

(Gallegos 1993)

It is not often that Anglos are memorialized in recuerdos, but Father Michael O'Brien was presented with a "testimonial" in Spanish that was published in the *Taos News*. The recuerdo testifies to his priestly ministry and thanks him for bringing the sacraments to the people of Taos (Torres 1993). Another recuerdo of note was offered to an attorney by a fellow Hispano attorney and was written in a non-corrido style. The memorial is a recuerdo because it recognizes the heroic in this man's good deeds, presents a *consuelo* to his family, expresses the writer's grief, and offers the writer's own despedida.

If a picture of a man with love and concern
for all is ever painted

I am sure that your kind, gentle, loving and
eternally youthful face will grace its four corners
To our dear departed friend, we say
"I love you, vaya con Dios."

("In Memoriam" 1991)

A master auto mechanic known for his patience and his precise and exacting workmanship was publicly eulogized in a newspaper by one of his children:

One Christmas, he gives my little sister a tool box just like his. It's not greasy yet, but it has tools. Her ruler has Mickey Mouse. Together they build a basket-weave fence around the yard. He wears his dark coveralls and his cap that says "ALLWOODS" and teaches her to nail and saw.

Standing at the lathe with my brother, he teaches him to cut threads. Again in blue coveralls, but this time his cap says "LOBO ENGINES." He tips his cap shielding his eyes from the light. Taking the micrometer from the box he tells my brother, "You must be accurate—at least to a thousandth of an inch."

When I first left home I had no tools or so I thought. I had no tire gauges, wrenches or pliers, or even a hammer, and I cried because I thought he didn't care. Later I realized the tools he gave me were not for shaping metal or sawing wood but rather for building character. He gave me quality, intelligence and diligence—TOOLS FOR SHAPING LIFE. ("Toolbox" 1987)

Epilogue

A sociology of everyday life can offer only a pale image of the despedida and its true meanings. I can only approximate these understandings by reflecting on some thoughts from the philosopher Nicolas Berdyaev. It is death alone that "gives true depth to the question of life. Life in this world has meaning because there is death. The meaning is bound in the end." And although we "rightly feel the horror of death and rightly regard it as the supreme evil, [people] are bound to connect it with the final discovery of meaning." Finally, meaning "is never revealed in an endless time; it is found in eternity. But there is an abyss between life in time and life in eternity; and it can only be bridged by the horror of the final severance" (Berdyaev 1959, 249–50).

CHAPTER 10

From Tombstones to *Star Trek:* *¡Qué poco soy! ¿No soy más?*

For all flesh is as grass, and all the glory of man as the flower of grass. The grass withereth and the flower thereof falleth away But the word of the Lord endureth forever.

1 Peter 1:24

Yo creo que la muerte es un gran sueño. (I believe that death is a long sleep.)

Pedro Ornelas, resident of Belen, New Mexico, at age ninety-five

JOSEPH CAMPBELL RAISES AN INTERESTING QUESTION ABOUT THE DIFFERING views of death in planting cultures, on the one hand, and hunting and forest cultures, on the other. Planting cultures turn to the plant as a metaphor for understanding death. The self-regenerative powers of the plant mean that its nature can be characterized as "continuing inbeingness." Pruning is helpful to a plant because it stimulates new growth. Out of the rot in a forest comes new life. Cut a branch from a tree, and new suckers appear in profusion. They are the "bright new little children who are part of the same plant." Campbell concludes, "So in the forest and planting cultures, there is a sense of death as not death somehow, that death is required for new life. And the individual is not quite an individual; he is a branch of a plant" (Campbell 1988, 102).

Some of what follows in this chapter is subjective. Subjectivity has been downplayed and derided, but subjectivity is as important as what is considered the objective with its scales, interview schedules, and so on. The reader is encouraged to read Mehan and Wood (1975) on the fallible in "objective research." This chapter and the other two *ciclo* chapters (chapters 11 and 12) are a search for meaning. If the objectivists want to create a *"ciclo"* scale, then so be it.

As farmers and stockmen, the Hispano people of northern New Mexico consider life, death, and resurrection within a framework of completing the harvest, the coming of the dark winter, and the blooming of flowers and trees in the spring. *El ciclo de vida y muerte* (the cycle of life and death) is based on the premise that flora die in the late fall, only to return in the spring. Antonio Medina, a social philosopher from Mora, New Mexico, originally proposed the *ciclo* idea, but he did not elaborate. This chapter is the first of a trilogy on the *ciclo de vida y muerte* and an attempt to give this typified idea more form. The chapter considers the flower motif, whereas chapters 11 and 12 are about light and darkness, and despair and transcendence, respectively. In enlarging the scope of this inquiry, we can begin to see that these symbols are laden with meaning from the everyday life of Hispanos.

We have to make clear that the *ciclo* dualism is incomplete. Octavio Paz deals with the dualism of life and death, though he also mentions but does not discuss the idea of resurrection (Paz 1961). His view is basically a pessimism that declares that both life and death are meaningless for the Mexican.

These three chapters will also leave the question of resurrection empty, as did Paz. This does not mean that a deep need does not exist to find a larger meaning than just the brute struggle for life, ending in death. Resurrection is implicit in the text of the three chapters. One is not advocating any particular denominational view to these important questions. Each chapter will deal with a major idea. In this chapter what is contrasted are ideas from a former planting culture; it asks a question that technology cannot answer. The thesis of this chapter is that Hispano culture *de más antes* (from olden days) attempts to provide answers to the deepest question, "Is this all I am? Is there nothing else?" asked by Mr. Spock, the logical Vulcan in the first of the *Star Trek* films. A subordinate theme in chapter 10 is to ask the question can technology answer the most crucial question about our purpose in life. Chapter 11 is about light and darkness as a metaphor for life and death. The subtext in this chapter concerns germination and creation of a new consciousness in darkness. Chapter 12 deals with the nature of struggle with despair and the liberation of transcendence. It also covers rituals of giving thanks (*dar gracias*). The subtitle for this chapter is the merger of psychology with religion. All three chapters need to be thought within a trifocal perspective of struggle, hope, and renewal. Perhaps this is why these chapters present a higher hope whether from faith or from psychology. All three chapters deal with life and death and implicitly with the belief in resurrection.

Planting Cultures

In the mid-1970s a series of interviews were conducted in northern New Mexico counties as part of an effort to collect oral history. Recordings of these interviews of older Hispanos living in villages in the 1920s and 1930s are kept in the Carnegie Library in Las Vegas, New Mexico. The interviews covered a great amount of information on a variety of topics, including daily life. Only information relating to living off the land is covered here. One interviewee, Cruz Sedillo Sr. from Las Vegas, remembers that people "helped each other out. There was no payment involved, it was voluntary. So the people lived in such a brotherly way. If a person was busy building a home others who weren't busy would help for free. It was an honest and beautiful life. There was love and fear of God. And we were happy to help each other without pay or anything" (Sedillo 1975, 21-2). The fear of God was a deterrent to bad behavior. The three cardinal values in this land-based culture were *respeto* (respect), *vergüenza* (personal honor), and *temor* (fear of God). This attitude of helping neighbors was similarly expressed by Lillian Sánchez of Buena Vista, who stated, "The people were closer. I remember that when we thrashed, all the neighbors would get together and do one's field, and then move off to the neighbors and so on, but all the people worked together. That way all the fields were thrashed before bad weather arrived. All those customs were very beautiful" (Sánchez interview 1973, 19-7). Sánchez related other information about making different food and included the means by which outside *hornos* (ovens) were prepared for making bread. John G. Moya, formerly from Pecos, New Mexico, talked about the importance of respect (*respeto*). He said, "People were very religious and had a lot of respect. The culture itself was geared for the benefit of the people. Respect was the number one priority that was taught at home. People dedicated a lot of their time to religious endeavors." He also stated, "Your surplus was bartered for something you needed" (Moya 1975, 11-1; 11-9). Moya stated that for Pecos, August 2 was reserved for Nuestra Señora de los Ángeles (Our Lady of the Angels). His understanding was that the *santo* (saint) was brought from Spain 400 years ago. Around 1617 the last Native American inhabitants of the pueblo of Pecos left to join the people of Jemez Pueblo. They gave the Nuestra Señora de los Ángeles to the community of Pecos, with the provision that once a year they would take the saint to Jemez Pueblo, a custom that is still observed (Moya 1975, 11-12).

More recently the community of Corrales near Albuquerque celebrated their village *función* (village feast day), the San Ysidro de Corrales festival. Matachine dancers performed a stylized dance depicting the war between good and evil, and a young woman played the role of La Malinche in the conquest of the Aztecs. Another story says that the dance represents the casting off of more than 800 years of Muslim Moorish rule by the Spanish in the early sixteenth century. There are other stories of its origins. The Bernalillo Parish, which is the mother church for San Ysidro de Corrales, has continued the matachine tradition for more than 300 years. Parishioners took the santo of San Isidro from the old church to the new one as part of the feast day activities. The term "matachines" comes from sixteenth-century French and Spanish and might be translated to mean "clowning" or "trickery" (Sánchez 2009, 4). Francisco Sena of Los Torres remembers dancing los Matachines with gourds and rattles. This man recited several poems of his own composition as well as the poetry of El Viejo Vilmas and the Poet, a philosophical and religious dialogue between these two characters. It is striking to find this poetry still extant in this very remote village along the Gallinas River in San Miguel County. Sena was eighty-eight at the time of these recitations (Sena 1975, 22–27).

Many cultures hold the idea that people come from the earth. The Pueblo peoples of New Mexico, for example, believed in the lake of emergence, the *sipapu*—a place in the center of the *kiva* from which the first people emerged. These places become sacred, "place[s] of spiritual relevance" (Campbell 1988, 94). In some places in New Mexico, creating life by planting is still seen as a sacred rite. In Villanueva, one panel of the 1976 Bicentennial tapestry in the village church depicts events in the life of the village, such as the coming of the teaching sisters, and one panel in particular depicts the Novenario. The Novenario is described as prayer and "pasear los santos para que venga la lluvia" (a procession of the saints to petition for needed rain). Many years ago, during a very dry summer, after the elderly participants of the Las Vegas foster grandparent program concluded their training on parenting, they decided that instead of a typical graduation, they wanted to do was to *pasear los santos* as part of their graduation ceremony. Many *santos* came off dashboards, from home altars, and some came out of special places of reverence and esteem. San Isidro is the patron saint of farmers. In San Miguel County, we have two villages named after this *santo* and probably many more villages across New Mexico. In earlier times many New Mexico communities were named after saints.

Referring to an even older culture, Marie-Louise von Frantz writes that the ancient Egyptians believed that if wheat grains sprouted, it was a sign that a dead person had successfully managed to reach "a completed resurrection" (1998, 32). Aguilar and Wood quote an ancient Aztec poem:

> We only came to sleep,
> we only came to dream;
> it is not true, it is not true
> that we came to live on the earth.
>
> We became the green growth of spring,
> Our hearts will again revive,
> they will again open the petals;

> but our body is like a rosebud,
>
> it gives a few flowers and withers.

> (Aguilar and Wood 1976, 50)

Aguilar and Wood believe that this poem represents the Mexican attitude toward death. The world is transitory ("transient" is their word); life is merely a passage from one state of being to another, something of greater significance, "somewhere [that] does not refer mainly to the Christian concept of everlasting life in some far off heaven, but indicates that in the cosmos there must be greater meaning and that death is merely a vehicle, a marker, on the road that must be traveled to achieve whatever awaits us" (Aguilar and Wood 1976, 50). Virgilio Elizondo in his piece on the book *Americanos* writes that "Latinos understand life as a pilgrimage, and when the pilgrimage stops, life comes to an end. This seems to be ingrained in our genes. From our most ancient memories, we remember being on pilgrimage. From Aztlan we marched toward the South until we arrived at the valley of the Anahuac people" (quoted in Olmos, Ybarra, and Monterrey 1999, 20).

THE GRIM REAPER

It is not surprising that the coming of death is conceived as a harvest by a grim reaper. The metaphor of someone's life as a grass or a flower to be scythed and gathered is not unusual for a people who have made their living farming and raising sheep and cattle. The reaper and scythe as a symbol for death dates back to ancient beliefs about the pre-Christian god Saturn, who was often depicted as a harvest god with a sickle (von Frantz 1998). A new weapon in the U.S. Air Force is called The Reaper. This unmanned drone can destroy "targets" thousands of miles from the command center located safely in the United States—surely death from above.

Review of Method

I start small by making an inquiry into the symbols of the growing season and into the New Mexico Hispano's view of life and death. I extend the *ciclo de vida y muerte* (cycle of life and death) to two other metaphors for life and death without referring to any particular religious ideology. Emulating but never surpassing Ernest Becker, I attempt to unite folk psychology with religion (Becker 1973). The larger view juxtaposes the old and the new. I consider film images to be the newer view, whereas older images from *aquellos años* (years ago) exist within the collective unconscious of a people. By attending to the new, I hope that young persons may see that even films deal with these cosmic images and themes. I turn to that human need to understand one's place in the cosmos, to attend to one's aging, and, in another sense, to honor one's own, *mi hermanita—la Flora que fue entregada a Dios* (my little sister, Flora returned to God).

Like the Hebrews of old, we became a great people for a brief period of time. Today we continue our pilgrimage to the North, to Denver, Cheyenne, Salt Lake City, and elsewhere. Regardless of the direction, we are a pilgrim people starting with the trek north from Mexico in 1598. The Hispano farmers were expelled out of New Mexico by the Pueblo Revolt of 1680. Twelve years later the Hispanos returned, with many families representing different strata from New Spain's southern provinces. This has been called the Entrada of 1692 and the root source of most of the Hispano families in New Mexico (Chávez 1973, xii).

Viewing these images in a broad and universal framework can teach us about the way Hispanos make sense of their history. Ethnomethodology is concerned with what people "make" of their everyday lives. It takes its cue from phenomenology and begins by inquiring about motives, purposes, beliefs, and attitudes in the structure and meanings of everyday life. It is a philosophy of the mundane, *la vida cotidiana.* In this way, all of life can be inquired into for deeper meaning. We need only open our eyes to ask questions. As Hispanos we can ask, Why do we believe these things? Robert Romanyshyn (2000) tells us that presence must precede meaning; one must be able to witness what appears to consciousness before one can ask what it means. This is the "intentionality of consciousness" discussed in chapter 1.

Tombstones

My exploration in this chapter was originally prompted by a need to understand certain symbols—specifically, stars—found on tombstones in scattered villages in northern New Mexico. Finding more of these symbols gave rise to larger questions. One would ordinarily dismiss these perceptions as a "given" and leave the cemetery without giving any thought to what one has seen. The tombstones are silent regarding the question, What was the carver's intent in the use of use of these symbols? And what do they indicate about the kinds of death images available to Hispanos in everyday life? We cannot make this request directly of these stones of remembrance—"Tell us with certainty about the implications of these symbols." Instead, we must be guided by Ricoeur's (1967) dictum, "The symbol gives rise to the thought!" We shall therefore follow these symbols to see where they lead us. I use

Plant tombstone in La Liendre Cemetery, San Miguel County, New Mexico (Carol Baldwin)

the work of Marie-Louise von Frantz and Carl Jung in developing my ideas about the cycle of life and death, its symbols, and the three ways it manifests.

Some of the simple headstones at the La Liendre cemetery illustrate the motifs of life and death. La Liendre was a village that flourished through the 1930s. It is located southeast of Las Vegas, New Mexico, on the Gallinas River. The name refers to a jackrabbit or long-eared hare. The sandstone headstones were carved from locally available sandstones for persons who died before the end of village life there. One of the gravestones depicts life in the form of a tree. The image depicts this person's new "life" in death as a living entity. La Liendre itself is now returning to the earth as the walls of its houses crumble and disintegrate. These walls served families of farmers and stockmen for many decades.

The images in the tombstones at La Liendre cemetery are from aspects of life on earth—birds, plants, and trees that flower and give life—and stars that give light. These images seem quite different from lambs, angels, Christ figures, and fancy engravings of names, dates, and relationships found on modern marble tombstones. The tombstones in La Liendre are hewn from the earth—quarried from local sandstone. Sandstone would be easy to carve with rough tools. We may not know precisely what the village carver intended by the images. All we can do is let perception guide our discussion as we attempt to draw meaning from this iconography, but we can assume that the images have to do with the everyday life of these village people.

THE FLOWER MOTIF

The beautiful Janice Medina recuerdo discussed in the previous chapter presents a young girl's death as God picking a flower. The taking of a young life is particularly painful because the young have not had the opportunity to grow, blossom, and flourish. Like young plants, they are full of promise of what they might become, the children they may bring into the world, and the contributions they may make to society. The reaper's "cutting down" of a life still in youth is the brutal, cold hand of death. And for the parents the heavy task remains of burying one of their own.

Octavio Paz describes a facet of the *ciclo de vida y muerte* when he writes, "The cult of life if it is truly profound and total, is also the cult of death, because the two are inseparable. A civilization that denies death ends by denying life" (1961, 60). Antonio Medina in an interview has also remarked on modern materialism and its insulating effect against the perception of the *ciclo de vida y muerte*: "The more insulated I am in materialism, the less conscious I become about death walking with me every step of the way" (Medina 1983). Brenner writes that a recurrent theme in Mexican thought is the "concern for the sheer facts of life. Life shifting from one form to the another, and all still the same . . . plants and people of necessity dying, at a definite fixed point, to be reborn. Hence, the constant consideration of death" (Brenner 1967, 15).

Marie-Louise von Frantz notes the importance of the death of vegetation as a symbol or image of both human death and resurrection. She writes, "Along with grass and grain, the tree often appears as a symbol for death's mysterious relation to life. . . . The tree is the unconscious life which renews itself and continues to exist eternally after human consciousness has ceased to exist." Dreams of trees represent both death and life after death (von Frantz 1998, 25). Moreover, "Man's dead body

Flower/star tombstone in La Liendre Cemetery, San Miguel County, New Mexico (Carol Baldwin)

also consists of inorganic matter only, and indeed—or so one hopes—living 'form' could arise from it again, as the vegetation imagery indicates" (von Frantz 1998, 37).

At a small college in New Mexico, Pablo Read, a well-liked worker, a husband, a father, a good and decent man, died in a fatal car accident. A tree was planted at the university as a living memorial for him. It was a native pine from the area, and Pablo's essence will continue to exist in it. This tree of life is also his tree of death.

THE CARVED FLOWER/STAR

Locally made gravestones in several northern New Mexico cemeteries are adorned with flowers. They are not the elegant roses or lilies carved by a computer-driven machine into a marble tombstone manufactured by a profit-making organization. They are more beautiful than those precisely etched symbols. What is important here are the images that a local person attempted to convey, however crude. The hard hands of someone hired by a villager, spouse, brother, uncle, or other family member provided their rendition of a flower cut into the sandstone. Some of these flowers have five or six points, others have eight. Some symbols are flowers that resemble stars; others are stars.

In antiquity, some cultures believed in the flower as a symbol of the soul. The soul, *ba*, in Egyptian thought was conceptualized as either a bird that flies or a flower with its petals fanning out like the rays of a star (von Frantz 1998). If a villager in La Liendre in the 1930s was trying to chisel a flower into a sandstone block, would not the "flower" come out looking like a star?

Do these flower-stars present a deliberate iconography? Would not the maker of such a tombstone believe that the dead person has now reached the stars—sparks of light in the darkness of eternity? In the Book of Daniel 12:1–3, the righteous are likened to stars when the dead are called out of the earth after the long sleep.

Von Frantz writes about the star in yet another way.

> The night chest is reminiscent of a coffin, the place of one's final sleep. But out of it comes flashes of light, that is, symbols of sudden illumination, pointing to a pale blue sky—a common image of the beyond—and to the sun, a symbol of cosmic source of the light of consciousness. The flashes remind us of Origen's concept of resurrection as *spintherismos*, defined as an emission of sparks from the corpse, the departure of the soul from the dead body. (1998, 60)

LAS ESTRELLAS: THE STARS

Stars are also often found in conjunction with crosses on tombstones. One tombstone I have seen has a star hovering above the cross. Both are enclosed in a *nicho* (niche). The *nicho* is very much a part of the New Mexico scene, where even upturned bathtubs are used to protect a beloved *santo* (saint) from the elements. These two symbols

Crucita, tombstone in Mora, New Mexico (Carol Baldwin)

of resurrection, the star and the cross, are distinct. The cross is the cross of Christ, whereas the star may represent the person, as if to say, "I am this day resurrected with Christ," "My star has risen," or "I have become as light, a star in the cosmos."

One tombstone is particularly intriguing. As shown in the photograph, the cross is in the background and a "blossoming effect" seems to occur in the presentation of the rosette. In the center is an eight-pointed star. The impression is one of movement captured in the stone, as if to suggest that the star is a product emanating from the center of the cross. The effect is striking, and the symbolism is communicated.

In the Mora cemetery, I found a cement cross that had six of the following signs marked with what looks like an asterisk on it, with long spikes radiating from each center. It, too, is a "star." On the tombstone, the name of the deceased is given as "Crusita," which is scratched on a homemade cement cross still bearing the striations of the box on which the cross was cast. *Cruz* (cross) is a common name for males, and *Crusita* is the diminutive feminine form. How appropriate that a homemade cross symbolizes the setting off of sparks or stars into the firmament where this person now dwells.

An enclosure surrounding the grave represents the family's love for their mother—the two powerful symbols coincide with each other. A large heart is laid out flat next to the headstone, representing her role as the heart of this family and the family's love for her. At the base is a large five-pointed star. It is presented as if to say, "This person's life is now diminished as a setting star" or "See, like the stars I have risen!"

And just as stars give light, candles represent a torch, as von Frantz (1998) has noted. A gravestone at the Calvario Cemetery in Las Vegas, New Mexico, has two lit candles engraved on the sides. Were they meant to light the way into the darkness of death?

In American society the star represents a person of special authority, position, or elevation. A western sheriff used to wear a "tin star" to symbolize his authority. His place was to keep order, catch evildoers, and jail them. In *High Noon*, Gary Cooper plays a sheriff who must face Frank Miller, fresh out of prison, and his gang, who are coming to town to kill him. His Quaker wife at first leaves him alone to battle this vicious group. No one in the town is willing to assist him, so his great challenge is to defeat the villains alone. When it is all done, the erstwhile hero throws his badge (star) on the ground and leaves the community, as if to say that the community does not deserve a sheriff because of their cowardice and unwillingness to support the rule of law (Zinnemann 1952).

A World War II four-star general had at least twelve stars, eight on his shirt, plus four more if he wore a "garrison cap" on his helmet. Chiefs of police in New Mexico wear at least eight stars, four to a cluster on each lapel (and, in one case, five stars). These badges of rank denote their elevated status and symbolically the upholding of the law. In this regard, they stand above other men and women. Liberty herself was enshrined by stars in much U.S. coinage, particularly in the nineteenth century. To conclude, important public ceremonies, such as on the Fourth of July, sparklers and fireworks shoot showers of stars to celebrate the concept of liberty and to light the very cosmos in the darkness of a July evening. In special ceremonies, the country

Blossom Effect, La Liendre Cemetery, San Miguel County, New Mexico (Carol Baldwin)

makes sure that Lady Liberty is showered by exploding firecrackers, for example, during the country's bicentennial.

Among Hispanos stars represent the cosmic. The blue mantel of Nuestra Señora de Guadalupe is studded with stars. She is cosmic in her presence. Even an angel is enlisted to support and present her as a moon goddess. Deeper still are the writings from the Book of Revelation that refer to the woman with child, which are cryptic, inspiring, and far-reaching.

The stars found in the Mora and La Liendre cemeteries tell us something about the elevation of the person to another status or life. He or she has crossed the divide between life and death. His or her star is rising. The spark of life no longer kindles the corporeal body, but is now an image, like a "shooting star" traveling across the firmament. On seeing a "shooting star" crossing the sky, Hispanos used to say, *Dios te guie y a mi me salve* (God guide you, and for me, salvation). Mircea Eliade writes, "It is the same thing to say that the sky manifests the sacred and to say that it signifies the most high, the elevated and the universal, the powerful and orderly, the clairvoyant and wise, the sovereign and the immutable" (Eliade 1949, quoted in Ricoeur 1967, 11).

Finally, the Book of Daniel tells us that the wise will shine like stars in the firmament.

> At time there shall arise Michael, the great prince, guardian of your people; It shall be time unsurpassed in distress since nations began until that time. At that time your people shall escape, everyone who is found written in the book. Many of those who sleep in the dust of the earth shall awake, some shall live forever others shall be an everlasting horror and disgrace. But the wise shine brightly like the splendor of the firmament, and those who lead the many to justice shall be like the stars forever. (Daniel 12:1–3)

The book of Daniel is apocalyptic in that it addresses the eschatological, or "the last things," as Berdyaev (1959) calls these questions. These discussions have to do with the end of time when we shall all be awakened from the ground and face *el día de juicio* (the day of judgment). More is said about apocalyptic ideas in chapter 12 in this book. Perhaps Hispanos understand the idea that we shall be like the stars, as we see many stars in older tombstones in Hispano cemeteries.

LAS FLORES DE LA MUERTE

What do Hispanos believe about death and flowers? Curtin tells us that the local name for the sunflower in New Mexico is *áñil* and its scientific name is *Helianthus annus L.* In New Mexico, it is also called *mirasol*—a marvelous or uncanny descriptive name for a flower that follows the sun: *mira* (see) and *sol* (sun). Sunflowers, along with the *áñil del muerto*, are abundant in cemeteries. From *helio* (sun) comes *helious*, or "sun giving light" and sustaining life (Curtin 1965). The New Mexican sunflower is common in middle to late summer along New Mexico's highways.

The flower called *el áñil del muerto* (the flower of death) is common in cemeteries. This flower is known also as gold weed, crownbeard, and *Verbesina enceliodes*, and, like the *mirasol*, it is from the aster family. It is used as a medicinal plant to cure stomach troubles, rheumatism, dropsy, and piles. Thus, the flower of death has healing or life-giving properties. Need one say more about the ironies of "*muerte giving life*"? Von Frantz makes the point that "vegetation . . . when cut down, or dried by the sun, always grows into a physical life again and continues to survive" (1998, 29). *Áñil del muerto* and the *mirasol* grow in profusion in New Mexico cemeteries.

Synchronicity

Jung's notion of synchronicity refers to "inner perceptions (forebodings, visions, dreams, etc.) [that] show a meaningful simultaneity with outward experiences, regardless of whether they are situated in the present, past or future" (Jacobi 1959, 62). For Jacobi and the Jungians, the explanation focuses on the "border zone" where the threshold of consciousness is lowered and elements from the unconscious spontaneously penetrate into the conscious mind. Jacobi writes that

> in a manner of speaking, they [inner perceptions] can be experienced and noted simultaneously, because the acausality and space-time relativity prevailing in the unconscious simultaneously enter and act upon the field of consciousness. What we have here is a linking of events which is not of a causal nature, but calls for a different principle of explanation. Their ultimate causes are no doubt the archetypes. (1959, 62–63)

Jung, as quoted by Jacobi, states that synchronicity is "a coincidence in time of two or more causally unrelated events which have a similar meaning." "However incomprehensible it may appear, we are finally compelled to assume that there is in the unconscious something like an *a priori* knowledge or an 'immediacy' of events which lacks any causal basis " (Jacobi 1959, 63). These coincidences may create consternation or amazement when they occur. In this regard I offer the following as examples cascading one upon the other as I worked on this chapter. We start with the dream.

ARE DREAMS PHENOMENA?

A dreamer tells us he had a dream in which he was walking in a dry alkali *playa*, as he had many years ago at Lucy, New Mexico, looking for arrowheads. In the dream, the flat playa was hot and dusty. The weeds and soil had the white encrustation of leached alkali salts. Along the way, the dreamer kept killing snakes with a snub-nosed revolver. He was not afraid but kept on walking and killing the serpents. On the way, he heard a voice that said, "Look upon this tree and you shall be saved."

The dreamer looked at the tree, which had outstretched branches like those of a dried apple tree. On the tree was a very large serpent supported by several of the branches. The serpent had huge fangs and looked at the walker. The dreamer woke up but was not frightened. Two days later he heard a passage from Numbers 21:6–9 read in a Catholic mass. This passage has to do with the children of Israel being bitten by serpents in the desert. They go to Moses to ask him to intercede on their behalf. Moses implores God, who tells him to place a brass serpent on a pole (cross, tree). And God says, "All who look upon this tree will be saved." The dreamer was incredulous that his dream and the reading of this particular passage should follow one after the other in time. This is a case of synchronicity.

The dream represents a change from the Mosaic way to that of Christ on his cross. The cross represents the defeat of man in terms of his tree of death, but also his transcendence in the tree of life. The symbol of the tree found in the cemeteries of La Liendre, San José (West Las Vegas), and Mora all attest to this double meaning.

Von Frantz quotes Jung's *Archetypes and the Unconscious* for a deeper understanding of the tree as a archetype:

> The alchemist saw the union of opposites under the symbol of the tree, and it is therefore not surprising that the unconscious of present-day man, who no longer feels at home in his world and can base neither his experience on the past that is no more nor the future that is yet to be, should hark back to the symbol of the cosmic tree rooted in this world and growing back to heaven—the tree that is also man. *In the history of symbols this tree is described as the way of life itself, a growing into that which eternally is and does not change; which springs from the union of opposites and by its eternal presence, also makes that union possible.* It seems as if it were only through an experience of symbolic reality that man, vainly seeking his own "existence" and making a philosophy out of it, can find his way back to the world in which he is no longer a stranger. (Emphasis by Jung. Von Frantz 1998, 27)

Other forms of art such as sculpture or poetry also depict the life and death transition as the next example shows.

OTHER EXAMPLES

Patrocino Barela (1908–1964) was a sculptor from the Taos area and did much of his work during the Writers and Artists Program during the 1930s (Gonzales and Witt 1996). Today his work is getting the recognition it never received in his lifetime. One of his pieces, in the Museum of International Folk Art in Santa Fe, is called *Resurrection.* It is a most unusual piece: It shows a central figure with outstretched arms ascending above three other figures. No cross holds up the figure, only the outstretched arms forming a cruciform figure with its body. A squatting figure to the lower left points to the ascending figure.

The gender of the three figures is unclear. Perhaps their dresslike tunics nullify one's attempt to differentiate gender. The figure to the viewer's right might be a woman, but then is that a cutaway of a dress? Another figure is enclosed in and superimposed on this standing figure. In cutaway, we sense an enclosed figure. Smaller than the other three, this figure might be a baby in a cocoon or in an embryonic state, representing birth. This scene may depict birth and death inextricably linked. Birth is cocooned in the embryo as death is cocooned in the earth. What is most striking is that the piece does not need the Christian cross to communicate its message because the ascending figure with its outstretched arms carries the message.

Death and Resurrection: An Elegiac View

The idea discussed in this section is not Hispano in origin, but like the previous themes can point back to the Hispano idea of *el ciclo de vida y muerte* (the cycle of life and death) and beyond. The act of rising upward can refer to both the physical experience and the sense of the transcendent. In the final movement of Gustav Mahler's Second Symphony, also called the Resurrection Symphony, a poem by eighteenth-century poet Friedrich Klopstock is used to point it to what is truly meaningful in the resurrection.

> Rise again, yea, thou shalt rise again,
> My dust, after short rest!
> Immortal life! Immortal life
> He who called thee will grant thee.
>
> To bloom again art thou sown!
> The Lord of the Harvest goes
> And gathers us like sheaves,
> Us who died.

The first stanza presents us with the belief in immortality and a promise of rising again. The second stanza presents us with the purpose of our lives—to bloom again. This second stanza also has changed the Reaper into the Lord of the Harvest, who gathers us as sheaves of grain—a reiteration of the flower theme. The horror of our ultimate end is transfigured by identifying death with the harvester instead.

In the seventh and eighth stanzas of Klopstock's poem, we find joy:

With wings which I have won me,
In love's fierce striving,
I shall soar upwards
To the light to which no eye has soared.
I shall die, to live!

The wings are the metaphorical release from all earthly cares. Flying is a metaphor for freedom, escape, soaring to the great light. The winning of wings is another metaphor—won in love's fierce striving—perhaps signifying the difficulty of life itself. The light that no eye has seen is the hoped-for great light. Death is transformed in the simple line, "I shall die [so as to] live." It takes death for us to find life, a new birth.

"With wings . . . I won me" promises the angelic. In *Greeting the Angels* (1992), Greg Mogenson puts forth the idea of mourning as a process in which the prosaic gives way to the poetic. We create the angels from our loved one's toil. I have gathered many death notices from New Mexico's leading newspapers that reflect this process, a practice for both Anglos and Hispanics in the Southwest (and perhaps elsewhere). For example, one person wrote about his or her mother:

> When God created you, dear one, He made a perfect thing that sent a gust of joy through Heaven and made the choirs sing. He took a ray of sunshine and a bit of angel's smiles. He dipped into the brightness of the cherub's star-dust pile. He added sweetest fragrance from the rose-bed of the sky, with a final dash of whiteness from a cloudlet passing by. If God had given me to choose my mother at my birth, I would have chosen you of all the mothers on the earth. ("Obituaries" 1999)

On the death of a three-year-old Hispano child, a local newspaper printed the following along with the child's picture.

> Open your heart to the Mystery of life
> As this Angel has a brief breath of life he has learned that life and death are one just as the river of life is an ocean all in one. In the valley of his soul he knows the knowledge of what is beyond. Drink from the temple . . . for God chose you to care for his sheep, brief that it has been. We love you and miss you very much.
> Mom, R. K., Grandma R., Uncle P., and Aunt A. ("Open Your Heart" 1999)

The river and the ocean are also significant symbols in the dream life as manifestations of death. Spanish poet Jorge Manrique wrote the following lines in 1476 upon the death of his father. It is called *Coplas a la muerte de su padre* (Stanzas upon the death of his father). The English translation was done by the American poet Henry Wadsworth Longfellow.

Nuestras vidas son los ríos	Our lives are rivers, gliding free
que van a dar en la mar,	To that unfanthomed, boundless sea,
que es el morir.	The silent grave!
Allí van los señoríos	Thither all earthly pomp and boast
derechos a se acabar	Roll, to be swallowed and lost
y consumir	In one great wave.
allí los ríos caudales,	Thither the mighty torrents stray,
allí los otros, medianos	Thither the brook pursues its way,
y más chicos,	And tinkling rill,
allegados, son iguales	There all are equal; side by side
los que viven por sus manos	The poor man and the son of pride
y los ricos.	Lie calm and still.

(Manrique 1982; English interpretation by Henry Longfellow)

In this *copla*, Manrique likens death to an ocean fed by many rivers, which are individual lives. Death takes the rich as well as those who work with their hands. Mogensen speaks about mourning as an elegy, a means for distilling what was good (and angelic) about the person who has been lost. Mourning, as a poetic process, attempts to free the impersonal from the personal in emotions and experiences. Much of what we recall about the dead is inconsequential so far as the psyche is concerned. Though the obituary may speak of the dead in terms of "time, place and, circumstance, cause and effect" (as the nineteenth-century poet Shelley put it), the aim of the elegiac mode is to individuate the dead from the arbitrary aspects of his or her simply given life, or, better, to show the soulful necessity that has organized these contingencies, the lines of character, on the face of fate. Above all, the bereaved, in their mourning, must take care to imagine the self-sustaining essence of the dead (Mogenson 1992, 35).

In the process of the dead separating from us in everyday life, we concentrate on selecting and distilling the good characteristics they possessed. We see this in obituaries when they speak about the person's good qualities. It is the first step in "soul making." Mourning is poetic when it creates what Mogensen calls "soul making": "Though death cancels the life of the physical body, the body of images which our loved ones made for themselves and lived from carries on. Mourning is a miracle of faith in the life of images" (Mogensen 1992, 35).

A woman by the name of Flora who has passed away is no longer the schizophrenic, the old woman who is ill clothed and toothless, who smokes endlessly, and walks all over town. Now she is remembered for her generosity. She is not dead, but her distilled good qualities live in our memory, as Mogenson has told us. She lives again and wears the green summer dress with its flowers of her youth as she comes back in a dream to reassure me she is all right now. In the last stanza of the Klopstock/Mahler piece, we are given an affirmation of what is to be:

> Rise again yea thou wilt rise again,
> My heart, in the twinkling of an eye!
> What thou has fought for
> Shall lead thee to God!

Love's striving is the same thing as what we have overcome in life—*las penas, las mortificaciones, las problemas, faltando de cosas, cuentas, enfermedades, chingaderas*, the pain of childbirth, and our death. All of that is behind us now as we make our way to the Light that no eye has seen. Purpose is given to life as we struggle. "Toriar la vida," said my father, as if life could be dealt with in the same way a bullfighter gracefully maneuvers and moves beyond the killing energy of the bull. Perhaps my father also meant that life is a series of dilemmas—to be on the "horns of a dilemma" and not to know which way to turn. Purpose or meaning in life is revealed at the end of time, said Berdyaev (1959), but first we must pass through the final horror—our death.

Is This All That I Am? Is There Nothing More?

We archive meaning by attending to symbols and signs. Specific scenes from two films suggest commonalities as they point to more ultimate concerns. These films involve death and resurrection, a new beginning, perhaps even for the human race.

Star Trek: The Motion Picture (Wise 1979) involves the story of an ominous cloud destroying everything in its path and heading toward Earth. Captain Kirk and the crew of the starship *Enterprise* must encounter it "out there" before it reaches Earth. The cloud captures and then returns Ailia, a Deltan and helmsperson, to the ship with a sensor implanted in the well of her throat. The crew quickly learns that she has been transformed into an automaton, a machine probe sent by "Viger" at the epicenter of the cloud to study the humans. Through Ailia, the crew learns that Viger considers humans as nothing more than "carbon units," inferior beings, an infestation of the ship and, worse, of Earth. It has come through many light years of time and space to transmit the information it has collected and link with its creator.

Viger knows that the creator is on the third planet of this solar system. Spock,

Is this all that I am, am I nothing more? (Carol Baldwin)

meanwhile, mind-melds with Viger and learns that it is essentially a machine. As Spock says, Viger is "a kindred brother." Spock tells us that Viger, like himself, is pure logic, but Viger is only a heartless machine.

Viger is an intelligent machine that has reached consciousness and like man has fashioned a god in its own image, and from that view judges all nonmachine forms of life. When Viger signals the planet to communicate with its creator on Earth, it receives no answer. It asks the question, "Why has the creator not responded?" Kirk plays out a gambit and tells Viger that the carbon units have the answer to Viger's inquiry. Viger protests and says, "It is illogical not to disclose the information!" and is relentless in its need for this information. Kirk gets it to withdraw the killer satellites. Viger leads the *Enterprise* and the earthmen closer to the center of its own mechanism. We see a familiar object there—a satellite with its concave dish.

As Kirk gets close up, he cleans with his hand the object's name plate. The name *Viger* gives way to V***ger and then to astonishment as Kirk, McCoy, and Spock discover the nonreadable parts on the satellite dish: *Voyager*! It is *Voyager 6*, which disappeared into a black hole three hundred years in the past. *Voyager 6* has returned as a conscious living machine. Its sole purpose is to transmit to its creator the information it has collected in its space mission and to merge with its creator. It has traveled the far reaches of space and countless light years to do this. Viger continues its request: "Kirk unit! Viger awaits the information." When Kirk tells Viger that the carbon units *are* the creators, it objects that this answer is illogical. Kirk says he will prove it by getting the earth code from the old NASA program that will allow Viger to complete its programming and give the information it was initially sent out to collect. Kirk calls the *Enterprise*, and the sequence of numbers is transmitted, but Viger refuses it and burns out the receiving antennae.

Meanwhile, Ailia/Viger is communicating a deeper need via her eyes at Decker, executive officer of the *Enterprise*. Decker also yearns for Ailia. We begin to sense that something else is afoot here. Decker surmises that Viger wants to meet, see, and join with its creator. Decker declares he will join with the entity Viger/Ailia. They come together, a union that produces an incredible burst of plasma energy that leaps and transcends into the cosmic realm as a stream of sparks fly.

McCoy makes the interesting comment that he, as a doctor, has helped to deliver a new entity. It is clear that Decker and Ailia have been consumed in the "fire" and been reborn as a new entity. Death becomes the passage into a new life. The idea that after death comes rebirth into another life is even found in this film, as well as in myths from many cultures. It is the basis of much of what is said at funerals.

We see the same unity of man and woman in a marriage-death motif, which is what von Frantz (1998) calls it. In the film *Like Water for Chocolate* (Arau 1992), Tita finally joins with her lover in this life-death marriage. Here too, the point of contact produces sparks and the *rancho* burns down from the intensity of this marriage of opposites. Films tackle the age-old question, what are we about? Are we star stuff, mere energy that needs to be returned to its source? Do we join with the creator?

In the film, these questions are asked by Viger, an intelligent machine, but they could just as easily have been asked by any human. As Spock puts it to his comrades, "Every person turns to someone: a parent, a brother, a sister, a god, and asks, 'Is this all that I am? Is there nothing more?'" Are we now angels who have "won our wings" by this release from our body and become sparks—the *spintherismos* posited earlier? A more subtle observation is to recognize that both Decker and Ailia have joined each other in death as well as in life, as have Tita and her lover. The film *Meet Joe Black* (Brest 1998) is filled with similar symbolic representations.

As death, Joe Black walks William "Bill" Parrish, the character played by actor Anthony Hopkins, across a bridge over a small stream as the sky is filled with exploding fireworks. This is Hopkins's human birthday and deathday and his deal with death must now be consummated.

The *conjunctio*, as Jung called it, is the marriage of opposites, death and birth. Jacobi (1959), writing about the *conjunctio*, states that

> the term applies only if this "marriage" is regarded as a perfect one, in which the two
> components are fused into an inseparable unity and wholeness and have become an

authentic "hemaphroditus." The soundness of this conception has been confirmed in innumerable fantasy and dream motifs, and in images and representations of all kinds, such as we find among mystics, alchemists, and painters, or such as are brought to the surface from the unconscious in the course of analytic work. (96)

This paragraph is most interesting in that what we are proposing at another level is the marriage with death. We embrace and marry into death as finality. We become dead and are inseparable from it. We learn that the unconscious is the progenitor of these images. We are aware of these images as surely as the filmmaker as artist "knows" these ideas.

A Personal Odyssey

In March 1994, our first and only grandchild was born in Denver. My wife and I drove to Denver in anticipation of meeting the newest member of the family. She was everything one would expect in a newborn. Her brown eyes were alert and open all the time. We took many pictures. It was a joyous occasion to go up the street to get another roll of film developed. We selected the best ones for enlargement and distribution to the great-grandparents and the rest of the family.

Later in the late afternoon I fed my grandchild a bottle, which she took with trust and aplomb. I was completely captivated by her. In the early evening, I plunged into a book, and read till late that night. I will keep the name of the book I was reading in check for now, but it plays into the story in a significant way. For some reason, I have 2:00 A.M. fixed in my mind. Fully asleep or in the half stupor of sleep, I felt the back of my leg being struck to awaken me or to at least lighten my sleep. A figure appeared and proclaimed that he/she was Rhianna's angel. I fell blissfully back to sleep.

Five weeks later I was at a conference in Albuquerque and going through the usual book vendor displays. I picked up a small book on angels and proclaimed, "That's the one, that's the angel I saw." People turned around to look at me. I was not embarrassed, but rekindled with warm feelings about this contact.

In June that year, another grandchild, this time a boy, was born. We drove to Las Cruces to meet him. He was presented to us, and I saw a jaundiced and wrinkled child. He seemed to be crying all the time. My other son, in his more lucid moments, likes to poke fun at everything and called him "shar-pei baby" because of his wrinkles. In the weeks that passed, I began to feel uneasy about my lack of relationship with this newest member of the family. I would get reports about his first accomplishments and developmental milestones. I was dispassionate about the whole thing. It began to dawn on me that I would be a lousy grandfather to this child because I had not bonded to him. It bothered me, but I could not get beyond the idea that he was just another entity in the world. I reflected on how distant my own grandfather and grandmother had been to me. The nagging questions about "bonding" with the new child remained. I was simply not involved in this fellow's life. I thought it interesting that he was developing according to plan, but I was not actively checking on his condition. His uncle started to call him "Eisenhower" because of his lack of hair, prominent head, and blue eyes.

I wondered about my lack of commitment and felt some despair in not being able to take on the role of a caring grandparent. I call my feeling "despair" because I wanted to be a good grandfather yet did not feel invested (really) in what the child was doing or was capable of doing.

One Wednesday afternoon, I thought it would be a good idea to go to Blockbuster and relax with a good film in the afternoon. My schedule was such that I usually worked on Sundays to get ready for back-to-back classes on Mondays, another class or two on Tuesday, an undergraduate class on Wednesday, and meetings with students between classes. Wednesday afternoon was the time for me to relax because the rest of the week would be the usual meetings.

At Blockbuster, none of the videos seemed particularly striking. I stopped at the science fiction section and halfheartedly picked *2001: A Space Odyssey* (Kubrick 1968). I first saw this film when it came out in 1968. Based on a story by Sir Arthur C. Clarke and directed by Stanley Kubrick, it tells a fascinating story with few clues as to its meaning. It is more of a visual treat with spectacular scenes punctuated with Richard Strauss's *Thus Spake Zarathustra*. The music that accompanies the film is meant to uplift and raise our consciousness. In the words of film critic Roger Ebert, "Its five bold opening notes embody the ascension of man into spheres reserved for the gods. It is cold, frightening, magnificent" (Ebert 2005).

The movie opens with a primal scene in which hominids are scrounging out a living in a bleak semidesert environment at the dawn of human time. A black monolith appears to these man-apes at dawn. They are astounded and screech in defensive postures against this strange thing. Finally, they come to touch it. In a following scene, other apes appear to take over a waterhole where "tapir" like creatures come to drink. A man-ape discovers that the long femur can be used as a weapon to kill. Dawning consciousness and a new thought have motivated an action to kill. Not only do these man-apes become better hunters, but because of the monolith they can now defeat other hominid groups that have not learned the advantage of the use of the long femur as a destructive weapon.

Dr. Heywood R. Floyd and other scientists are sent out to the Earth's moon to investigate a monolith that has been found on its surface. The scientists have the temerity to touch the monolith. An alignment of planets ensues, and an eerie piercing sound seems to be coming from the monolith. This scene directs man to Jupiter, where a mathematically precise obelisk (its sides all prime numbers, as we learn in the sequel film called *2010* [Hyams 1984]) is next to be found. The action jumps to a long, tedious, endless journey to Jupiter space by several astronauts that takes many months to complete. We are introduced to Commander Bowman, the protagonist in the story.

A point of interest in the journey, though, is an encounter with HAL 9000, a computer that has decided to terminate the lives of the crew members. This highly intelligent machine concludes that human beings are a threat to the mission and that it and its programming can deliver the data on the nature of the obelisk without humans involved. HAL shuts down life-support systems, killing the rest of the crew, who are in deep hibernating sleep. When Commander Bowman, who has been outside the ship in a maneuverable pod to repair an antennae, attempts to enter the ship, HAL (H + 1, A + 1, L + 1 = IBM) refuses him entry. Commander Bowman will die in the pod if he cannot get HAL to open the pod bay doors. Bowman succeeds in overcoming the obstacles that HAL has set up and shuts down the computer's higher functioning, but something has happened to Bowman in Jovian space. If the film has been thin on an easily understood narrative up to this point, it now becomes even more difficult to comprehend or follow.

In 1994, I was again going through the slow paces of the film. I was half watching and semidozing. The film takes us through splashes of color and form, sometimes formlessness. It is accompanied by eerie and dissonant music. The visual forms come at us in dizzying frequency, likened to a bad acid trip. The images slow down and make a return to earthlike features, waves, rivers, and mountains, except that the colors are fractal and do not resemble the familiar. Some hues are glaring, others soft. We have no clue as to what we are seeing. Have we seen a universe beyond Jupiter, what no eyes have seen? What looks like the iris of an eye appears, but it, too, is the wrong color—lavender then green, as if to say we have seen all this and more. And then we see something tangible, a window to a white room, a Victorian room with the space pod in which Commander Bowman would have died if had not outwitted the killer computer. We next see Bowman in his red space suit. He is ghostly, wide eyed, almost frightened. He seems incredulous as he walks in the room. He sees himself much older, with lines on his face that appear to be those of a fifty-seven-year-old (myself at the time) man. We hear the mechanical noise like a man breathing in a space suit. Bowman gets the sense that he is not alone. He turns and goes toward a doorway, where he sees an old man eating alone. The man's back is toward us, and he stops eating as if to listen to the intruder. Bowman about age fifty-seven contemplates another much older self, another Bowman perhaps in his early seventies. The heavy, emphasized breathing stops. The old man gets up to see who is in the next room. He walks to the room, sees nothing, and returns to his lunch or dinner. He drinks from a goblet. In his movement, he breaks the goblet. The old man leans forward to contemplate its meaning. As he leans forward, we again hear the heavy mechanical breathing. He turns to see a much older man (Bowman?) in a bed, probably dying. The film shows us a shoulder shot of the old man contemplating, perhaps, his own death. The man in bed has labored breathing. He raises his arm slowly and begins to point with his finger toward an object—the monolith! This thing that has transformative powers is here in this room. We see it from different angles.

Then the resounding musical theme begins to build as the first notes from *Thus Spake Zarathustra* are heard again—slowly building to a climax. As if to connect one scene with another (the death scene), a radiant light appears on the bed and within it an embryonic figure. Death has become birth, a creature in a protective cocoon. Next we see the pale blue of Earth. It is basking in white brilliant light. As the music theme develops, behold the child—blue eyes, profound, transcendent. As the theme reaches crescendo, we have full sight of the star child. It is ethereal, bathed in a soft blue-hued embryonic protective sac, a beautiful child whose wondrous eyes behold Earth. The film ends.

2001: A Space Odyssey is a wonderful, visually uplifting film that profoundly altered my thinking as I saw it again in 1994, despite my dozing. I was filled with tears and emotions as I rewitnessed the last few minutes, and *I understood!* I understood the meaning of my despair, and the sudden release resulted in a transcendent feeling. A dawning consciousness of new wonder filled me. My thoughts became quite clear and coalesced into two ideas, one in Spanish, the other in English: *Tu eres mi otro yo* (You are my other me) and *I shall live through you*. My grandson and the film had solved one of the most profound mysteries of being and continuity. I thought this mystery was like Cooley's (1922) idea about the looking-glass self. We are reflected in other people's thoughts. This idea means much more to me now as I understand that I shall continue in my grandson, in the genes he has received, in his intelligence, and in his life. Klopstock's "I shall die so as to live" is a promise that my grandson will fulfill for me. I was ecstatic and joyous. I understood! As Hispanos we have to deal with these ultimate questions. Religion is available to fill in and provide a sense of continuity into another time, space, or place. We read it in the many recuerdos I collected from the *Taos News* over the years in which Mrs. Gallegos brought comfort to her neighbors by reminding them of what lies beyond.

Transcendence has to come after despair if some of the mysteries of living and dying are to be broached. This process is the basis of Christian teaching: the conquering of death and the finding of new life. After the *2001* experience, other ideas began to connect in my mind as in the Jungian synchronicity. I see my grandson's blue eyes, and I see the same hues in my daughter's eyes and in my grandfather's eyes. I see my grandfather looking back at me through time, as Bowman contemplates himself in the film. What a sense of continuity! I found myself writing a very long letter to my grandson, which I have stowed to be opened when he is a young adult. It will be a way to transcend time as I write to him from the past to reach him in the future. In the last part of this chapter I take up these concerns in a current theory of gerotranscendence.

When I first saw *2001*, I tried to understand it in terms of space-time and relativity. Today I see it as a personal statement of my own aging and end. It was a way to get beyond what hampered my bonding to my grandchild. Today I have considerable interest in his comings and goings. He is fun to be with, and I enjoy him a great deal. He is bright and articulate. He learned to read early, and I look to his promise in the future, as I do for the rest of little ones in the family. He will be a "star child," whereas Rhianna will remain an angel to me.

Fast forward to 2005, and another "Eisenhower" who has made his way into the world. He is mellow and sweet. He is on the verge of one of the greatest achievements for a biped—to walk upright. The book I was reading when I met Rhianna's angel is also by Arthur C. Clarke and is called *2061*, the third book in Clarke's odyssey. The main hero is still Heywood R. Floyd of the *2001* film and the film *2010*. He is now 109 in this book. Now how is that for synchronicity?

Much has been made of the film *2001*. I read somewhere that after its debut people went to church and asked for guidance. Does the imposed ambiguity in the film imply that people can assign many different meanings to it? Film critic Roger Ebert wrote that "the film creates its essentials out of visuals and music. It is meditative. It does not cater to us, but wants to inspire us, enlarge us":

> Only a few films are transcendent, and work upon our minds and imaginations like music or prayer or a vast belittling landscape. Most movies are about characters with a goal in mind, who obtains it after difficulties either cosmic or dramatic. "2001: A Space Odyssey" is not about a goal but about a quest, a need. It does not hook its effects on specific plot points, nor does it ask us to identify with Dave Bowman or any other character. It says to us: We became men when we learned to think. Our minds have given us the tool to understand where we live and who we are. Now it is time to move on to the next step, to know that we live not on a planet but among the stars, and that we are not flesh but intelligence. (Ebert 2005)

Gerotranscendence

Lars Tornstam has found evidence for a concept in both qualitative and quantitative studies. He calls this concept *gerotranscendence*. It is marked by a cosmic and transcendent view of life in the aging process. The gerotranscendent individual has a new understanding of fundamental existential questions—a feeling of cosmic communion with the spirit of the universe, a redefinition of time, space, life, death, and self to others, an affinity with past generations and a decrease in the interest in superfluous social interaction. According to Tornstam, there are three dimensions of gerotranscendence: the cosmic, the self, and social and individual relationships. The cosmic is particularly relevant to our discussion. In time and space, there is a transcendence of borders between past and present. There is a connection to earlier generations—an increasing attachment to them. There is also a diminishing fear of death and a new comprehension of life and death. The last of the subcomponents of the cosmic dimension is an acceptance of the mystery in life and a joy in experiencing the macrocosmos in the microcosmos (Tornstam 1997).

There is a growing interest in the field of social gerontology in dealing with end-of-life questions as personal meanings. It seems to me to be part of other phenomena that lift and help us see a much greater view of life. Looking at the larger perspective called the *ciclo de vida y muerte y muerte en la vida* (cycle of life and death and death in life) offers us one more opportunity to reflect on these phenomena. They repeat what Medina (1983) said about living *consciente de la muerte*, in the light of death. Becker tells us how our American culture has been built around the denial of death. It is the terrible paradox of individuality within finitude. We are symbolic selves, "a creator with a mind that soars out to speculate about atoms and infinity, who can place himself imaginatively at a point in space and contemplate bemusedly his own planet. This immense expansion, this dexterity, the ethereality, this self-consciousness gives to man literally the status of a small god in nature, as the Renaissance thinkers knew." And, as if to mock us, Becker reminds us that we are also in nature: "Man is a worm and food for worms." Our splendid uniqueness, he writes, is that we "stick out of nature with a towering majesty, and yet [we go] into the ground a few feet in order blindly and dumbly to rot and disappear forever. It is a terrible dilemma to be and to have to live with" (Becker 1973, 26).

This comment brings us back to what prompted my inquiry in this chapter in the first place, and that is the star-flowers. Perhaps, as *2001* shows us, we belong to the stars, the last emissions of *spintherismos*, of life itself, as it oozes out of us. Maybe when the tombstone makers in La Liendre and in Mora carved their iconographic

Julian joins the space race (Parents)

symbols, they were trying to say that we return as energy, light, intelligence, and soul to the creator. How else to reckon these strange symbols?

One important issue, in terms of the theory of gerotranscendence, is the arrival at a cosmic place after distressing and difficult struggles, the recognizing of a different state of being, and the awareness of things cosmic. This recognition would entail a different perspective on one's place in the generations. Maybe this is love's struggle, as proposed in Klopstock's poem. As one listens to the ever-developing dynamics in the last movement in the Resurrection Symphony of Mahler, one thinks, "Open your eyes and ears. Listen to this great feat of music and let it uplift you. Let your soul be open to greater things. Go beyond where you are!"

We see some of this awareness in many Hispano families where the oldest male is called *tata* for "father" and the oldest female is called *nana* for "mother." I believe they are better terms for *abuelo(a), bisabuelo(a), or tatarabuelo(a)* (grandparent, great-grandparent, great-great-grandparent). It seems a better recognition of what age and the patriarchy and matriarchy mean in many families. Perhaps it is deeper reckoning of what grandparenthood should mean. We have not given much attention to the role of older members in Hispano families, much less in other families. If recognition of a transcendent experience as a part of aging is a goal for older persons, how do we incorporate it into the psychologies that deal with older persons? Are materialism, television, bingo, gambling, alcohol, and illnesses obstacles and distractions to seeing this dimension of human growth? How does achieving the phenomenon of the gerotranscendent help one to deal with death issues if one is confined to a modern high-tech hospital with its the capacity for keeping one alive beyond reason? In its work with the dying, has the palliative care movement approach moved us toward accepting gerotranscendence? And, finally, who cares?

It seems now that confronting my own end meant a cosmic transformation. The new life around me in my nephews, nieces, some *hijitas* and *hijitos* gained from baptisms and confirmations testify strongly to the importance of *familia*. Robert Henry, Michaela, Caroline, Ryan Christian, Dillon, Angela, Angelo Isaiah, Ezekial, Nickolas, Khallen, Rhianna, Julian, Kennan, "John John" are stellar cases because these little ones attest louder than any symphony to the beauty of creation. I am convinced that joy is the emotion of the transcendent. It is the joy of first-time parents as the ordeal of labor is ended and a new entity comes into the world, hungry, squealing, put upon, and seeking union with his/her creators. Joseph Campbell puts on the finishing touch when he asks and answers his own question: "Is the machine going to crush humanity or serve humanity? Humanity comes not from the machine but from the heart" (1988, 18).

CHAPTER 11

Seeking Light after the Great Night: *Tinieblas*

Este mundo es el camino para el otro, que es morada sin pesar; mas cumple tener buen tino para andar esta jornada sin errar.

Jorge Manrique

THE TINIEBLAS, FROM THE LATIN *TENEBRAE*, IS THE LAST CEREMONY BEFORE Easter Sunday conducted by the *La Cofradía de Nuestro Padre Jesús Nazareno* (also known as *Los Hermanos Penitentes*) [the Penitent Brotherhood]).* Tinieblas is conducted on Holy Thursday or on Good Friday and always after sunset in darkened *moradas* (lay chapels) in northern New Mexico and southern Colorado.† The term *tinieblas* (darkness and death) provides a contrast between light and darkness, sin and death, perdition and eternal life. This contrast can be subsumed under *el ciclo de vida y muerte* (the cycle of life and death) in New Mexico (Medina 1983). Under the general rubric of *el ciclo de vida y muerte*, one can subsume three contrasts: death and regeneration, darkness and light, and grief and praise (or, in more general terms, despair, trial, and tribulation compared to transcendence and joy). In this chapter, I consider the contrast between light and darkness as a metaphor

---

*New Mexico historian Fray Angelico Chávez makes the point that Jesús Nazareno and the *nazarenos* do not derive their names from Jesus of Nazareth but from "Nazarite," a Hebrew term applied to one "consecrated to God." One exterior feature of the Nazarites is that they never trimmed their hair. Sampson and Samuel were Nazarites (Chávez 1954, 118–19).

† The word *morada* (dwelling place or lodge) is from the verb *morar* (Chávez 1954, 122).

for life and death. As Jung has shown, the contrast between light and darkness is primordial and archetypal:

> When the great night comes, everything takes a note of deep dejection, and every soul is seized by an irrepressible longing for light. That is the pent-up feeling that can be detected in the eyes of primitives, and also in the animal's eyes, and we never know whether that sadness is bound up with the soul of the animal or is a poignant message which speaks to us out of that still unconscious existence [unreflective consciousness]. That sadness also reflects the mood of Africa, the experience of its solitudes. It is a maternal mystery, this primordial darkness. That is why the sun's birth in the morning strikes the natives as so overwhelmingly meaningful. That *moment* in which light comes *is* God. That moment brings redemption, release. To say that the *sun* is God is to blur and forget the archetypal experience of that moment. . . . In reality a darkness altogether different from the natural light broods over the land. It is the psychic primal night which is the same today as it has been for countless millions of years. The longing for light is the longing for consciousness. (Quoted in von Frantz 1998, 66–67)

This paragraph has all the elements for the analysis of *tinieblas.* All of the themes in Jung's vision are rife with meaning and symbolism. The themes are applicable in a consideration of Hispano thought and spirituality and have applications to other cultural groups as well. The task involves the need to amplify—in the Jungian sense—the symbolism of darkness and light to reach the deeper intentionality of *tinieblas.* Consciousness is always intentional, which is to say that consciousness is always "consciousness of" something (Stewart and Mickunas 1974, 64). This concept from phenomenological philosophy refers to that mechanism by which consciousness—as awareness or a perception of an object or a state of being—cannot be disrelated from the object or from the concern of the moment. How does the experience of *tinieblas*, either the ceremony or the broader sense of darkness, affect a participant's consciousness? What do people experience when they participate in such a ceremony? Does this ceremony, conducted in darkness, bring a new consciousness of spiritual meanings? How do immersions in total darkness affect the modern person?

One of the first tasks in this inquiry involves the need to amplify the ideas of light and dark as metaphors for life and death as well as for resurrection. One needs to "suspend one's belief," to use the phenomenological method of "bracketing" and, as noted in earlier chapters, to hold in abeyance what we think we know to be the reality of everyday life. In the mundane rising and setting of the sun we rarely think of comparing light and dark. It is part of the taken-for-granted reality of everyday life. What would happen if the night became prolonged or if the sun never "set"

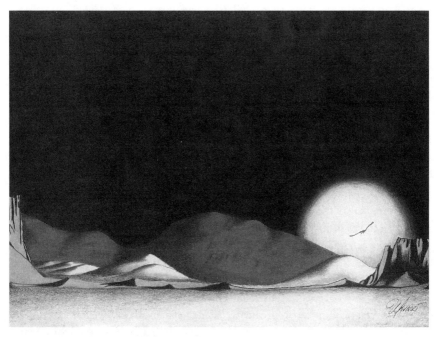

In the still of the night (Gilbert Ulivarrí)

on a particular day? Our perception of this happening would involve surprise and incredulity, and we would have to question Kepler's laws of planetary motion or resort to placations to the Almighty.

The closest we come to experiencing such events is in the darkening of the earth in a full solar eclipse. We handle the eclipse as information flow from newscasters and government agencies that inform us of the extent of the event. We are told by the National Oceanic and Atmospheric Administration not to look directly at the sun and are provided with alternatives for seeing the event. We experience the event as a darkening of the day. The newscasters tell us what areas of the country will be affected, where the umbra will pass, and how long the eclipse will last. If we are so disposed, we can travel to regions of the world so affected. It is all predictable but it still conjures up wonder. We can also note in passing that full solar eclipses happen every 410 years in any given area of the earth. If one has been so fortunate to see a full solar eclipse, then the chance of again seeing such a spectacular celestial happening is minimal.

Eclipses have had an impact on human history. The earliest recorded eclipse was on October 22, 2134 B.C.E., in China. When the royal astronomers His and Ho failed in their duty of predicting the event, the emperor, taken by surprise, beheaded them.

The ancient belief was that the sun had been devoured by a dragon. Drummers beat their drums, and archers shot arrows into the sky to set things right. An eclipse is recorded in the Bible in Amos 8:9, "'And on that day' says the Lord God, 'I will make the Sun go down at noon, and darken the Earth in broad daylight.'" The day was June 15, 763 B.C.E. A more famous eclipse ended a five-year war between the Lydians and the Medes. The two Middle Eastern armies were in battle when "the day turned into night." The date was May 28, 585 B.C.E. Both parties stopped fighting at once. They agreed to a peace treaty ("Eclipses" 1998). Darkness has always been a premonition of impending doom, whether it is the darkness of a world gone awry or a celestial event.

Sometime between 1806 and 1816, parts of New Mexico were shadowed by a full umbra. An elderly informant described in a letter in 1967 (Baca 1967) what her mother had told her about such an event. Her mother lived 105 years and had witnessed the event in the area near Anton Chico, New Mexico. When the eclipse occurred, people stopped work in the fields; others ran to their homes thinking that the end of the world was near. Many, according to this account, implored God to set the day straight.

We fear such events because they confront us with the prospect of our own death. Yet American culture is in a perpetual "denial of death," as Becker (1973) noted. Finality brings on the full collapse of the ego, and all that is left is "food for worms" as discussed in the last chapter (Becker 1973, 28).

The Rising Sun

Hispanos of the previous generation greeted the dawn by singing "La alba." Children would be roused out of bed to sing:

Ángel de mi guardia,	Guardian Angel,
noble compañía,	noble company,
vélame en la noche	watch over me at night
y guardame en el día.	and guard me in the day.
Cantemos la alba	We shall sing the morning song
Ya viene el día,	Day is breaking,
Deremos gracias,	Let us give thanks,
Ave María.	Hail Mary.

An angel watches over the person at night and is implored for help during the day. As dawn breaks, thanks are offered for the new day. It is interesting that the word *vélame* (watch) appears in the song. Writing about the 1940s Lucero-White said that a deceased person would not be left alone at night before his or her burial, and some family members or neighbors were appointed to *velar* or *vigilar el muerto* (to watch over him or her). This act was called *el velorio* (wake), after the term for *vela* (candle) (Lucero-White 1945, 255). Jaramillo tells us that in the past it was not uncommon to *velar el muerto* in the home. *Canticos* (religious chants) would go on all night. In the morning, "La alba" would be sung, mass said, and the dead person taken to his or her rest (Jaramillo 1941).

In a family prayer still used in some *moradas*, the parent asks a series of questions: "¿Quien es el dueño de la fe?" Followed by the response, "José." "¿Quien llena la casa de alegría?" "María." "¿Quien en esta casa da luz?" Followed by the answer, "Jesús." (Who is the keeper of the faith? Joseph. Who fills it with happiness? Mary. Who gives light to this house? Jesus). It is best not to answer "the REA" (Rural Electric Association) to the last question or one might get a quick smack on the mouth!

Some Hispano last names attest to the idea of light. For example, *Vigil* refers to the vigil and vigilance. *Velarde* means *vela arde* (light that burns). Some have attributed the *Velarde* name to a crypto-Jewish origin. *Lucero* is a common last name with roots that go to one of the first colonial families of New Mexico, Lucero de Godoy. It is the name of the morning star or the white star on a horse's head. Lucero means "splendor" or "brilliance." People would arise to do chores to *el lucero de la mañana*, a star in the east, that is, Venus. Women's names such as Aurora, Lucia, Estrella, Estella, and Luz also mean "dawn," "light," and "star." *Luz* is more than a woman's name—it also means "to bring to the light" in the process of giving birth. *Lucifer* means "light," even though it implies wickedness, and Lucifer is called *el ángel de las tinieblas* (the angel of darkness).

The theme of light and dark is also apparent in celestial configurations in the folk lexicon of the 1930s–1940s as presented to us by Cordóva. *Las Tres Marías*, mentioned in Cordóva's *No lloro pero me acuerdo* (1976), are identified in Jaramillo's *Shadows of the Past* as the three stars in Orion's belt (Jaramillo 1941). *Las Tres Marías* were seen in the east at the beginning of winter and moved to the west by summer. Jaramillo writes that other aspects of the night sky were also important to Hispanos of the 1940s: *El Carrito del Cielo* (heaven's carriage); *Los Ojitos de Santa Lucia* (St. Lucy's eyes) were tiny, evenly matched stars named after Santa Lucia; and *Las Cabrillas* (the goats) were a group of small stars bunched together like a herd of goats. As for *Las Tres Marías*, folk astronomy might have been a way to understand the night by making it familiar, by identifying stars with saints. Or perhaps there is nothing more to it than a simple identification of three stars.

Hispanos as spiritual people have oriented themselves to God and belief in their own salvation. "La alba" tells us that Jesus is the light of the world and the Word Incarnate in the fifth and seventh stanzas.

5. En una pobreza	In such poverty
ya parió María	Mary gave birth
al Verbo Encarnado	to the Word Incarnate
para amparar y guía	for help [light] and guidance

7. Ya parió María	Mary has given birth
para el consuelo	for the consolation
de los pecadores	of sinners
y luz del día.	and the light of day.

Mary's son is seen as the source of light (*luz del día*, the light of day). Sin is contrasted with the light of day. *Luz* is both light and, in the Hispano meaning system, the act of giving birth—*dando luz*. Mary gives birth to Jesus: Only women can give light! The eleventh stanza is of particular interest because of the idea that the light of day is a blessed gift, like life itself. Light comes from a blessed source.

Bendito sea	Blessed be
la luz del día	the light of day
bendita sea	blessed be
quien nos la envía.	the one who gives it.

Finally, the sun itself, rising in the East, is seen as blessed, as are the things of the earth and the firmament. The theories of Jung and Hispano natural philosophy coincide in the stanzas below, where it is recognized that "the *moment* in which light comes *is* God" (von Frantz 1998, 66).

13. Bendito sea	Blessed be the
sol refulgente,	brilliant sun,
bendito sea	blessed be the
sol del oriente.	eastern sun.

The purpose of singing "La alba" is provided in the fourteenth stanza.

14. Quien al el alba canta	He who sings "La alba"
muy de mañana	early in the morning
las indulgencias	the indulgences
del cielo gana.	of heaven gains.

The contrast between darkness and light is applied to other aspects of the human experience. An older psychology, for example, the work of Eugene Minkowski, speaks of "clear" and "dark" space as subtypes of attuned space. Clear space is not only the space of the horizon, perspective, and distinctiveness, it is also what Minkowski called the "distance vècue" (experienced distance)—the distance between individuals. This "free space" refers to the emotionally neutral, and it results in a certain "amplitude of life." Dark space is experienced as obscurity or a fog. It is more than the mere absence of light, horizon, or perspective. "Phenomenologically, darkness is a black, thick and gloomy substance. Because the 'experienced distance' disappears, there is no more 'life amplitude' and vital space is narrowed, space is desocialized, it surrounds the individual and even penetrates his body" (Minkowski, quoted by Ellenberger 1967, 111). Minkowski and this older school of psychoanalysts were concerned with how psychopathology distorted time, space, and body perception. Indeed, Minkowski associates this "dark space" with paranoia and delusions of persecution (Minkowski, quoted by Ellenberger 1967, 111).

Becker notes that the psychiatric and religious perspectives of reality are intimately related. He notes that "psychiatric experience and religious experience cannot be separated either subjectively in the person's own eyes or objectively in the theory of character development" (1973, 67). Consider what is said in the Gospel of Matthew and its connection to "dark space": "The eye is the lamp of the body. If your eyes are good, your whole body will be full of light. But if your eyes are bad, your whole body will be full of darkness. If then the light within you is darkness, how great is that darkness!" (Matthew 6:21–23). The "eye" is the light of the soul.

The Passage

The fourth chapter of von Frantz's *On Dreams and Death* has the odd title of "The Dark Birth Passage and the Spirit of Discouragement" and relates two seemingly unconnected themes, death as a passage and "birth" into another existence. The work of Dr. Raymond Moody has captured the public attention in its descriptions of people who have had near-death experiences, that is, have "died" and then "come back" to relate that death was like a passage through a tunnel. They saw a light ahead. Some report a state of happiness, others of seeing dejected forms without substance (Moody, in von Frantz 1998, 57–58). Some have reported that they were "sent back" after being informed that this was not their time. Moody writes that he has not conducted cross-cultural studies on this phenomenon and hence cannot comment on its universality. Critics of Moody's work have suggested other reasons for the phenomenon he describes, in particular an oxygen-starved brain (Moody 1980).

An interesting image comes from a person who "died" and was "brought back to life."

I turned over and tried to get into a more comfortable position, but just at that moment a light appeared in the corner of the room, just below the ceiling. It was just a ball of light, almost like a globe, and it was not very large. . . . It was a feeling of complete peace and utter relaxation. I could see a hand reach down for me from the light and the light said, "Come with me, I want to show you something." So immediately, without any hesitation whatsoever, I reached up with my hand and grabbed onto the hand I saw. . . . Now, at this time, as soon as I left my body, I took on the same form of light. (Moody, quoted in von Frantz 1998, 75)

More interesting is the survivors' experience of the "passage" from life to death. The death of someone close to us floods us with emotions, some of which can be identified as depression, dejection, and even despair, especially if we consider the death "meaningless," such as those deaths caused by violence. What is important is how a transition is made not only by the dying, but by the survivors. Ceremonies and rituals assist in making the passage from despair to transcendence, from travail to joy, such as in a funeral ceremony and the activities designed to let the loved one "go." An old Hispano admonishment to someone who has been grieving too long and in an uncontrolled way is to say to them, *Ya no piensas tanto de Fulano, deja lo ir* (Don't be thinking so much about Fulano, let him go), or *Ya dejalo ir, no puede hallar descanso si sigues pensando tanto de el* (Let Fulano go, he will not be able to find rest [or make his way] if you continue to wail and cry for him so). The idea is that unless one ends mourning after an appropriate period of time, the deceased will not be able to go on her or his way—the dead is seen as *siguen penando* (our grief for him will not let him rest). Most cultures, therefore, have provided important ceremonies as a mechanism for "soul release." For Hispanos, the one-year anniversary, called *la misa del cabo de año* (the end of the year mass), is offered for the repose of the soul. The *misa de ocho días* (a mass at eight days) is also offered to assist family members early in their travail. Thus a ceremony is used to mark the end of grieving and to let the spirit go.

A prayer published in a northern New Mexico periodical is intriguing in its symbolism of one outstretched hand grasping another (Moya 2001, 40). The prayer recognizes the transition from life to death and from the darkness of *tinieblas* to this life. It is reminiscent of Michelangelo's Sistine Chapel fresco in which the hand of God reaches to touch Adam to give him life. In Moya's prayer the supplicant asks the Father to take him by the hand and lead him into the next life:

Dame Señor, tu mano, pa' que pueda yo cruzar	Give me your hand oh Lord so that I can cross
de esta vida hasta la otra,	from this life to the next,

Crescencio, Abiquiui Cemetery (Jeremy Herrera)

Como yo una vez cruce a esta vida	as once I crossed to this life from the
con la ayuda de tu mano.	other with the help of your hand.

The theme of one hand shaking the other also appears in two Hispano village cemeteries. One tombstone varies the theme by showing a hand pointing to heaven as if to say, "I have gone that way." At the Tecolote Cemetery, near Las Vegas, New Mexico, I observed a crystal hand positioned as if emerging from the burial mound.

The Absence of Light: The Tinieblas Ceremony

La Cofradía de Nuestro Padre Jesús Nazareno (Confraternity of our Father Jesus the Nazarene, the *Penitente* brotherhood) evolved during the early decades of the nineteenth century. The brotherhood was influenced in part by the lay Third Order of St. Francis. The Third Order was established by St. Francis in 1221. The order was to serve men and women who for some reason or another could not enter the cloister in the first and second order and so was midway between these orders and the world. The order was designed to follow the Rule set up by St. Francis. In the late eighteenth century, village men in New Mexico organized themselves into local chapters to provide support to families and individuals because there were few priests to minister to communities. Beyond the support they offered, the men sought a deeper state of oneness with God by emulating Christ's pain and suffering. The ritual of Tinieblas is performed in a darkened *morada* (chapel) on Good Friday evening. The absence of light has a profound impact on participants. I observed the ritual at six different times.

In one instance, the *morada* was situated in an open field in a village deep in the mountains in northeastern Mora County, New Mexico. There were no outside lights, so that making one's way to the *morada* meant adjusting one's eyes to the darkness. After entering the threshold, one was greeted warmly by an *hermano* (a *Penitente* brother) and escorted to benches against the far wall. An altar lit with many candles and adorned with *bultos* (handmade representations of Christ and the saints) and store-bought *santos* (saints) was located in the front of the *morada.* A large figure of Christ was covered in a dark purple mantle to remind the viewer of the gravity of Lent and the absence of Jesus. It presented an eerie cast. The candles provided the only source of light. Rael notes that in some *moradas*, one finds a skeletal, sculptural rendition of death, sometimes seated on her death cart (*la carreta de la muerte*) holding a bow and arrow. Rael notes that she is referred to as *nuestra comadre Sebastiana* (our friend Sebastiana) (Rael 1951, 12). Sebastiana was the name given to death.

The floor was without carpets or linoleum; only warped bare boards that creaked as one walked across them. An old pot-bellied stove provided heat. People came in and were greeted, and some would go to the altar, kneel, make the sign of the cross, and pray. Silently they took their seats. A privileged anteroom was attached to the main *morada.* At the beginning of the ceremony, the altar candles were snuffed out. Only the candles of a homemade "candelabra"—the *tinieblario*—were used to light the chapel. The *tinieblario* was a triangular object made of pine furring strips (two-by-two-inch boards). It stood about waist high on a pedestal with fourteen

Abandoned *morada*, Manuelitas Canyon (Jeremy Herrera)

lit candles, which were secured on the top beam of this apparatus. A small group of *hermanos* stood in front of the lit candelabra. After each stanza was recited, a candle was snuffed out. The *hermanos* moved the *tinieblario* back a few feet after each stanza and eventually to the back of the *morada*. The recitations continued until all fourteen candles had been extinguished. The increasing darkness in the *morada* and the recitations reminded observers of the blackness of sin and the eternal night of the long, dark sleep. As the last candle is put out and after a pause, the *morada* explodes into a din. I heard heavy foot stomping, the whirling, dry, wooden sound of the *matraca*, and a banging on the *morada*'s outside door as if demons of hell had come to claim one's soul. Fear gripped me because there was no other sensory input in this darkened room. Then a voice in back of the main room asked, "¿Estan salvados?" (Are you saved?). After a pause to give the guests a chance to collect their wits, one candle was brought to the main altar to reignite all the altar candles, and a long recitation of prayers for the villagers ensued.

The contrast of darkness and light created a sense of transcendence as persons realized that they had somehow "survived" the noisy onslaught and the disorientation

A *tinieblario*, "La Luz en La Noche" (Father José Vigil)

of the darkness and found themselves alive on "this" side, in the light of life. In capturing the contrast between light and darkness, life and death, repentance and sin, the ceremony is meant to invite one to a more perfect life. After the disorienting darkness, the light is welcomed. It is the life-sustaining light, *la luz*. In this little chapel in the middle of a large field, without electric lights, and deep in the mountains of

New Mexico, both the literal and the symbolic passages from darkness to light were enacted. Leaving the *morada*, I was struck with the brilliance of the stars unobscured by city lights and smog, the majesty of the night sky, and with renewed feelings of well-being.

Oh, sangre de mi Jesús, a text published in northern New Mexico with all the *alabados* and the *hermanos'* recitations, sheds further understanding on the ceremony I witnessed. It illustrates how the *hermanos* have kept faith with practices that came from Spain more than 500 years earlier. At matins and in the Tenebrae, the monks would recite fourteen psalms from the Book of Psalms. They use fifteen-candle candelabra for the Good Friday matins service. They extinguish a candle after every psalm until all fourteen candles are blown out. The monks then make holy noise by banging their Psalters against the pews. After the noise is over, the fifteenth or Christ Candle is brought in, having been lit to signify the resurrection of Christ (*Oh Sangre de mi Jesús* 1999, 170).

This compilation of prayers and songs published by the *hermanos* tells us that the prayer chanted during Tinieblas is called *El miserer* (The one who gives mercy). It has fourteen stanzas to coincide with the fourteen candles. After the fourteenth verse, the brothers recite the *Ofrecimiento del Credo*, and the holy noise begins in the dark. The first verse is this:

El cielo y tierra Dios mío,	The earth and the sky my God,
se pasma viendo el amor	are stunned seeing the love
con que por salvar al hombre,	with which in wanting to save mankind
Dais vuestra vida, Señor.	you gave your life, Lord.
Sentenciado al inocente	The innocent was sentenced
por librar al pecador.	in order to save the sinner.
Pues con tierno llanto todos,	Thus with tender lament
Te rogamos: "Audimos (oyenos)	we all pray to you: Hear us
In te Domino sperabis"	in you, Lord, we hope"
No me confundas, Señor	Do not confuse me, Lord
Lávame, lávame y purifícame.	wash me, wash me, and purify me.

The *Enciclopedia universal ilustrada* tells us that *tenebrae* means the lack of light and, more interesting, to be in a state of ignorance and confusion because a person has not attained understanding (1930, 1361). Another definition is that there is a lack of light (*luz*) in the understanding of abstract or moral ideas. Tenebrae is also the last three days of Holy Week—the *Tridium*. The *Enciclopedia* entry also refers to the *Ángel de Tinieblas* (the dark and delivering angel), describes the ancient rites in the church during Holy Week, and includes a picture of the *Tinieblario de la Catedral de Jaén* in Spain. The ornate stand has places for fourteen candles surrounding a centerpiece much like a pie plate, with church ornamentation about its edges. It is incredible that the Tinieblas practices could have such a long and rich history. Indeed, the *hermanos* have been the keepers of the light in New Mexico. I have been told that a distinction should be made between the brothers of light and the *hermanos de sangre* (brothers of blood), who used to practice flagellation and macerations of the body.

Von Frantz reminds us that the light of torches and candles has a deeper meaning with regard to death: a new life and an awakening to a new consciousness granted to the deceased (1998, 67). No wonder that one sees candles on tombstones. The Tinieblas ceremony has the deeper significance of moving the participant from the "darkness" of present consciousness to the light of a new and dawning consciousness.

Another Tinieblas ceremony in a *morada* in another part of New Mexico used a different text in its services, and offered a different contemplation of the end of all things. This service was also held deep in the mountains away from traffic, city lights, and from unwanted intrusion. A camping light greeted the participants; there was no other source of light in these woods. The interior of the main service altar was lit by two candelabras, each with seven candles. The ceremony began with several *hermanos* kneeling in front of the altar and some kneeling away from the main altar, aligned along the right side of the room. The audience-participants sat on comfortable pews on the left side of the room. The Profession of Faith was followed by this chant:

Mira, mira pecador,	Look [pay attention], sinner,
que si vives en pecado,	if you live in sin
puedes anochecer bueno,	you might go to bed well
y amanecer condenado.	But wake up condemned.
Amanecer condenado.	Wake up condemned.

To add gravitas and underline the frightening message, the other *hermanos* functioned as chorus participants, repeating the last word of each stanza, in this case *condenado* (condemned). The mighty passage forces the penitent to contemplate *el cabo del mundo* (the final judgment)—her or his own judgment. Penitence here is reserved for the participants, including the *hermanos*. Does one want to go to bed some night only to awaken condemned to eternal night? The second stanza from "Mira, mira, pecador" (Beware, beware, sinner) says:

Mira que breve es tu vida	See how short is your life,
y que vas muy a la posta,	and walking with a single purpose,
caminando hacia la muerte	walking toward death,
piénsalo bien que te importa	Think carefully that it concerns you.
. . . que te importa.	. . . that it concerns you.

The penitent must take heed because life is too short, and we all will be consumed by death. "Que te importa" (think carefully) is repeated for a grave effect. The last event in life is depicted in the next stanzas.

3. Triste, turbado y confuso,	Sad, upset, and confused,
temeroso y aún temblando	fearful and even trembling
entre batallas y penas	between battles and pains
estaras agonizando	you will be at your death bed
. . . agonizando.	. . . agonizing.

4. Piénsalo bien que te importa,	Think carefully that it concerns you,
para que enmiendes tu vida,	so that you amend your life
y lo hagáis en cuanto antes,	and you do it as soon as possible
porque ya estas de partida	Because you are about to die
. . . de partida.	. . . to die.

Agonizando is substantive in Spanish. It connotes the last moments of life as Hispanos understand them. It is the *gorgoritos* (the death rattle of the dying) (see Moya 2001 for a discussion of the *gorgoritos*). The stanzas continue their dire predictions, and each stanza is sung with its lingering one-word ominous coda. In the ceremony I observed, after each four-line stanza, a candle was snuffed out, and the room became darker and darker. The penitents were told how the death rattle will sound in their chest and how they will be laid in the ground.

5. Cuando agonizando estás	When you are dying
y roncandote ya el pecho,	and death rattles in your chest
y con la vela en la mano,	and with the candle in your hand
y que quisieses haber hecho	you think of what you should have done
. . . haber hecho.	. . . you should have done.

8. Piénsalo bien que te importa,	Think carefully that it concerns you
y mira que sepultado,	and see that once buried
entre tierra, polvo y huesos	among the earth, dust, and bones

has de quedar olvidado	You shall remain forgotten
. . . olvidado.	. . . forgotten.

10. Piénsalo bien que te importa,	Think carefully that it concerns you
pues si vives descuidado,	because if you live carelessly
puedes ser, por tu descuido,	you may be, due to your carelessness,
en el juicio condenado—	at the judgment condemned
. . . condenado.	. . . condemned.

11. En perpetuos alaridos	In never-ending howls
están allí en el infierno,	they are there in hell
echando a Dios maldiciones,	casting curses upon God
y rabiando en fuego eterno	and raging in eternal flames
. . . fuego eterno.	. . . eternal flames.

The recitation called "Mira, mira, pecador" has twenty-seven stanzas. But it takes a different tone after the thirteenth stanza. The four-line stanzas now proclaim the glory and beauty to be found in heaven. The sixteenth stanza proclaims the eternal light:

16. Nunca es noche, siempre es día,	It is never night, always day,
en esa hermosa ciudad,	in that beautiful city
porque la luz que le alumbra,	because the light that shines
es de Dios su claridad.	is from God's glory.

After the fourteen candles on the candelabra were snuffed out, we heard the din of a heavy chain in the darkness. The effect was disconcerting and compelling because I had just heard stanzas about being enchained (*encadenado*) by sin. What a powerful and profound effect to equate the message with its sound in the darkened chapel!

In the darkened room, the *hermanos* began to name persons who had died and for whom special prayers had been requested. After announcing a person's name, a repetitive prayer followed asking forgiveness for his sins. This list continued for a long time because each brother presented many names. I recognized some of these names as belonging to people who had died within the past year. Perhaps the petitions had been made to individual *hermanos* in the community and brought to this assemblage. Finally, when it seemed as if the list was exhausted, the prayer leader implored the participants sitting in the pews to render names. He said repeatedly, "Piden, piden" (ask, ask). New names were now offered by the participants. Each name was identified in this "communion of saints" and added to the long list of the departed. Many were remembered, and their plight implored before God.

Rael noted that the twelve yellow candles of the *tinieblario* represent the twelve apostles and that the thirteenth (Weigle states that there are thirteen candles, compared to the fourteen used in conjunction with the fourteen stanzas in the *miserer* discussed above), a white candle, represents Jesus (Rael, cited in Weigle 1971, 400). Rael continued his description thus:

> When the church is dark, the *rezador* [prayer leader] shouts: "Salgan vivos y difuntos a acompañar con el amor de Dios" ("All ye living and dead persons come forth to join us, for the love of God"). . . . Immediately after the *rezador* recites the Apostles' Creed three times in a low voice . . . the members of the congregation make all kinds of loud noises with wooden clappers, chains, drums, and flutes. . . . At the end of the recitation of the Creed, the *rezador* gives the signal for silence. Prayers for the living and the dead are recited then: Hail Mary's, Our Father's, the *Salve Regina*, and certain prayers known as *sudarios* (in reference to the shroud in which Our Lord was wrapped). When these prayers are terminated, the noises are resumed once more. This alternation of prayers and loud noises is repeated three times. When the noises are suspended the fourth time, at a signal given by the *rezador* the lighted candle is brought once more into the room, and all the candles on the tenebrae candelabrum are lighted again from its flame. (Rael 1951, 15)

According to Weigle, the noise represents the moment of Jesus' death, when "there was darkness over the whole land until the ninth hour, when the sun's light failed" (Luke 23:44–45) and "the curtain of the temple was torn in two, from top to bottom; and the earth shook, and the rocks split; the tombs were opened, and many bodies of the saints who had fallen asleep were raised, and coming out of the tombs after the resurrection they went into the holy city and appeared to many" (Matthew 27:51–53; Weigle 1971, 399).

Praying in the dark allows one to pray without distraction. In my own experience, a deep feeling ensued that, by identifying with the departed in the dark, I was somehow linked to them. It was as if prayers from the faithful would move the deceased persons from where they were (perhaps a purgatory?) to what Andelecia Gallegos has called *una mansión hermosa* (a beautiful mansion), or the final glory (Gallegos 1996, 62). Praying in the dark for the lost souls also puts one in that same dark eternity. It is a means of imploring God to take to him those for whom prayers are offered. It is not often that we can be part of the amorphous nature of the deep night. Praying in the dark is a primordial experience in which we are put in touch with the universal elements we have lost in our well-lit cities and streets.

Dando Luz

The relationship between birth and death is subtle and far-reaching. Von Frantz writes: "The image of a dark, narrow passage also belongs among those archetypal motifs which anticipate the course of death" (1988, 56). In the Hispano worldview, however, there is even more to this idea.

A sad recuerdo written by the poet Ricardo Montoya in 1937 is a despedida on behalf of a mother's grief. (As noted in chapter 9, the despedida as leave-taking is best exemplified in folk poetry and folk psychology; see chapter 9 and Korte 1999a). It begins, characteristically, by giving the date.

Año de mil nuevecientos	The year was nineteen hundred
agregando el tres y siete,	and thirty-seven,
presente tengo la fecha	I know the date
por ser marzo el vienteisiete.	it was March twenty-seventh.
A las siete en la mañana	It was seven in the morning
Las Vegas el hospital,	at the Las Vegas hospital,
pa' que la muerte llegara	so that death would come
destinó Dios el lugar.	God destined the place.
Estrella Patrón Perea	Estrella Patrón Perea
enferma allí se incontraba,	was ill in the hospital,
quien a la hora de su muerte	at the time of her death
vienteitrés años contaba.	she was twenty-three years old.
En nombre de ella diré	In her name I will say,
adiós mi esposo querido,	good-bye to my loving husband,
mi padre, madre y hermanas	my father, mother, and sisters
mis tíos, ya me despido.	my uncles, I take my leave.
Adiós mis niños gemelos	Good-bye, my twin infants,
por ellos pido clemencia,	I ask for God's clemency,
once días de edad tenían,	they were eleven days old
es su estado de inocencia.	in their state of innocence.
Cuando luz a ellos di	When they were born
nunca pensado tenía,	I never thought that

que quedaran huerfanitos	they would become orphans
pero así Dios lo quería.	but that was what God wanted.
Adiós mis padres políticos	Adios to my in-laws
pa,' quien cariño guardaba,	whom I loved,
adiós a mis dos hermanos	good-bye to both my brothers
quienes ausentes se hallaban.	who were not around.
Le encargo mamá querida	Dearerst Mother, I ask of you,
a Refugio mi hermanito,	my brother Refugio,
mi esposo José D. Perea	and my husband, José D. Perea,
cuida bien a mis hijitos.	to take good care of my children.
Por todos pidiré a Dios	For all, I ask in God's name
ques les envíe consulo,	for consolations
y que gracia nos concede	and His grace we shall receive
para vernos en el Cielo	to see each other again in Heaven.
No parece de sentirse	It is difficult to feel
un caso como el presente,	a case like the present,
sinembargo yo los siento	because I feel for
a su esposo y los dolientes.	her husband and the bereaved.
Estos versos no travo	I do not write these versus
para mostrar sentimiento,	to present sentiments
sino que fui suplicado	but because I was asked
dar el acontecimento.	to provide the farewell eulogy.
Al componer estos versos	In order to write these versus
no es pues por fama gozar,	it was not to gain fame,
sólo es para describir	but only to describe
un caso de lamentar.	a lamentable case.
29 de abril, 1937.	April 29, 1937.

(Arellano and Vigil 1985)

In this tragic recuerdo, birth and death are closely tied together. As Estrella gives *luz* (the light of birth) to her twins, she suffers her own death. The poet tells us that on her behalf he will ask for God to send is *consuelo* (consolation) and his grace to her family with the hope that they will see each other in heaven at the final resurrection.

Luz y Entregas

Because we are alive, we give light to others. In death, we see the end of life and our birth into a new light. We northern New Mexicans express this idea in our *pesames* (condolences). We see life as *prestado* (on loan). In condolence, we say about a father or mother's death, *Se lo (la) prestaron por tantos años* (Your father [or mother] was lent to you for so many years). We should be grateful for this revelation of life before us. If life is on loan, so it can be *entregada* (returned) to its creator. Life and the gift of personhood can be returned with joy, as some newspaper obituaries proclaim. As noted in chapter 9, all *entregas* seem to have a dark side as well as a light and happy side. This includes the *entrega* for marriage (*la entrega de novios*), wherein parents give a final despedida, as well as the *entrega de difuntos* (the eulogy). It is a joyous occasion tinged with a dark side, because the bride and groom are reminded that the life they have chosen for themselves may be difficult (see also Korte 1999a). Another *entrega* is the joyous one of bringing a child home from church after his or her baptism. Like in the *entrega de novios*, the new *padrinos* (godparents) make a ritual proclamation as the child is returned to them. The child is no longer in *tinieblas*. A short version of this proclamation, from Truchas, New Mexico, says:

Compadre y Comadre	Cofather and Comother
Reciban a esta niña(o) con	Receive this child
todo nuestro rendimiento;	with our best compliments;
La sacamos de tinieblas con	We have rescued him/her from
el primer sacramento.	darkness with the first sacrament
En la pila del bautismo con	In front of the baptismal font
toda fe nos paramos	we took our place
Y allí del primer abismo	and from that abyss
también la descautivamos	was rescued
Dios les dé a su merced buen	God give you his
fin para doctrinala.	grace to teach her.
Nos dispensan las molestias, y	Please excuse this intrusion
con cariño reciban la	and with love receive this
Niña que se llama María	child who is called María
Tranquilina.	Tranquilina.

(Quoted in Torres 1963, 6).

An aside in Torres's citation is that newly baptized children were allowed to sweat so that the sacrament would permeate flesh and bones. Baptismal records of the nineteenth century indicate that many children were named "María," as in María Teresa, María Juanita, María Louisa, María Rita, or as shown above.

To say that one gives light (e.g., *dar luz, sacar a luz*) is to beg the question, What lies on the other side of *luz?* A letter written in Mora County, New Mexico, on October 12, 1880, provides some perspective on this question. In very formal Spanish, a couple in territorial Mora County asks another couple to be godparents for a newly arrived baby boy. They ask for the *padrinos* (godparents) to "sacar de tinieblas a la luz de la Gracia por medio de las aguas regeneradoras del Santo Bautismo a un infante que Dios nuestro Señor ha sido servido de darnos a luz" (to take this child from *tinieblas* into the light of grace through the regenerative waters of holy baptism, an infant that the Lord our God has seen fit to bring to light). The couple were first-generation German immigrants asking another first-generation German immigrant couple to baptize their newborn son, José Edwardo Korte, my grandfather (Korte and Metzger 1880).

What the baptism and the ceremony of *Tinieblas* have in common is the process of coming out of the darkness and the journey into the light the knowledge of good and evil, light and darkness—the living of one's life in a good way so that at the end one is not a formless soul, lost forever in the darkness. When working on this chapter I was told that Latino(a)s in southern Texas keep a light (or candle) burning all night where a newborn infant sleeps and turn it off (or put it out) only after baptism (Trujillo 2002). This fits within the discussion in this chapter.

One final comparison of light and dark comes from a stanza from another *entrega de bautismo* as presented by Anselmo Arellano (1995).

Nuestro Señor Jesucristo	Our Lord Jesus Christ
Con su mano bondadosa,	With his mercy
Ya le cerró el negro abismo,	Has now closed the dark abyss
Y le abrió su Santa Iglesia.	And has opened his Holy Church.

The basic definition of *tinieblas* in the *Enciclopedia universal ilustrada* (1930) says it all: "Suma ignorancia y confusión, por falta de conocimientos" ([It is] the sum of ignorance and confusion because of a lack of understanding). Isn't this what Jung was trying to tell us: that the darkness, like unconsciousness, will bring understanding and light? Cooper comments that

> darkness is not essentially evil since it is the ground of the light which emerges from it, and in this sense it is unmanifest light; the pre-cosmogonic, pre-natal darkness precedes

both birth and initiation and darkness is associated with states of transition as in death and initiation; germination and creation occur in darkness and everything returns to darkness in death and dissolution. (1978, 50)

CHAPTER 12

Giving Thanks: *Dando Gracias*

I am not a Catholic myself, I was not brought up in that faith; but at least one-third of my army are Catholic and I respect a good Catholic as much as a good Protestant.

Proclamation of Brigadier General Steven W. Kearney, to the people of
Las Vegas, August 15, 1846, Plaza Park West, Las Vegas, New Mexico

He who learns must suffer. And even in our sleep, pain which we cannot forget falls drop by drop until, in our own despair, against our will, comes wisdom through the awful grace of God.

Robert F. Kennedy, quoting Aeschylus' *Agamemnon* on the
death of the Martin Luther King Jr., April 4, 1968

When you are joyous, look deep into your heart and you shall find it is only that which has given you sorrow that is giving you joy.

Kahlil Gibran

There can be no comfort in the thought that we shall be immortal in our children and that our work will last forever, for the end is coming to all consolations that are in time. Apocalypse is a paradox of time and eternity that cannot be expressed in rational terms. And when the end comes there shall be no more time. And therefore we must paradoxically think of the end of the world both as in time and eternity. The end of the world, like the end of each individual man, is an event both immanent and transcendent. Horror and anguish are caused by this incomprehensible combination of the transcendent and the imminent, the temporal and the eternal.

Nicholai Berdyaev

THE APOCALYPSE IS CONSIDERED THE END IN ALL PERSPECTIVES OF RACIAL OR cosmic immortality; at the apocalypse the entire world faces the judgment of eternity. In this final reflection, I present the themes of despair and transcendence as another facet of the *ciclo de vida y muerte*. I expand the dualistic metaphor of *el ciclo de vida y muerte* but recognize that there is a need to reintroduce the idea of resurrection as a trifocal view. I also look at the question of an Hispano eschatology. "Eschatology" refers to the "the last things," for example, heaven, hell, and redemption. In this chapter we take up the question of what a folk psychology says about the last things.

During my research for this chapter, I found three Hispano "end of the world" texts that deal with "last things." These texts are interesting in their own right, and I discuss them after I develop the idea of *dando gracias.* In the last section of the chapter, I take a closer look at several Hispano views of apocrypha.

Berdyaev reminds us that the "apocalyptic mood is one in which the thought of death reaches its highest intensity, but death is about the death that is experienced as a way to a new life" (1959, 260). I begin by considering the simple ceremony of *dando gracias*, thanking both the deceased for his or her life as well as the community for the good things it has done for a bereaved family.

Dando Gracias at the Cemetery

Dando gracias, the giving of thanks at the burial site at the cemetery, is an important event. It is the act of giving thanks for the person's contribution to the community as a person, father, mother, employee, and other roles. During the eulogy, the person's talents and good traits are extolled. Perhaps this is the first step in "soul making."

The last official act by a family in the funeral rites is to give thanks to those who brought food, provided care and love, provided prayers on behalf of the loved one, and gave the eulogy. The burial site is usually the place where the family gives thanks to members of the community for their help. The family invites everyone to come to the house or a local hall (e.g., Veterans of Foreign Wars) for a gathering of friends for a repast. This last rite might be called *dar gracias*, but it is more than that when we extend the definition. *Dando gracias* is the giving of thanks not only to the community, but also to God for a life and a soul that manifested itself among us. In an interview Medina (1983) proposed that "las gracias son a Dios por una vida, por una alma que se revelo adelante de nosotros como una encarnación" (thanks are given to God for a soul that manifested itself bodily among us).

At one funeral, the deceased man's capacity for music was emphasized by his brother, another musician, who sang his departed brother's signature song, a tender love song. It was interpreted as the deceased man's *despedida* to his wife. There is something of the tragic and the triumphant in these events: tragic because we will no longer enjoy this person's talents or feel his or her presence; triumphant because the person no longer suffers the disease that killed him or her and is now free from future pain. As one gravestone proclaims, the person is "sheltered and safe from sorrow," and no longer feels even the sting of death. Both the tragic and the triumphant are also present in the funeral mass. The last words in the "Libera me" (Deliver me) and the "In paradisium" (In paradise, both covered later in the chapter) in the funeral mass reflect both the frightful day of judgment (*el día del juicio*) and the triumphant entry into paradise.

Thanksgiving and Recognition

After a struggle has occurred, thanksgivings and recognition ceremonies follow. Struggles can include a course of study, labor, or the birth of a child. These experiences suggest a transition from one state to another. Recognition ceremonies mean more if there has been a great effort to attain the next stage of development or the achievement of some great goal. In the training of military recruits, the newcomers are berated with such appellations as "meathead," "slime worm," and "sewer mouth." The drill instructor (DI) in the 1987 Stanley Kubrick film *Full Metal Jacket* told recruits that they were "lower than grabasstic amphibian shit." As the initiate grows in military bearing and skills, he reaches a point in the training where he "makes it" and is recognized by a new title. The DI proclaims to his charges, "As of this date, you are now a marine. You will always be a marine; you are part of a brotherhood. You will not die, as the Marine Corps lives forever!" How confident the DI is of his indoctrination! Graduation from boot camp and assignment to a unit marks the newly achieved status. In all fields, the completion of a course of study leads to the wearing of special clothing that distinguishes the former candidate. Other ceremonies provide for the awarding of honors, societal recognition, and special initials after the honoree's name. Commonly at college or high school graduations, the ceremony of recognition is heralded by Elgar's first *Pomp and Circumstance March*, bringing closure to the struggle. It is experienced as a joyful event with the academic community, family, and relatives witnessing the change.

War recognitions are similar in that a victorious army passes through some ceremonial place to mark the end of the struggle. U.S. soldiers passed through the Arc de Triomphe after the liberation of Paris from the Nazis. The Eighty-second Airborne marched in a parade on Broadway in New York to mark the end of World

War II. In *Star Wars, Episode III* (Lucas 1977), the destruction of the Deathstar was followed by a large celebratory by the protagonists. All these recognition ceremonies evoke the human need for this theatrical staging.

The first Thanksgiving Day was a time to give thanks to the Almighty for bringing the colony through the ordeal of a difficult winter. New Mexico's first Thanksgiving occurred on April 30, 1598, when 400 armed settlers and 130 women and children led by Capitan General y Governador don Juan de Oñate took possession of the colony of Nuevo Mexico after a difficult march from present-day El Paso, Texas (Armenta 1994). Likewise, days are set aside everywhere for the harvest ceremonies that give thanks after a grueling summer of toil.

It is in their contrast that these two facets of life are made manifest: overcoming an obstacle and offering thanks for being able to do so. Beethoven's Pastoral Symphony provides a similar type of contrast in the fourth and fifth movements. The dark side of the storm in the fourth movement is contrasted with the giving of thanks by the country folk after the light of day returns in the fifth movement. The music changes from dark tonal qualities to a lovely, light, upbeat tempo. How well Beethoven understood the idea of change and transcendence!

The *Triquetra*

As noted in chapters 10 and 11, Octavio Paz tells us that *vida y muerte* (life and death) are one. I take the same tack here but amplify this idea. Despair and transcendence are part of *vida y muerte*, and they are inseparable from each other. If one exists, so does the other. The quote from Kahlil Gibran at the beginning of this chapter adds to this idea. The theme of the last three chapters of this book is the *ciclo de vida y muerte*. The Indian *mandala* is a good symbol for *vida y muerte*: two fish chase each other within a circle such that one fish blends into the other, symbolizing how each is essential to the other. This fish image is not without significance. I discovered a *mandala* that had three interlocking fish. Representing each fish in its basic form and interlocking them gives us a symbol called the *triquetra*. If the symbol is the thought, as Ricoeur (1967) writes, then adding an interlocking ring to the fish allows us to add another concept. With the circle representing God—or the circle of life—and the interlocking fish representing the universe, the whole figure incorporates both *vida y muerte* and *resurrección* (resurrection.)

The *triquetra* has been attributed to the Celtic Christian church, although some modern pagan groups also claim it. It has, however, also been called an ideal Christian symbol composed of three interlocked *vesica pisces* and thus is a symbol of the Holy Trinity, showing the "three in one" of Christian unity beliefs

A *triquetra* (Wikipedia)

("Triquetra" 2006). Here it illustrates *vida, muerte, y resurrección* held together in the divine circle.

Despair and Transcendence: Diverse Sources

Despair and transcendence, like the duality of *vida y muerte,* belong on the same coin. They depict a truth found in all kinds of writing, both prose and music. Personal triumph cannot exist without some travail. The struggle when one is in despair leads to the joy of transcendence when despair dissipates. We find this in Scripture, personal histories, and psychotherapy. We see it most clearly in the passion and death of Christ at Easter. His cross is his defeat, but the cross also carries the larger message of resurrection in glory. This message is sometimes communicated by an empty wooden cross with an earthly garment wound about the crossbeams: *Es la Esperanza,"* the last hope at the end of life.

Examining examples of despair and transcendence in life experiences can help us determine what these experiences have in common. As noted earlier, I use a Jungian articulation and amplification approach.

Scripture reads:

Blessed are they that mourn, for they shall be comforted. (Matthew 5:4)

They that sow in tears shall reap in joy. He that goeth forth and weepeth, bearing precious seed, shall doubtless come again with rejoicing, bringing his sheaves with him. (Psalms 126:5–6)

In Psalms 126:5–6, weeping is followed by rejoicing. The promise is there for all to see that after the travails comes joy. Joy is the emotion of the transcendent undergoing a marked change in status.

The Book of Mormon also recognizes that despair and transcendence are part of the same coin. One cannot have one without the other:

And now, behold, if Adam had not transgressed he would not have fallen, but he would have remained in the Garden of Eden. And all things which were much have remained in the same state in which they were after they were created; and they must have remained forever and have no end.

And they would have no children; wherefore they would have remained in a state of innocence, having no joy, for they knew no misery, doing no good, for they knew no sin.

But behold, all things have been done in the wisdom of him who knoweth all things.

Adam fell that man might be; and men are, that they might have joy. (2 Nephi 2:22–25)

The key point in number 23 is that one needs to know misery and to struggle through it in order to know joy. Without misery, there can be no growth, future, or change, and therefore no experience of joy. Joy comes after misery in the struggle for something. It is experienced as a release from despair and grief.

The Night of a Prisoner

The book *Blessed Are the Soldiers*, about Hispano soldiers from the Belen, New Mexico, area who served in World War II and Korea, shows how the experience of war encapsulates the theme of despair and transcendence (Lopez 1990). Combat is a tremendously difficult travail with many deprivations, stresses and fears. In World War II, many New Mexico soldiers from the 200th Coast Artillery and its "daughter" organization, the 515th Coast Artillery, became prisoners of war (POWs) when the

Bataan Peninsula in the Philippine Islands was overrun and captured by the Japanese in April 1942. They were forced to march sixty miles to Camp O'Donnell. On their way, they were deprived of rest, food, and water. They were beaten because their enemy thought it was contemptible to surrender. They were forced to carry their wounded and sick comrades suffering from malaria, beriberi, and dysentery. If a person fell in the "death march," he was shot or bayoneted on the spot. Conditions in Camps O'Donnell and Cabanatuan were worse. Lack of medical facilities, shortages of food, and beatings on work details were prisoners' daily fare. Toward the end of the war, many were put in the holds of ships on their way to Japan to work in the mines or in factories. Conditions on these "hell" ships were deplorable, with little food and water. Starvation and lack of warm clothing took their toll. Many died in the camps, in the hell ships, or in the work camps in Japan (Cave 2006). Thus, when the men who had suffered but survived were finally freed, they experienced a joyful transcendence. About his liberation as a POW, Pete A. Gonzales said:

> Before the American transport trucks came, the American Navy planes flew over and dropped a supply of candy, cigarettes, and other goodies. The supplies were dropped by American Bombers with colored parachutes of red, white and blue, so some of the guys made an American flag from out of them. One of our great joys was removing the Japanese flag and raising our own flag that flew proudly over the prison camp that held us captive for so long. There were tears falling down our faces and it was a very emotional time for all of us, a time of great joy and thanksgiving. When our military personnel arrived with the medics, they immediately began to care for the sick. (Quoted in Lopez 1990, 112–13)

Soldiers lay down their lives for their comrades, making it the greatest sacrifice anyone can be called to make. It is a pure act of dedication to the group, a selfless act made so that others may live. It may be the "best tradition of the service" and in several cases has been recognized by bestowing the medal of honor on soldiers such as SP4 Daniel Fernandez from Los Lunas, New Mexico, who courageously threw himself on a grenade in Vietnam, thus saving the lives of his squad. It is also the highest calling in the Christian tradition. And those who perform these acts are "blessed," as Lopez emphasizes in the title of her book.

Despair and Therapy

May takes on the relationship between despair and joy:

> Authentic despair is that emotion which forces one to come to terms with one's destiny. It is the great enemy of pretense, the foe of playing ostrich. It is a demand to face the reality

of one's life. The "letting go" that we have noted in despair is a letting go of false hopes, of pretended loves, of infantilized dependency, of empty confusion which serves only to make one behave like sheep huddled in a flock because they fear the wolves outside the circle. Despair is the smelting furnace which melts out the impurities in the ore. Despair is not freedom itself, but is a necessary preparation for freedom. (May 1981, 235)

This position has tremendous import in therapy for people who hide behind false selves that they have created. They must confront these false selves to secure their freedom. Alcoholics Anonymous states that the alcoholic will not be cured until he or she has fallen into complete despair. One has to hit bottom and confront the lies about one's drinking. If one confronts oneself and one's lies, then another step awaits. Sometimes this is the step to freedom.

May continues:

When a person has "hit bottom"—i.e., when he has reached ultimate despair—he can then surrender to eternal forces; this is the dynamic in all authentic conversions. I would describe this process as giving up the delusions of false hope and, thus acknowledging fully the facts of destiny. Then and only then can this person begin to rebuild himself. (May 1981, 236)

Two essential steps follow. First is the discovery of hidden talents and coping mechanisms that assist the person in the struggle. "Despair is essential to the discovery on the part of the client of his or her hidden capacities and basic assets. . . . The function of despair is to wipe away our superficial ideas, our delusionary hope, our simplistic morality." The second step is happiness. "Those who feel healthy despair are often those who also can at the same time experience the most intense pleasure and joy. . . . human freedom and human joy also begin on the far side of despair" (May 1981, 237).

The philosopher of despair is Søren Kierkegaard, who held that man is a synthesis of the finite and the infinite. "The self is a synthesis in which the finite is the limiting factor, and the infinite the expanding factor" (Kierkegaard 1954, 163). If a human being were not a synthesis, she or he would not find her- or himself in despair. R. D. Laing takes this idea further by proposing that dread (i.e., despair) is the condition of the schizoid selves who find themselves in a condition in which other people's reality threatens their ontologically (i.e., bodily) insecure selves (Laing 1976). They find they cannot withdraw from society because they need social others to "feel real." Hence, one sense of dread in the schizoid condition involves the need to be with people to feel real and authentic while avoiding them because their weighty presence is a threat to an insecure and threatened self. Thus, Laing undergirds Kierkegaard by pointing out that the existential situation creates "splits" in the self and thus the sense of dread. "In so far as the self does not become itself, it is not its own self; but to be one's own self is despair. Infinitude's despair is therefore the fantastical, the limitless" (Kierkegaard 1954, 163). May says that the worst condition of all is to boast about never having been in despair, for that means that the person has never been authentically conscious of himself (May 1981, 238). Kierkegaard understood the despair captured in the childhood prayer "I dread the loss of Heaven and the pain of Hell" as the position of a person between the finite and the infinite. In this condition, the person confronts the contradiction of entering into or contracting despair yet never passing through it.

Kierkegaard writes,

> So also we can demonstrate the eternal in man from the fact that despair cannot consume his self, that this precisely is the torment of contradiction in despair. If there were nothing eternal in man, he could not despair; but if despair could consume his self, there would still be no despair. . . . Death is not the last phase of this sickness [unto death], but death is continually the last. To be delivered from this sickness by death is an impossibility, for the sickness and its torment . . . and death consist in not being able to die. (Kierkegaard 1954, 153–54)

Those who suffer panic attacks will recognize something of the truth of these statements. In Laingian psychology, the false self comes to be seen as the dead center of the self, and life is experienced as unreal and fantastical and never grounded as body experience. As my (mentally ill) sister once said, "For many years I could not realize myself." To live with phantoms and fantasy is to live an unreal, unembodied life. To live fully embodied is to live a life with others, hence the possibility of realizing one's own potential.

THE CHURCH CALENDAR

These ideas are reflected twice a year on occasions in which the Roman Catholic Church might be said to juxtapose despair and transcendence. Epiphany is the dark time before the celebration of Christmas. It is a time of waiting and praying for the coming of a great savior. The shortened days of winter and longer periods of darkness makes this a period of waiting as one hears such hymns as "O Come Emmanuel." When the great event occurs after the long night of waiting, joy, celebration, and a great light break forth. Similarly, the Lenten period involves many observances that provide the contrast of dark and light. The brothers of the *Cofradía de Nuestro Padre Jesús Nazareno* enact the *via cruces* (the fourteen Stations of the Cross) on Fridays during Lent. This is a time of personal reflection to remind the participants of the great suffering of Christ bringing redemption and change. The great renewal of Easter is a season of great light and a strong reminder of the defeat of death by Christ's resurrection. Because it coincides with the new plant growth of spring, it offers the promise of a new life and joy in Christ.

The Nature of Joy

We need to reiterate that the importance of joy is a promise of a new life. When examining joy, one should compare it to happiness.

> [J]oy is living on the razor's edge; [whereas] happiness promises satisfaction with the present state, a fulfillment of old longings. . . . Joy is a thrill of new continents to explore, and unfolding of life, of new continents emerging within oneself. Happiness is the absence of discord; joy is the welcoming of discord as a basis for higher harmonies. . . . .

May concludes that:

> What I am emphasizing is the joy that follows rightly confronted despair. Joy is the experience of possibility, the consciousness of one's freedom as one confronts one's destiny. In this sense despair, when it is directly faced, can lead to joy. After despair the one left is possibility. (May 1981, 242)

This transition is why one can speak of attaining a new state of being.

The future is open to us. Milton tells us in *Paradise Lost* that Adam and Eve, after their great despair following the loss of Eden and the rebuke of God, began to experience human consciousness and the pains and joys of life.

> Some natural tears they dropped, but they wiped them soon;
> The world was all before them, where to choose
> Their place of rest, and Providence their guide.
> They, hand in hand, with wandering steps and slow
> Through Eden took their solitary way.
>
> (As cited in May 1981, 242)

The Apocalyptic View

Apocalyptic views are important for Hispanos since they provide an end in time, called *el cabo del mundo*, the end of the world. In another context this has been called *el día del juicio*, the day of judgment. These views are important in defining the nature of good, of evil and what happens if one fails to lead a good life. Is there a final reward? a hell? Will God punish the evildoers at the end? Along with Scripture these texts provide a rationale for an end of time. There is a piece of common wisdom that says *No salemos de este mundo sin pagar las que debemos* (We do not leave this life without paying what we owe).

In this section these questions are brought to central consciousness by reflection on their meanings. The apocryphal texts mentioned in this section are the "Dies Irae," some texts from the *Penitente* prayer book, a piece that came out of Ribera, New Mexico, presented by Adán Gonzales (1959), and the "Poesía alfabética" (Alphabetical poetry), by Fernando Baca of Anton Chico, New Mexico (1843–1918). Aside from their historical significance, perhaps they are important in understanding *temor* as "the fear of God" and the judgment at the end of time.

"Dies irae, dies illa" is the first line of the medieval Latin poem "Dies Irae," which was once part of the Catholic funeral mass. It also used to be sung at the mass of All Souls Day (*In Commemoratione Omniuum Fidelium Defunctiontorum*) or at anniversary masses for the dead. The "Dies Irae" is attributed to Thomas of Celano in the thirteenth century. It is a Latin poem of fifty-seven lines and nineteen stanzas in accentual (nonquantitative), rhymed, trochaic meter ("Dies Irae" 2009).

The poem is no longer used in Catholic services. Archbishop Annibale Bugnini said that following the Second Vatican Council, the Catholic Church would rid itself of text that smacked of "negative spirituality from the Middle Ages" (Bugnini 1990, 773). The texts he refers to are the "Libera me," the "Domine," and the "Dies Irae," as well as others that "overemphasized judgment, fear, and despair. These were replaced with texts urging Christian hope and giving more effective expression to faith in the resurrection" ("Bugnini, Annibale" 2007; see also Bugnini 1997).

I have had a lifelong interest in the "Dies Irae," so the change in policy came as a surprise and a personal disappointment. The mass for the dead no longer has its onerous and heavy, emotional cast. Like the American funeral, it has been "sanitized" and made more uplifting. One no longer hears the *requiebros* from another time. The *requiebro* was the wailing and carrying on of people in their grief and loss whether at the rosary or funeral mass. Montoya wrote about the *requiebros'* more intentional and unintentional comedic aspects. Often a bereaved person would emote about the deceased's sexual infidelity or drinking problems. For example, one survivor lamented loudly "Tanto que te aflojaba la lengua ese vinito, Allí estás ahora estas muy calladito" (How that wine loosed you tongue. Look how quiet you are now). A woman who was tired of seeing her drunken husband staggering through life cried out, "Tanto que trastraviastes en esta vida. Mira como allí estan tan tiesesito" (How you staggered when you were alive. Look at you now, so stiff) (Montoya 1992, 71).

One has to make a distinction between the text of the "Dies Irae" and its melody. Part of the text is presented below. Perhaps one of the best sources to hear the melody is in the "Dream of the Witches' Sabbath" in the Symphonie Fantastique by Hector Berlioz. In popular culture, the "Dies Irae" can be found in a scene in the film *Sleeping with the Enemy* (Ruben 1991). In the film actress Julia Roberts plays an abused wife who lives with a domineering man. In one scene of marital rape, the husband puts on the "Dies Irae" theme as he leads her upstairs and forces sex on her. The "Dies Irae" theme is used to create the sense of horror and fear. In *The Shining* Jack Nicholson plays a would-be writer who becomes deranged in an isolated resort closed down because of the winter months. There are evil forces that exist in the hotel. Nicholson uses an axe to terrorize his wife while the musical theme of the "Dies Irae" is played (Kubrick 1980). Several stanzas of the "Dies Irae" follow in the next section.

> Days of wrath and doom impending,
> David's word with Sibyl's blending
> Heaven and Earth in ashes ending!
>
> Oh, what fear man's bosom rendereth
> when from heaven the Judge descendeth
> On whose sentence all dependeth!
>
> Wondrous sound the trumpet flingeth,
> throughout earth's sepulchers it ringeth
> All before the throne it bringeth.
>
> Death is struck and nature quaking,
> All creation is awaking,
> To its judge an answering making.
>
> ("Dies Irae" 2009)

The "Dies Irae" differs from other apocalyptic forms in that it does not promise eternal life in its last stanzas, but pleads for man's placement among the sheep with Jesus and not among the goats *en el día del juicio* (on the day of reckoning or judgment). The "Dies Irae" does not contrast an eternity filled with light and joy with the darkness of sin, death, and despair. The "Dies Irae," along with the other three apocryphal texts presented in the next sections, are reflective of another time when social control on Hispanos seemed to be more severe. More emphasis is placed on the salvation and making amends before the day of judgment. Even though there are references to a judgment in the gospels, one does not hear this language of a final verdict. The texts typify another historical time when even the "Dies Irae" was played at Catholic funeral masses. Today it is a theme thundering through several symphonies, requiems and tone poems.

The "Dies Irae" is more than music portending imminent danger in a horror film or for funeral masses. The "Dies Irae" is about eschatology, the end times. The "Dies Irae" is apocryphal—it depicts the expectation of a cosmic cataclysmic end in which God destroys evil and delivers the righteous to life in a messianic kingdom.

OF THE END TIMES

Hispanos are concerned with eschatology, the end of things and of time. An elderly lady from Anton Chico said just prior to her death, "¡Todo se está acabando!" (Everything is ending!) She was expressing an eschatological belief that everything was ending, including her own life. For Hispanos the *cabo del mundo* (the end of the world) is their eschatological event. Beliefs about the end of the world, whether based on Scripture or folklore, tie into the fundamental belief that if you live your life righteously, you will be rewarded in a better life. The idea ties to the subject of this chapter's discussion: if you deal with despair by putting your faith in a larger purpose you will attain salvation and eternal joy. Life can be said to be a series of tests of one's basic nature, and hence like Job if one does not despair of one's God, one will be rewarded. In this section I examine some examples in folklore by discussing three *cabo del mundo* pieces.

One *cabo del mundo* poem in the form of a corrido was found at the New Mexico Highlands University library in a master's thesis by Adán Gonzales (1959). "El cambio de los años" was sung as a corrido for Gonzales by a singer from San Miguel del Bado in the Villanueva, New Mexico, area.

Aquí me pongo a cantar	Here I begin my song
por los cambios de los años;	of changing times;
la seña que está en el cielo	the sign is in the sky
es negocio muy extraño.	it is a strange business.
Muy triste están en el mundo	Things are sad in the world
Es triste estar en la tierra;	it is sad to be on earth;

Con las señas en el cielo	as one sees the signs in the sky
Platican que va a haber guerra.	they say there will be war.
Ya no creemos en Dios	We no longer believe in God
ya el mundo se está chisquiando;	the world has gone to pot;
el mundo se va a cabar	the world will end
no vamos a saber cuándo.	we do not know when.
Lo que siento es a mis padres	I feel for my parents
Y también a mi persona;	as well as for myself;
Que si se prende la guerra	if there is war
Ya va a quedar en roña.	we will all be in it.
Ya nosotros hoy en día	And all of us today
ya no olvidamos el vicio;	do not let go of our vices;
el día se va llegando	the day is coming
el triste día del juicio.	that day of judgment.
Un día lo creeremos	One day we believe
Que no va a haber esperanza;	there will be no more hope;
Jesucristo va a venir	Jesus Christ will come
A recibirnos con ansias.	to anxiously receive us.
Se volverá pura lumbre	All will be consumed in fire
Como a media noche oscura;	at midnight;
Se levantarán los muertos	the dead will arise
Del plan de la sepultura.	from the depth of their graves.
Juzgará vivos y muertos	The living and the dead will be judged
por todos sus malos hechos;	for their evil deeds;
mentiras, y todo saldrá	lies and all will be made clear
del alma de nuestro pecho.	from our souls and heart.
Ya nos vamos a quemar	We will all burn
A causa de la perdición;	we are all in perdition;
Porque cuando van a misa	because when we go to church
Ya no tienen devoción.	we are not devoted.
Aquí terminamos todo.	We end all this here.

Porque es la pura verdad;	Because it is the pure truth;
El que no quiera creer	he who does not believe
Algún día lo pasará.	he will see it one day.

(Gonzales 1959, 27).

Gonzales defines some special terms used here: "Chisquiando: que hay mucho desorden en el mundo. El roña: cuando una persona está en contra de otro. Plan: del fondo" (*Chisquiando:* that there is much disorder in the world. *El roña*: when a person is against another both get dirtied in the process. *Plan*: From the bottom up) (Gonzales 1959, 27).

This simple, undated poem foretells the start of a war that will destroy everything. Our vices and inauthentic behavior in church are seen as precursors to the coming of Christ and the day of judgment (*el día del juicio*). Some will find a place with him, but others only everlasting fire.

MIRA, MIRA, PECADOR: THE LATTER STANZAS

The *Penitente* chant "Mira, mira, pecador" (Listen, listen, sinner) is the second of the three apocryphal offerings. It, too, is an instance of Hispanos' awareness of the connection between despair and transcendence. I already discussed the first stanzas of this *alabado* (hymn), which calls the sinner to repentance, in chapter 10; here I take a closer look at the final stanzas. These last stanzas seem *gloriosas* (glorious). They speak of the attributes of heaven. Stanza 16 presents us with a view of heaven:

Nunca es noche, siempre es día,	It is never night, always day,
en esa hermosa ciudad,	in that beautiful city
porque la luz que le alumbra,	because the light that shines
es de Dios su claridad.	is from God, his clarity.

Stanza 18 is about the angels:

Cual será la vista y bella	What shall be that vista and beauty
de los ángeles y los santos	of the angels and the saints
que más que el sol resplandecen,	that they shine more than the sun
siendo sin número tantos.	and more than all [of them], glorious.

And stanza 20 tells us about Christ:

Ahí, cuando el alma vea,	There the soul shall see
a Jesús, flor de las flores	Jesus, flower of flowers,
deliciando con fragrancia,	delighting with fragrance
y esparciendo resplandores.	and scattering his brilliance.

The last stanzas exhort the sinner to consider well his situation. Stanza 26 tells the sinner:

Estudia todos los días,	Study[heed] this everyday
en este despertador	this wake-up call,
aborrecerás los vicios	you should hate all vices
aun siendo muy pecador.	even though you are a sinner.

And the last stanza reads:

Y si cuidadoso lo haces,	And if carefully you do it
y lo consideras bien,	and you consider it well
conseguirás buena vida	you shall attain a good life
y buena muerte también.	and a happy death as well.

(*Oh sangre de mi Jesús* 1999, 81–82)

The final apocryphal offering was written by Fernando Baca from Anton Chico, New Mexico, His "Poesía alfabética" used the Spanish alphabet to head each of the stanzas. There are no stanzas with "*ñ*" or "rr." The letter "x" is reserved for Satan. The "Poesía alfabética" has eight lines for each of the letters of the alphabet for a total of 224 lines. It is a remarkable piece of poetry in that the author found terms not used in local New Mexico Spanish anymore except by persons with great expertise in the language. This "wise knight of faith," as Kierkegaard (Becker 1973, 257–58) would have called him, served in the House of Representatives in the eighty-second New Mexico Legislature in 1882, when new schools were being funded. He was the representative for San Miguel County. He was the son of Juan de Jesús Baca and Ramona Lucero of Puertecito, New Mexico. He is buried in the old Anton Chico cemetery.

THE "POESÍA ALFABÉTICA" BY FERNANDO BACA

The "Poesía alfabética" starts each stanza with a letter from the Spanish alphabet. *A* is alpha, the birth of Christ, and *Z* for Zagala, the shepherd lady. The Spanish alphabet has twenty-seven characters, although Baca used only twenty-five. He makes no representations for *k*, *w*, or *ñ*. Instead Baca used *ll* as in "Llorará todo viviente."

POR LA PRIMERA APARICIÓN DEL MENSAJERO DEL SAGRADO CORAZÓN: POESÍA ALFABÉTICA

Al Mensajero brillante

Let us welcome

Del Sagrado Corazón

The brilliant messenger

Démosle la bienvenida

Of the Sacred Heart

Cual á un astro iluminante

Like an illuminating star

Que despertando al instante

That instantly awakens

Al dormido pecador

The dormant sinner

Lo defiende sin temor

Without fear he defends them

Del enemigo alarmante.

From the alarming enemy.

Bien vamos todos, cofrades,

We are all on the right path, brothers,

Todos vamos en unión

We all go together

A enarbolar las banderas

To raise our flags

Del Sagrado Corazón:

Of the Sacred Heart

Los Siervos y Asociados

Servants and associates

Cuales Soldados de Sión

Like soldiers of Zion

Aparejad los borricos

Get ready the donkeys

En que montó el Salvador.

Upon which our Savior mounted.

Cuando nació el Redentor

When the Redeemer was born

Un astro anunció en oriente,

A star announced in the East

Y los tres reyes al frente

And the three kings in the forefront

Se marchan sin detención.

March without hesitation

Dejan todos su nación

They all leave their nation

Sin vacilar un momento

Without hesitation for a moment

Para salir al encuentro

In order to meet

A adornar al Salvador.

And to adorn the Savior.

Del nacimiento de Cristo

About the birth of Christ

Todo el mundo conoció,

The whole world became aware

Desde el cielo hasta a la tierra,

From the heavens to the earth

Pues Herodes se turbó:

For Herodotus was mistaken

Con toda prisa indagó

In a hurry he asked

En manera muy formal

In a very formal manner

Para ir también á adorar

With the intent of also going to adore

Al niño Rey que nació.

The child King that was born.

Era el mes de Diciembre

It was the month of December

Cuando la estrella brilló

When the star was shining

Sobre la Belén humilde	Over humble Bethlehem
Que a los Ángeles unió.	And which gathered the Angels.
Gloria á Dios en las Alturas	Glory to God in the Highest
Pues el Mesías nació	For the Messiah was born.
A dar la paz a los hombres	To bring peace to men
Que por buenos escogió.	Who for being good were chosen.
Fué este tiempo en que el profeta	This was the time in which the prophet
Daniel había anunciado	Daniel had announced
Que nacería el Salvador	That the savior would be born
De todo el mundo esperado	Which the whole world awaited
Satanás desesperado	As the frustrated Satan
Pone trabas y sofismas	Laid out traps and deceptions
Que se convierte en cismas	Which were converted into schisms
Que al mundo traen engañado.	Which have fooled the world.
¡Gracias demos a Jesús!	Let's give thanks to Jesus
¡Gracias demos a María!	Thanks also to Mary
Gracias demos a José	Let's give thanks to Joseph
De su amable compañía.	For his sympathetic company
Gracias demos en unión	Let's give thanks together
Los Cristianos a porfía	All Christians unwavering
Que ha nacido nuestro guía	That our guide has been born
Para nuestra salvación.	For our salvation.
Hombres cuantos han nacido	As many men as have been born
Desde Adán hasta el presente	From Adam to the present
Todos toman de la fuente	They all drink from the fountain
De Cristo recién nacido.	From Christ recently born.
Todo el mundo ha conocido	The whole world has recognized
Que el verdadero sendero	That the true path
Por librarnos del infierno	That will free us from Hell
Es Cristo recién nacido.	Is Christ recently born.
Israel, fuiste escogido	Israel you were chosen
Como el pueblo predilecto	As the preferred nation
El profeta más perfecto	The most perfect prophet
Tu seno lo ha concedido	Has permitted your bosom
De tus tribus traes contigo	From the tribes you bring with you

Al caudillo sempiterno,	The perpetual leader
Siendo Dios desde el eterno	Being God from eternity
Y del Señor el Ungido.	And from our Lord anointed.
Josefat, eres el valle	Josefat, you are the valley
Del gran teatro universal	Of the grand universal theater
En donde se ha de congregar	Where there will congregate
El orbe con cuanto se halle	The world with whatever is found
Rodeado de bien y mal.	Surrounded by good and evil
El espíritu infernal	The infernal spirit
Nos estará allá aguardando	Will be awaiting us
Procurándonos ganar.	In order to win us over.
Las almas que en este día	The souls which this day
Hayan sido reprobadas	Have been condemned
Se verán precipitadas	Will be seen hurled
Al infierno noche y día.	To hell night and day
Solo la conciencia pía	Only the pious conscience
Permanecerá constante	Will remain constant
Con vestido muy brillante	With brilliant clothing
De salvación y de vida.	Of salvation and life.
Llorará todo viviente:	All living beings will cry;
Hombres, niños y mujeres.	Men, children and women,
Clamarán todos los seres	All beings will clamor
Y las cosas cual sufrientes.	And things from which they suffer.
Los clamores de las gentes	The uproar of the people
Se disputarán la palma.	Will not give them victory
Los que tengan pura la alma	Those who have a pure soul
Descansaron para siempre.	Will rest forever.
Mas ay de los reprobados	But woe to the condemned
¡Que se hallarán á la izquierda!	They will find themselves to the left!
Ningún recurso les queda	No recourse do they have
De sus actos mal obrados.	For ill-conceived acts.
Al contrario los salvados	On the contrary the saved ones
Que á la derecha se vean:	That to the right will be:
Estos de por sí posean	These for themselves possess
Como bienaventurados.	The benefits of good fortune.

Nunca hubo día tan cruel	There never was a day
Como el de la Ira de Dios.	As the one of God's wrath.
En el cual cerró su voz	On which he set his judgment
El tentador Lucifer.	On the tempter Lucifer.
Los ángeles han a ejercer	The angels will exercise
El poder que Dios les dió	The power that God gave them
De separar la semilla	To separate the seed
Que la cizaña infectó.	Which discord infected.
¡Oh Dios de misericordia!	Oh merciful God!
Los justos proferirán,	The just will utter;
Ya Dios quiso castigar	God already wished to punish
La soberbia Babilonia	The Babylonian arrogance,
Esta ciudad tan glotona	This very gluttonous city
Que se embriagó con el vicio:	Which became inebriated with vice:
Ya vino el día del juicio	Judgment day has arrived
De que era merecedora.	Of which she was deserving.
Pueblos todos figurados	All countries foretold
Por montañas gigantescas,	Throughout their gigantic mountains
Llegaron horas funestas	Baneful hours arrived
En que serás desolados.	During which they will be forlorn.
¡Desconsolados los malos!	The evil afflicted!
Se acabó la gran Ramera	The Great Harlot will be finished
Que con su gula y blasfemia	Who with gluttony and blasphemy
Los tenía encadenados.	Had them in bondage.
Quiera Dios tener piedad	May God have mercy
De toda su fiel criatura,	On all his faithful creatures
Que haciendo una vida pura	Who make a pure life
Y viviendo en santidad,	And live in sanctity,
Es infalible verdad	The infallible truth being
Que Dios prometió y nos dijo	That God promised and told us
Que el que escuchara á su Hijo	That he who listened to his Son
Poseería su heredad.	Will possess his inheritance.
Raras veces se convierten	Rarely are converted
Los que viven en el vicio.	Those who wallow in vice.
La idea del último juicio,	The idea of a final judgment,

Búrlense de ella y divierten,	They mock it and amuse themselves
Por su culpa se pervierten,	Through their fault they're perverted
No hallando paz ni reposo	Not finding peace nor repose
Hasta que el proceloso	Until the tempestuous evil
Les ha brindado su suerte.	Has brought them their due.
Se eximen de toda la ley	They exempt themselves from every law
Y á Dios quieren ya negar.	Wanting to deny God
Del juicio particular	Of the particular judgment
Búrlanse muchos también,	Many a mockery of it make
Y poniéndose al nivel	And lowering themselves to the level
De los demás reprobados	Of the others that are condemned
Quédense así descarreados	As such they remain astray
Por seguir se parecer.	For following their beliefs.
Todo estará sumergido	Everything will be submerged
A la voz de su Creador.	Upon the Creator's voice
Todos con gran atención	All will be very attentive
Concurrirán al sonido	They will convene to the sound
Que las trompetas entonces	That the trumpets, then
Los Angeles tocarán	The angels, will play
Para poder congregar	In order to congregate
Con ellas todos los hombres.	With them all mankind.
Una sola la sentencia	There is one sole sentence
Que contra cada uno habrá.	That against each one will be.
Apelación no tendrá,	There will be no appealing
Pues concluye la paciencia	Endeavor now for patience
Con Dios en su gran Clemencia	That God in his great Clemency
Tenía por su piedad	Had for his mercy
En la gran eternidad	In the great eternity
No hay más que la Omnipotencia.	There is only Omnipotence.
Virgen, Hija del Altísimo	Virgin, daughter of the Most High
Y madre del Redentor,	And mother of the Redeemer
Que por tu fruto Santísimo	That for your most holy fruit
Quebrantaste aquel dragón	You debilitated that dragon
Que asechaba á tu talón	That lurked at your heels
Con toda descendencia:	With complete linkage

De la gran Omnipotencia	Of the Great Omnipotence
Recibiste el galardón.	You received your just reward.
Xerodonte satánico astuto,	Most devious, satanic and astute one
Ya tu poder expiró	Your power has now expired
De tentador de las almas	For being a tempter of souls
Que Dios para sí las crió.	Which God for himself created
El infierno te tragó	In Hell he swallowed you
Todos tus asociados:	With all your associates
Y á los bienaventurados	And all the blessed
El Cielo los recibió.	Were received in Heaven.
Y la Iglesia ha sido triunfante	And the Church has triumphed
Con su esposo Jesucristo:	With her husband Jesus Christ
Al impostor anticristo	For the imposter Antichrist
Con su astudea represante	With his reproaching ascent
Ya no le queda un instante	He does not even have an instant
De su poder infernal	Of his infernal power
Para llevarnos al mal	To lead us to evil
Sobre manera alarmante.	In an extremely alarming way.
Zagala, eres tú la fuente	Shepherd lady, you are the fountain
Del paraíso celestial	Of the celestial paradise
Contra el poder infernal	Against the infernal power
Te escogio el Omnipotente:	The Omnipotent chose you
Y del Paraíso terrestre	And the earthly paradise
También fuiste protectora.	You were also the protector.
Vos sois la Reina y Señora	You are the Queen and Lady
Del Rebaño eternamente.	Of the flock of all eternity.

(Baca n.d.; trans. Jorge Thomas)

Baca's "Poesía" is concerned with the triumph of good over evil, as is all eschatology, and it raises some important questions. The forces of good will establish a new order upon the earth. Judgment shall be passed, and all will have to make an account of their life. Baca's poem is a Christmas story, the coming of the savior, and an Easter in which death is finally conquered—an end-of-the-world story. It is a story of events in the past, but also of those in a distant, triumphant future. The beginning is the end, the alpha and the omega. It is the drama that was played out at the beginning

Fernando Baca Anton, Chico, New Mexico (inmate artist, California Penal System)

of time and that will be played out in the end of time. It is the cycle of the years of each person's life.

Lest one think that Baca's "Poesía" is arcane and obsolete, one can turn to the film, *The Stand* (Garris 1994), based on the novel by Stephen King. Within *The Stand* the same themes are played out. *The Stand* is a story of about two groups of survivors of a pandemic, a horrific superinfluenza that was mistakenly released from a military base. Most of the world dies from this superflu. Some of the survivors begin receiving dream messages from an elderly African American woman. Mother Abigail, similar to the *zagala* (shepherd lady) in Baca's "Poesía," beckons the dreamers to come to

Boulder, Colorado (the Free Zone), where other good persons will be gathering. Others are summoned to Las Vegas, Nevada, by a demonic individual called Randall Flagg. Flagg uses his "trabas y sofismos" (to use Baca's terms) to entice Nadine Cross, a modern-day Eve, to play on Harold Lauder's hatred of his nemesis in Boulder to make a bomb to destroy the Free Zone. In one scene Cross tells Lauder, "We are dammed!" Flagg is a ruthless and deceiving leader (not unlike Baca's Xerodonte) of the opposition who rapes Cross, sending her into a catatonic state. *The Stand* is about the confrontation between the forces of good and evil. The end comes when an atomic bomb is detonated in Las Vegas by one of Flagg's followers—a crazed man called Trashcan Man.

BUT FROM WHENCE COMES EVIL?

The personification of evil in Baca's poem is called "Xerodonte," a word or name I have not found in any dictionary or resource thus far. It seems to be a made-up name for the leader of the hordes of evil demons, "made up" simply because so few words start with x in Spanish. Whatever the origin of this name, it is clear that evil is present in the world, but what are we to make of evil that interrupts our lives directly?

Berdyaev questions the idea that God allows evil to exist. Does that mean God is powerless over evil? One hears that God uses evil to create good. If so, then is God responsible for the evil and suffering in the world? Berdyaev finds this assertion objectionable as well. And to the idea that evil is nonbeing, Berdyaev replies, "[The] sources of evil lie outside being which is altogether under an all-powerful God, i.e. in an existential and uncreated freedom. . . . This is only a philosophical interpretation, a philosophical interpretation of the ultimate mystery related with freedom and evil" (1965, 186). We are led to the idea of freedom and evil coexisting by the experience of evil in the world and by the recognition of creativity in the world. "The escape from evil is in the suffering of God himself, that is in Christ. Not in God the All-mighty, but in God the redeemer, the God of sacrificial love. I think that herein lies the essence of Christianity" (Berdyaev 1965, 186–87). Dostoyevsky put the same idea into these words: "Evil is inexplicable without freedom. Evil is the child of freedom" (quoted in Berdyaev 1965, 188).

Both Baca's "Poesía" and the *cabo del mundo* poem-corrido previously quoted, "El cambio de los años," are concerned with the ultimate triumph of good over evil. It has been *the* eschatological issue for as long as *Homo sapiens* have been self-aware. Berdyaev writes:

> Man's last hope is connected with death, which manifests so clearly the power of evil in the world. This is the greatest paradox of death. According to the Christian religion death

is the result of sin and is the last enemy, the supreme evil which must be conquered. Spiritual enlightenment and an extraordinary intensity of spiritual life are needed to give us the right attitude towards death. (1959, 249)

Hope and transcendence are born from the conquering of despair. The final despair is death. We conquer death by linking our highest aspirations to a transcendent idea far greater than us. Because we are both spirit and body, the latter must give way to the former and to the belief in immortality. Berdyaev comments,

> There is no such thing as immortality of man as a natural being, born in the generic process; there is no natural immortality of his soul and body. In this world man is a mortal being. But he is conscious of the Divine image and likeness in him and feels that he belongs not only to the natural but to the spiritual world as well. What is eternal and immortal in man is not the psychical or the physical element as such but the spiritual element, which, acting in the other two, constitutes personality and realizes the image and likeness of God. Immortality has to be won by the person and involves struggle for personality. (1959, 255)

What seems required in life is transcendence. It is clear even in the simplest words from St. Paul, St. Francis, and Thomas Merton, that we need to redeem despair and suffering and transform it into the transcendent. Antonio Medina said once, "La muerte es la última mortificación y no hay mas que sufrir la (There remains nothing but to suffer death as the final mortification). St. Paul, in his Second Letter to the Corinthians, proclaims: "but he said to me, 'My grace is sufficient for you, for power is made perfect in weakness.' I would rather boast most gladly of my weakness, in order that the power of Christ may dwell in me. Therefore, I am content with weaknesses, insults, hardship, persecutions, and constrains, for the sake of Christ, for when I am weak, then I am strong" (II Corinthians 9–10). In this passage, the promise of finding the transcendent Christ is possible even when one is in the throes of despair.

More to the point is a discussion between Brother Leo and St. Francis in Nikos Kazantzakis's life of St. Francis. Brother Leo says,

> In order to mount to heaven, you used the floor of the Inferno to give you your momentum. "The further down you gain your momentum," you used to tell me, "the higher you shall be able to reach. The militant Christian's greatest worth is not his virtue, but his struggle to transform into virtue the impudence, dishonor, unfaithfulness, and malice within him. One day Lucifer will be the most glorious archangel standing next to God; not Michael, Gabriel, or Rafael—but Lucifer, after he has finally transubstantiated his terrible darkness into light." (Kazantzakis 1962, 21)

And Thomas Merton tells us:

> The desert is the home of despair. And despair, now is everywhere. Let us not think that our interior solitude consists in the acceptance of defeat. We cannot escape anything by consenting tacitly to be defeated. Despair is an abyss without bottom. Do not think to close it by consenting to it and trying to forget you have consented.
>
> This, then, is our desert: to live in despair, but not to consent. To trample it down under hope in the Cross. To wage war against despair unceasingly. That war is our wilderness. If we wage it courageously, we will find Christ at our side. If we cannot face it, we will never find Him. (Merton 1958, 41)

All this returns us to where we started in this chapter: death and *dando gracias*. The meaning of suffering as an existential question was answered by an old man in Mora. "Hay nomás que llegar al punto donde todo lo que queda es hacer la voluntad de Dios" (Romero 1983): "One has to come to a point where all that remains is to do God's will." The mystery at the heart of death is to give thanks for life and cross over to a new life via our death. These expectations are echoed in the "Libera me" and "In paradisium" from the Catholic ordinary of the mass for the dead. As noted earlier, the "Libera me" was sometimes used in funeral masses in the past and in this example from Fauré's *Requiem*.

DELIVER ME

Deliver me, O Lord, from the eternal death in that awful day when heaven and earth shall be moved, when Thou shall come to judge the world by fire. Trembling, I stand before Thee, and I fear the trial that shall be at hand and the wrath to come. That day, a day of wrath, of calamity and of misery, a great day and exceeding bitter. Eternal rest grant them, O Lord, and let perpetual light shine upon them. (Fauré 1987)

In the funeral service, the faithful are reminded of God's love and his infinite mercy. In the Catholic tradition, the faithful are reminded that on the day of their baptism they were inducted into Christ's death (see also Romans 6:3–4 in New American Bible 2005, 1216). Incense and holy water are used in the service to purify the deceased, but the incense is also like prayers rising to the Eternal. The final words tell the deceased to take leave of us, to leave this place. The hymn "Que los Angeles te Lleven al Paraíso" by Arsenio Córdova (1991) is the Hispanic version of "In paradisum." It was most gratifying to hear a duet with guitars sing this version of the " In Paradisium" in Spanish at the end of a funeral mass for Antonio Romero in Mora, New Mexico, in 2007.

Que los ángeles del cielo te encuentren	May the angels of heaven greet you
Y te lleven al paraíso del Señor	and take you to God's paradise
Que los ángeles del cielo te encuentren	May the angels of heaven greet you
Y los santos y los mártires tambien.	as well as the saints and martyrs.

The words are confident and resurgent in expressing hope.

Gracias démosle a mi bisabuelo, Fernando Baca, por la lección en la fe. Thank you, great-grandfather, Fernando Baca, for your lesson on faith.

When these last three chapters were first conceived I intended to create a "natural" view of the larger questions of live and death, *el ciclo de vida y muerte*, and to stay away from any one denominational view. These ideas are not just a "Catholic" perspective but a larger human need to understand one's place in the cosmos. I find that my ignorance of other denominations limits my understanding. The more I studied these concerns the more I had to reconnect with the deeper target about ideas of resurrection. What is offered in this last chapter is only one of many perspectives. Today as I write these pages a profound gushing of ideas from across Native America has been on the radio for the last hour. Native America Calling broadcast from Albuquerque, New Mexico, has had a number of Native Americans callers talking today about light and darkness, sacred teachings, epistemologies, 2012, and comments on this the eve of a lunar eclipse associated also with the winter solstice. The hour has enriched me and other listeners as these epistemologies from the Native American cultures are presented and elaborated. These folks, too, are making sense of this celestial event and providing perspectives that broaden one's own framework. One can appreciate the human need to make sense of this event and as one recognizes the humanness of the Native American cultures in this country.

CHAPTER 13

Final Thoughts:
Pensamientos Últimos

THERE ARE SEVERAL GOALS IN THIS CHAPTER. ONE GOAL IS TO COVER SOME OF the main findings by linking them back to some basic ideas from phenomenology. Another goal is to connect some of what has been uncovered in the previous chapters to the work of others. In the latter part of the chapter some consideration is given to applications in mental health. For example, it is noted that bracketing from phenomenological philosophy finds applications in mental health work, particularly in the study of empathy. Specifically we note that empathy is used by Husserl to understand the consciousness of another human being. It is important to extend some of what was learned in this study and to relate it to other possible sources of Hispano typifications and research.

We started this book by asking a question that Roberta Imre and others have proposed. Her comments can also apply to those who use interpretive methods to study Hispanos. Imre wondered why the helping professions had not adopted a different ideology for practice given that helping professions deal with a variety of people with various and differing worldviews. In her view, it did not make much sense to use a perspective that came from the physical sciences. Client epistemologies (i.e., their ways of knowing the world) are derived from many nationalities, subgroups, and ethnicities. Imre reasoned that some "knowledges" that come from Western cultures are assumed to be highly developed, "civilized," and superior. Imre proposed that

> studying other cultures with an open mind to possibilities, and a reflective attitude towards one's orientation, leads to other ways of knowing. Such reflective methods often incorporate phenomenological approaches involving the effort to bracket preconceptions in order to make it possible to see differences not encompassed by present theories. (1995)

This book assumes that an Hispano epistemology exists and is deserving of study through the use of interpretative methods. Plenty of material surfaced during my research. Several core ideas merged, such as the three manifestations of the *ciclos* in chapters ten, eleven, and twelve. Amplifying the concept using a variety of media extends the core idea, giving it a generalizability. By using multiple examples one reduces the question to its elemental forms, a type of reduction reaching the essence of the concept.

The book has focused on some well-known Hispano typifications, such as *envidia*, envy, *joda*, and other areas of discourse. Perhaps it was this latter idea that surprised the author. I did not give it a full discussion in the desmadre chapter, but will append it to this chapter. It is likely that there are many examples of *joda* as "being badly off" and more social interactional than one of its more vulgar connotations. *Se muele la idea hasta que algo sale* (It is a matter on chewing on the cud, or the kernel of an idea until one can situate it better in social life). This is in keeping with sociologist Denzin's idea of linking concepts to social interaction (Denzin in Douglas 1970).

This study might also be considered to be existential phenomenology because it is primarily concerned with the meaning of everyday events, activities, attitudes, feelings, and behaviors important to Hispanos of northern New Mexico. I proposed in chapter 1 that intentionality of consciousness, meaning, intersubjectivity, reflection, bracketing (i.e., the suspension of belief of the natural attitude), freedom, the lived body, are all part of an existential phenomenology framework. Each of these categories is endorsed in the large sections devoted to them in the *Encyclopedia of Phenomenology* (1997).

I have been calling these conceptual ideas categories (concepts) and identified them as useful for any study of Hispanos. These categories are often not discrete but are still useful in anchoring categories in phenomenological philosophy. Intersubjectivity, body, and consciousness come to mind as they are interdependent and will be considered below. The categories are useful in understanding typifications so that one does not deal with "mind things" or "body things" as separate entities.

Ethnomethodology provided the license to take seriously elements of everyday life, talk, and conversation and the methods people use to make the social world understandable. It focuses on what is important as people make sense of their social reality. It seems to me that ethnomethods are less about theory than about depiction of the social. Chapter 7, where inmates in a prison argue about what it is to be a *veterano pinto*, qualifies as an ethnomethods study. We need to understand what is going on in situations, what is promoting social order or disorder. Ramos's work in dealing with a confrontation is a case in point (Ramos 1973). He helps us to understand what people are taking into account in everyday scenes as one family "battles" the social agencies in a community. One needs to bracket for the moment what one is observing in order to develop understanding, focusing less on making theory or trying out methods. In the sections to follow I take up the formal language of these concepts, for example, the phenomenological reduction as used by other scholars. The review in this chapter should provide a deeper theoretical understanding of several of the categories, for example, intentionality of consciousness, the phenomenological reduction, intersubjectivity, and the lived body.

Typifying in Daily Life

A typification is often the essence of a concept. An example of the *mancornadora* came from a janitress who typified the concept and added that it meant "one woman and two men"—the essence of the typification. She learned about these concerns from singing *mancornadora* songs with her brother. Her knowledge is the knowledge of everyday life. There is more to this idea (as chapter 5 offers), the idea of being *mancornado* (cuckold) as the real issue, despite the *mancornadora* songs that blame women as instigators and betrayers. This is especially true when one works with Hispano domestic violence offenders.

USING THE CATEGORIES

Perhaps one can say that when studying phenomena one should ideally be able to address them by playing out all the phenomenological categories. In this book, however, not all the categories were played out because some were more important than others in a given chapter. Some of the categories moved to the periphery of the analysis; others did not surface in a cogent way. For example, body is an important concept in phenomenology yet only surfaced in the description of Mrs. Benites in the mortification chapter (chapter 3). The premise of the lived body is the recognition that other bodies exist in one's consciousness, and this is the basis for intersubjectivity (read interaction). For example, the body feelings expressed by Mrs. Benitez in the chapter on *mortificacíon* were described as listlessness and *sin animo* (lacking drive), among others. Her perception of her toxic relationship (intersubjectivity) with her son-in-law was experienced in her lived body—and explicated by language—as being *mortificada*. Another important phenomenological concept is freedom of choice. It was important in the description of bulimic meaning systems in Klein's (1985) study, but never surfaced as a central concept in any of the other chapters. Perhaps this is a limitation on the part of the author or on the method.

EXPERIENCE WITH THE MODEL

I have used the phenomenological categories described above with graduate students over the course of many years of teaching. In one master's seminar thirteen students were asked to suspend their use of the *DSM-IV* and do a "phenomenological inter-view" with their clients. Many reported a very different experience in understanding their client's life by using a phenomenological framework. Others had difficulty in bracketing and letting go of what they knew of the *DSM-IV* and its typology of human problems.

Phenomenological Research

Clark Moustakas's phenomenological research methods are important in gaining a deeper understanding of the application of phenomenology in doing research and treatment of individual problems. In addition, I will extend some ideas by considering the work of Moustakas on what he calls heuristic research:

> Heuristics is a way of engaging in scientific search through methods and processes aimed at discovery; a way of self-inquiry and dialogue with others aimed at finding the underlying meaning of important human experiences. The deepest current of meaning and knowledge takes place within the individual through one's senses, perceptions, beliefs, and judgments. This requires a passionate, disciplined commitment to remain with a question intensely and continuously until it is illuminated or answered. (1994, 18)

Heuristics tells us that the goal is to reach closure on a topic. The primary idea in this book has been to find, within the interviews, published material, music, and poetry, statements that captured the essence of the typifications as phenomena. This is also the idea of thick description covered in chapter 1. The essence of some typifications was clear from the outset. For example, the essence of *envidia* (envy) is found in comparing oneself with others and finding that one is wanting in these comparisons. The succinct statement rendered by Sandoval (1996) about *envidia* is a case in point. In the chapter on *mortificación* insight came not from a textbook but from a janitress in the building where I worked, from her common everyday knowledge gained from singing *mancornadora* songs with her brother. Persons know about these conflicts as typified in experience under the term *mancornando.* It is important to discard the idea of *mancornadora*, which focuses on women as instigators and betrayers. More to the point is the need to focus more on the man who is feeling a sense of loss and gets the invidious label of *mancornado*, a scoundrel.

Edmund Husserl, who created phenomenology, referred to essence as "the things themselves." For Husserl "things" meant any phenomena of which one was conscious. And anything of which one is conscious is a legitimate field of inquiry. Thus, Husserl was returning to Aristotle, who proposed that "it is the mark of an educated man to look for precision in each class of things just so far as the nature of the subject admits" (Stewart and Mickunas 1974, 22–23).

INTENTIONALITY REVISITED

In this book, the concept of the intentionality of consciousness is taken primarily from the applied psychotherapeutic work of Rollo May (1969) and from Stewart and Mickunas (1974). The application of intentionality to alleviating people's problems should draw the attention of mental health workers. May attaches great store to the confrontation of the daimonic in people's lives. He shows that even the "psychotherapy" as used by "primitive" peoples was based on the idea of confronting their personal limitations (May 1969). It is important to point out that the root of intentionality is *intendere*, which means "caring." We care, that is, we mind what happens to us (see chapter 1). "Mind," in this understanding, is the active sense of the intentionality of consciousness itself.

Moustakas presents a philosophic definition of the intentionality of consciousness. First, consciousness is dealt with from an Aristotelian perspective: the orientation of the mind toward its subject; that is, the object exists in the mind in an intentional way (Moustakas 1994, 28). Then Moustakas defines intentionality as "the internal experience of something; thus the act of consciousness and the object of consciousness are intentionally related" (1994, 28). Stewart and Mickunas make the point that consciousness is always directed toward an object. But the notion of a distinct subject perceiving a separate object is so ingrained in our everyday thinking that it makes it difficult to see Husserl's view as revolutionary (Stewart and Mickunas 1994). How a subject makes contact with an object is no longer a problem. There is no such thing as consciousness as essentially empty any more than there is an unexperienced object. Husserl talked about it as "ego-cogito-cogitatum; the 'I' (ego) is inconceivable from its conscious life (cogito), and there is no conscious life apart from the content of consciousness (cogitatum)" (Stewart and Mickunas 1974, 37). Moreover, Husserl developed additional ideas concerning the intentionality of consciousness. In order to underscore the phenomenological view of consciousness and to nullify the dualism of subject and object, Husserl introduced the term "noesis," from the Greek meaning "mental perception, intelligence, or thought," and "noema" from the Greek meaning "that which is perceived, a perception, a thought" (the adjectival forms are "noetic" and "noematic," respectively). (Stewart and Mickunas 1974, 37). Moustakas used these terms when he wrote that the noema is the "perceived as such" and the noesis is the "perfect else-evidence." "For every noema there is a noesis: for every noesis there is a noema. On the noematic side is the uncovering and explication, the unfolding and becoming distinct, the clearing of what is actually presented in consciousness. On the noetic side is the explication of the intentional processes itself" (Husserl's *Cartesian Meditations*, quoted in Moustakas 1994, 30). Returning to Stewart and Mickunas, we round out this piece by their observation that noetic activity cannot be identified with psychological activity, for it deals with the meaning of psychic processes themselves. Likewise, "the noematic cannot be identified with the empirical object, for it deals not with the physical experience but with the meaning of that experience.. . . This unity of meanings is another indication of the importance of the intentionality of consciousness" (Stewart and Mickunas 1971, 37). In sum, the intentionality of consciousness is a meaning-ascribing activity. Typifications are words developed to identify a type of behavior, event, or attitude (broadly speaking) that strikes or has stricken consciousness in the present or the past.

The intentionality of consciousness has been found a useful concept attuned to meanings in persons' lives. In recent years there have been many articles and books that argue that clients (or others we are studying) are the best source of information about their world. There are advocates who support the client's worldview in social work (e.g., Ruth Dean 1993), psychology (e.g., Keen 1975), and nursing (e.g., Benner and Wrubel 1989; Benner 1994).

Moustakas concluded his discussion of intentionality by providing a captivating idea that he tied to methodological considerations: (1) explicating the sense in which our experiences are directed; (2) discerning the features of consciousness that are essential for the individuation of objects (real or imaginary) in consciousness (the noema); (3) explicating how beliefs about such objects (real or imaginary) may be acquired, and how it is that we experience what we experience (noesis); and, most interesting, (4) integrating the neomatic and the noetic correlates of intentionality into meanings and essences of experience (Moustakas 1994, 31–32).

Three major ideas follow from intentionality. First is *epoche*, which is a Greek term that means "to refrain from making a judgment, to abstain from or stay away from the everyday, ordinary way of perceiving things" (Moustakas 1994, 33). This is what was called "bracketing the natural attitude" in chapter 1. Second, Moustakas develops what he calls the "transcendental-phenomenological reduction." This is a "textural description of the meanings and essences of the phenomena, the constituents that comprise the experience in consciousness, from the vantage point of an open self" (34). Third, the crux of the matter is that "the content of experience is dependent on myself as subject; experience presents itself to me its claim to validity: I must certify this claim . . . I, as subject, [am] . . . not only the source of validity of experience, but also its significance" (Schmitt, quoted in Moustakas 1994, 34). The following excerpt is from an interview of a Latina (from a South American country) whom we will call Pilar, dealing with being told she was HIV positive. What follows may be applicable to many persons from many walks of life experiencing the shock of receiving this diagnosis. In Pilar's words:

> Yes, at that time I cried, the day they gave me the results. I did not take it well because it was a very strong word ["positive for HIV"]. . . . That is one thing that I never thought would happen to me. Supposedly, I had done the right thing by deciding to stay in this country. I had found a partner. Maybe for my family he was not the ideal thing, because he was not a professional. He was not a handsome man, was married twice, and had a daughter in each marriage, but I felt that I had found support after what had happened with my first husband. So then when they told me what I had, I did not assume much until [the man who later became] my husband . . . [had a poor] chance of survival because he [had] cancer of the lymphatic system and also AIDS. His chance of survival was very small.
>
> Then when he began to recover and started to live with the disease. That is when I felt the burden of being [HIV] positive because I supported him a lot. I was a spoiled daughter. I did not know how to wash the dishes and the clothes. I did not have those obligations because I worked and went to the university. I had some money that I could give to my mom. I did not come to this country for economic necessity, as many do.
>
> So when [the man who became] my husband began abusing me physically, verbally and even psychologically . . .I felt the burden of the disease because I would say, okay, I already have this disease and I no longer have a chance with another person. I no longer have the opportunity to rebuild my life with another person because I [can't] start anything. In the job where I am working a lot of guys that were American would look at me and I cannot even give them a chance because I cannot lie to them about what I have. Perhaps, I could act like I do not have it and begin a relationship, but I am not capable of passing an illness that was passed to me . . . of maybe killing that person. Then I continued the relationship with him. In fact, we decided to get married. (Yudilevitch 2009, 112–19)

In this situation the phenomenological reduction, as depicted in the first person, focuses on making a decision on the issue of continued relationships with men. Pilar decides not to seek further relationships with men but will try to salvage her life. One area of the human condition that seems to be neglected (except in anthropology) is the issue of defilement. This is an old term that basically refers to contact with something unclean (Ricoeur 1967). What projects do people create in order to "feel whole" or "clean" after they have been defiled? The work with HIV-positive persons would be appropriate for these kinds of studies. Is becoming HIV-positive a modern form of defilement?

Finally, with the concept of "imaginative variation" we reach the structural essence of experience. Moustakas, citing Husserl, says that the goal is to arrive at a *"structural differentiation among the infinite multiplicities* of actual and possible *cognitiones,* that relate to the object in question and thus somehow go together to make up the unity of the identifying synthesis" (Husserl, quoted in Moustakas 1994, 35). An abbreviated example of the experience of anxiety follows:

> Initially, becoming and being anxious in either of these situations means that one experiences a sudden loss of momentum, a sense of being blocked, and an inability to move forward undividedly. Confronted with multiple, problematic, and often contradictory meanings of the situation, one is captured, at least temporarily, by its ambiguity, its lack of a univocal meaning. Expressing the sense of being blocked and captured is a burgeoning uncertainty as to what to do, for that matter, as to one's ability to do anything effectively. (Moustakas 1994, 35–36)

This example of imaginative variation is what I have been calling an "essence," in this case that of the experience of anxiety. The transcendental-phenomenal reduction and the imaginative variation are both examples of a methodology for studying psychological states such as anxiety or depression (Keen 1984), useful in a variety of types of research such as on insomnia, suspicion, the psychotherapist's experience of presence, searching for life's meaning, emerging from depression, midlife change of career, longing, adults abused as children, traumatic head injury, women in transition and self-development, mother-daughter relationships, women's experience of power, undergoing coronary artery bypass surgery and the source of guilt. Many of the preceding examples come from doctoral dissertations (Moustakas 1994, x–xi). Other examples of the use of this methodology include von Gebsattel's (1938, 1967) study of a compulsive person plagued with imaginary urine smells. Jerry Jacobs (1979) studied the process by which a person progresses to the point of suicide. The latter study used suicide notes and survivor interviews to develop a ten-step process model by which people come to commit suicide. It is a useful model to use when evaluating suicide potential. Von Gebsattel's and Schwartz and Jacob's studies fit within the definition of imaginative variation. Imaginative variation could be used to study such topics as the experience of *nervios* (nerves) (Chavez 1979), *congoja*, and *soledad* (solitude) (Romero 1980). In the appendices of the *DSM-IV* are listed folk illnesses that are familiar to Hispanos. Particularly interesting for analysis are familiar illnesses such as *ataque de nervios, locura, susto, espanto, pasmo,* and *perdidio del alma* (*DSM-IV* 2000, 899).

INTERSUBJECTIVITY REVISITED

How do I know the other? Do social others share the same ideas I have? How is it possible to interact with another? These are vital questions that Husserl tackled, and which led to his exploring the concept of "intersubjectivity." In chapter 1 it was defined as social interaction, but there is more to it. To say that there are social others who share typifications with me is to focus on the problem: I share a world (that I understand) with others, and I assume they share the same world with me. In other words, I can assume that others think like I do. In chapter 7, a discussion group of convicts, under the supervision of researcher-therapists, became embroiled in a conflict over a petition. When a petition was circulated, some signed whereas others did not, creating an issue but also an opportunity to determine what convicts took into account in dealing with each other. One of the leaders saw the problem in this way: "If I am a convict, then it is all right to back a man's petition against a guard. It is the convict thing to do." But others, including his crime partner, did not share that view, which led to a lot of talk about what constitutes being a convict. Ramos (1973) advocated using these "naturally occurring troubles" as an investigative device that could be used to highlight the background of taken-for-granted assumptions in social encounters.

Intersubjectivity is the agreement between one's own consciousness and another's consciousness, or between one's conscious "world" and that of another. The experience of the body of another, the experience of the psychic experiences of another, and social communication between them are intersubjective (Kern 1997). Husserl tackled the problem of intersubjectivity through the use of two transcendental reductions. The first reduction involves the sense of one's ego and the perception of egos alien to oneself. In Husserl's words, "That my own essence can be at all contrasted for me with something else (who is not I but someone other than I), presupposes that *not all my own modes of consciousness are modes of my self-consciousness*" (Husserl 1972, 423). Consciousness of others is an "experience of something alien (something that is not I), is present as experience of an Objective world and [with] others in it (non-Ego in the form: other Ego)"; and continuing the reduction is "An important result of the ownness-reduction performed on these experiences was that it brought out a substratum belonging to them, an intentional substratum in which a reduced 'world' shows itself, as an 'immanent transcendency'" (424). "Immanence" is that which is within consciousness, whereas "transcendence" refers to that to which consciousness points (Stewart and Mickunas 1974, 38). These ideas are presented to give the reader a sense of the work of consciousness in defining something as difficult as the presence of others and as the philosophical basis of empathy.

In the second reduction, a major point of this section, Husserl makes use of the idea of "empathy." Husserl came to the problem of empathy through the insight "that no fields of sensation can be empathetically experienced *immediately* in a body that is externally perceived, and that this happens only insofar as the outer body becomes experienced as a living body *for the other* through the RE-PRESENTATION of that alien point of view" (Kern 1997, 356).

One of the tenets of Keefe's model of empathy is that good therapists experience a greater physiological arousal than nontherapists. Like the two reductions noted above, Keefe's model begins with the perception of behavioral cues emanating from the client. The second reduction occurs when the body of the therapist registers a somatic (bodily) response that communicates reflection of his or her state back to the client (Keefe 1976). Note that in the Keefe model "holding in abeyance" means bracketing (the epoche) feelings, thoughts, and judgment one may have about the other, be it a client, patient, someone who I have just met, or a person from another culture. In Keefe's model high levels of empathic response is predicated on (1) allowing one's perception of the client to be unfettered by cognitive and feeling responses in oneself; (2) the therapist's feelings remaining as free as possible from cognitive distortions, for example, stereotypes, making value judgments, or analyzing perceptions according to a fixed theoretical construct; (3) cognition and somatic responses being triggered in the social worker, although it is incumbent on the worker to hold cognition in abeyance; (4) attending to somatic feelings aroused in oneself (as Husserl identified with his reduction, people arouse bodily responses in oneself); (5) separating feelings held by the therapist from those sensed and shared with the client; and (6) establishing a feedback loop with the client as feelings shared with the client are communicated back to the client (Keefe 1976, 12). Both Keefe's model and Husserl's work point to the body as important in intersubjectivity. Other people arouse bodily responses in oneself, causing a person to question his or her perception of the other. Empathetic response means that the social worker communicates that he or she is "in touch" with what the client, patient, other is experiencing. It is central to establishing proper rapport with the other person.

It will be recalled in chapter 7 that Omni was very angry that some of the men differed on the petition that was being passed around. If we conceptualize the problem in terms of empathy, we can note that Omni was unable to empathize with those who did not sign the petition and was therefore incapable of taking into the account the position of these others. Instead, he clung to the idea that being a convict meant supporting any antisocial ploy planned against the guards. The clash of perspectives supports the idea that in interactions with others one's inability to take the role of the other may lead to further problems. This can destroy the values of *respeto* (respect) in social interactions with others (see chapter 4). It is important to emphasize that bodily perceptions are also those of consciousness. Empathy as discussed above shows that consciousness registers in the lived body.

THE LIVED BODY

The body is an important consideration in phenomenology. The phenomenological definition of "body," however, is different from the conventional meaning. First, in English, "body" has a limited definition. In German, there are two words: *das Leib* and *der Körper. Das Leib* means "lived body," whereas *der Körper* is "physical body," and sometimes "material body" or "object body" (Behnke 1997, 66). The terms "lived body" and "lived experience" are appropriate for a phenomenological perspective. The lived body is the necessary condition and center for all active experience. Everything is seen from the perspective of one's body. The lived body is the means by which consciousness experiences the world and through which it is situated in space and time. The body is intimately connected to the intentionality of consciousness (Stewart and Mickunas 1974, 97–98).

The body functions as a center of orientation, the bearer of felt sensations, and the original means for motility: it is the primordial organ or mechanism of all action, perception, and expression (Behnke 1997, 66). Felt meanings are important cues to our relations with others, our experiences in the world, and they are where we store memories of unpleasant past events (Gendlin 1978). According to Becker,

> It seems that we will not gain an understanding of man until we cogitate within the broadest possible framework needed to describe his [or her] action. This means not only that mind is a function of behavior, it means much more. We saw above that growth and development of the organism takes place by shaping reactive behavior to a well-defined object world. In other words, the world that exists *outside* the organism, and the experience *within* the organism, are complementary aspects of one transactional behavioral process. (1964, 18)

As a result, "In order for an object to exist on any level, in order for it even to be perceived as a perceived object, the organism must be able to call up a response to it" (Becker 1964, 19). Bergson as described by Becker, came to an important conclusion, that is, that the past is stored in the organism (person) in two forms: (1) as motor mechanisms, and (2) as personal memory-images. Motor mechanisms bring memories to bear on the present in the form of total organismic action. Memory-images are more autonomous, more divorced from present action. Memory-images merely "represent" the past. The motor-memory "acts the past" in the present. Becker concedes that the "body-memory" of Bergson is insufficient as a model for understanding how experience anchors meaning (1964, 19–20). The purpose of the material below is to flesh out Becker's discussion of a body memory so we can move beyond the mind-body dualism that prevails in our thinking, particularly in the human services.

BULIMIA AND THE LIVED BODY

A master's thesis by Martha Klein applied the phenomenological concept of the lived body to the problem of bulimia. Bulimia is defined as a loss of control over food, binging on large quantities of food, followed by a purging cycle of vomiting, the use of diuretics, or heavy exercise. "Secret eating" was another common theme associated with the self-definition (Klein 1985, 2). The "body physical" is perceived to be too "large." "The body physical is altered although the perception of the body is left intact. The bulimic's self-image is of one who is grotesque, lazy and undesirable. This cognitive pattern of perceiving herself as fat is maintained" (5). Klein discovered, however, that bulimic women's mothers had placed an inordinate importance on becoming and remaining thin. Two women recalled their interactions with their mothers as being a series of double binds. One said, "I felt caught in a double-bind because I would diet to please [mom] and yet she'd fix a lot of food at mealtimes. In both situations she said she did it because she loved me" (38). Klein's conclusion about the structure of consciousness of a bulimic (imaginative variation) is that of a distortion of the body physical, in that "being bodily" can be

> seen as being the vehicle through which all experiences occurs; a perception being separate from one's body sets up a schism between the actual physical reality of the body and one's perception of it. In this splitness, a perception that is distant from the regulating center of a person results in a fragmented perception of self. A sense of connectedness is important in viewing the self in a manner more congruent with the reality of the situation. Due to the lack of a constructive relationship with their bodies, these women viewed themselves as heavy when even according to physical measurements they would not be considered to be overweight. (43)

Dreyfus (1983) relates some ideas from Merleau-Ponty's emphasis on the need for a different definition of repression, one not based on psychoanalytic theory but on phenomenology. Merleau-Ponty proposed that repression consists in the subject's entering upon a certain course of action—a love affair, a career, a piece of work—in his encountering on this course some barrier, and, because he has the strength neither to surmount the obstacle nor to abandon the enterprise, he remains imprisoned in the attempt and uses up his strength indefinitely renewing it. . . . Time in its passage does not carry away with it these impossible projects; it does not close up on traumatic experience; the subject remains open to the same impossible future, if not in his explicit thoughts, then in his actual being. (Merleau-Ponty, quoted in Dreyfus 1983, 5)

Dreyfus continues, "The body as correlative with the world remains frozen in a certain stance which then distorts everything that shows up" (7). Dreyfus makes some suggestions regarding the type of therapy that would be appropriate for these types of characterological problems. Becker's *Angel in Armor* (1969) is a study of Freudian characterology based on the defense mechanisms.

FELT MEANING

Eugene Gendlin's work in *Focusing* (1978) can teach us something of the mind-body continuum. The book is based on Gendlin's "explication method." Gendlin developed a six-stage process ("movements") that leads one to the solution of a personal problem or the release of psychic pain lodged in a body memory. I will not present the entire process, but highlight three of the five movements as important ideas. The first movement is called "clearing a space" so that the work of focusing can occur. The second movement is called the "felt sense" of the problem. This requires that the self-lectures (e.g., What's the matter with me?), analytical theories, clichés, one's "squawking and jabbering" about the problem have to be put aside (bracketing). The "felt sense" (felt meaning) of the problem has to come through. Gendlin calls us to feel "the single great aura that encloses all of it" (1978, 53–54). These two movements can be seen as a suspension of belief (holding in abeyance the "squawking and jabbering")—that is, the phenomenological bracketing of the problematic experience—so that the internal dialogue can be quieted until the sense of the problem—that is, the felt meaning—can be reexperienced (i.e., re-membered, reconnected). The third movement is closely tied to the felt sense. It involves putting a "handle" on the problem, that is, naming the problem or concern in a few words. Letting the felt meaning arise on its own means allowing oneself to see the problem changing, and it may differ from what one expected. The third movement involves an intentionality-of-consciousness state in which the object of consciousness is the structure of the problem within one's body-memory. The fourth movement is to experience the handle and the felt meaning together to ensure a good fit of the name with the feeling being excited in consciousness. This is a confirming event in that the feeling is that of a "just right" fit. If it doesn't come, then one tries to sense more accurately as more exact words come from the feeling. In this fourth movement, if the fit is good, the sense of rightness is a check on the handle. What this brings is a change in the body that is felt as releasing, processing, and moving. This is called a "body shift" and signifies a change in the problem. Gendlin writes, "The body shift is mysterious in its effects. It always feels good, even when what has come to light may not make the problem look any better from a detached, rational point of view" (1978, 59). With a body shift one is "next" to the problem but not in it, hence the sense of release, which assists coping and managing behavior in the fifth step ("receiving") (Gendlin 1978, 60). The pain carried in the body-memory is reduced or gone. This example, like the ones below, is provided to underscore the importance of the body in phenomenological studies, as in the use of those methods in mental health.

Antiquated Terms

Some readers may have had problems with the older terms used as major typifications in the book. They may consider the terms antiquated and be unable to reach an understanding of what mortification really means. One needs to return to the basic premise in each of the chapters. Mortification occurs when the adult son or daughter is suffering from chronic unemployment, mental illness, or drug and alcohol problems and the parent is unable to act in that role. *La mortificación* is a deformation of the role of a parent. It is an inability to act, and one experiences a sense of the death of the self. The reader should be able to extract the characteristics of the situations. The examples are of a kind: typal, not specific. Mortification is about a class of behaviors and one's inability to take action to nullify its effects.

The term *mortificación* largely expresses a "felt meaning," a human situation and the emotions linked to it. When a former colleague mentioned my essay on *mortificación* to someone, that person immediately launched into a tale of *un huevon* (lazy, shiftless individual) who was living off his parents' Social Security income. The colleague had successfully extracted the elements of the behavior implied in the typification.

The Stranger and Bracketing

Schutz (1964) writes that the stranger is in the best position to see cultural mores, societal mores, or folkways. As Schwartz and Jacobs also point out,

Such a role necessitates an attitude which in many ways is the opposite of the natural attitude. While there can be numbness of attention for those with member's knowledge, the stranger must be on the edge of his cognitive seat. There is no problem in being constantly suspicious of his own view of what's going on because he literally does not know what's going on and is continually rediscovering this awkward fact. (Schwartz and Jacobs 1979, 248)

I have taken these comments to heart in this work. In the penitentiary studies, particularly on the role of the *veterano*, we used strangers—that is, non-Hispano members of the group who were in a position to report on Hispano *pintos*—to provide some reliability regarding what was being observed. In addition, as mental-health workers we had to bracket our own biases. It was too easy to go to these interviews and see these men in terms of a *DSM-IV* category (e.g., sociopath).

I first heard the term *mortificación* from my parents concerning the task of dealing with my mentally ill sister. I heard it next in a classroom discussion when as a first step I bracketed the term and began to ask about people who use this term. I was referred to an elderly foster grandparent. I set up an appointment to collect her story. She was living with a man who would threaten her with an ax. Once the term had been socially situated, I turned to the literature on shame and guilt to further extrapolate the term.

When I began my research on *mancornando*, I began to collect newspaper stories about situations in which an old boyfriend assaults or kills his former girlfriend and her new lover. Sadly someone got killed, usually the girlfriend and the new boyfriend in a double homicide, or in some cases the rejected suitor commits suicide. I used Mexican music from an earlier time but still in vogue to explicate the concepts. The men understood the central tenet of a relationship between one woman and two men and they identified additional music such as Garth Brooks's "Mama Loved Papa," Jimi Hendrix's "Hey Joe," and one of the songs by The Sparx, a northern New Mexico female vocal group. A colleague extended the musical ideas by offering the ballad by Lyle Lovett. More compelling was a comment made by a participant at a convention of psychoanalysts and psychotherapists in Santa Fe.

The participant pointed out that the opera *Carmen* was also a case of *mancornando* (i.e., the cuckolded man). I latched on to the idea of the impaling horn (the knife used to kill *Carmen*) as the chorus sang "Toreador, toreador . . .") in the background. The *mancornado* man suffers internal pain, as he too is losing what he loves (see the loss equals violence formula in Denzin 1984a). Jacobi views the sword as symbolic of "the penetrating principle," which is both destructive and fruitful, an "inciter" that either promotes development or brings death (Jacobi 1959, 154).

For each of the examples given in this chapter and elsewhere in this book, my concern was to explicate the methods needed to generalize the core concept. One means of doing this was to use a wider set of examples (e.g., the music sources above) so that a kind of generalizability would ensue in these types of descriptive studies. This is not quite similar to sampling in more traditional research.

THE STRANGER IN A CULTURE

Working in areas where two or more cultures live side by side and freely interact can provide opportunities for learning about a new culture or one's own. New Mexico offers many opportunities, given the interactions between the many peoples of New Mexico. My experiences when making a decision about a child welfare placement of a Navajo child brought me face-to-face with Navajo culture. Sometimes one is unprepared to deal with these interdictions, as Ricoeur (1967) calls these encounters. It is in these interchanges where one must hold in abeyance or bracket for the moment what one thinks one knows about other people whose culture is unknown. Often these interdictions uncover the stereotypes that pass for knowledge or in many cases ignorance about another culture on our part. Bias and stereotypes should not govern the interactions or services between peoples but true respect (*respeto*) and a highly attuned empathetic response. As a stranger sometimes one has to work the interactional ground between two distinct groups when "naturally occurring trouble" happens (Ramos 1973).

Having to explain one's cultural behavior brings about reflection and learning. A student from Michigan asked to go into the community of Mora. She wondered what preparations she should make. We asked her to suspend her beliefs (bracket them for the moment) as she entered the community and try to answer the question of what gives people a sense of community. Doing phenomenology is "bearing witness with fidelity" to the things of the world" (Romanyshyn 1992).

Extending the Typifications

The chapters in the book focused on typifications. There are other sources of social life that are or could be sources of typifications. These sources are also "meaningful" but in very different ways than language or written text. In this section some attention is given to identifying areas of possible research activity.

El Bote Afamado (the famed garbage can) across the street from El Rialto Restaurant on Bridge Street in Las Vegas, New Mexico.

ART AND IMAGES

Each chapter in this book presented an image. Some images were developed to assist the reader to understand certain ideas. In one example, a drawing of a *morada* outside of Manuelitas, New Mexico, was used to give the reader an idea of what these structures look like. If readers are curious about the inside of these *moradas*, they can find pictures in Rael's 1951 book. A *morada* as an image is more compelling when it involves the creation of an internal "indwelling" of love. The *encuentro*, an encounter between Jesus and Mary on the way to Calvary, is a *los Penitentes* Good Friday Lenten play performed in Abiquiu, New Mexico. The *encuentro* narrator told the audience of the existing *morada* between Jesus and his mother.

The images presented in this book were important because of the need to get as wide a collection of material on New Mexico as possible. The image selected for *desmadre* was of a trash can with the term *desmadre* written in gang graffiti style (see figure). What is important is the graffiti writer's message to convey a thought via a word.

Images join poetry, text, interviews, narratives, music, pictures, newspaper stories, films, and material things to help us understand what is being studied in this book. In a single painting, drawing, sculpture, or photo an artist can present us with powerful and evocative images in astonishing ways. Las Vegas, New Mexico, artist and scholar David Escudero creates vibrant and dazzling *chamisos* (sagebrush) in late summer that lack only the distinctive wooden, pungent scent. One sees the bright yellow flowers of these plants along the highway into Santa Fe in the magnificent light of autumn. They seem distinctively New Mexican and iconic of the landscape. Escudero captures the stark beauty of large landscapes of the Cañon del Agua in San Miguel County.

A Taos artist, Alex Chávez, created what I believe to be an excellent depiction of *el ciclo de vida y muerte.* Chávez's work is based on the Indian *mandala* and presents his subject surreally. He calls his work "digital photo montage." Some of his work is based on Catholic icons and might be called "electronic *retablos.*" He fuses the icon of the modern age, the power of the computer with the folk art of the New Mexico *retablo* (in general, images of saints painted on wood). One image is the *Santo Niño* (infant Jesus) surrounded by a *mandala* of flowers and other images hovering over a New Mexico mesa.

In the *Day of the Dead*, Chávez portrays a death scene where a real cemetery and trees are used for background for a phantasmagorical scene. On one tombstone is depicted the Guadalupana with the name of its inhabitant, the *cucui* (sometimes "cucuy"), which is another name for the "bogeyman." The *cucui* is described as the man who carts off bad children in a rice sack (del Pilar Muñoz 2002, 30). The central figure is *muerte*, dressed in black, depicted with its white face and *huesos* (bones) and holding a live child. The child reaches out to touch this hideous but compelling winged figure. The piece is reminiscent of the great masters' depictions of the Madonna and Christ child. Both figures are superimposed on a black cross. Above the cross where one normally sees "INRI" is an inscription that reads "La Madre de Vida" (The mother of life). Below the arm of the cross are right- and left-facing women each with one arm uplifted as if to say, "Behold!" Fire surrounds both of them. Perhaps they burn in hell. Seven festive yellow flowers surround the central figures. Are these flowers *el áñil del muerto* (goldenrod), which are found in cemeteries? Adding to this festive bouquet is a group of monarch butterflies with a human skeleton for a body. These are very strange angels. Two guitarists at the bottom of the flower bouquet contribute to the festive nature of the piece.

If *vida y muerte* are one, as Paz (1961) contends, then Chávez has captured this idea succinctly. It is the fiesta of life, which is both festive and sad. *Day of the Dead* made a huge impression on me because it seemed that he had captured in a single image what I was attempting to describe in the final three chapters of this book.*

---

*The reader is referred to http://www.newicons.com to view his remarkable and imaginative work. It is important to see art also as typifying some vital element of social life. There are many talented Hispano(a) artists in New Mexico.

Film is another medium that helps us reflect on Hispanos. In the film *My Family / Mi Familia* (Nava 1995) a scene is presented in which José Sanchez, the father, receives a call from the police regarding his son Chucho. This scene is important in that Chucho's marijuana dealing creates a schism in the Sanchez family. The schism allows us to explore Mexican American family values. The son creates trouble for his father by selling marijuana. The father creates trouble for the son because he disapproves of selling *mota*. It allows one to discover the taken-for-granted assumptions of everyday scenes typical in ethnomethods studies (*respeto, vergüenza*), like the graffiti writer's attempt to convey a thought via a word. In one scene Mr. Sanchez waits for his son to come home so he can confront him about the police call. While he waits he drinks tequila. When Chucho shows up, Mr. Sanchez asks where he has been. Chucho responds "Out." "Out?" "Selling *mota*?" inquires the father. Then he accosts Chucho with the following: "Don't you have respect? I didn't raise you to be a *delinquente. ¡Un sinvergüenza! ¿Que no tienes dignidad?*" (Don't you have dignity?). To which Chucho responds angrily "Fuck your *dignidad!*" and, holding up a wad of money, says, "This is what is respected in this country!" A fight breaks out between father and son; the mother intervenes, stopping Chucho from punching his fallen father. A traditional belief has it that if you strike your parent your hand will wither. Chucho is told to get out of the house as the father yells "*¡Alargate!*" (get out) and then throws the wad of money at Chucho. The point is that a value conflict ensues: the father believes in the dignity of work, whereas the son espouses the value of "Get it while you can." The nature of conflict is a tool for all manner of interaction studies, such as family studies, that take us beyond the veneer of everyday life. This idea can be found in the family dynamics literature (Jackson 1970).

Evidently the director and his wife, who wrote the script, fell back on these typified values of *respeto, vergüenza* and *dignidad* to film this scene and to present the larger story of the Sanchez family. It was a pleasant surprise to see these values played out in this 1995 film since the author first wrote about these values in a paper on *carría* in 1976. To see them played in the film also meant that the discussion on these values extend to a greater Mexican American community. The concepts no longer exist in a historical vacuum because the film gave it a confirmation in the present, at least in 1995. What is still an open question in the family's conflicting values is the extent to which these values are still extant in northern New Mexico.

Berg's study of mixed identity is a topic that resonates for many of mixed parentage and identity. Being of mixed parentage, Berg is particularly sensitive to these issues in film and in discrimination studies. Berg's major contribution has to do with the changing image of Latinos as portrayed in Hollywood films of the past and in the present. Another major contribution has to do with the subtle images of the "alien" (symbolized as undocumented Mexican persons) in science fiction genre films (Berg 2002). The film *Alien* (Scott 1979) is relevant because the "mother" beast guards hordes of unborn alien creatures that will invade the solar system (Berg 2002). Berg's view is that the film is code for all the undocumented aliens that have yet to penetrate the border and invade the United States. Film is a great medium for the study of identity, roles played by Hispanics and Latinos in society, and social presentation. For example the film *American Me* (Olmos 1992) provides poignant examples of the dictum *No te rajes* as well as loyalty to the group and the convict code. It is a very compelling and disturbing film.

RITUAL AND MYTH

There are many religious rituals that are important to New Mexico's Hispanos. Many make the Lenten pilgrimage to El Santuario de Chimayo or to Tomé Hill across the river from Los Lunas in Valencia County. Thousands make the walk to Chimayo. The walk up to Tomé Hill was begun by a returning World War II veteran by the name of Edwin Berry. Albuquerque resident Carmen Baldonado of the 877th Quartermaster, Army Reserve, climbed the hill in honor of her friends in Kuwait. Frank Aragón of Albuquerque moved a seventy-five-pound cross in honor of his brother, who had died recently. Father Albert Gallegos and two youth ministers and a small flock did the Stations of the Cross that Jesus walked bearing his own cross ("Good Friday" 2004–5). In Las Vegas, youth are encouraged to do the ten-mile round trip to Tecolote. These are ripe areas for participant research. Suspending belief and asking people why they do the walk would reveal many individual meanings and would enlighten us about Hispano spirituality. What does the walk have to do with spirituality? How is this manifested? What individual meanings do people attribute to walking during this period of the year? Some are fulfilling *mandos*—that is, in the past it may have been a promise to a saint to make the walk every year for bringing a person back from the Vietnam War or from one of the Iraq wars. Perhaps others are thanking a special saint for helping them conquer alcoholism or drug abuse. How one typifies the numerous responses would create a typology of considerable interest (the "survey" portion of such a study). For example I noticed pictures of National Guard Hispano(a) soldiers just before the first Iraq war at the Santuario de Chimajo. These are silent testimony to a *mando*, an *encomienda* put forth by worried parents or relatives to bring back their children safe from war. An *encomienda* is the act of putting the loved one in God's hands for his or her safe return from war. A research question would be to explore via a descriptive study the nature of these *encomiendas* and a study on faith. Newspapers provide stories about Hispanos making the Lenten pilgrimages or putting up *altares* (which seems to be spreading) on *el día de los muertos* (day of the dead, November 2—All Souls' Day). In a related area is the question whether *quinceañeras* (fifteenth-birthday coming-out party for young women) are on the increase in northern New Mexico. Do these rituals extend the kin network of *madrinas y padrinos* (godparents) for the young person.

TYPIFICATIONS IN GEOGRAPHY, OCCUPATION, AND AGE

In this section we take up typifications related to geography, occupation, and age. By geography we mean place and place attachment. New Mexico's varied geography has led to distinct and unique lifestyles. One needs to work and live in distinct geographic areas to appreciate the importance of this type of life space.

Of course, occupations lead to typifications based on work occupations and their special language. One needs only to consult McWilliams (1961) to appreciate the contributions that Spanish vaqueros (from *vaca*, cow, becoming "cowman," "cowboy," or "cowgirl") gave to the cattle industry. These men gave the American cowboy/cowgirl the language and skills he or she needed to do ranch work. Such terms as "lariat," "rodeo," "chaps," "quirt," "stampede," "bronco," "ten-gallon hat," and other accoutrements of cowboy life come from Spanish. In addition, names for different kinds of horses and cows also have their precursor Spanish names (McWilliams 1961, 153–55). If typifications involve the naming of things in an occupation, then the vaquero has triumphed in this area of endeavor.

THE IMPORTANCE OF PLACE

Place has received considerable attention in psychology and social gerontology. Key concepts from this area are called "attachment to place," "place attachment," and "aging in place." Place makes sense for existential phenomenology because it involves the attachment of personal meanings and feelings. DeBuys (1985) typifies three ways of looking at "place." To the Pueblo peoples of New Mexico, the landscape was special because it was imbued with spirituality. The mountains were sacred locales of spiritual energy, the lakes were places of contact with the underworld, and the land and the sky were living things that the Pueblo people supplicated through ritual to ensure the orderly progression of the seasons. For the Hispanos of New Mexico the land was not a sacred thing as with the Pueblos but a mother protector of a subsistence pastoralism. Some lands were designated as communal, belonging not to individuals but to a village, supplying wood, rock, and pasture. In contrast, the Anglo view of land was that it was a commodity to be bought and sold, although by the end of the nineteenth century this view changed somewhat: mountain forests would be held in trust for all members of society in order to protect water quality and timber (deBuys 1985). These differing views have led to conflict among the three groups. Nevertheless, the point is that the land is endowed with meaning, whether as a spiritual place, a maternal life sustaining the community, or a commodity to be bought and sold. The maternal view is often expressed as *¡La tierra es madre, no la vendan!* (The land is our mother, don't sell it!). *Acequias* (water-delivering ditches) were designated *acequia madre* (the mother ditch); some *acequias* are given the names of specific saints. For Hispanos June 24 was *el día de San Juan* (after St. John the Baptist), when the waters were supposed to be sacred and holy. Traditionally no river bathing was allowed until after *el diá de San Juan.* Some communities still have a procession to bless the waters on this special day. In one community *paciar los santos* was a procession with each person carrying a *santo* for the purpose of eliciting rain. These ideas are part of the "planting culture" epistemology described in chapter 10. There was a procession in June 2011 whereby elderly Las Vegans carried their household cantos to bring much-needed rain.

In recent years a growing body of literature has developed around the concept of "attachment to place." Rowles's study of small-town elderly is a case in point. Rowles proposes that place is central to a sense of well-being and belonging. "Such identity and belonging may represent a basic human need" (1990, 106). Place attachment can intersect various fields, for example, geography, psychology, anthropology, and psychiatry (Fullilove 1996). Fullilove tells us that place connotes the geographical center, site, situation, or locations for events.

> In this regard human survival depends on having a location that is "good enough" to support life. It is a biological imperative that viable settings provide people with ready, equitable access to food, water and safe shelter; offer appropriate facilities for the disposal of wastes; and limit human exposure to toxic chemicals or other harmful substances. (1996, 1517)

Fried elaborates on the importance of this place to identity.

> We may say that a sense of *spatial identity* is fundamental to human functioning. It represents a phenomenal or ideational integration of important experiences concerning environmental arrangements and contacts in relation to the individual's conception of his own body in space. It is based on spatial memory, spatial imagery, the spatial framework of current activity, and the implicit spatial components of ideals and aspirations. (Quoted in Fullilove 1996, 1520)

Hispanos identify themselves often in relation to the spatial dimension, that is, a geographical place. A recent book on northern New Mexico focuses on place identification and identity (Gonzales 2007).

Hispanos used terrestrial landmarks to mark off the adjoining landholder's properties. "The size of rural land was predicated upon the basis of social and use-value consideration, including the status of the person(s) being granted the land, the use to which the land was to be put, the character and quality of the land in question, and the established needs of the person(s)" (Van Ness and Van Ness 1980, 9). Boundary disputes are still common today because no grid system existed to identify boundaries.

It is important to draw out some ideas of lived space as applied to Hispanos and other peoples with long tenure on the land. The following is offered:

- A long tenure with the land either by birthright or historical precedent
- Identification with the particular features of the land geography
- Work and effort put into the building up or restoration of the economic value of the land
- Family events celebrated within the confines of the family space
- Extended family relationships, sometimes living multigenerationally
- The social cultural meaning of place attachment
- A sense of continuity, longevity and tenure

Tenure on the land may have been brought about by birthright or historical precedent (i.e., multiple generations living on the land). Hispanos' identification with the land may go back multiple generations when the land was given to the original settlers in either the Spanish colonial period (1598–1820) or the Mexican period (1821–48). For Native Americans land tenure goes back millennia. An identification with geographic features (e.g., water or terrain) is important. A connection to these features—such as through the spiritual—may be used to relate a lived experience with the details of the land. For example, for many decades the Taos Pueblo people rightly fought to get back Blue Lake, a place considered to be of great significance to Taos Pueblo spirituality and worldview. It was finally returned to them during the Nixon administration and its return celebrated. One might note the vocabulary that exists in regard to an understanding of, and use of, land features. Giving a ranch a name, identifying areas for grazing with a specific name, are part and parcel of living in the plenitude of the land.

The American occupation of New Mexico after 1846 found the majority of Hispanos living in small, self-sufficient farm villages. They were engaged in subsistence agriculture. Many of these villagers were related to each other by blood or marriage and by the *compadrazgo* system. Land use was given special meanings according to how the lands were used. The communal lands adjacent to the village were called the *ejido.* These lands provided grazing, hunting, firewood, and timber (Knowlton 1967, 2–3). The town was laid out around a central plaza. Land needed for home sites was called *sitios* or *solares.* Each individual recipient of a home lot was also given an allotment called a *suerte.* After a given period of occupancy the *suerte* became the private property of the grantee. This was one way in which the community land grant was plotted out. Land could also be identified as *temporal*—not under irrigation but planted with the expectation that rains would provide the needed moisture and *de regadillo* under irrigation (White et al. 1972).

Even household places were given meaning by designating special names for the buildings in these farms and *ranchitos* (small ranches). Consider the description of this multigenerational household living in Tecolotito prior to 1918.

> My grandparents, my father, uncles and families lived in a big adobe home made in length as a block long and divided into many rooms. Uncle Guadalupe and his family had three good sized rooms; my grandparents and three spinster sister aunts four rooms; my father and family three rooms; Uncle Narciso four rooms. It was a big family living like neighbors.
>
> In the back of the residence was a big long rock wall all around a big patio or plazuela. Inside was another room "el galero" where bales of alfalfa were piled up in order. There was another room "el granero" where corn, beans, wheat and other grains were stored. Then the "tropa" room, which was half full of apples. Then a tiny niche . . . "Palomar" made . . . with some [bricks] missing alternatively . . . [f]or doors in an inside corner of the wall where a lot of doves would live and roost. Outside this plazuela was a big corral made of latas (peeled posts) tied up and standing where the cows and horses were fenced.
>
> In the front of the residence, a few yards away, ran the community ditch. Near this "acequia" stood another small house called "la mielera," where our people used to grind cane. They had a machine to squeeze juice out of the cane. . . . The cane juice would be boiled and made into syrup. (Korte, 1999b, 49)

One might call this the "*terrenito* lifestyle." Today it may be rare to find multi-generational families living together. This author knows of two such families in the southern part of the state and one in the northern part of the state. One student at New Mexico Highlands University wrote a paper on the *ranchito* lifestyle in Taos County (Archuleta 1980). Such a lifestyle means living in a small rancho with some cows, perhaps designating some fields for cultivating vegetables or apples, as well as holding down a regular job as a teacher, state employee, or working in the university.

A goal was to live *una vida buena y sana* (a good life), which meant plenitude in another time. A seventy-three-year-old man recalls:

> In Mora much wheat was produced and many oats, alfalfa, and all kinds of seed one planted in the soil. The land produced good quantities. The way of life in that genera-tion was to live from one's own work and produce, what I mean by *de por si* [on your own], because of every ten persons that lived in a home, easily two or three worked for someone else. All from the same family worked together planting and cultivating and harvesting their fields, as I said before, because the blessings of God were all over us. (Martinez ca. 1973)

For others the loss of the land base meant migration out of the Hispano homeland. One of Zantelle's respondents, in her study of land loss, put it this way.

> They took it for taxes . . . yes my grandfather on my father's side, they lost all their land, and they owned a lot [of land] of Cebollita. See in his family there were 13 children and they owned a lot of land, a lot of land, my grandfather used to go to work in Wyoming and he would send my grandmother money to pay the taxes, but she didn't understand things like that, so they lost this beautiful land and now it's taken away by the Anglos, they have subdivided and subdivided and subdivided. (Zantelle 2005, 203)

Another elder recalls, "This is not to glorify the past, for there were difficult days brought on by bad roads, the unpredictivity of weather, drought, and excess rains, [which] made for a difficult life. It took two days and an overnight camping to go from Pecos to Santa Fe on a wagon, a distance of twenty-five miles" (Moya ca. 1973).

Another man remembered another unpleasant incident in the 1930s. This ninety-year-old man said that he and his "primo-in-law" went to Santa Rosa to sell cabbage. The truck broke down and due to lack of money they were forced to sleep in the back of the truck and eat cabbage for four days until parts could be ordered and the truck fixed (Baca 2005).

This section was intended to give some "body" to the idea of a "planting culture" by focusing on the land. It was by no means as easy a life as Moya describes, but it had its moments of plentitude, even in a New Mexico that would be hit by drought and depression in the 1930s. This section recognizes the history of a people living a difficult existence yet creating meaning, a rich folklore, and a resiliency in the history of a rural people. Eventually large-scale out-migration occurred as the Great Depression put its full weight on these people. Today we have elements of the old and elements of urban culture in a composite of systems of belief and attitude. Clark

Knowlton proposed that the major events experienced by many Hispano families in New Mexico can be considered within a broad framework. The 1920s can be seen as a period of migration out of the heartland, the 1930s were years of discrimination, urbanization after World War II, assimilation in the 1950s, and, finally, again, urbanization. The goal is to develop these ideas along with family histories in order to embody these ideas.

Afterthoughts on *Joda*

There are various considerations as one thinks about *joda* (*hoda*). When I wrote the *desmadre* paper (Gonzales 2007) I had come to the conclusion that I did not want to dwell on the *chingar* theme, as Octavio Paz had already made due course with it. In analyzing the roles in a three-party interaction, I had discerned that the person "carrying" gossip would be called the *mitotero(a)*; the person presenting the bad information about oneself would be the *pendejo* for not verifying its veracity. What was one to call the "victim" in this real-life minor drama at the senior center I witnessed in Socorro, New Mexico, many years ago? (See chapter 8.) It came to me to call the situation of such a person so victimized as *me jodieron.* One might say after one of these situations, *Me jodieron.*" In this sense the term *jodido* means simply "being badly off," as Rubén Cobos (2003) put it in his New Mexico dictionary. But the person doing the hurting is also linked into this micro interaction by being branded a *jodido(a)* (someone who hurts people) in return. We often say, *Como es jodido(a) tal y tal* [reference to a person] *por que me jodio* (That person is a real *jodido(a)* because he or she did me in). In that sense we are indeed left badly off.

Recently on the Internet a person from Medellin, Colombia, was looking for a Spanish term to mean annoying, pesky, bothersome. A Florida professor with incredible credentials answered him saying that the term he was looking for was *jodiendo.* He gave as an example *Estos mosquitos estan jodiendo.* In New Mexico we would call the mosquito by the name *jején* (Cobos 2003). In Medellin as in New Mexico we are bothered by mosquitos, or by humans who "bug" us, calling it *mortificaciones* by people or situations. Once I met a student from Argentina who proclaimed in my classes many years ago that her mother would use the word *jodiendo* with added gravity on the syllable *jo-*.

¡A que joda llevamos! (We were worked hard) is also found in the dictionary of New Mexico and Colorado Spanish (Cobos 2003). Montoya's definition of the word sees life as a series of *jodas*, to be endured, tolerated, and lived. It is the work of a struggle in life. One of José Montoya's best-known poems is about *El Louie*, a Korean War veteran who came back to the barrio with polished black boots, as used in the

Airborne. Equally "La Jefita" (little mother) is also captivating. Until recently I was unaware of Montoya's book called *In Formation: 20 Years of Joda*. Each of twenty years of his poetry is presented to us year by year. It was a joy to discover this series of poems because Montoya's work is to release "subjugated knowledge" from the barrio.

Montoya is originally from a place called Escoboza, New Mexico, in the East Mountains near Albuquerque. Montoya was also a founding member of RCAF, the Royal Chicano Air Force, a group of poets, artists, and musicians in Sacramento, California.

In the preface to the book Montoya tells that he too will honor Paz by not dwelling on the *chingar* term. Instead he has fun with the word "Xoda" (*joda*) and he intends to torment Spanish-language purists. *Joda* he says is better suited to describe struggle and resistance than *chinga*. He says, "Watch 'em [linguists, purists] try to sound the 'J' like in 'jay,' which is pronounced Jowda. Sounds too much like *chora*, barrio slang for phallus. And yora sounds like a lament, which is close, but it is simply *joda*, like in *jodidos*—which brings us the 'H' sound—'odidos'?" He concludes, "Chicanos find love—a gem stone called culture, which unlike the rock of Sisyphus, carries us up and down the hill. *Y seguimos jodiendo until los jodidos nos oigon.* Ho!" (Montoya 1992, viii–ix).

This little lament was found in a tile on a wall in a Mora restaurant. It proclaims simply, "Hace un dia precioso, veras como viene alguno y lo 'joda'" (Today is a beautiful day, watch how someone comes and screws it up).

Respectfully, Dr. Tomás Atencio will be given the last word. He offers a philosophical rationale for developing an electronic network to provide discourse on Hispanos. The *resolana* was a place on the south side of a house where men (*los resolaneros*) gathered in midwinter to discuss the nature of the social world about them. Basing his work on the Socratic method, Atencio compares his *resolana* to the light of enlightenment, offering a discourse on the interpretation of everyday life (Atencio 1988). In his teaching Atencio extended the *resolana* concept to the computer-driven teaching-learning environment of the modern university student—a way of pulling together for the enlightenment of the modern era. It may help us survive the end of the industrial age as we move into the information age.

Glossary

A

abuelo(a) grandfather/grandmother

acompañamiento accompaniment of the dead

adivinansas a type of riddle

agonizando death rattle

alcahuete panderer

amistad friendship

ángel de la guardia guardian angel

áñil del muerto goldenrod, a tall, flowering plant with yellow blooms (genus *Solidago*)

animado(a) animated

animo(a) animated person

artistico polished form of ballad (a type of romance)

asesino assassin; "El asesino" is a song

atender to attend to someone's needs, to take care of someone

atole gruel, porridge

ausente absence

B

baile a dance
balsamo de consuelo God's healing balm, especially after a death in a family
bisabulo(a) great-grandfather/great-grandmother
boquinete white sucker (fish), *Catostomus commersoni*
borrachera drunken, inebriated
borracho(a) drunken person
bulto image of a holy person carved in the round (see Cobos 2003)
burla, burlado making fun of someone, being rebuffed

C

cabo del año the traditional Christian mass marking the end of a year of mourning
cabo del mundo end of the world
cabrón intruder (as defined in this book), cuckold, pimp (Cobos 2003)
cabula (cabuya) an insult to a person such that he or she does not recognize the
    insult
café coffee, as in the *trovo* between *café* and *atole*
calor heat; to be incited
carilucio shiny or glossy face
carinegro swarthy complexion
carilla small face
carría joking game marked by repartee and played by New Mexico Hispanos
carrillera metallic chin strap on a helmet
carrillo one with prominent cheeks
carrilludo(a) having a plump face
camaradas comrades
carnales brothers (slang "bros")
carnalismo brotherhood
casa prison argot for one's cell;, otherwise house, home
chingaderas bothersome problems
chingado to be f****d over
chisme gossip
chiste story with a funny ending; a joke
chotas barrio term for police
ciclo cycle
ciclo de vida y muerte cycle of life and death
clerico ballad written by a cleric (a type of romance)

Cofradía de Nuestro Padre Jesús Nazareno, La The Penitent Brotherhood, a religious group of men in many New Mexico communities who provide Lenten services and help to community members

comadre, compadre ritual co-parent; mother or father of one's godchild

comportamiento comportment, behavior

condenado someone who is condemned

confianza trust, trust building

consejo wise counsel

consideración consideration of others

consuelo consolation; "Consuelo" is a common woman's name

copendeja(o) co-dependent person (slang term coined by Loretta Maez)

coplas couplets, a type of exchange where one presenter challenges another with jest

coplas y versons verses in a light exchange set with music

corrido a type of ballad patterned after the medieval romance of Spain (Cobos 2003)

crianza upbringing

criar to create or to provide upbringing

crucita little cross

cuerno horn

D

dame tu mano give me your hand

dando or **dar carría** to engage others to make light of someone's personal value or traits

dando or **dar gracias** giving thanks, thanksgiving

danza dance

dar or **dando luz** give birth

deber an obligation, such as to care for one's aged parents

décima type of poetry of ten lines

delgadina medieval play concerning a father's incest

des- prefix meaning "without"

desabrochar to untie, e.g., a shoe

desaigre, desaigrado rebuff, slight

desanimado loss of interest in life

desatar to untie something, such as a shoe or rope

descanso roadway cross marking where someone died

descarado "without face," a shameless person

desde abajo "from below," from the people

desmadrado badly beaten (slang) (Cobos 2003)

desmadrando assault on someone

desmadrazgos poet and writer Richard Sanchez's word meaning "disordered life"

desmadre to separate small animals from their mothers, disorder

despedida parting from an interaction, farewell

despedirse to make one's partings in a social exchange

deprimido(a) name for depression, including *aguitado(a), acongojado(a), aburrido(a), desanimado(a),desesperado(a)*

diablo devil

dicho folk proverb used to provide a moral lesson

E

educación family upbringing

ejemplo a moral example (a type of corrido)

Eme, La "M": the Mexican mafia

en aquellos tiempos in the old days

encabronado violently angry

encadenar to link together

encendido someone who is all agitated

enfermedad illness

enfermero a male nurse

enfermo(a) sick person

entendimiento accord or agreement with someone

entrementido intruder, someone who gets into other people's business

entregada(o) returned to God

entrega de muertos return of the dead person's soul to God

entrega de niños bautisados return of children by the *compadres* from baptism

entrega de novios turning of newlyweds toward each other at a wedding party

envidia envy

estar de acuerdo to be in accord with someone

¿Estas salvado? Are you saved?

F

falta de cosas lack of material things

falta de educación lack of family upbringing

familia family

Fenomenología del relajo philosophical book on embarrassment by Mexican philosopher Jorge Portilla

feria money (slang)

flor que fue entregada a Dios Flora (the author's sister) upon her death, a flower returned to God

formal formal, serious

G

genio demeanor, genius, as in having a special talent

gorgoritos the death rattle

grito titanic yell, an expression of great excitement

guardan el luto (for the generation that lived from, approximately, 1905 to 1975) to preserve a period of bereavement by family members, usually one year

"güera Chavela, La" song in which Chavela (a variant of "Isabel") is a blond

güero (huero) refers to a blond person, in some cases a swarthy person

H

hermano brother; more formally a member of the *Cofradía de Nuestro Padre Jesús Nazareno* (Penitente Brotherhood)

Hispano(a) used by some Spanish-speaking people in northern New Mexico to refer to themselves

Historia ballad covering a historical event (a type of corrido)

hija(o) daughter/son

hombrecito "little man"

hombres jodidos neologism referring to philandering husbands, boyfriends, colleagues, or persons who "do one in"

I

importamadrismo someone who does not care what happens to him or her

J

joder to "mess" with someone's head, to bother someone, be a pest

jodiendo bothersome mosquitoes, or people

jodido one who has "done one in," a person without social concern for others who use them to get ahead, or get "one up" on the other

jodio to be done in by someone, to do someone in

L

"Lagunas de pesar" A song; *lagunas* refers to lakes and *pesar* means heavy, nightmarish problems

lambe, lambiscon a bootlicker

Libro de San Cipriano, El A book of hexes, incantations, and spells attributed to Jonas Sufurino

llega a mi canton "come to my house" (a prison cell)

Llorona, La mythic story of a woman who drowns her children so she can be with another man

loco crazy, insane

Lucero common last name in New Mexico

lucero de la mañana morning star (Venus); white spot on a horse's forehead

luminarias festive lights, generally at Christmas

luz light; "Luz" is a common woman's name

luz del día daylight; the coming of the new day

M

mala fe person of bad faith

malas intenciónes person who has bad intentions toward us

mala voluntad acting in bad faith

maldecido someone who has been cursed; a malediction

maleficio being the subject of a curse or hex; a curse, hex, spell

mañanitas birthday greeting (a type of corrido)

mancornado(a) a person who has been cuckolded

mancornadora interaction, usually with a violent outcome, in which one woman is involved with two men

mano y cuerno literally, "hand to horn"; metaphor for *mancornadora* songs

más antes in earlier times

más vale . . . literally: "what is more important . . ."

matraca wooden box with a wooden toothed spindle that makes a dry, whirling sound, used in *Penitente* Lenten services

mentiras lies

mester de clerecía minstrel who sang erudite poetry

mester de joglaría minstrel who sang popular form of poetry of the common people

mirasol sunflower

misa del cabo del año Christian mass at the end of a year of mourning (traditional)

mitote gossip

mitotera(o) person who engages in gossip

morada chapel usually in rural areas used by the *Penitentes* to conduct Holy Week and other religious services

mortificación the state of being mortified

mortificar el cuerpo to mortify the body

mosca fly

movida deceitful behavior; hustle; to hustle someone

muerte death

muerto dead person

N

nadismo from *nada*, meaning nothing, nothingness, a nihilistic perspective

nana endearing term for a female, elderly person, a matriarch

narración narration, such as a comic story (a type of corrido)

necesidad necessity

nicho niche in which saints are placed

norteño(a) a northern New Mexican

no tener crianza to lack family upbringing

no te rajes, no rajarse to crack; to break down; to be unable to comply

O

orale slang for "hi," also meaning "okay"

orejón someone with large ears, someone who does not hear gossip about himself

Ormiga, Colorado Unlike Mosca, Colorado, a fictional community in southern Colorado

P

paciar los santos a community religious observance in which the church's saints are taken out to the fields to implore God for rain; also called a *novenario*

paloma negra literally a black dove: heroine in a song; dark portends

palomas pigeons; a *paloma blanca* is a white dove

paño handkerchief, in this case a type of prison art using a handkerchief for a canvas

pariente a relative

parranda drunkenness

pelado pealed, someone from the lower classes

pena worry; a worrisome situation

persona person

persona de consideración considerate person, respectful person

pesadilla a nightmare

pesado heavy oppressive person, also called *sangrón*

pésame the offering of condolences

pesar heavy-weightedness

pinche a cussword meaning "crummy," "wretched" (Cobos 2003)

pinto a penitentiary inmate, self-reference term

pisca del betabel work at harvesting in the sugar beet industry

platica warm, friendly conversation

pobreza poverty

ponerese en la cabuya to catch the drift of a conversational topic

preso prisoner

"Preso número nueve" "Prisoner Number Nine," a Joan Baez song

prestado(a) to be on loan; as in the idea that life is on loan

problema problem

pucieron los cuernos having the horns put upon one

punche wild tobacco

Q

que joda what a mess!

quemadota a "sting"

R

ranchera a type of Mexican song

rata a snitch, a "rat" in prison who snitches to authority

recuerdo remembrance; memorial for a deceased person (a type of corrido)

refrán proverb

relajo insult game in Mexico

"Renunciacíon" a Javier Solis song

reo prisoner

requiebro wailing sound made at funerals in the past

respetable respectful of others

respetados to be respected

respeto respect

respetuoso respectful
resurrección resurrection
rezador(a) person acknowledged for his or her ability to pray at public events
romance See *corrido*.
roña dirt; to be soiled or dirtied
"Rosita Alvirez" A corrido about a woman who is killed at a dance

S

sangrón oppressive person; a "heavy"-blooded person; see *pesado*
San Isidro Saint Isidore, patron saint of farmers
santo saint
Santo de la Escoba, El San Martín de Porres; his title refers to his job of cleaning the monk's cells with his broom
sin fondo without bottom; without end
sipapu emergence myth of the Pueblo peoples of New Mexico
serio, seriedad, falta de seriedad serious; serious deportment; lack of serious behavior
simpatía sympathetic
sin oficio a person without a serious social purpose
sinvergüenza a person without shame; shameless
shaquegüe a type of porridge made from blue corn meal

T

tantiando developing an intent
tata endearing term for father or God as in *Tata Dios*
tatarabuelo(a) great-great-grandfather/grandmother
tejido woven as in a net
terco stubborn; obnoxious drunk
¿Tienes feria? Do you have money?
tinieblas darkness; Tenebrae ceremony during Lent
tinieblario object used in Tinieblas ceremony to hold lit candles
toriar la vida to take on life like a bull
trabajando duro doing hard manual labor
traición treasonous behavior
traidora female who is treasonous; *traidor* is male traitor
tragedia tragedy (a type of corrido)

trovo poem where one person/entity challenges another to respond with an equally compelling argument

tú, tu you, thou

U

una veintela a song with twenty lines

usted formal term for "you"

V

valse chiquiado a musical form in which verses are exchanged, a waltz

vamos acompañar to accompany usually the dead

vato jodido a traitor

vergüenza shameful behavior; in Pitt-Rivers's book (1971), innocence

veterano pinto an experienced penitentiary inmate

vida cotidiana daily life

viejito(a) an elderly person

velando el (la) enfermo(a) vigil provided a dead person (traditional)

Velarde person's last name; *vela arde* is a lit candle, place-name in New Mexico

velorio wake for the dead; also *velorios* for the saints

versos y coplas verses in a light exchange set with music (a type of corrido)

vestirse en luto to wear dark clothing; to be in mourning

viejo traditional ballad (a type of romance)

volando flying out of control

vulgar common people's ballad or song (a type of romance)

References

INTERVIEWS AND CORRESPONDENCE

Baca, Belarmino. 2003. Interview by the author, Fontana, Calif., July 31.

Baca, Benjamin. Ca. 1973. Interview No. 28, Santa Rosa, N.Mex. Oral History Interviews. Carnegie Public Library, Las Vegas, N.Mex. Tape 35/Baca. P. 28-2.

Baca, George. 2005. Interview by the author, Las Vegas, N.Mex., April 12.

Baca, Marta. 1967. Letter to Antonia Baca. In author's possession.

Korte, Henry, and Juanita Metzger de Korte. 1880. Letter to Andreas and Lenore Laumbach, October 12. In possession of the author.

Maes, Juan. 1998. Interview by the author, Las Vegas, N.Mex., April 13.

Martinez, Jesús. Ca. 1973. Interview No. 4, Mora, N.Mex. Oral History Interviews. Carnegie Public Library, Las Vegas, N.Mex. Tape 3/Martinez. P. 4-1.

Medina, Antonio. 1983. Interviews by the author, Mora, N.Mex., December 13 and 22.

Moya, John. Ca. 1973. Interview no. 11, Pecos, N.Mex. Oral History Interviews. Carnegie Public Library, Las Vegas, N.Mex. Tape 7/Moya. P. 11-8.

Romero, Antonio 2003. Interview by the author, Mora, N.Mex., August 17.

Romero, Moises Mano 1983. Interview by A. Medina, Mora, N.Mex., December 23.

Sánchez, Juan. 1991. Interview by the author, Las Vegas, N.Mex., November 10.

Sánchez, Lillian. Ca. 1973. Interview No. 19, Buena Vista, N.Mex. Oral History Interviews. Carnegie Public Library, Las Vegas, N.Mex. Tape 23/Sánchez. P. 19-7.

Santistevan, Pablo. 1979. Interview by the author, Las Vegas, N.Mex., September 27.

Sedillo, Cruz, Sr. Ca. 1975. Interview Number 21, Las Vegas, N.Mex. Oral History Interviews. Carnegie Public Library, Las Vegas, N.Mex. Tape 24/Sedillo. P. 21-2.

Sena, Francisco. Ca. 1975. Interview Number 22, Los Torres, N.Mex. Oral History Interviews. Carnegie Public Library, Las Vegas, N.Mex. Tape 25/Sena. P. 22-7.

Trujillo, Rosario. 2002. Interview by the author, Las Vegas, N.Mex., October 11.

Valdez, Facundo. 1979. Interview by the author, Las Vegas, N.Mex., October 2.

WORKS

Abeyta, Carlos. 1995. "La Herencia es Nuestra Lengua." *La Herencia del Norte*, Spring, 39.

Abrahams, Roger D. 1972. "Joking: The Training of the Man of Words in Talking Broad." In *Rappin' and Stylin' Out: Communication in Urban Black America*, ed. Thomas Kochman. Chicago: University of Chicago Press.

"Affidavits Filed in Slaying Case." 2005. *Journal North*, November 11, 4.

Aguilar, Ignacio, and Virginia N. Wood. 1976. "Therapy through a Death Ritual." *Social Work* 1 (January): 49–54.

American Heritage Spanish Dictionary, The. 1986. Boston: Houghton Mifflin.

Andrada, Patsy, and Alvin O. Korte. 1993. "En aquellos años: A Reminiscing Group with Hispanic Elderly." *Journal of Gerontological Social Work* 20, nos. 3–4: 25–42.

Archuleta, Michael. E. 1980. "Mexican American Elderly in Hondo-Seco Area in Northern New Mexico: A Reality or Myth." M.S.W. thesis, New Mexico Highlands University

Arellano, Anselmo. 1976. *Los pobladores nuevo mexicanos y su poesía, 1889–1950*. Albuquerque, N.Mex.: Pajarito Publications.

———. 1995. "Entrega de Bautismo: Celebrating the First of Many Sacraments." *La Herencia del Norte*, Summer, 41.

Arellano, Anselmo, and Julian Vigil. 1985. *Las Vegas Grandes on the Gallinas 1835–1985*. Las Vegas, N.Mex.: Editorial Telaraña.

Arellano, Estévan, ed. 1972. *Entre verde y seco*. Dixon, N.Mex.: La Academia de la Nueva Raza.

———. 1986. "Descansos." *New Mexico Magazine*, February, 42–45.

———. 1992. *Inocencio: Ni pisca ni escarda pero siempre se como el mejor elote*. Mexico City: Consejo Nacional Para la Cultura y las Artes.

———. 2010. "La Abundancia del Jardin Rizo: The Bounty of the Natural Garden." *Green Fire Times*, September, 28.

Arau, Alfonso. 1992. *Like Water for Chocolate*. Mexico City: Arau Films International.

Armenta, Steve. 1994. "Giving Thanks in April: Northern New Mexico's First Thanksgiving Day." *La Herencia del Norte*, Spring, 42–43.

Atencio, Tomás. 1972. "La Academia de La Nueva Raza Sus Obras." *El Cuaderno (De vez en cuando)* 2, no. 1: 6–13.

———. 1988. "La Resolana: A Chicano Pathway to Knowledge." Third Annual Ernesto Galarza Commemorative Lecture. Stanford Center for Chicano Research, Stanford University.

Aviera, Aaron. 1996. "'Dichos' Therapy Group: A Therapeutic Use of Spanish Language Proverbs with Hospitalized Spanish-Speaking Psychiatric Patients." *Cultural Diversity and Mental Health* 2, no. 2: 73–87.

Baca, Alegario. 1930. Untitled despedida. *El Independiente* (Las Vegas, NM), April 1.

Baca, Antonia. Ca. 1977. "My Life in Tecolotito," In in "A Journey Through Antón Chico's Past," by Alvin O. Korte. *La Herencia del Norte* 24 (Winter 1999): 49.

Baca, Fernando. n.d. "Poesía Alfabética," in "La Poesía Alfabética de Fernando Baca," by Korte, Alvin O. and Luisa Baca. *La Herencia* 44 (Winter2004): 20-21.

Becker, Ernest. 1964. *The Revolution in Psychiatry*. New York: Free Press.

———. 1969. *Angel in Armor: A Post-Freudian Perspective on the Nature of Man*. New York: George Braziller.

———. 1971a. *The Birth and Death of Meaning: An Interdisciplinary Perspective on the Problem of Man*. 2nd ed. New York: Free Press.

———. 1971b. *The Lost Science of Man*. New York: George Braziller.

———. 1973. *The Denial of Death*. New York: Free Press.

———. 1975. "The Self as a Locus of Linguistic Causality." In *Life as Theater: A Dramaturgical Source Book*, ed. Dennis Brisset and Charles Edgley. Chicago: Aldine.

Behnke, Elizabeth A. 1997. "Body." In *Encyclopedia of Phenomenology*, ed. Lester Embree et al. Dordrecht: Kluwer Academic Publishers.

Benner, Patricia. 1994. *Interpretive Phenomenology: Embodiment, Caring and Ethics in Health and Illness*. Thousand Oaks, Calif.: Sage.

Benner, Patricia, and Judith Wrubel. 1989. *The Primacy of Caring: Stress and Coping in Health and Illness*. Menlo Park, Calif.: Addison-Wesley.

Berdyaev, Nicholai. 1959. *The Destiny of Man*. New York: Harper Torchbooks.

———. 1965. *Christian Existentialism: A Berdyaev Anthology*. Trans. Donald A. Lowrie. New York: Harper Torchbooks.

Berg, Charles Ramirez. 2002. *Latino Images in Film: Stereotypes, Subversion, Resistance*. Austin: University of Texas Press.

Berger, Peter L., and Thomas Luckmann. 1966. *The Social Construction of Reality: A Treatise in the Sociology of Knowledge*. New York: Doubleday.

Blumer, Herbert. 1969. *Symbolic Interactionism: Perspective and Method*. Berkeley:

University of California Press.

Brenner, Anita. 1967. *Idols behind Altars.* New York: Biblio and Tanner.

Brest, Martin. 1998. *Meet Joe Black.* Los Angeles: City Lights Films.

Bugnini, Annibale. 1990. *The Reform of the Liturgy: 1948–1975.* Trans. Matthew J. O'Connell. Collegeville, Minn.: Liturgical Press.

"Bugnini, Annibale." 2007. Wikipedia. Available at http://www.en.wikipedia.org/ wiki/Archbishop_Annibale_Bugnini.

Butler, Alban. 1962. *Butler's Lives of the Saints: Complete Edition.* Ed. Herbert Thurston and Donald Attwater. Vol. 3. New York: J. P. Kenedy & Sons.

Buytendijk, J. F. F. 1960. "The Phenomenological Approach to the Problems of Feelings and Emotions." In *Feelings and Emotions: The Mooseheart Symposium,* ed. Martin Reymert. New York: McGraw Hill.

Campa, Arthur L. 1946. *Spanish Folk-Poetry in New Mexico.* Albuquerque: University of New Mexico Press.

Campbell, Joseph, with Bill Moyers. 1988. *The Power of Myth.* Ed. Betty Sue Flowers. New York: Doubleday.

Cave, Dorothy. 2006. *Beyond Courage: One Regiment against Japan, 1941–1945.* Santa Fe: Sunstone Press.

Chang, Tung-Sun. 1970. "A Chinese Philosopher's Theory of Knowledge." In *Social Psychology through Symbolic Interaction,* ed. Gregory P. Stone and Harvey Farberman. Waltham, Mass.: Xerox College Publishing.

Chávez, Fray Angélico. 1954. "The Penitentes of New Mexico." *New Mexico Historical Review* 29, no. 2: 97–123.

———. 1973. *Origins of New Mexico Families in the Spanish Colonial Period.* Albuquerque: University of New Mexico Press.

Chávez, Nelba. 1979. "Mexican American's Expectations of Treatment, Role of Self and of Therapist: Effects of Utilization of Mental Health Services." In *La Frontera Perspective: Providing Mental Health Services to Mexican Americans,* ed. Patricia Preciado Martin. Tucson: Old Pueblo Printers.

Clark, Margaret. 1970. *Health in the Mexican American Culture.* Berkeley: University of California Press.

Clavel, James. 1975. *Shogun: A Novel of Japan.* New York: Atheneum.

Cobos, Rubén. 1973. *Refránes Españoles del Suboeste / Spanish Proverbs of the Southwest.* Cerillos, N.Mex.: San Marcos Press.

———. 1974. "Cantares Familiares." *El Cuaderno (De vez en Cuando)* 1, no. 3: 41.

———. 2003. *A Dictionary of New Mexico and Southern Colorado Spanish.* Santa Fe: Museum of New Mexico Press.

Coles, Robert. 1973. *The Old Ones of New Mexico.* Garden City, N.Y.: Anchor Press.

Compendio de Folklores Nuevo Mejicano. N.d. Santa Fe: Sociedad Folklorico de Santa

Fe, Nuevo Méjico.

Cooley, Charles H. 1922. *Human Nature and the Social Order.* New York: Scribner

Cooper, Jean C. 1978. "Darkness." In *An Illustrated Encylopaedia of Traditional Symbols.* New York: Thames and Hudson.

Córdova, Arsenio. 1991. "Que los Ángeles te Lleven al Paraíso." In *Flor y Canto,* ed. Owen Alstott. Portland, Oreg.: OCP Publication.

Córdova, Arsenio, and Alvin O. Korte. 2001. "El Día de los Manueles." *La Herencia,* Winter, 16–17.

Córdova, Benito. 1972. *Bibliography of Unpublished Materials Pertaining to Hispanic Culture.* Santa Fe: Bilingual-Bicultural Communication Arts Unit, State Department of Education.

Córdova, Gilbert Benito. 1970. "A Hispano Tale from Abiquiú, New Mexico." *Aztlan* 1, no. 2: 103–10.

Córdova, Josephine M. 1976. *No lloro pero me acuerdo.* Dallas: Taylor.

Curtin, L. S. M. 1965. *Healing Herbs of the Upper Rio Grande.* Los Angeles: Southwest Museum.

Davidson, Theodore R. 1983. *Chicano Prisoners: The Key to San Quentin.* Prospect Heights, Ill.: Waveland Press.

Dean, Ruth. 1993. "Teaching a Constructivist Approach to Clinical Practice." In *Revisioning Social Work Education A Social Constructionist Approach,* ed. Joan Laird. Binghamton, N.Y.: Haworth Press.

deBuys, William. 1985. *Enchantment and Exploitation: The Life and Hard Times of a New Mexico Mountain Range.* Albuquerque: University of New Mexico Press.

de Córdova, Lorenzo. (Lorin Brown). 1972. *Echoes of the Flute.* Santa Fe: Ancient City Press.

del Pilar Muñoz, María. 2002. "El Cucuy." *La Herencia,* Summer, 31.

del Río, Yolanda. 2007. *Rancheras.* CD Compacto Siglo XXI Inc. 1070 Tijuana, B.C. Cp. 60417.

Denzin, Norman K. 1970a. "The Methodologies of Symbolic Interaction: A Critical Review of Research Techniques." In *Social Psychology through Symbolic Interaction,* ed. Gregory P. Stone and Harvey Farberman. Waltham, Mass.: Xerox College Publishing.

———. 1970b. "Symbolic Interaction and Ethnomethodology." In *Understanding Everyday Life,* ed. Jack Douglas. Chicago: Aldine.

———. 1984a. "Meaning and Method in Phenomenological Research." *Field Notes: A Newsletter on Qualitative Research in Human Services* 1, no. 2: 1–2.

———. 1984b. "Toward a Phenomenology of Domestic, Family Violence." *American Journal of Sociology* 90, no. 3: 483–513.

Dewey, John. 1922. *Human Nature and Conduct.* New York: Henry Holt.

Diagnostic and Statistical Manual of Mental Disorders (DSM-IV). 2000. 4th ed. Arlington, Va.: American Psychiatric Association

"Dies Irae." 2009. Wikipedia. Available at http//en.wikipedia.org./wiki/Dies_Irae.

Dollard, John. 1939. "Dialectic of Insult." *American Imago* 1:3–25.

Dorson, R. 1964. "Corrido de la muerte de Antonio Mestas." In *Buying the Wind*. Chicago: University of Chicago Press.

Douglas, Jack. 1970. "Understanding Everyday Life." In *Understanding Everyday Life*, ed. Jack Douglas. Chicago: Aldine.

Dreyfus, Hubert. 1983. "Alternative Philosophical Conceptualizations of Psychopathology." Available at http://socrates.berkeley.edu/~hdreyfus/html/paper_alternative.html.

Ebert, Roger. 2005. "2001: A Space Odyssey" Available at http://www.palantir.net/2001/other/ebert.html.

"Eclipses in History and Literature." 1998. Available at http://www.earthview.com/ages/history.htm.

Edelman, Sandra. 1998. *Turning the Gorgon*. Woodstock, Conn.: Spring.

Eggan, Fred. 1975. *Essays in Social Anthropology and Ethnology*. Chicago: University of Chicago Press.

Eliade, Mircea. 1949. *Traité d' historie des religions*. Paris: n.p.

Ellenberger, Henri F. 1967. "A Clinical Introduction to Psychiatric Phenomenology and Existential Analysis." In *Existence: A New Direction in Psychiatry and Psychology*, ed. Rollo May, Ernest Angel, and Henri F. Ellenberger. New York: Simon and Schuster.

"El Mitote Cora: Música, Danza y Fiesta Ritual Que se Repite Año con Año en el Nayar." 2003. Available at http://conaculta.gob.mx/saladeprensa/2003/12nove/mitote.htm.

Enciclopedia universal ilustrada. 1930. Madrid: Espasa-Calpa, S.A.

Espinosa, Aurelio M. 1913. "New Mexican Spanish Folk-Lore. IV Proverbs." *Journal of American Folk-Lore* 26, no. 100: 97–122.

———. 1914. "New Mexico Folk-Lore VI. Los Trovos del Viejo Vilmas." *Journal of American Folk-Lore* 27, no. 104: 105–47.

———. 1926. "Spanish Folk-Lore in New Mexico." *New Mexico Historical Review* 1, no. 2: 135–55.

"Ex-Boyfriend Held after Shooting." 1992. *Albuquerque Journal North* (Sunday edition), April 20.

Fauré, Gabriel. 1987. *Requiem, Opus 48*. Orchestre symphonique de Montréal. St. Eustahe, Z Montreal. London Records.

Foster, George. 1978. "Relationships between Spanish and Spanish American Folk Medicine." In *Hispanic Culture and Health Care: Fact, Fiction, Folklore*, ed. Ricardo

Arguijo Martínez. St. Louis: C. V. Mosby.

Fuller, B. A. B. 1955. *A History of Philosophy.* 3rd ed. New York: Henry Holt.

Fullilove, Mindy Thompson. 1996. "Psychiatric Implications of Displacement: Contributions from the Psychology of Place." *American Journal of Psychiatry,* December, 1516–23.

Gallegos, Adelecia. 1985. "En memoria de Janice Medina." *Taos News,* January 11.

———. 1987. "En memoria de una jovencita hermosa." *El Crepúsculo* (Taos, N.Mex.), September 3.

———. 1993. "Para recordarte, adios Teresita, Hermosa." *El Crepúsculo* (Taos, N.Mex.), February 23.

———. 1996. *Memorias y Recuerdos del Valle de Taos.* S.O.M.O.S. (Society of the Muse of the Southwest Taos). Taos, N.Mex.

Galván, Robert A., and Richard V. Teschner. 1977. *El diccionario del español Chicano / The Dictionary of Chicano Spanish.* Silver Springs, Md. :Institute of Modern Foreign Languages.

García, M. 1978. "Preparing to Leave: Interaction at a Mexican American Family Gathering." Paper presented at the National Conference on Latino Discourse Behavior, Princeton, N.J., April.

Garfinkel, Harold. 1967. *Studies in Ethnomethodology.* Englewood Cliffs, N.J.: Prentice-Hall.

———. 1973. "Background Expectancies." In *Rules and Meanings: The Anthropology of Everyday Knowledge,* ed. M. Douglas. New York: Penguin.

———. 1974. "The Origins of the Term 'Ethnomethodology.'" In *Ethnomethodology: Selected Readings,* ed. Roy Turner. Baltimore: Penguin Education.

Garris, Mick, director. 1994. *The Stand.* Stephen King. Author. Television miniseries. ABC.

Geertz, Clifford. 1973. *The Interpretation of Cultures: Selected Essays.* New York: Basic Books.

Gendlin, Eugene. 1978. *Focusing.* New York: Everest House.

———. 1979. "Experiential Explication." In *Phenomenology and Existentialism,* ed. Robert C. Solomon. Lanham, Md.: University Press of America.

———. 1997. *Experiencing and the Creation of Meaning: A Philosophical and Psychological Approach to the Subjective.* Evanston, Ill.: Northwestern University Press.

Gibran, Kahlil. 1970. *The Prophet.* New York: Alfred A. Knopf.

Goffman, Erving. 1959. *The Presentation of Self in Everyday Life.* Garden City, N.Y.: Doubleday Anchor.

———. 1961. *Asylums: Essays on the Social Situation of Mental Patients and Other Inmates.* Garden City, New York: Anchor Books.

———. 1967. *Interaction Ritual.* New York: Doubleday.

———. 1972. "Embarrassment and Social Organizations." In *Down to Earth Sociology: Introductory Readings,* ed. James Henslin. New York: Free Press.

Gonzales, Adán. 1959. "El corrido de Nuevo México." Master's thesis, New Mexico Highlands University.

Gonzales, Edward, and David L. Witt. 1996. *Spirit Ascendant: The Art and Life of Patrocino Barela.* Santa Fe: Red Crane Books.

Gonzales, Phillip, ed. 2007. *Expressing New Mexico: Nuevomexicano Creativity, Ritual, and Memory.* Tucson: University of Arizona Press.

"Good Friday Pilgrimage Walkers Come from All across State to Make Trek to Top of Tomé Hill." 2004–5. In *Welcome to Valencia County.* Belen, N.Mex.: Valencia County News-Bulletin.

Gross, Edward, and Gregory P. Stone. 1970. "Embarrassment and the Analysis of Role Requirements." In *Social Psychology through Symbolic Interaction,* ed. Gregory P. Stone and Harvey A. Farberman. Waltham, Mass.: Xerox College Publishing.

Gutiérrez, Patricia A. N.d. *Con esa boca comes: An Innovative Look at Gang Lexicon.* Vacaville, Calif.: California Prisons, Voces de Germania.

Halleck, Seymour L. 1971. *The Politics of Therapy.* New York: Science House.

Hartman, Ann. 1994. *Reflection and Controversy: Essays on Social Work.* Washington, D.C.: NASW Press.

Hendrix, Jimi. 2001. "Hey Joe." On *The Jimi Hendrix Experience Live in Ottawa.* Seattle, Wash.: Dagger Records.

Herrera-Sobeck, María. 1982. "The Treacherous Woman Archetype: A Structuring Agent in the Corrido." *Aztlan* 13:135–48.

———. 1990. *The Mexican Corrido: A Feminist Analysis.* Bloomington: Indiana University Press.

Hopkins, Gerard Manley. 1962. *Poems and Prose of Gerard Manley Hopkins.* Ed. W. H. Gardner. Baltimore: Penguin.

Horney, Karen. 1948. "The Value of Vindictiveness." *American Journal of Psychoanalysis* 2:3–12.

Husserl, Edmund. 1979. "Fifth Meditation." In *Phenomenology and Existentialism,* ed. Robert C. Solomon. Lanham, Md.: Rowman and Littlefield.

Hyams, Peter, director. 1984. *2010: The Year We Make Contact.* Los Angeles: MGM/UA Entertainment Company, Production Company.

Ichheiser, Gustav. 1970. *Appearance and Realities: Misunderstanding in Human Relations.* San Francisco: Jossey-Bass.

Imre, Roberta W. 1995. "The Epistemological Basis for Ethnographic Research." Paper presented at the Conference on Ethnographic Research and Urban Policy Problems Conference, Howard University, December 8–9.

"In Memoriam of James Hardgraves, September 2, 1991, by Arthur L. Bustos, Your

Friend." 1991. *Las Vegas Daily Optic,* September 5.

Jackson, C. C., and G. P. Davidson. 1986. "The Anorexic Patient as a Survivor: The Denial of Death and Death Themes in the Literature on Anorexia Nervosa." *International Journal of Eating Disorders* 5, no. 5: 821–35.

Jackson, Don. 1970. "The Study of the Family." In *Family Process,* ed. Nathan W. Ackerman. New York: Basic Books.

Jacobi, Jolande. 1959. *Complex Archetype Symbols in the Psychology of C. G. Jung.* Trans. Ralph Manheim. Princeton, N.J.: Princeton University Press.

Jacobs, Jerry. 1979. "A Phenomenological Study of Suicide Notes." In Howard Schwartz and Jerry Jacobs, *Qualitative Sociology: A Method to the Madness.* New York: Free Press.

James, William. 1958. *Varieties of Religious Experience: A Study in Human Nature.* New York: Mentor.

Jaramillo, Cleofas. 1941. *Shadows of the Past.* Santa Fe: Ancient City Press.

Jones, Ernest. 1951. *On the Nightmare.* New York: Grove Press.

Kalish, R. A., and D. K. Reynolds. 1981. *Death and Ethnicity.* Farmingdale, N.Y.: Baywood.

Kany, Charles E. 1960. *American Spanish Euphemisms.* Berkeley: University of California Press.

Kazantzakis, Nikos. 1962. *Saint Francis.* Trans. P. A. Bien. New York: Simon and Schuster.

Keefe, Thomas. 1976. "Empathy, the Critical Skill." *Social Work,* January, 10–14.

Keen, Ernest. 1975. *A Primer on Phenomenological Psychology.* New York: Holt, Rinehart and Winston.

———. 1984. "Emerging from Depression." *American Behavioral Scientist* 27, no. 6: 801–12.

Kenny, Michael. 1965. "Poise and Counterpoise in the Presentation of the Spanish Self." *Anthropological Linguistics* 7, no. 4: 79–91.

Kern, Iso. 1997. "Intersubjectivity." In *Encyclopedia of Phenomenology,* ed. Lester Embree et al. Dordrecht: Kluwer Academic Publishers.

Kierkegaard, Søren. 1954. *Fear and Trembling* and *The Sickness unto Death.* Trans. Walter Lowrie. Garden City, N.Y.: Doubleday.

Klein, Martha. 1985. "A Descriptive Study of Meaning Systems among Bulimic Women." M.S.W. thesis, New Mexico Highlands University.

Knowlton, Clark S. 1967. "Land-Grant Problems among the State's Spanish-Americans." *New Mexico Business Reprint,* June, 1–13.

Korte, Alvin O. 1999a. "Despedidas as Reflections of Death in Hispanic New Mexico." In *La Familia: Traditions and Realities,* ed. Marta Sotomayor and Alejandro Garcia. Washington, D.C.: National Hispanic Council on Aging.

———. 1999b. "A Journey Through Antón Chico's Past." *La Herencia del Norte* 24 (Winter): 49.

———. 2010. "Idiomatic Expressions." Unpublished manuscript.

Korte, Alvin O., and Luisa B. Lucero. 2004. "La Poesía Alfabética de Fernando Baca." *La Herencia* 44 (Winter): 20–21.

Kubrick, Stanley, director. 1968. *2001: A Space Odyssey.* Los Angeles: Metro-Goldwyn-Mayer.

———. 1980. *The Shining.* Aylesbury, England: Hawk Films.

———. 1987. *Full Metal Jacket.* New York: Natent.

Laing, R. D. 1969. *Self and Others.* New York: Pantheon.

———. 1976. *The Divided Self.* New York. Penguin.

Lauria, Anthony, Jr. 1964. "Respeto, Relajo, and Interpersonal Relations in Puerto Rico." *Anthropological Quarterly* 37 (April): 54–67.

Lawrence, Nathaniel, and Daniel O'Connor, eds. 1967. *Readings in Existential Phenomenology.* Englewood Cliffs, N.J.: Prentice-Hall.

Leiter, Kenneth. 1980. *A Primer on Ethnomethodology.* Oxford: Oxford University Press.

Lemert, Edwin. 1970. "Paranoia and the Dynamics of Exclusion." In *Social Psychology through Symbolic Interaction,* ed. Gregory P. Stone and Harvey A. Farberman. Waltham, Mass.: Xerox College Publishing.

Lewis, Helen B. 1971. *Shame and Guilt in Neurosis.* New York: International Universities Press.

Loeffler, Jack, with Katherine Loeffler and Enrique R. Lamadrid. 1999. *La Música de los Viejitos Hispano Folk Music of the Río Grande del Norte.* Albuquerque: University of New Mexico Press.

Lopez, Angie S. 1990. *Blessed Are the Soldiers.* Albuquerque: Sandia.

Lovato, Alberto "Morgan." 1974. "Agusa'o con los velices." *El Cuaderno (De vez en Cuando)* 3, no. 4: 42–44.

Lovett, Lyle. 1990. "L.A. County." On *Pontiac.* Nashville, Tenn.: UNI/MCA.

Lucas, George, director. 1977. *Star Wars: Episode IV.* Los Angeles: Twentieth Century Fox.

Lucero-White, Aurora. 1945. "Wakes for the Dead and the Saints." *El Palacio* 52, no. 12: 255–58.

Luquin, Edwardo. 1961. *Analisis espectral del Mexicano: El lambiscon, el madrugador, el picapedrero, el pistoler; ensayo.* Mexico City: Costa-Amic.

Lynd, Helen M. 1958. *On Shame and the Search for Identity.* New York: Harcourt, Brace and World.

"Mancornar." 1930. In *Enciclopedia universal ilustrada.* Madrid: Espasa-Calpa, S.A.

Manrique, Jorge. 1982. "Coplas por la muerte de su padre." In *Antologia general de la literatura española: Verso, prosa, teatro,* ed. Angel del Rio. New York: Editorial Mensaje.

"Manrique, Jorge." 2007. Wikipedia. Available at http://www.en.wikipedia.org/wiki/Jorge_Manrique.

Mares, L. 1986. "Platicando." *Taos News,* May 15.

Martinez, L. V. N.d. "Despedida, Española, New Mexico." Unpublished song manuscript.

May, Rollo. 1969. *Love and Will.* New York: Norton.

———. 1981. *Freedom and Destiny.* New York: Norton.

McWilliams, Carey. 1961. *North from Mexico: The Spanish-Speaking People of the United States.* 2nd ed. New York : Monthly Review Press.

Mead, Margaret, ed. 1955. *Cultural Patterns and Technical Change.* New York: New American Library.

Mehan, Hugh, and Houston Wood. 1975. *The Reality of Ethnomethodology.* New York: John Wiley and Sons.

Mellinkoff, Ruth. 1970. *The Horned Moses in Medieval Art and Thought.* Berkeley: University of California Press.

Mendoza, Vicente T. 1974. *El Corrido mexicano.* Mexico City: Fondo de Cultura Económica, Secretaría de Educación Pública, Cultura SEP.

Mérimée, Ernest. 1930. *A History of Spanish Literature.* Translated, revised, and enlarged by S. Griswold Morley. New York: Henry Holt.

Merton, Thomas. 1958. *Thoughts in Solitude.* New York: Farrar, Straus and Cudahy.

Mills, C. Wright. 1970. "Situated Actions and the Vocabularies of Motive." In *Social Psychology through Symbolic Interaction,* ed. Gregory P. Stone and Harvey Farberman. Waltham, Mass.: Xerox College Publishing.

Mogenson, Greg. 1992. *Greeting the Angels: An Imaginal View of the Mourning Process.* Amityville, N.Y.: Baywood.

Mondragón, Roberto. 2000. "Saber adivinar no es difícil." *El Norteño Semenal, Journal North,* September 24, 5.

Mondragón, Roberto, and Georgia Roybal. 1994. "La Cultura Nuestra: Outline of Our Hispanic Culture." *La Herencia del Norte,* Spring, 7.

Montaño, Mary C. 2001. *Tradiciones Nuevomexicanas: Hispano Arts and Culture in New Mexico.* Albuquerque: University of New Mexico Press.

Montiel, Miguel. 1970. "The Social Science Myth of the Mexican American Family." *El Grito* 3, no. 4: 56–63.

Montoya, José. 1992. *Information: 20 Years of Joda.* San José, Calif.: Chusma House Publications.

Montoya, M. 1992. "Mourning: The Process of Revealing *Requiebros." New Mexico Magazine,* October, 68–73.

Moody, Raymond. 1980. "Questions." In *Death: Current Perspectives,* 2nd ed., ed. Edwin S. Shneidman. Palo Alto, Calif.: Mayfield.

Moustakas, Clark. 1994. *Phenomenological Research Methods.* Thousand Oaks, Calif.: Sage.

Moya, E. 2001. "Learning from Nuestros Ancianos." *La Herencia del Norte,* Fall, 40.

Natanson, Maurice. 1974. *Phenomenology, Role, and Reason: Essays on the Coherence and Deformation of Social Reality.* Springfield, Ill.: Charles C. Thomas.

Nava, Gregory. 1995. *My Family / Mi Familia.* Agora Hills, Calif.: Ana Thomas.

New American Bible, The. 2005. Wichita, Kans.: Fireside Catholic Publishing.

New Catholic Encyclopedia. 1967. New York: McGraw-Hill.

New Revised Velásquez Spanish and English Dictionary. 1985. Clinton, N.J.: New Win.

"Nicotine." 2008. Wikipedia. Available at http://en.wikipedia.org/wiki/Nicotine.

Nuttin, Josef. 1950. "Intimacy and Shame in the Dynamic Structure of Personality." In *Feelings and Emotions: The Mooseheart Symposium,* ed. Martin L. Reymert. New York: McGraw-Hill.

"Obituaries." 1999. *Albuquerque Journal,* February 23.

Oh, sangre de mi Jesús; Oh, lagrimas de María! Cuaderno de alabados y oraciones comúnmente cantados y rezadas por los hermanos y hermanas de la Cofradía de Nuestro Padre Jesús Nazareno. 1999. Compiled and translated by Los Hermanos Cofrados de la Morada de Nuestra Señora de Guadalupe de La Madera, Nuevo Méjico. Albuquerque: Creative Designs.

Olmos, Edward James, director. 1992. *American Me.* Los Angeles: Universal.

Olmos, Edward James, Lea Ybarra, and Manuel Monterrey. 1999. *Americanos: Latino Life in the United States / La vida latina en los Estados Unidos.* New York: Little, Brown.

"Open Your Heart to the Mystery of Life." 1999. *Las Vegas Daily Optic,* March 10.

Pacheco, Dorothy. 2008. *La perla y el diamante.* Written note. Las Vegas, New Mexico.

"Para despedir al Padre O'Brien la última vez." 1993. *Taos News,* February 18.

Parsons, Jack. 1990. *Straight from the Heart: Portraits of Traditional Hispanic Musicians.* Albuquerque: University of New Mexico Press.

Paz, Octavio. 1961. *The Labyrinth of Solitude: Life and Thought in Mexico.* Trans. Lysander Kemp. New York: Grove Press.

Péristiany, J. G., ed. 1966. *Honour and Shame: The Values of Mediterranean Society.* Chicago: University of Chicago Press.

Pitt-Rivers, Julian A. 1966. "Honour and Shame: The Values of Mediterranean Society." In *Honour and Shame: The Values of Mediterranean Society,* ed. J. G. Péristiany. Chicago: University of Chicago Press.

———. 1971. *The People of the Sierra.* 2nd ed. Chicago: University of Chicago Press.

Polsky, Ned. 1969. *Hustlers, Beats, and Others.* Chicago: Aldine.

Portilla, Jorge. 1966. *Fenomenología del relajo*. Mexico City: Ediciones Era, S.A.

Rael, Juan B. 1951. *The New Mexico Alabado*. Stanford, Calif.: Stanford University Press.

———. 1977. *Cuentos Españoles de Colorado y Nuevo Mexico*. 2nd ed. 2 vols. Santa Fe: Museum of New Mexico Press.

"Rage Earns 'Madelino' 4.5 Years." 1992. *Rio Grande Sun*, July 17.

Ramos, Reyes. 1973. "A Case in Point: An Ethnomethodological Study of a Poor Mexican American Family." *Social Science Quarterly* 53, no. 4: 905–19.

———. 1979. "Movidas: The Methodological and Theoretical Relevance of Interactional Strategies." In *Studies in Symbolic Interaction*, ed. Norman Denzin, vol. 2. Greenwich, Conn.: Jai Press.

———. 1982. "Discovering the Production of Mexican American Family Structure." *De Colores Journal* 6, nos.1–2: 120–34.

Ramos, Samuel. 1965. *El perfil del hombre y la cultura en México*. Mexico City: Espasa-Calpe Mexicana, S.A.

Reynolds, D. 1970. "A Funeral in México." *Omega* 1:259–69.

Ricoeur, Paul. 1967. *The Symbolism of Evil*. Trans. Emerson Buchanan. Boston: Beacon Press.

———. 1979. "Motive and Value." In *Phenomenology and Existentialism*, ed. Robert C. Solomon, 297–302. New York: Modern Library.

———. 1986. *Fallible Man*. Trans. Charles A. Kelbley. New York: Fordham University Press.

Rilke, Rainer Maria. 1948. *Letters of Rainer Maria Rilke*. Vol. 2, *1910–1926*. Trans. Jane Bannard Greene and M. D. Herter Norton. New York: Norton.

Rodríguez-Puértolas, Julio. 1975. "La problemática socio-política chicana en corridos y canciones." *Aztlan* 6, no. 1: 97–116.

Romano, Octavio V. 1960. "Donship in a Mexican American Community in Texas." *American Anthropologist* 62:966–76.

Romanyshyn, Robert. ca. 1992. Lecture delivered at Pacifica Graduate Institute. Audio cassette.

———. 2000. "Psychology Is Useless; Or, It Should Be." *Janus Head*, Fall 3, no. 2. Available at http://www.janushead.org/3-2/romanyshyn.cfm.

Romero, Estevan E. 1980. "La Soledad." Course papers, Spring semester, New Mexico Highlands University. In possession of the author.

Romero, José Rubén. 1983. *La Vida Unútil de Pito Pérez*. Mexico City: Editorial Porrua.

Ross, Jeffrey Ian, and Stephen C. Richards. 2002. *Behind Bars: Surviving Prison*. Indianapolis: Alpha Books.

Rowles, Graham. 1990. "Place Attachment among Small-Town Elderly." *Journal of*

Rural Community Psychology 11, no. 1: 103–19.

Rubel, Arthur. 1960. "Concepts of Disease in Mexican-American Culture." *American Anthropologist* 62: 795–814.

Ruben, Joseph, director. 1991. *Sleeping with the Enemy*. Los Angeles: Twentieth Century For.

Sagel, Jim. 1990a. *On the Move Again / Otra Vez en la Movida: New and Collected Poems of Jim Sagel*. Albuquerque: West End Press.

———. 1990b. "Pasión y Tradición: Los Músicos del Pueblo." In Jack Parsons, *Straight from the Heart: Portraits of Traditional Hispanic Musicians*. Albuquerque: University of New Mexico Press.

Salazar, Abel, director. 1978. *Picardía mexicana*. Mexico City: Cima Films.

Saleeby, Dennis. 1995. Presentation to the faculty School of Social Work, New Mexico Highlands University. April 12.

Sánchez, Aurelio. 2009. "Corrales Pageant Honors Patron Saint of Farming." *Albuquerque Journal*, April 30, 4.

Sánchez, Ricardo. 1995. *Canto y grito mi liberación y lloro mis desmadrazgos*. Pullman: Washington State University Press.

Sandoval, Frederick. 1996. "*La Envidia* Keeps Us from Getting Ahead." *La Herencia del Norte*, Winter, 37.

Sands, Roberta G. 1983. "The DSM-III and Psychiatric Nosology: A Critique from the Labeling Perspective." *California Sociologist*, Winter, 77–87.

Sartre, Jean-Paul. 1965. *The Philosophy of Jean-Paul Sartre*. Ed. Robert Denoon Cumming. New York: Vintage.

Scheff, Thomas J. 1984. *Being Mentally Ill*. 2nd ed. Chicago: Aldine.

Schneider, Carl D. 1979. *Shame, Exposure, and Privacy*. Boston: Beacon Press.

Schoeck, Helmut. 1969. *Envy: A Theory of Social Behavior*. New York: Harcourt, Brace and World.

Schrag, Clarence. 1961. "A Preliminary Criminal Typology." *Pacific Sociological Review* 4, no. 1: 11–16.

Schutz, Alfred. 1964. "The Stranger." In *Collected Papers*, vol. 2, *Studies in Social Theory*. The Hague: Martinus Nijhoff.

———. 1971. *Collected Papers*. Vol. 1, *The Problem of Social Reality*. The Hague: Martinus Nijhoff.

Schwartz, Howard, and Jerry Jacobs. 1979. *Qualitative Sociology: A Method to the Madness*. New York: Free Press.

Scott, Ridley, director. 1979. *Alien*. Shepperton Studios, England: Brandywine Productions.

Searles, H. 1956. "The Psychodynamics of Vengefulness." *Psychiatry* 19:31–39.

Sifuentes, Roberto. 1982. "Approximaciones al 'Corrido de los hermanos Hernández ejecutados en la Cámara de Gas de la penitenciaría de Florence, Arizona, el día 6 de julio de 1934.'" *Aztlan* 13:95–110.

Sisneros, José A. 2000. "Consciousness of Difference: A Grounded Theory of Everyday Experience in Living in a Latino/a Family in the Contemporary United States." Ph.D. diss., University of Denver.

Solomon, Robert C., ed. 1979. *Phenomenology and Existentialism.* Washington, D.C.: University Press of America.

Sparx, The, with Lorenzo Antonio. 2007. *Corridos Famosos.* Albuquerque: Striking Music. CD.

Stewart, David, and Algis Mickunas. 1974. *Exploring Phenomenology: A Guide to Its Literature.* Chicago: American Library Association.

Sufurino, Jonas. N.d. *El libro de San Cipriano: Libro completo e verdadera magia o sea tesoro del hechicero.* Mexico City: Biblioteca Ciencias Ocultas.

Sykes, Gersham M. 1966. *The Society of Captives: A Study of a Maximum Security Prison.* New York: Atheneum.

Sykes, Gersham M., and Sheldon L. Messinger. 1960. "The Inmate Social System." In *Theoretical Studies in Social Organization of the Prison,* ed. Richard A. Cloward, Donald R. Cressey, George H. Gorsser, Richard McCleery, Lloyd E. Ohlin, Gersham M. Sykes, and Sheldon L. Messinger. New York: Social Science Research Council.

Szasz, Thomas. 1961. *The Myth of Mental Illness.* New York: Dell.

Taymor, Julie, director. 2002. *Frieda.* Los Angeles: Handprint Entertainment.

Toch, Hans. 1977. *Living in Prison: The Ecology of Survival.* New York: Free Press.

"Tony's Adiós." 1992. *Santa Fe New Mexican,* September 14.

"Toolbox." 1987. *Las Vegas Daily Optic,* October 1.

Tornstam, Lars. 1997. "Gerotranscendence in a Broad Cross-Sectional Perspective." *Journal of Aging and Identity* 2, no. 1: 17–36.

Torres, Jeramías. 1963. "Costumbres folklóricas de Truchas, Nuevo México." Master's thesis, New Mexico Highlands University.

Torres, Larry. 1993. "Para despedir al padre O'Brien la última ves." *El Crepúsculo,* Feb. 18, 4.

"Triquetra." 2006. Wikipedia. Available at http//en.wikipedia.org./org/wiki/Triquetra.

Tuck, D. 1977. "The Corrido of the Mexican Revolution." *Greater Llano Estacado Southwest Heritage* 7 (Spring): 20–46.

Valdez, Facundo. 1979. "Vergüenza." *The Survival of Spanish American Villages,* ed. Paul Kutsche. Colorado College Study no. 15. Colorado Springs: Colorado College Research Committee.

Valle, Ramón, and Lydia Mendoza. 1978. *The Elder Latino.* San Diego: Campanile Press.

van Manen, Max. 1977. "From Meaning to Method." *Qualitative Health Research* 7, no. 3: 345–69.

———. 1990. *Researching Lived Experience: Human Science for an Action Sensitive Pedagogy.* Albany: State University of New York Press.

Van Ness, John R., and Christine Van Ness. 1980. *Spanish and Mexican Land Grants in New Mexico and Colorado.* Manhattan, Kans.: Sunflower Press.

Velázquez: A New Pronouncing Dictionary of the Spanish and English Languages. 1973. Compiled by Mariano Velázquez de la Cadena, with Edward Gray and Juan L. Iribas Rev. ed. Englewood Cliffs, N.J.: Prentice-Hall.

Vida del Lazarillo de Tormes. 1965. Ed. Angel Gonzalez Palencia. 2nd ed. Madrid: Editorial Ebro.

Vigil, Cleofas. 1991. "En memoria de James C. Martinez." *El Crepúsculo* (Taos, N.Mex.), September 9.

Vigil, M. E. 1984. "Sociedad de San José Prepares for Centennial Celebration." Unpublished manuscript.

Vine, W. E., Merrill Ungar, and William White Jr. 1996. *Vine's Complete Expository Dictionary of Old and New Testament Words.* Nashville: Thomas Nelson Publishers.

von Frantz, Marie-Louise. 1998. *On Dreams and Death: A Jungian Interpretation.* Trans. Emmanuel Kennedy-Xipolitas and Vernon Brooks. Chicago: Open Court Press.

von Gebsattel, V. E. 1938. "The World of the Compulsive." *Monatsschrift fur Psychiatrie and Neurologie* 99:10–74.

———. 1967. "The World of the Compulsive." In *Existence: A New Direction in Psychiatry and Psychology,* ed. Rollo May, Ernest Angel, and Henri F. Ellenberger. New York: Simon and Schuster.

Warner, C. Terry. 1986. "Anger and Similar Delusions." In *Social Construction of Emotions,* ed. Rom Harre. New York: Blackwell.

Weider, Lawrence. 1974a. *Language and Social Reality: The Case of Telling the Convict Code.* The Hague: Mouton.

———. 1974b. "Telling the Code." In *Ethnomethodology: Selected Readings,* ed. Roy Turner. New York: Penguin.

Weigle, M. M. 1971. "Los Hermanos Penitentes: Historical and Ritual Aspects of Folk Religion in Northern New Mexico and Colorado." Ph.D. diss., University of Pennsylvania.

"What's a Convict?" 1983. *Santa Fe Prison News* 2, no. 1: 3. This is/was an inmate-run newspaper and does not reflect the views of the former or current administration of this institution. The newspaper gave permission to quote the code verbatim.

Whitehead, Alfred North. 1961. *The Aims of Education.* New York: Mentor Books.

White, Koch, Kelly and McCarthy Attorneys at Law and the New Mexico State Planning Office. 1972. *Land Title Study: Technical Report, Prepared by White, Koch, Kelly & McCarthy, for the New Mexico State Planning Office.* Santa Fe: State Planning Office.

White, Leslie A. 1943. "Punche: Tobacco in New Mexico History." *New Mexico Historical Review* 18 (October): 386–93.

Williams, Kim, and Garth Brooks. 2005. "Papa Loved Mama." On *Ropin' the Wind.* Nashville: Pearl Records.

Wilmer, Harry A. 1965. "The Role of the 'Rat' in the Prison." *Federal Probation* 29:44–49.

Wise, Robert, director. 1979. *Star Trek: The Motion Picture.* Los Angeles: Century Associates.

Woods, Richard Donavan, and Grace Alvarez-Altman. 1978. *Spanish American Surnames in the Southwestern United States.* Boston: G. K. Hall.

Wrong, Dennis H. 1970. "The Oversocialized Conception of Man in Modern Man." In *Social Psychology through Symbolic Interaction,* ed. Gregory Stone and Harvey Farberman. Waltham, Mass.: Xerox College Publishing.

Yudilevitch, Sandra. 2009. "Living with HIV/AIDS: Exploring Latina Women's Narratives." Ph.D. diss., University of Georgia, Athens.

Zantelle, Yoly. 2005. "Psychological Implications of Land Loss among Hispanos of Northern New Mexico." Ph.D. diss., Walden University.

Zinnemann, Fred, director. 1952. *High Noon.* Los Angeles: Stanley Kramer Productions.

Zuniga, María E. 1992. "Using Metaphors in Therapy: Dichos and Latino Clients." *Social Work* 37, no. 1: 55–60.

Index